The Enforceability of the Interim Measures Granted by an Emergency Arbitrator in International Commercial Arbitration

Junmin Zhang

The Enforceability of the Interim Measures Granted by an Emergency Arbitrator in International Commercial Arbitration

Springer

Junmin Zhang
Department of Law, College of Philosophy,
Law and Political Science
Shanghai Normal University
Shanghai, China

ISBN 978-981-97-6535-5 ISBN 978-981-97-6536-2 (eBook)
https://doi.org/10.1007/978-981-97-6536-2

This work was supported by Shanghai Planning Office of Philosophy and Social Science (grant number 2023ZFX006).

This Springer imprint is published by the registered company Springer Nature Singapore Pte Ltd.
The registered company address is: 152 Beach Road, #21-01/04 Gateway East, Singapore 189721, Singapore

Acknowledgements

This book is based on my doctoral research completed at Maastricht University, the Netherlands, in 2020. I appreciate all the guidance, support, and encouragement I had during this struggling but incredible journey. I am very grateful to all my colleagues, friends, and families who made it ever possible.

I give my sincere and foremost gratitude to Prof. René de Groot and Dr. Stephan Rammeloo, for the detailed comments and precious suggestions, for the trust they have put in me, for the generous support, and most importantly, for their academic integrity and enthusiasm that made me know what kind of academic I want to be. Their understanding and efforts helped me to achieve the standard for defendable academic work. Many thanks also go to Prof. Chuanli Wang. She gave me the very initial support when I told her that I wanted to pursue a doctoral degree. I must also thank my doctorate committee members, Prof. Dr. Michael Faure, Prof. Dr. Marta Pertegás Sender, Prof. Dr. Bas van Zelst, Prof. Dr. Jacques Rinkes, and Prof. Dr. Yuwen Li. Their insightful comments inspired me to present a better version of this book.

My gratitude also goes to my friends and colleagues who accompanied me during these years. We shared numerous great moments together in so many places. It is impossible to name them all here. Although we might be in different geographical locations, I felt we always stayed together.

To my parents, I gratefully acknowledge their infinite love and encouragement. Their confidence in me and endless support gave me the strength and courage to make this happen. No words can describe my appreciation for their understanding.

Contents

Abbreviations

AAA	American Arbitration Association
ACICA	Australian Centre for International Commercial Arbitration
ADR	Alternative Dispute Resolution
BAC	Beijing Arbitration Commission
Cap.	Chapter
CIETAC	China International Economic and Trade Arbitration Commission
CISG	United Nations Convention on Contracts for the International Sale of Goods
CMAC	China Maritime Arbitration Commission
Co.	Company
CommonLII	Commonwealth Legal Information Institute
ECOSOC	United Nations Economic and Social Council
EU	European Union
FTZ	Free Trade Zone
HCCH	Hague Conference on Private International Law
HKIAC	Hong Kong International Arbitration Centre
IBA	International Bar Association
ICC	International Court of Arbitration of the International Chamber of Commerce
ICCA	International Council for Commercial Arbitration
ICDR	International Centre for Dispute Resolution
ICSID	International Centre for Settlement of Investment Disputes
INC	Incorporation
LCIA	London Court of International Arbitration
LLC	Limited Liability Company
LLP	Limited Liability Partnership
Ltd/Ltd.	Limited Company
PhD	Doctor of Philosophy
SAR	Special Administrative Region
SCC	Stockholm Chamber of Commerce

SHIAC	Shanghai International Economic and Trade Arbitration Commission
SIAC	Singapore International Arbitration Centre
UNCITRAL	United Nations Commission on International Trade Law
U.S./USA	United States of America

Chapter 1
Introduction

Interim measures, also known as provisional measures, conservatory measures, emergency relief, and other similar terms, are used to protect parties' rights in a dispute pending the final decision.[1] In international commercial arbitration, owing to the complexity of disputes, an arbitral tribunal needs enough time to grant a satisfying final award. Under such circumstances, parties expect to have a very effective mechanism for interim measures in order to guarantee a meaningful final award. Most of the arbitral institutions adopt the emergency arbitrator mechanism for this purpose.

The emergency arbitrator mechanism enables parties to seek interim measures before the constitution of an arbitral tribunal when the facts ask for such relief.[2] During the last 18 years since the introduction of the mechanism of interim measures by the International Center for Dispute Resolution (ICDR) in 2006, most arbitral institutions, such as the Hong Kong International Arbitration Centre (HKIAC), the London Court of International Arbitration (LCIA), the International Court of Arbitration of the International Chamber of Commerce (ICC), the Arbitration Institute of the Stockholm Chamber of Commerce (SCC), and the Singapore International Arbitration Centre (SIAC) have adopted this approach of using interim measures. The increasing popularity of the emergency arbitrator mechanism in international arbitration points to the need for interim measures and the concerns raised by the business community in this regard.

---

[1] Ali Yesilirmak (2005), *Provisional Measures in International Commercial Arbitration*, Kluwer Law International, p. 5.

[2] The emergency arbitrator mechanism in the book is not the summary arbitral proceedings adopted in the Netherlands according to the NAI and the Dutch Code of Civil Procedure. The emergency arbitrator mechanism discussed in the book is a generally accepted concept in institutional rules and arbitration laws. More details regarding the Dutch summary arbitral proceeding can be found in Rogier Schellaars & Martje Verhoeven-de Vries Lentsch (2020), *Arbitral Emergency Proceedings—à la Hollandaise: Twenty Years of Practice*, Tijdschrift voor Arbitrage, pp. 15–18.

J. Zhang, *The Enforceability of the Interim Measures Granted by an Emergency Arbitrator in International Commercial Arbitration*,
https://doi.org/10.1007/978-981-97-6536-2_1

However, the proliferation of emergency arbitrator mechanisms is not without problems. The enforceability of the interim measures granted by an emergency arbitrator is seen as the "Achilles' Heel" of the arbitration system.[3] In the 2015 International Arbitration Survey by the Queen Mary University of London and White & Case LLP, 79% of the participants hesitated to use this mechanism, because of the uncertainty and unpredictability of the enforceability of the interim measures issued by an emergency arbitrator.[4] The ability to enforce decisions made by emergency arbitrator is a critical concern for the choice of seat of arbitration.[5] Not only in practice but also academically, the enforceability of interim measures granted by emergency arbitrators has been under dispute since the introduction of the emergency arbitrator mechanism.[6]

This research evaluates the enforceability of the interim measures granted by the emergency arbitrator in international commercial arbitration. It starts with comparisons between various emergency arbitrator provisions in arbitral institutions and between relevant arbitration laws in different jurisdictions. Based on the comparisons and legal practice, the legal status and competence of an emergency arbitrator, the legal criteria for an emergency arbitrator to decide on the request, and the essential elements necessary to enforce the interim measures by an emergency arbitrator will be analyzed. After the assessment, suggestions to improve the current emergency arbitrator mechanism will be proposed.

---

[3] Erin Collins (2012), Pre-Tribunal Emergency Relief in International Commercial Arbitration, 10 *Loyola University Chicago International Law Review* 116; Jason Fry (2013), The Emergency Arbitrator—Flawed Fashion or Sensible Solution?, 7 *Dispute Resolution International* 180.

[4] Queen Mary University of London and White & Case LLP, 2015 International Arbitration Survey: Improvements and Innovations in International Arbitration, p. 28, available at http://www.arbitration.qmul.ac.uk/media/arbitration/docs/2015_International_Arbitration_Survey.pdf (18 December 2023).

[5] Queen Mary University of London and White & Case LLP, 2021 International Arbitration Survey: Adapting Arbitration to a Changing World, p. 8, available at https://arbitration.qmul.ac.uk/research/2021-international-arbitration-survey/ (1 June 2024).

[6] Baruch Baigel (2014), The Emergency Arbitrator Procedure under the 2012 ICC Rules: A Juridical Analysis, 31 *Journal of International Arbitration* 9; Cavinder Bull (2013), Commencing Arbitration, in Albert Van den Berg, *International Arbitration: The Coming of a New Age?*, 17 *ICCA Congress Series* 163; Diana Paraguacuto-Maheo & Christine Lecuyer-Thieffry (2016), Emergency Arbitrator: A New Player In The Field-The French Perspective, 40 *Fordham International Law Journal* 761; Fabio G. Santacroce (2015), The Emergency Arbitrator: A Full-Fledged Arbitrator Rendering An Enforceable Decision?, 31 *Arbitration International* 302–312; Ali Yesilirmak (2005), *Provisional Measures in International Commercial Arbitration*, Kluwer Law International, pp. 114–157.

1.1 Background of the Research

Interim measures are not a recent development. Dating back to the Middle Ages,[7] possessory assizes were used to "mitigate the long delay which occurred between the issuance of a writ of right and the trial—a delay which was due to the solemnity of the writ of right".[8] The introduction of interim measures into the world of international commercial arbitration is related to the growth of international trade and business. From the beginning of the twentieth century until the early 1980s, attempts to improve international arbitration had little success, partially because of the restrictions on the free movement in commercial activities after the Second World War.[9] However, during this time period, important conventions were established in legal practice on the recognition and enforcement of arbitration agreements and awards internationally,[10] in particular, the Convention on the Recognition and Enforcement of Foreign Arbitral Awards 1958 (New York Convention),[11] the European Convention on International Commercial Arbitration 1961.[12] The fall of the Berlin Wall from 1989 marked the beginning of a new era of globalization.[13] Restrictions on international trade and business were gradually removed. The developments in the international market called for a mature mechanism of international commercial arbitration, which gave rise to advances in arbitration practices. The use of interim measures in international commercial arbitration was one of these developments. The United Nations Commission on International Trade Law (UNCITRAL) already introduced its Model Law on International Commercial Arbitration in 1985, including Article 17 regulating interim measures by an arbitral tribunal. The purpose of the model law is "to assist States in reforming and modernizing their laws on arbitral procedure",[14] taking the needs of international commercial arbitration into account.

---

[7] W. W. Buckland & A. D. McNair (1965), *Roman Law and Common Law: A Comparison in Outline*, Cambridge University Press, pp. 420–423.

[8] Jerome B. Elkind (1981), *Interim Protection: A Functional Analysis*, Martinus Nijhoff Publishers bv, p. 27.

[9] Geoffrey Jones (1996), *The Evolution of International Business: An Introduction*, Routledge, pp. 46–52.

[10] Ali Yesilirmak (2005), *Provisional Measures in International Commercial Arbitration*, Kluwer Law International, p. 21.

[11] Convention on the Recognition and Enforcement of Foreign Arbitral Awards, New York, 10 June 1958, United Nations Treaty Series, vol. 330, p. 3, available at https://treaties.un.org/Pages/ViewDetails.aspx?src=TREATY&mtdsg_no=XXII-1&chapter=22&clang=_en (18 December 2023).

[12] European Convention on International Commercial Arbitration, Geneva, 21 April 1961, United Nations Treaty Series, vol. 484, p. 349, available at https://treaties.un.org/Pages/ViewDetails.aspx?src=TREATY&mtdsg_no=XXII-2&chapter=22&clang=_en (18 December 2023).

[13] Loukas Mistelism (2000), Regulatory Aspects: Globalization, Harmonization, Legal Transplants, and Law Reform—Some Fundamental Observations, 34 *International Lawyer* 1055.

[14] UNCITRAL, UNCITRAL Model Law on International Commercial Arbitration (1985), with amendments as adopted in 2006, para.1, available at https://uncitral.un.org/sites/uncitral.un.org/files/media-documents/uncitral/en/07-86998_ebook.pdf (18 December 2023).

In 2006, the UNCITRAL Model Law was amended, extending the article to a whole chapter for interim measures.

Historically speaking, "national law [has] not infrequently denied arbitrators the power to order interim measures"[15] based on the rationale that arbitrators could not issue coercive measures because of public policy concerns.[16] With the development of international arbitration, and the increasing need for interim measures, "[s]tates began to view the courts' role as supportive of arbitration, rather than considering them separately".[17] The prohibition against arbitrators granting interim measures has "rightly been almost universally abandoned".[18] Nevertheless, the constitution of the arbitral tribunal is time-consuming, and this can have serious consequences, such as evidence becoming or irreparably damaged, which can result in meaningless final awards with little effect. To prevent these situations, some arbitral institutions introduced various mechanisms in order to provide fast and valid interim measures without having to go to state courts. In 1990, the ICC provided the possibility for interim measures before the constitution of a tribunal, namely the Rules for a Pre-Arbitral Referee Procedure. While the emergency arbitrator mechanism adopts an opt-out approach, which means that, if the parties agree to arbitrate under a specific set of institutional rules, then the included emergency arbitrator mechanism will automatically apply, the ICC Rules for a Pre-Arbitral Referee Procedure adopts an opt-in approach, which means that parties who want to apply the pre-arbitral referee procedure have to agree on the rules expressly. Unfortunately, mainly due to the opt-in approach,[19] the procedure is rarely used, and it is to a great extent unknown to the public.[20] In 1999, the American Arbitration Association (AAA) created the Optional Rules for Emergency Measures of Protection. Similar to the ICC Rules for a Pre-Arbitral Referee Procedure, the AAA Optional Rules used the same opt-in approach, which has led to difficulties in practice by requiring parties to agree on those rules separately.[21] In 2006, the ICDR, which is an international branch of the AAA, developed the emergency arbitrator mechanism in its International Dispute

---

[15] Gary B. Born (2021), *International Commercial Arbitration*, Kluwer Law International, p. 2610.

[16] Dana Bucy (2010), How to Best Protect Party Rights: The Future of Interim Relief in International Commercial Arbitration under the Amended UNCITRAL Model Law, 25 *American University International Law Review* 588.

[17] Dana Bucy (2010), How to Best Protect Party Rights: The Future of Interim Relief in International Commercial Arbitration under the Amended UNCITRAL Model Law, 25 *American University International Law Review* 588.

[18] Gary B. Born (2021), *International Commercial Arbitration*, Kluwer Law International, p. 2611.

[19] Article 2.1.1, ICC Rules for a Pre-Arbitral Referee Procedure 1990, available at https://iccwbo.org/news-publications/arbitration-adr-rules-and-tools/rules-pre-arbitral-referee-procedure/ (18 December 2023).

[20] Gary B. Born (2021), *International Commercial Arbitration*, Kluwer Law International, p. 2632; Emmanuel Gaillard & Philippe Pinsolle (2004), The ICC Pre-Arbitral Referee: First Practical Experience, 20 *Arbitration International* 13.

[21] G Lemenez & P Quigley (2008), The ICDR's Emergency Arbitrator Procedure in Action, 63 *Dispute Resolution Journal* 62; G. Smith (2015), The Emergence of Emergency Arbitrations, Dec. *Arbitrator & Mediator Journal* 2, available at http://www.gordonsmithlegal.com.au/resources/Emergency%20Arbitrations%20(12082016).pdf (18 December 2023).

Resolution Procedures 2006. The ICDR emergency arbitrator mechanism follows the opt-out approach.[22] After nearly 15 years of developments, most of the world's leading international arbitral institutions, like the ICC,[23] the LCIA,[24] the SIAC,[25] the HKIAC,[26] and the SCC,[27] have adopted the emergency arbitrator mechanism with an approach like the ICDR.

The emergency arbitrator mechanism is used upon the request of the parties for interim measures to be granted before the constitution of the arbitral tribunal, without prejudging the merits of the dispute.[28] 93% of the participants in the 2015 International Arbitration Survey were in favor of the emergency arbitration being included in the arbitration rules.[29] 38% of the participants would even have preferred to have a mandatory rule in place.[30] Despite its widespread acceptance, the emergency arbitrator mechanism has quite unique features.

The emergency arbitrator mechanism is extremely efficient,[31] which is a high priority in issuing interim measures considering the urgency at issue. Taking the

---

[22] Article 7, ICDR International Dispute Resolution Procedures (ICDR Arbitration Rules) 2021, available at https://www.icdr.org/sites/default/files/document_repository/ICDR_Rules_1.pdf?utm_source=icdr-website&utm_medium=rules-page&utm_campaign=rules-intl-update-1mar (1June 2024).

[23] Article 29 & Appendix V, ICC Arbitration Rules 2021, available at https://iccwbo.org/dispute-resolution/dispute-resolution-services/arbitration/rules-procedure/2021-arbitration-rules/ (18 December 2023).

[24] Article 9B, LCIA Arbitration Rules 2020, available at https://www.lcia.org/Dispute_Resolution_Services/lcia-arbitration-rules-2020.aspx#Article%209B (18 December 2023).

[25] Article 30 & Schedule 1, Arbitration Rules of the Singapore International Arbitration Centre (SIAC Arbitration Rules) 2016, available at https://siac.org.sg/siac-rules-2016 (18 December 2023).

[26] Article 23 & Schedule 4, HKIAC Administered Arbitration Rules (HKIAC Arbitration Rules) 2024, available at https://hkiac.org/arbitration/rules-practice-notes/hkiac-administered-2024 (1June 2024).

[27] Article 37 & Appendix II, SCC Arbitration Rules 2023, available at https://sccarbitrationinstitute.se/en/resource-library/rules-and-policies/scc-rules (18 December 2023).

[28] Peter L. Michaelson, Emergency Arbitration: Fast, Effective and Economical, available at https://www.ccarbitrators.org/wp-content/uploads/2021/06/PLMichaelson-Emerg-ArbABA-JustResolutions-03-2016final-complete.pdf (18 December 2023); Diana Paraguacuto-Maheo & Christine Lecuyer-Thieffry (2016), Emergency Arbitrator: A New Player In The Field-The French Perspective, 40 *Fordham International Law Journal* 763; Sarah Zagata Vasani, The Emergency Arbitrator: Doubling as an Effective Option for Urgent Relief and an Early Settlement Tool, available at https://www.lexology.com/library/detail.aspx?g=e786221a-8823-4f25-8307-d28df1078fdc (18 December 2023).

[29] Queen Mary University of London and White & Case LLP, 2015 International Arbitration Survey: Improvements and Innovations in International Arbitration, p. 29, available at http://www.arbitration.qmul.ac.uk/media/arbitration/docs/2015_International_Arbitration_Survey.pdf (18 December 2023).

[30] Queen Mary University of London and White & Case LLP, 2015 International Arbitration Survey: Improvements and Innovations in International Arbitration, p. 29, available at http://www.arbitration.qmul.ac.uk/media/arbitration/docs/2015_International_Arbitration_Survey.pdf (18 December 2023).

[31] Chan Leng Sun & Weiyi Tan (2013), Making Arbitration Effective: Expedited Procedures, Emergency Arbitrators and Interim Relief, 6 *Contemporary Asia Arbitration Journal* 350.

SCC Arbitration Rules 2023 as an example, the appointment of an emergency arbitrator takes place within 24 h, and the decision of the emergency arbitrator shall be made within 5 days after the application.[32] The statistics show that, in two relevant SCC cases in 2022, an emergency arbitrator was appointed within 24 h, and the decisions made by those emergency arbitrators were issued on average within 8 days.[33] In 2021, the decision rendered on average after 6.6 days in 7 SCC emergency arbitrator proceedings.[34] Additionally, the emergency arbitrator mechanism guarantees confidentiality and impartiality. An emergency arbitrator is appointed by an arbitral institution, which is neutral. Parties also have the right to challenge an improper appointment.[35] Meanwhile, providing parties the opportunity to seek interim measures rendered by an emergency arbitrator instead of state courts respects the initial willingness of parties to resolve disputes through arbitration. Furthermore, the emergency arbitrator mechanism is easily accessible. Unlike the ICC Rules for a Pre-arbitral Referee Procedure, the emergency arbitrator provisions are included in the institutional rules. If parties do not explicitly exclude the emergency arbitrator provisions, the mechanism will apply automatically.[36] Additionally, using the emergency arbitrator mechanism for interim measures does not require a specialized knowledge of another unfamiliar legal system and procedures. Spending time and making efforts on foreign legislation could end up causing a considerable delay in the arbitral proceedings, leading to a meaningless final award.

1.2 Enforcement of the Interim Measures Granted by an Emergency Arbitrator: Characterization, Questions and Challenges

Despite all the advantages discussed, the emergency arbitrator mechanism and, like all other mechanisms, it is no exception as it also encounters practical problems as followed.

There is no widely accepted definition of what constitutes an emergency arbitrator. The Hong Kong Arbitration Ordinance (Cap. 609) refers it as "an emergency arbitrator appointed under the arbitration rules (including the arbitration rules of a permanent arbitral institution) agreed to or adopted by the parties to deal with the

[32] Articles 4 & 8 of Appendix II, SCC Arbitration Rules 2023.

[33] SCC, Statistics 2022, Emergency Arbitrator Proceedings 2022, available at https://sccarbitrationinstitute.se/en/about-scc/scc-statistics (18 December 2023).

[34] SCC, Statistics 2021, Emergency Arbitrator Proceedings 2021, available at https://sccarbitrationinstitute.se/sites/default/files/2023-02/scc-statistics-2021.pdf (18 December 2023).

[35] Article 3 of Appendix V, ICC Arbitration Rules 2021; Article 7 of Schedule 4, HKIAC Arbitration Rules 2024, Article 4 of Appendix II, SCC Arbitration Rules 2023.

[36] Christopher Boog (2018), Chapter 4, Part II: Commentary on the ICC Rules, Article 29 [Emergency arbitrator], in M Arroyo (ed), *Arbitration in Switzerland: The Practitioner's Guide*, Kluwer Law International, p. 815.

parties' applications for emergency relief before an arbitral tribunal is constituted".[37] Whether an emergency arbitrator is a fully-fledged arbitrator is still in dispute. Some scholars argue that an emergency arbitrator has the same power as a regular arbitrator with regard to issuing interim measures, being both of a jurisdictional and contractual nature.[38] Others insist that an emergency arbitrator shall not be considered the same as an arbitrator.[39] A tribunal, enjoying broader power than an emergency arbitrator, can issue interim measures, and more importantly, it can modify or even nullify the interim measures granted by an emergency arbitrator in the same dispute, which may lead to conflicting results on the same issue.

The status of the decisions made by an emergency arbitrator is not clear. An interim measure granted by an emergency arbitrator, without addressing the merits of the dispute, is, by its nature, provisional, which brings uncertainty in terms of enforcement. For example, it is believed that, in order to be recognized and enforced by state courts under the Convention on the Recognition and Enforcement of Foreign Arbitral Awards 1958 (New York Convention), the award needs to be "final and binding".[40] The interim measures granted by an emergency arbitrator seem to fail this "finality" test. The standard for an emergency arbitrator to decide on the request of interim measures is undetermined. The ICC Arbitration Rules 2021 state that an emergency arbitrator "shall conduct the proceedings in the manner which the emergency arbitrator considers to be appropriate, taking into account the nature and the urgency".[41] The LCIA Arbitration Rules 2023 and the SCC Arbitration Rules 2023 adopt a similar approach.[42] Without providing a specific standard, an emergency arbitrator has broad discretion in the issuance of interim measures. As a consequence, there is an increase in the unpredictability of the decisions.

There are no international conventions and only little legislation addressing the emergency arbitrator mechanism in most jurisdictions. Currently, no international

---

[37] Section 22A, Arbitration Ordinance (Cap. 609) 2015, available at https://www.elegislation.gov.hk/hk/cap609 (18 December 2023).

[38] Fabio G. Santacroce (2015), The emergency arbitrator: a full-fledged arbitrator rendering an enforceable decision?, 31 *Arbitration International* 292; see also William G. Bassler (2016), The Enforceability of Emergency Awards in the United States: or when interim means final, 32 *Arbitration International* 574; Christoph Muller& Sabrina Pearson (2015), Waving the Green Flag to Emergency Arbitration under the Swiss Rules: the Sauber Saga, 33 *ASA Bulletin* 814; Ank A. Santerns& Jaroslav Kudrna (2017), The State of Play of Enforcement of Emergency Arbitrator Decisions, 34 *Journal of International Arbitration* 10.

[39] Baruch Baigel (2014), The Emergency Arbitrator Procedure under the 2012 ICC Rules: A Juridical Analysis, 31 *Journal of International Arbitration*; K. Berger (2005), Pre-Arbitral Referees: Arbitrators, Quasi-Arbitrators, Hybrids, or Creature of Contract Law?, in G. Aksen, (eds), *Global Reflections on International Law, Commerce and Dispute Resolution: Liber Amicorum in Honor of Robert Briner, International Chamber of Commerce*; J.P. Beraudo (2005), Recognition and Enforcement of Interim Measures of Protection Ordered by Arbitral Tribunals, 22 *Journal of International Arbitration.*

[40] Jonathan Hill (2018), Is an Interim Measure of Protection Ordered by an Arbitral Tribunal an Arbitral Award?, 9 *Journal of International Dispute Settlement* 594.

[41] Article 5(2) of Appendix V, ICC Arbitration Rules 2021.

[42] Article 9.7, LCIA Arbitration Rules 2020; Article 7 of Appendix II, SCC Arbitration Rules 2023.

conventions include the issue of interim measures, without even mentioning the emergency arbitrator mechanism. States take various approaches when facing the request to enforce interim measures granted by an emergency arbitration, which leads to legal conflicts. In some jurisdictions, the power to grant interim measures belongs exclusively to state courts. For example, arbitral tribunals need to submit the applications for interim measures to state courts in Mainland China.[43] The situation is also similar in the Czech Republic.[44] With only a few jurisdictions recognizing the enforceability of interim measures granted by an emergency arbitrator, it is far from enough for the future development of this mechanism.

1.3 Structure and Content of the Book

This book concentrates on the current situation and future development of the emergency arbitrator mechanism with a specific focus on the enforceability of interim measures granted by an emergency arbitrator in international commercial arbitration.

According to the scope of influence and applicability, from affecting only parties to different jurisdictions,[45] this book starts with institutional rules in Chap. 2. It focuses on a comparison of arbitration rules. Six international institutions, including the ICC, the ICDR, the LCIA, the HKIAC, the SIAC, and the SCC, were chosen for the study. By comparing the rules, the common legal framework of the emergency arbitrator mechanism will be provided, presenting several unique innovation rules adopted by different arbitral institutions. For example, the LCIA allows *ex parte* interim measures, which means that, under some circumstances, an emergency arbitrator could issue the decision without consulting the other party.[46] Additionally, other solutions for interim measures that can be used before the constitution of a tribunal will also be discussed.

Chapter 3 tries to discover the essential requirements to enforce interim measures granted by an emergency arbitrator by conducting a comparison among international conventions, and a comparison among three selective jurisdictions—Singapore, Mainland China and the United States of America. These three jurisdictions represent three different attitudes toward the emergency arbitrator mechanism. The current legal practice concerning the emergency arbitrator mechanism in these jurisdictions will be discussed, including arbitration laws and case law. Chapters 4, 5, and 6 discuss the potential barriers to enforce the interim measures granted by an emergency arbitrator summarized in the comparisons.

---

[43] Article 68, Arbitration Law of the People's Republic of China 2017, translation available at http://en.pkulaw.cn/display.aspx?cgid=83c8fbd6da8a6eb8bdfb&lib=law (18 December 2023).

[44] Section 22, Act of the Czech Republic No. 216/1994 Sb. on arbitration proceedings and on enforcement of arbitration awards, available at https://is.muni.cz/el/1422/jaro2008/SOC026/um/216-1994_EN.pdf (18 December 2023).

[45] Margaret L. Moses (2017), *The Principles and Practice of International Commercial Arbitration*, Cambridge University Press, p. 6.

[46] Article 9.7, LCIA Arbitration Rules 2020.

In Chap. 4, the discussion will be mainly based on the legal status and jurisdiction of an emergency arbitrator, which is the premise and foundation determining the enforceability of the interim measures granted by an emergency arbitrator. The chapter will engage in the debate to discover the true nature and the source of jurisdiction of an emergency arbitrator.

Chapter 5 focuses on the standards required for an emergency arbitrator to issue interim measures before the constitution of the arbitral tribunal based on empirical study mainly based on the SCC emergency arbitration decisions. Moreover, the emergency arbitrator mechanism requires that there is no prejudgment of the merits of the dispute involved in the decision. However, in order to grant interim measures, the basic facts of the dispute must be examined. The boundary between taking the merits into account and prejudging the merits will also be discussed in this part.

Chapter 6 deals with the binding nature of interim measures rendered by an emergency arbitrator, dealing with several controversial elements that could probably cause adverse effects on their enforceability. Those elements include arbitrability of claims related to the request for interim measures, the possibility to modify, terminate, or annul by an arbitral tribunal, setting aside by state courts at the seat of arbitration, the finality test for enforceable arbitral awards, and public policy concerns.

Chapter 7 will summarize the assessment of the emergency arbitrator mechanism and discuss whether harmonizing the enforceability of interim measures granted by emergency arbitrators is necessary. If necessary, suggestions to improve the enforceability of the interim measures granted by an emergency arbitrator mechanism will be proposed.

1.4 Methodology and Limitation of the Research

The book takes a doctrinal and comparative approach, mainly based on descriptive and normative research. The comparative studies include a comparison among the different emergency arbitrator provisions of specific arbitral institutions and a comparison among arbitration laws and legal practice, including case law in the chosen jurisdictions.

It must be noted that the research has limited the scope and number of the comparisons carried out, Due to the limited time, the comparison will not cover every arbitration rule from all existing arbitral institutions or every arbitration law from all existing jurisdictions. Owing to the confidentiality required in international commercial arbitration, cases are generally not open to the public. The cases discussed in the book are limited and not exhaustive. This research will analyze and discuss the most representative ones available.

Chapter 2
Comparison Among Institutional Arbitration Rules

In this chapter, six arbitral institutions that have emergency arbitrator mechanisms in their rules will be compared regarding the emergency arbitrator proceedings. They are the International Court of Arbitration of the International Chamber of Commerce (ICC), the International Center for Dispute Resolution (ICDR), the Hong Kong International Arbitration Centre (HKIAC), the London Court of International Arbitration (LCIA), the Singapore International Arbitration Centre (SIAC), and the Arbitration Institute of the Stockholm Chamber of Commerce (SCC). This comparison starts with a general introduction to these arbitral institutions and current statistics regarding the emergency arbitrator cases (Sect. 2.1), then a comparison of the different stages of the emergency arbitrator procedure will be carried out, including the application to initiate the emergency arbitrator mechanism (Sect. 2.2), the appointment of an emergency arbitrator (Sect. 2.3), the emergency arbitration proceedings (Sect. 2.4), the decision of an emergency arbitrator (Sect. 2.5), and the costs of emergency arbitration (Sect. 2.6). Lastly, a brief introduction will be given to some alternative solutions for interim measures before the constitution of an arbitral tribunal other than the emergency arbitrator mechanism in the institutional arbitration rules (Sect. 2.7).

2.1 Current Situation of the Emergency Arbitrator Mechanism in Arbitral Institutions

After nearly 20 years of development since 2006, arbitral institutions already have some experience in practice regarding the application of the emergency arbitrator mechanism. This section begins with a brief introduction to the ICC, the ICDR, the HKIAC, the LCIA, the SIAC, and the SCC, as representatives of existing arbitral institutions. Subsequently, facts and statistics concerning the emergency arbitrator mechanism in these arbitral institutions are provided.

J. Zhang, *The Enforceability of the Interim Measures Granted by an Emergency Arbitrator in International Commercial Arbitration*,
https://doi.org/10.1007/978-981-97-6536-2_2

2.1.1 World's Leading Arbitral Institutions

In line with the continuous growth of international commercial arbitration, arbitral institutions are also expanding at the same time.[1] The different arbitral institutions vary in the quality of the services provided. As a result, parties tend to choose an institution with a better reputation and well-established arbitration rules.

The ICC is "one of the best-known and most prestigious arbitral institutions",[2] established in Paris in 1923. Although called a "court", the ICC "exercise[s] judicial supervision of arbitration proceedings",[3] but it does not issue judgments as a regular judicial authority would. In the 2021 International Arbitration Survey, the ICC ranked at the top in the preferences for arbitral institutions among respondents to the survey.[4] Although there is a tendency that parties like to choose institutions in the region in which they are based, the respondents still commented that the "ICC would also be agreeable to both them and their counterparties".[5]

Two distinguishing features of the ICC arbitration practice may play a role in its success. First, the "Terms of Reference" needs to be drafted at the outset of an arbitral procedure. The Terms of Reference list all the information related to the relevant dispute, ensuring that all parties and the ICC have the same knowledge basis at the beginning of the arbitration proceedings.[6] Second, all the awards made by an arbitral tribunal are reviewed by the ICC before they are given to the parties in order to guarantee the quality of the awards.[7] In the emergency arbitrator mechanism, the ICC also has the power to decide on the *prima facie* jurisdiction of an emergency arbitrator before the procedure.[8]

---

[1] Margaret L. Moses (2017), *The Principles and Practice of International Commercial Arbitration*, Cambridge University Press, p. 11.

[2] Margaret L. Moses (2017), *The Principles and Practice of International Commercial Arbitration*, Cambridge University Press, p. 11.

[3] ICC, ICC International Court of Arbitration, available at https://iccwbo.org/dispute-resolution-services/arbitration/icc-international-court-arbitration/ (16 June 2020).

[4] Queen Mary University of London and White & Case LLP, 2021 International Arbitration Survey: Adapting Arbitration to a Changing World, p. 9, available at https://arbitration.qmul.ac.uk/research/2021-international-arbitration-survey/ (1 June 2024).

[5] Queen Mary University of London and White & Case LLP, 2015 International Arbitration Survey: Improvements and Innovations in International Arbitration, p. 17, available at http://www.arbitration.qmul.ac.uk/media/arbitration/docs/2015_International_Arbitration_Survey.pdf (16 June 2020).

[6] Article 23, ICC Arbitration Rules 2021; Margaret L. Moses (2017), *The Principles and Practice of International Commercial Arbitration*, Cambridge University Press, p. 12.

[7] Alan Redfern & J. Martin Hunter (2022), et al., *Redfern and Hunter on International Arbitration*, Oxford University Press, p. 45.

[8] Article 1(5) of Appendix V, ICC Arbitration Rules 2021.

The American Arbitration Association (AAA) is responsible for the administration of domestic arbitration inside the United States, including inter-state arbitrations.[9] The ICDR is an international branch of the AAA established in 1996 with "exclusive responsibility" to deal with international arbitrations.[10] The ICDR also cooperates with other arbitral institutions, for example, the SIAC,[11] which can have the result of promoting Singapore as an important seat of arbitration in Asia. Both the AAA and the ICDR's rules are drafted based on the UNCITRAL Model Law on International Commercial Arbitration (1985), with amendments as adopted in 2006, intending to allow "a maximum of flexibility and a minimum of administrative supervision".[12]

The HKIAC was established in 1985 under Hong Kong arbitration laws.[13] After more than 30 years of expansion and growth, the HKIAC now "represents the most popular arbitral institution outside of Europe".[14] The HKIAC also received Global Arbitration Review's innovation award of 2014, which reflects the fact that it is "constantly at the forefront of innovative arbitration practice".[15]

The LCIA was founded in 1892,[16] known as "the oldest existing international arbitration institution".[17] As one of the world's leading arbitration centers, the LCIA's international character can be found in the fact that "over 80% of parties in pending LCIA cases are not of English nationality".[18] The LCIA and the ICC have been "the acknowledged market leaders for well over a decade".[19] The reasons for parties to choose the LCIA as a dispute resolution center were for the "reputation, neutrality and expertise".[20]

The SIAC, which was established in 1991, is another leading arbitral institution located in the Asian region. Similar to the HKIAC, the SIAC "has been cited by

---

[9] Alan Redfern & J. Martin Hunter (2015), et al., *Redfern and Hunter on International Arbitration*, Oxford University Press, p. 49.

[10] Gary B. Born (2021), *International Commercial Arbitration*, Kluwer Law International, p. 204.

[11] Margaret L. Moses (2017), *The Principles and Practice of International Commercial Arbitration*, Cambridge University Press, p. 12.

[12] Gary B. Born (2021), *International Commercial Arbitration*, Kluwer Law International, p. 205.

[13] HKIAC, About HKIAC, available at http://www.hkiac.org/about-us (16 June 2020).

[14] Margaret L. Moses (2017), *The Principles and Practice of International Commercial Arbitration*, Cambridge University Press, p. 12.

[15] HKIAC, At A Glance, available at https://www.hkiac.org/about-us (16 June 2020).

[16] LCIA, History, available at http://www.lcia.org/LCIA/history.aspx (16 June 2020).

[17] Margaret L. Moses (2017), *The Principles and Practice of International Commercial Arbitration*, Cambridge University Press, pp. 12–13.

[18] LCIA, Introduction, available at http://www.lcia.org/LCIA/introduction.aspx (16 June 2020).

[19] Queen Mary University of London and White & Case LLP, 2015 International Arbitration Survey: Improvements and Innovations in International Arbitration, p. 17, available at http://www.arbitration.qmul.ac.uk/media/arbitration/docs/2015_International_Arbitration_Survey.pdf (16 June 2020).

[20] Queen Mary University of London and White & Case LLP, 2010 International Arbitration Survey: Choices in International Arbitration, p. 24, available at http://www.arbitration.qmul.ac.uk/media/arbitration/docs/2010_InternationalArbitrationSurveyReport.pdf (16 June 2020).

practitioners and arbitrators for making great strides in the overall quality of the services it provides".[21] Singapore is also considered to be the seat of arbitration that has improved the most.[22] Although the SIAC is a very young arbitration institution compared to those based in Europe, it has excellent potential to play a "prominent" role in the international commercial arbitration community.[23]

The SCC was established in 1917 to deal with both Swedish domestic and international disputes.[24] The SCC is outstanding at resolving the disputes in East–West arbitrations.[25] Additionally, by developing into a unique role in international investment disputes, the SCC has become "the world's second largest institution for investment disputes",[26] following the World Bank's International Center for Settlement of Investment Disputes (ICSID).

2.1.2 Facts and Statistics Concerning the Emergency Arbitrator Mechanism in Arbitral Institutions

Since the ICDR adopted the emergency arbitrator mechanism in 2006, its position in the international commercial arbitration community has been under development for over 15 years, reflected in its latest version of rules in 2021. The SCC amended its rules in 2010 by adding the emergency arbitrator provisions. In 2023, the SCC introduced the latest version of its arbitration rules. The SIAC adopted the emergency arbitrator mechanism in 2010 and amended it in both 2013 and 2016. The ICC introduced the emergency arbitrator mechanism in 2012 and amended its institutional rules in 2021. The HKIAC used the same approach of providing for the emergency arbitrator mechanism in 2013 and thereafter updated its arbitration rules in 2018 and 2024. The LCIA made a similar adjustment in 2014 in its arbitration rules, and in its newly amended rules in 2020.

Although those arbitral institutions have provided the possibility for interim measures to be issued by emergency arbitrators, the current caseload of emergency arbitration varies among the institutions. The ICC had enabled parties to apply the emergency arbitrator mechanism in 154 cases since the introduction in 2012 by the

---

[21] Margaret L. Moses (2017), *The Principles and Practice of International Commercial Arbitration*, Cambridge University Press, p. 13.

[22] Queen Mary University of London and White & Case LLP, 2015 International Arbitration Survey: Improvements and Innovations in International Arbitration, p. 2, http://www.arbitration.qmul.ac.uk/media/arbitration/docs/2015_International_Arbitration_Survey.pdf (16 June 2020).

[23] Margaret L. Moses (2017), *The Principles and Practice of International Commercial Arbitration*, Cambridge University Press, p. 13.

[24] SCC, About the SCC, available at http://www.sccinstitute.com/about-the-scc/ (16 June 2020).

[25] Margaret L. Moses (2017), *The Principles and Practice of International Commercial Arbitration*, Cambridge University Press, pp. 13–14; SCC, About the SCC, available at http://www.sccinstitute.com/about-the-scc/ (16 June 2020).

[26] SCC, About the SCC, available at http://www.sccinstitute.com/about-the-scc/ (16 June 2020).

end of 2020.[27] Between 2006 and the end of 2022, there were 92 applications under the ICDR emergency arbitration provisions.[28] The SIAC administrated 152 requests for the emergency arbitrator mechanism since 2010 so far, consolidating the SIAC as another leader in the emergency arbitrator proceedings.[29] Since the introduction of the emergency arbitrator mechanism in 2010, the SCC managed 73 applications for interim measures by an emergency arbitrator in total.[30] Since 2013, 35 arbitration cases were filed with the HKIAC as using the emergency arbitrator mechanism.[31] 22 cases before the LCIA called for an emergency arbitrator since 2014.[32]

The 2015 International Arbitration Survey indicated that 32% of the participants considered the "arbitral rules applicable to the dispute"[33] and this was within the three most important factors that were taken into account when choosing whether to apply for the emergency arbitrator mechanism for interim measures. With the differences in the number of applications for the emergency arbitrator mechanism, it is essential to analyze the institutional rules in the various arbitral institutions. This chapter analyzes the general framework of the emergency arbitrator mechanism in order to present a full picture of the proceedings, also including specific regulations from individual arbitral institutions.

The discussion here covers all the different stages of emergency arbitrator proceedings in the chosen arbitral institutions (the ICC, the ICDR, the HKIAC, the LCIA, the SIAC, and the SCC), including the application, the appointment of an emergency arbitrator, the emergency arbitrator proceedings, and the decision made by an emergency arbitrator. When analyzing those rules, the different versions will be identified to map out the developments of the emergency arbitrator mechanism within each institution over time. The arbitration rules include the ICC Arbitration Rules 2012,2017, and 2021, the ICDR Arbitration Rules 2006, 2009, 2014, and 2021, the HKIAC Arbitration Rules 2013, 2018, and 2024, the LCIA Arbitration Rules 2014, and 2020, the SIAC Arbitration Rules 2010, 2013 and 2016, the SCC Arbitration Rules 2010, 2017, and 2023.

---

[27] ICC, ICC Dispute Resolution 2020 Statistics, available at https://jusmundi.com/en/document/publication/en-2020-icc-dispute-resolution-statistics (25 May 2024).

[28] ICDR, 2022 ICDR Case Data Infographic, https://www.adr.org/sites/default/files/document_repository/AAA430_ICDR_Case_Data_2022.pdf (25 May 2024).

[29] SIAC, SIAC Annual Report 2023, p. 42, available at https://siac.org.sg/wp-content/uploads/2024/04/SIAC_AR2023.pdf (25 May 2024).

[30] SCC, SCC Statistics 2010–2023, available at https://sccarbitrationinstitute.se/en/about-scc/scc-statistics-0 (25 May 2024).

[31] HKIAC, 2023 Statistics, available at https://www.hkiac.org/about-us/statistics (25 May 2024).

[32] LCIA, Reports, available at https://www.lcia.org/lcia/reports.aspx (25 May 2024).

[33] Queen Mary University of London and White & Case LLP, 2015 International Arbitration Survey: Improvements and Innovations in International Arbitration, p. 28, available at http://www.arbitration.qmul.ac.uk/media/arbitration/docs/2015_International_Arbitration_Survey.pdf (16 June 2020).

2.2 Application for Starting the Emergency Arbitrator Procedure

Although the detailed rules are not the same in the various institutions, the emergency arbitrator provisions share a similar goal, which is to deal with the requests for interim measures in an efficient way. In order to meet this aim, the arbitration rules provide for a short period to react to such applications. The following aspects of an application for the emergency arbitrator procedure will be discussed in detail: timing, the default nature and the essential content of an application.

2.2.1 *Timing*

Generally, an application for the emergency arbitrator mechanism commences before the constitution of an arbitral tribunal. However, the starting point of the application varies in the different institutions.

Article 29 (1) of the ICC Arbitration Rules 2021, 2017 and 2012 requires parties to initiate an application for the emergency arbitrator mechanism before the file is submitted to a constituted arbitral tribunal.[34] It is "irrespective of whether the party making the application has already submitted its Request for Arbitration".[35] Meanwhile, the ICC Arbitration Rules 2021, 2017 and 2012 all state that the Request for Arbitration must be received within ten days after the application for the emergency arbitrator mechanism has been made. If not, the ICC will terminate the application.[36] Lastly, for an effective emergency arbitrator procedure, the arbitration agreement under the ICC rules shall be concluded on or after 1 January 2012 to be subject to these rules.[37]

The ICDR requires the party who needs an emergency arbitrator for interim measures to submit a written notice to the institution and all the other parties "concurrent with or following the submission of a Notice of Arbitration".[38] The applicable version of rules for a particular emergency arbitration will be the ICDR Rules "as in effect at the date of commencement of the arbitration".[39] In the ICDR Arbitration Rules 2009, the use of the emergency arbitrator procedure is limited to arbitration agreements entered into on or after 1 May 2006, unless parties agree otherwise.[40]

According to the HKIAC Arbitration Rules 2018, a party can apply for the emergency arbitrator mechanism "(a) before, (b) concurrent with, or (c) following the

[34] Article 29(1), ICC Arbitration Rules 2021, 2017 and 2012.

[35] Article 29(1), ICC Arbitration Rules 2021, 2017 and 2012.

[36] Article 1(6) of Appendix V, ICC Arbitration Rules 2021, 2017 and 2012.

[37] Article 29 (6), ICC Arbitration Rules 2017 and 2012.

[38] Article 7(1), ICDR Arbitration Rules 2021; Article 6(1), ICDR Arbitration Rules 2014.

[39] Article 1(1), ICDR Arbitration Rules 2021 and 2014.

[40] Article 37(1), ICDR Arbitration Rules 2009.

filing of a Notice of Arbitration, but prior to the constitution of the arbitral tribunal".[41] Under the previous HKIAC Arbitration Rules 2013, parties were not able to apply for an emergency arbitrator before a request for arbitration.[42] In order to apply the HKIAC emergency arbitrator provisions, the notice of arbitration needs to be submitted to the institution on or after 1 November 2013, unless the parties to the dispute agree otherwise.[43]

The LCIA does not require a request for arbitration before an application for the emergency arbitrator proceedings. Any party can apply for an emergency arbitrator "at any time prior to the formation or expedited formation of the Arbitral Tribunal".[44] The LCIA also provides that the parties need to conclude the arbitration agreement after 1 October 2014, or as agreed otherwise, in order to use the provisions.[45]

The emergency arbitrator mechanism conducted under the SIAC rules is required to be applied "concurrent with or following the filing of a Notice of Arbitration but prior to the constitution of the Tribunal".[46] The SIAC Arbitration Rules 2016 concerning the emergency arbitrator mechanism came into force on 1 August 2016[47] and applies to "any arbitration started on or after that date"[48] unless parties agree otherwise. Similarly, the starting time-limit to apply the relative provisions has not changed from the SIAC Arbitration Rules 2010 and the SIAC Arbitration Rules 2013, since the introduction of the emergency arbitrator mechanism. In the SIAC Arbitration Rules 2013, the commencing date to use the emergency arbitrator mechanism is 1 April 2013.[49] In the SIAC Arbitration Rules 2010, the date was 1 July 2010.[50]

There is no requirement to submit a request for arbitration before applying for the emergency arbitrator mechanism under the SCC rules, as long as the application is made before the case has been referred to an arbitral tribunal.[51] It regulates that "the parties shall be deemed to have agreed that the following rules, or such amended rules, in force on the date of the commencement of the arbitration, or the filling of an application of the appointment of an [e]mergency [a]rbitrator" apply unless the parties have agreed otherwise.[52]

[41] Article 23.1 & Article 1 of Schedule 4, HKIAC Arbitration Rules 2024 and 2018.

[42] Article 23.1 & Article 1 of Schedule 4, HKIAC Arbitration Rules 2013.

[43] Article 1.5, HKIAC Arbitration Rules 2018; Article 1.3, HKIAC Arbitration Rules 2013.

[44] Article 9.4, LCIA Arbitration Rules 2020 and 2014.

[45] Article 9.16, LCIA Arbitration Rules 2020; Article 9.14, LCIA Arbitration Rules 2014.

[46] Article 1 of Schedule 1, SIAC Arbitration Rules 2016.

[47] Article 1.2, SIAC Arbitration Rules 2016.

[48] Article 1.2, SIAC Arbitration Rules 2016.

[49] Article 1.2, SIAC Arbitration Rules 2013.

[50] Article 1.2, SIAC Arbitration Rules 2010.

[51] Article 1 of Appendix II, SCC Arbitration Rules2023, 2017 and 2010.

[52] Preamble, SCC Arbitration Rules 2023, 2017 and 2010.

2.2.2 *Default Nature of the Emergency Arbitrator Mechanism*

Unlike the 1990 ICC Pre-Arbitral Referee Procedure and the 1999 AAA Optional Rules for Emergency Measures of Protection, which provide an opt-in approach, the emergency arbitrator mechanism adopts an opt-out approach. The opt-out approach means that if parties agree to arbitrate under a set of specific institutional rules, and if the emergency arbitrator mechanism is included in these rules, then the mechanism will apply automatically.

However, if parties wish to exclude the application of the emergency arbitrator mechanism, they have to make that choice expressly. For example, the ICC Arbitration Rules 2021 provides a model clause as "[t]he Emergency Arbitrator Provisions shall not apply".[53] The ICC Arbitration Rules 2021 also excludes the application of the emergency arbitrator mechanism in a dispute arises from a treaty.[54] While under the ICC Arbitration Rules 2017, if parties have chosen an alternative pre-arbitral procedure for interim measures, then the emergency arbitrator provisions will no longer be applicable.[55]

The framework is quite similar concerning the relations between emergency arbitrators and state courts in terms of granting interim measures. The ICC Arbitration Rules 2021 make it clear that the emergency arbitrator mechanism is "not intended to prevent any party from seeking urgent interim or conservatory measures from a competent judicial authority at any time".[56] Such action will not be regarded as an infringement or a waiver of the arbitration agreement, but parties must notify the ICC.[57] The ICDR also allows parties to ask for interim measures from a judicial authority, which will not be incompatible with its emergency arbitrator mechanism, as well as the right to arbitrate.[58] The HKIAC takes a similar approach. Seeking interim measures from a judicial authority is possible at any time during arbitration.[59] The LCIA does not preclude any parties from seeking interim measures from legal authorities before the constitution of an arbitral tribunal. Such applications to a court and the court's order regarding interim measures "shall be communicated promptly in writing to the Emergency Arbitrator, the Registrar and all other parties".[60] The rules in the SIAC state that "[a] request for interim relief made by a party to a judicial authority prior to the constitution of the Tribunal, or in exceptional circumstances thereafter is not compatible with these Rules".[61] The SCC stipulates

---

[53] ICC Arbitration Clauses, ICC Arbitration Rules 2021, 2017 and 2012.

[54] Article 29(6), ICC Arbitration Rules 2021.

[55] Article 29(7), ICC Arbitration Rules 2017 and 2012.

[56] Article 29(7), ICC Arbitration Rules 2021, 2017 and 2012.

[57] Article 29(7), ICC Arbitration Rules 2021, 2017 and 2012.

[58] Article 7(7), ICDR Arbitration Rules 2021; Article 6(7), ICDR Arbitration Rules 2014; Article 37(8), ICDR Arbitration Rules 2009 and 2006.

[59] Article 23.9, HKIAC Arbitration Rules 2024, 2018 and 2013.

[60] Article 9.13, LCIA Arbitration Rules 2020; Article 9.12, LCIA Arbitration Rules 2014.

[61] Article 30.3, SIAC Arbitration Rules 2016; Article 26.3, SIAC Arbitration Rules 2013 and 2010.

that the request for interim measures to a judicial body is not incompatible with the arbitration agreement and the rules regarding the emergency arbitrator provisions.[62]

2.2.3 *Content of Applications for the Emergency Arbitrator Procedure*

The rules are different in the six institutions in terms of the content of an application initiating the emergency arbitrator proceedings. The following subsection firstly gives the detailed provisions of each arbitral institution and then provides a comparison based on the different required elements.

2.2.3.1 Detailed Regulation in Each Arbitral Institution

The ICC Arbitration Rules 2021 list the necessary elements to be included in an application for the emergency arbitrator mechanism very clearly in Article 1(3) of its Appendix V. They include (a) the details of all parties in the dispute; (b) the details of the representatives; (c) the circumstances resulting in the application for the emergency arbitrator mechanism and the underlying dispute; (d) the statement of the interim measures sought; (e) the reasons the applicant needs the interim measures so urgently; (f) the arbitration agreement and other related agreements; (g) any agreements concerning the place, the applicable law or the language of arbitration; (h) the proof of payment for the costs of the emergency arbitrator proceedings; and (i) the Request for Arbitration if any.[63] The applicant is welcome to submit any documents which are useful for the emergency arbitration. The elements needed in an application for the emergency arbitrator mechanism under the ICC Arbitration Rules 2017 and 2012 are the same as in the Arbitration Rules 2021.[64]

In the original rules containing the emergency arbitrator provisions, Article 37(2) of the ICDR Arbitration Rules 2006 states that the following elements need to be fulfilled: a) written notification that the administrator and all other parties have been informed or the steps have been taken in good faith; b) the nature of the interim measures sought; c) the reasons the interim measures are needed urgently; and d) the reasons for the applicant to be entitled to the requested interim measures.[65] The ICDR Arbitration Rules 2009 are the same.[66] In the ICDR Arbitration Rules 2014, one extra element was added, which is the concurrent submission of a Notice of Arbitration.[67] The ICDR Arbitration Rules 2021 clearly listed four elements required

[62] Article 37(5), SCC Arbitration Rules 2023 and 2017; Article 32(5), SCC Arbitration Rules 2010.
[63] Article 1(3) of Appendix V, ICC Arbitration Rules 2021.
[64] Article 1(3) of Appendix V, ICC Arbitration Rules 2017 and 2012.
[65] Article 37(2), ICDR Arbitration Rules 2006.
[66] Article 37(2), ICDR Arbitration Rules 2009.
[67] Article 6(1), ICDR Arbitration Rules 2014.

in an application: "a) the nature of the relief sought; b) the reasons why such relief is required on an emergency basis before the tribunal is appointed; c) the reasons why the party is likely to be found to be entitled to such relief; and d) what injury or prejudice the party will suffer if relief is not provided."[68]

The HKIAC regulates the required elements to initiate an application for the appointment of an emergency arbitrator in detail. The information shall include (a) the contact information of the parties and their representatives; (b) the relevant circumstances leading to the application and the underlying dispute; (c) the statement of the interim measures sought; d) the reasons the applicant needs the interim measures urgently; (e) the reason for the applicant to be granted the interim measures applied; (f) the arbitration agreements and other related agreements; (g) the agreement on language, the applicable law, and the seat of emergency arbitration; (h) the proof of payment; and (i) the confirmation that the documents have been delivered to all parties.[69] Other materials containing any relevant information can also be submitted. The HKIAC Arbitration Rules 2018 and 2024 add some additional disclosure requirements regarding the third-party funding provision in Article 44, which are "the existence of any funding agreement and the identity of any third party funder".[70]

Under the LCIA Arbitration Rules 2014, an application for emergency arbitration shall be in writing including: (a) a copy of Request or Response of Arbitration; (b) the notification to all parties; (c) the reasons for asking for the appointment of emergency arbitrator; (d) the claim for interim measures with reasons; and (e) the written proof of payment.[71]

Both the SIAC Arbitration Rules 2010 and 2013 require the applicant to provide the following supporting materials: (a) the nature of the interim measures sought; (b) the reason the applicant needs the interim measures on an emergency basis; (c) the reasons the appointed emergency arbitrator shall support the claim; (d) the confirmation that all parties have received a copy of the application or similar steps have been taken in good faith; and (e) the proof of payment.[72] The SIAC deleted the second element in the Arbitration Rules 2016.[73]

The SCC did not change the content of the requirements for an application for the emergency arbitrator mechanism in its Arbitration Rules 2017. An application shall include (a) the contact information of all the parties and the counsel; (b) the summary of the related dispute; (c) the statement for the interim measures sought and the reasons; (d) the arbitration agreement or any other related agreements; (e) any agreement on the seat, the applicable law, and the language of the emergency arbitrator proceedings; and (f) the proof of payment.[74]

---

[68] Article 7(1), ICDR Arbitration Rules 2021.

[69] Article 2 of Schedule 4, HKIAC Arbitration Rules 2013.

[70] Article 2(i) of Schedule 4, HKIAC Arbitration Rules 2024 and 2018.

[71] Article 9.5, LCIA Arbitration Rules 2020 and 2014.

[72] Article 1 of Schedule 1, SIAC Arbitration Rules 2013 and 2010.

[73] Article 1 of Schedule 1, SIAC Arbitration Rules 2016.

[74] Article 2 of Appendix II, SCC Arbitration Rules 2023, 2017 and 2010.

2.2.3.2 Common Grounds and Differences Regarding the Content of an Application for the Emergency Arbitrator Mechanism

Ten elements appear in the rules of the chosen institutions regarding the content of an application for the emergency arbitrator mechanism. This subsection compares these common grounds and differences regarding the content of an application for the emergency arbitrator mechanism.

(a) **The Contact Details of the Parties and Their Representatives**

The ICC, the HKIAC and the SCC specifically require this as the first element in their arbitration rules. However, the LCIA also requires a copy of a Request for Arbitration or a copy of Response. The contact information of parties and their representatives should also be provided in detail. The Notice of Arbitration, including contact information, is a mandatory element under the ICDR Arbitration Rules 2021 and 2014 in order to start the proceedings for the emergency arbitrator mechanism. The situation is similar in the SIAC Arbitration Rules. To sum up, the first element, the contact details of the parties and their representatives, are required either expressly or it is implied for the requested submission of a Notice of Arbitration, Request for Arbitration, or Response.

(b) **The Circumstances Giving Rise to the Application and the Dispute Being Referred to Arbitration**

The ICC, the HKIAC, the LCIA, and the SCC ask for the inclusion of the circumstances giving rise to the application for the emergency arbitrator mechanism and the dispute that is being referred to or that will be referred to arbitration. The ICDR and the SIAC do not include this second element in their arbitration rules. However, both the ICDR and the SIAC require the applicant to apply the emergency arbitrator mechanism "concurrent with or following"[75] the Notice of Arbitration, which includes giving information on the dispute in detail. Therefore, this element is necessary for an application for the emergency arbitrator mechanism.

(c) **A Statement of the Interim Measures Sought**

As the core element in applying for the emergency arbitrator mechanism, all institutions ask for a statement of the requested interim measures in their arbitration rules, starting from the very beginning of the introduction of the emergency arbitrator mechanism in the ICDR Arbitration Rules 2006.[76]

(d) **A Statement of the Interim Measures Sought**

---

[75] Article 1 of Schedule 1, SIAC Arbitration Rules 2016, 2013, and 2010; Article 6(1), ICDR Arbitration Rules 2014.

[76] Article 37(2), ICDR Arbitration Rules 2006; Article1(3)(d) of Appendix V, ICC Arbitration Rules 2017 and 2012; Article 2(c) of Schedule 4, HKIAC Arbitration Rules 2024, 2018 and 2013; Article 9.5(ii), LCIA Arbitration Rules 2014; Article 1 of Schedule 1, SIAC Arbitration Rules 2016, 2013, and 2010; Article 2(iii) of Appendix II, SCC Arbitration Rules 2017 and 2010.

The ICC, the ICDR, the HKIAC, and the LCIA explicitly state in their arbitration rules that parties must provide the reasons that interim measures are urgently needed. The ICC asks for "the reasons why the applicant needs urgent interim or conservatory measures that cannot await the constitution of an arbitral tribunal".[77] The ICDR states as "the reasons why such relief is required on an emergency basis".[78] The HKIAC uses similar wording to the ICC.[79] The LCIA combines this element with the second by providing that "the specific grounds for requiring, as an emergency, the appointment of an Emergency Arbitrator".[80] The SIAC and the SCC do not include such an element in their rules. However, due to the nature of the emergency arbitrator mechanism, it is essential to establish in an application that the need for interim measures is very urgent considering the arbitration rules as a whole.[81]

(e) **The Reasons an Applicant is Entitled to the Interim Measures Sought**

Neither the ICC Arbitration Rules 2012, 2017 nor 2021 require the reasons that an applicant is entitled to the interim measures sought, which makes the ICC the only institution that does not require that element. The other five arbitral institutions request that the reasons the applicant is entitled to the interim measures be included in a written application.[82]

(f) **Relevant Agreements Between Parties Including the Arbitration Agreement**

The ICC, the HKIAC and the SCC require the applicant to submit the relevant agreements, especially the arbitration agreement. The ICDR asks for a Notice of Arbitration, which includes the arbitration agreement, when applying for emergency relief since 2014. The LCIA and the SIAC adopt a similar approach as the ICDR. The existence of an arbitration agreement is the basis of international commercial arbitration, as well as the emergency arbitrator mechanism. This element is essential, and its inclusion is not surprising.

(g) **Any Agreed Seat, Applicable Law and Language of Emergency Arbitrator Proceedings**

The ICC, the HKIAC and the SCC make clear that the applicant should submit any agreement concerning terms of the seat of emergency arbitration, applicable law

---

[77] Article 1(3)(e) of Appendix V, ICC Arbitration Rules 2021.

[78] Article 7(1), ICDR Arbitration Rules 2021.

[79] Article 2(d) of Schedule 4, HKIAC Arbitration Rules 2024, 2018 and 2013.

[80] Article 9.5(i), LCIA Arbitration Rules 2020.

[81] Fabio G. Santacroce (2015), The emergency arbitrator: a full-fledged arbitrator rendering an enforceable decision?, 31 *Arbitration International* 285; G. Smith (2015), The Emergence of Emergency Arbitrations, Dec. *Arbitrator & Mediator Journal* 6, available at http://www.gordonsmithlegal.com.au/resources/Emergency%20Arbitrations%20(12082016).pdf (1 June 2024).

[82] Article 6(1), ICDR Arbitration Rules 2014; Article 37(2), ICDR Arbitration Rules 2009 and 2006; Article 2(e) of Schedule 4, HKIAC Arbitration Rules 2024, 2018 and 2013; Article 9.5, LCIA Arbitration Rules 2014; Article 1 of Schedule 1, SIAC Arbitration Rules 2016, 2013, and 2010; Article 2(iii) of Appendix II, SCC Arbitration Rules 2017 and 2010.

and the language of the emergency arbitration proceedings.[83] The ICC uses "place" instead of "seat" in its rules.[84] The President of the ICC will determine the place of the emergency arbitration proceedings when an agreement to that effect between the parties is absent, without prejudice to the determination of the seat of arbitration.[85] The HKIAC points out that, in the case there is no agreement regarding the seat of the emergency arbitrator procedure, referring to Article 14.1 of the HKIAC Arbitration Rules 2024, 2018 and 2013 concerning the seat of arbitration, the seat shall be Hong Kong.[86] The SCC regulates that the seat of emergency arbitrator proceedings shall be the place agreed upon by parties as the seat of arbitration. Otherwise, the institution will make a choice.[87] The ICDR is silent regarding these issues. The LCIA states that, in the default of any agreement about the seat of emergency arbitration, the seat shall be London.[88] The SIAC provides that the seat of arbitration shall be the seat of emergency arbitration. Otherwise, it shall be Singapore without prejudice to the determination of the seat of arbitration.[89] For other issues, the LCIA and the SIAC are both silent.

(h) **Proof of Payment**

The ICDR is the only institution that does not require proof of payment for the application of the emergency arbitrator mechanism. The other five institutions ask for proof of payment to be included in an application for the emergency arbitrator mechanism.

(i) **Relevant Submissions**

The relevant submissions include the Notice of Arbitration, the Request for Arbitration, the Response, and all the other submissions relating to the dispute. The ICDR, the SIAC and the HKIAC require the submission to be made at the same time as or before an application for the emergency arbitrator mechanism. The LCIA requires the applicant to submit a copy of the submissions while applying to appoint an emergency arbitrator. The ICC only asks for the Request for Arbitration to be made within ten days of the receipt of the application for the emergency arbitrator mechanism, while the SCC does not rule on the necessity of submissions for applying the emergency arbitrator proceedings.

(j) **Confirmation that All Parties Have Been Served Documents Regarding the Application**

---

[83] Article 1(3)(g) of Appendix V, ICC Arbitration Rules 2021, 2017 and 2012; Article 2(g) of Schedule 4, HKIAC Arbitration Rules 2024, 2018 and 2013; Article 2(v) of Appendix II, SCC Arbitration Rules 2017 and 2010.

[84] Article 1(3)(g) of Appendix V, ICC Arbitration Rules 2021.

[85] Article 4(1) of Appendix V, ICC Arbitration Rules 2021.

[86] Article 9 of Schedule 4, HKIAC Arbitration Rules 2024 and 2018; Article 10 of Schedule 4, HKIAC Arbitration Rules 2013.

[87] Article 5 of Appendix II, SCC Arbitration Rules 2023.

[88] Article 16 & 9.14, LCIA Arbitration Rules 2020; Article 16 & 9.13, LCIA Arbitration Rules 2014.

[89] Article 4 of Schedule 1, SIAC Arbitration Rules 2016.

The ICDR, the HKIAC, the LCIA, and the SIAC specifically mention that all parties have sent a copy of the emergency arbitrator proceeding to the other parties in the dispute. The ICDR also accepts the alternative of "an explanation of the steps taken in good faith to notify all parties".[90] The ICC only requires that the applicant needs to prepare and submit the copies necessary to be provided to all parties. The SCC puts the responsibility on the SCC Secretariat to send the documents related to the application of emergency relief to all the parties.

2.3 Appointment of an Emergency Arbitrator

Due to the nature of the emergency arbitrator proceedings, all the institutions start to appoint an emergency arbitrator very rapidly after an application is submitted. This section discusses the period for appointing an emergency arbitrator, the requirements for a potential emergency arbitrator, and the challenge of an appointed emergency arbitrator in each of the institutional arbitration rules.

2.3.1 Time for the Appointment of an Emergency Arbitrator

The ICC appoints an emergency arbitrator normally within two days, as soon as possible after the receipt of an application for emergency relief.[91] The ICDR takes one business day to appoint an emergency arbitrator after the receipt of an application.[92] The HKIAC reduced the appointment period from two days in the previous Arbitration Rules 2013[93] to 24 h after the application for an emergency arbitrator in the latest Arbitration Rules 2024 and 2018.[94] The LCIA mentions three days as the time limit for the appointment of an emergency arbitrator by the LCIA Court.[95] The SIAC stipulates one day for the appointment of an emergency arbitrator,[96] and the SCC grants only 24 h for the appointment of an emergency arbitrator.[97] In general, the time allowed for the appointment of an emergency arbitrator in all the six institutions is very short.

[90] Article 7(1), ICDR Arbitration Rules 2021.

[91] Article 2 of Appendix V, ICC Arbitration Rules 2021, 2017 and 2012.

[92] Article 7(2), ICDR Arbitration Rules 2021; Article 6(2), ICDR Arbitration Rules 2014; Article 37(3), ICDR Arbitration Rules 2009 and 2006.

[93] Article 5 of Schedule 4, HKIAC Arbitration Rules 2013.

[94] Article 4 of Schedule 4, HKIAC Arbitration Rules 2024 and 2018.

[95] Article 9.6, LCIA Arbitration Rules 2020 and 2014.

[96] Article 3 of Schedule 1, SIAC Arbitration Rules 2016.

[97] Article 4(1) of Appendix II, SCC Arbitration Rules 2023, 2017 and 2010.

2.3.2 *Requirement for a Possible Emergency Arbitrator*

Like a normal arbitrator, an emergency arbitrator needs to be independent and impartial during the emergency arbitrator proceedings. The ICC requires the appointed emergency arbitrator to sign "a statement of acceptance, availability, impartiality and independence".[98] The ICDR requires a potential emergency arbitrator to "disclose to the Administrator any circumstances that may give rise to justifiable doubts as to the arbitrator's impartiality or independence",[99] which is the same approach as the SIAC takes.[100] The LCIA refers to the requirement that general arbitrators must sign a written declaration, including any justifiable doubts as to impartiality and independence.[101] The HKIAC also requires the emergency arbitrator to submit a statement to confirm impartiality and independence and to disclose all circumstances that may bring justifiable doubts regarding impartiality and independence.[102] The SCC does not have a similar requirement.

Except for the LCIA, the five other arbitral institutions stipulate that an appointed emergency arbitrator may not act as an arbitrator in future arbitral proceedings relating to the same dispute.[103] The ICC also does not provide the possibility that parties can agree on the appointment of an emergency arbitrator as an arbitrator while the ICDR, the HKIAC, the SIAC, and the SCC allow this possibility when all parties agree.[104] The LCIA is silent regarding this issue.

2.3.3 *Challenge of an Emergency Arbitrator*

All the six institutions provide the opportunity for parties to challenge the appointment of an emergency arbitrator based on doubts regarding impartiality and independence, or other requirements in the applicable rules and arbitration agreements.

---

[98] Article 2(5) of Appendix V, ICC Arbitration Rules 2021, 2017 and 2012.

[99] Article 7(2), ICDR Arbitration Rules 2021; Article 6(2), ICDR Arbitration Rules 2014; Article 37(3), ICDR Arbitration Rules 2006 and 2009.

[100] Article 5 of Schedule 1, SIAC Arbitration Rules 2016; Article 3 of Schedule 1, SIAC Arbitration Rules 2013 and 2010.

[101] Article 5.4 & 9.6, LCIA Arbitration Rules 2020 and 2014.

[102] Article 11, HKIAC Arbitration Rules 2024, 2018 and 2013.

[103] Article 2(6), ICC Arbitration Rules 2021, 2017 and 2012; Article 7(5), ICDR Arbitration Rules 2021; Article 6(5), ICDR Arbitration Rules 2014; Article 37(6), ICDR Arbitration Rules 2006 and 2009; Article 19 of Schedule 4, HKIAC Arbitration Rules 2024 and 2018; Article 21 of Schedule 4, HKIAC Arbitration Rules 2013; Article 6 of Schedule 1, SIAC Arbitration Rules 2016; Article 4(4) of Appendix II, SCC Arbitration Rules 2023, 2017 and 2010.

[104] Article 2(6), ICC Arbitration Rules 2017 and 2012; Article 7(5), ICDR Arbitration Rules 2021; Article 6(5), ICDR Arbitration Rules 2014; Article 37(6), ICDR Arbitration Rules 2006 and 2009; Article 21 of Schedule 4, HKIAC Arbitration Rules 2013; Article 6 of Schedule 1, SIAC Arbitration Rules 2016; Article 4(4) of Appendix II, SCC Arbitration Rules 2023, 2017 and 2010.

The ICC allows three days for parties to challenge the appointment of an emergency arbitrator after the notification of the appointment, or after the circumstances arise that call for the challenge.[105] After the challenge, an opportunity is given to the emergency arbitrator and all the other parties for written comments to be submitted within a reasonable time.[106] The ICDR limits the period for challenging the appointment to one business day after the appointment of an emergency arbitrator and the disclosure of the circumstances.[107] The HKIAC, as the ICC, grants three days for the parties to notify the challenge of an emergency arbitrator after confirming the appointment or becoming aware of the circumstances concerning impartiality, independence, qualifications, or an inability to undertake the responsibility.[108] After a successful challenge, the HKIAC shall appoint a substitute emergency arbitrator within 24 h according to its Arbitration Rules 2018,[109] and within two days according to the Arbitration Rules 2013.[110] The proceedings are paused at the same stage unless the other emergency arbitrator decides otherwise.[111] The LCIA refers to Article 10 of its Arbitration Rules 2014 to regulate the situation of challenging an emergency arbitrator. Within 14 days of the appointment or after being made aware of related circumstances, the parties can refer to resignation, capacity, impartiality, and independence to challenge the appointment of an emergency arbitrator.[112] The LCIA gives the challenged emergency arbitrator a chance to comment.[113] If all parties agree to challenge an emergency arbitrator, the LCIA will revoke the appointment.[114] Otherwise, the LCIA makes a final decision.[115] In urgent situations, parties can apply for the expedited appointment of a replacement arbitrator, as set out in Article 9C of the LCIA Arbitration Rules. The SIAC amended the time to challenge the appointment of an emergency arbitrator from one business day in the SIAC Arbitration Rule 2013 and 2010[116] to two days after the communication of appointment and the circumstances are disclosed in the SIAC Arbitration Rules 2016.[117] The SCC only accepts a challenge to the appointment of an emergency arbitrator within 24 h after the related circumstances regarding impartiality, independence or qualification

---

[105] Article 3(1) of Appendix V, ICC Arbitration Rules 2021, 2017 and 2012.

[106] Article 3(2) of Appendix V, ICC Arbitration Rules 2021, 2017 and 2012.

[107] Article 7(2), ICDR Arbitration Rules 2021; Article 6(2), ICDR Arbitration Rules 2014; Article 37(3), ICDR Arbitration Rules 2009 and 2006.

[108] Article 11, HKIAC Arbitration Rules 2024 and 2018, 2013.

[109] Article 8 of Schedule 4, HKIAC Arbitration Rules 2024 and 2018.

[110] Article 9 of Schedule 4, HKIAC Arbitration Rules 2013.

[111] Article 8 of Schedule 4, HKIAC Arbitration Rules 2024 and 2018; Article 9 of Schedule 4, HKIAC Arbitration Rules 2013.

[112] Article 9.6, 10.1, & 10.3, LCIA Arbitration Rules 2020 and 2014.

[113] Article 10.5, LCIA Arbitration Rules 2020; Article 10.4, LCIA Arbitration Rules 2014.

[114] Article 10.4, LCIA Arbitration Rules 2020; Article 10.5, LCIA Arbitration Rules 2014.

[115] Article 10.5, LCIA Arbitration Rules 2020; Article 10.6, LCIA Arbitration Rules 2014.

[116] Article 3 of Schedule 1, SIAC Arbitration Rules 2013 and 2010.

[117] Article 5 of Schedule 1, SIAC Arbitration Rules 2016.

of a specific emergency arbitrator are made known to the parties.[118] The challenged emergency arbitrator and the parties have an opportunity to comment on the challenge.[119] Only when all parties agree on the challenge, the emergency arbitrator will resign or the SCC will step in and make a final decision.[120]

2.4 Emergency Arbitrator Proceedings

Regarding the emergency arbitrator proceedings, the different institutions have their own rules while maintaining the essential feature of a general shared regulatory framework. This section examines the jurisdiction issue, the procedural timetable, procedural fairness, and the discretion of an emergency arbitrator.

2.4.1 Jurisdiction of an Emergency Arbitrator

Except for the SCC leaving the determination of the jurisdiction of an emergency arbitrator to the Board,[121] the five other institutions provide an emergency arbitrator with the power to decide on his or her own jurisdiction. In the ICC arbitration rules, an emergency arbitrator has the power to determine his or her jurisdiction and whether the application of interim measures is admissible.[122] The ICDR expressly states that the emergency arbitrator "shall have the authority vested in the arbitral tribunal", including the authority to rule on its own jurisdiction, and "shall resolve any disputes over the applicability".[123] The HKIAC also gives the power to rule on the jurisdiction issue to an emergency arbitrator, including "any objections with respect to the existence, validity or scope of the arbitration clause(s)",[124] and the arbitrator shall resolve any disputes regarding the application of the emergency arbitrator provisions. For the jurisdiction issue, the LCIA refers to Article 23 of its Arbitration Rules 2014 concerning the jurisdiction of an arbitral tribunal.[125] Similar to an arbitral tribunal, an LCIA emergency arbitrator has the power to rule on the jurisdiction issue.[126] The

[118] Article 19(1), Article 4(3) of Appendix II, SCC Arbitration Rules 2023 and 2017; Article 15(1), Article 4(3) of Appendix II, SCC Arbitration Rules 2010.
[119] Article 19(4), SCC Arbitration Rules 2023 and 2017; Article 15(3), SCC Arbitration Rules 2010.
[120] Article 19(5), SCC Arbitration Rules 2023 and 2017; Article 15(4), Article 4(3) of Appendix II, SCC Arbitration Rules 2010.
[121] Article 4(2) of Appendix II, SCC Arbitration Rules 2023 and 2017.
[122] Article 6(2) of Appendix V, ICC Arbitration Rules 2021, 2017 and 2012.
[123] Article 7(3), ICDR Arbitration Rules 2021; Article 6(3), ICDR Arbitration Rules 2014; Article 37(4), ICDR Arbitration Rules 2009 and 2006.
[124] Article 10 of Schedule 4, HKIAC Arbitration Rules 2024 and 2018; Article 11 of Schedule 4, HKIAC Arbitration Rules 2013.
[125] Article 9.14, LCIA Arbitration Rules 2020; Article 9.13, LCIA Arbitration Rules 2014.
[126] Article 23.1, LCIA Arbitration Rules 2020 and 2014.

SIAC points out that an emergency arbitrator "shall have the powers vested in the Tribunal", "including the authority to rule on his own jurisdiction, without prejudice to the Tribunal's determination".[127] The SCC does not expressly state that an emergency arbitrator has the power to decide on the jurisdiction issue, but it provides that "[a]n emergency arbitrator shall not be appointed if the SCC manifestly lacks jurisdiction over the dispute".[128] In the introduction to the Board of the SCC, it makes clear that the function of the Board includes the determination of the jurisdiction of the SCC arbitration procedure.[129]

The jurisdiction of an emergency arbitrator ceases when the dispute is referred to a fully functional arbitral tribunal. The ICC stipulates that "[n]o emergency arbitrator shall be appointed after the file has been transmitted to the arbitral tribunal".[130] The ICDR provides that an emergency arbitrator will not have further power as long as the arbitral tribunal is formed.[131] The HKIAC uses a similar expression that the emergency arbitrator has "no further power to act once the arbitral tribunal is constituted".[132] The LCIA regulates the applicable period of the emergency arbitration in Article 9.4 of the LCIA Arbitration Rules 2014, which is "at any time prior to the formation or expedited formation of the Arbitral Tribunal".[133] The SIAC also terminates the power of an emergency arbitrator with the constitution of an arbitral tribunal.[134] The SCC draws the line with the referral of the case to an arbitral tribunal.[135] As soon as the constitution of an arbitral tribunal or the referral of the dispute to an arbitral tribunal has taken place, the jurisdiction of an emergency arbitrator terminates immediately.

In the newly revised HKIAC Arbitration Rules 2024, it allows an HKIAC emergency arbitrator to "have the power to make any preliminary or interim order the emergency arbitrator deems necessary before making the Emergency Decision referred".[136] This clarification confirms that an emergency arbitrator administrated by the HKIAC to issue interim measures pending its "main" emergency order, *i.e.*, an "interim" interim measure.

---

[127] Article 7 of Schedule 1, SIAC Arbitration Rules 2016; Article 5 of Schedule 1, SIAC Arbitration Rules 2013 and 2010.

[128] Article 4(2) of Appendix I, SCC Arbitration Rules 2023, 2017 and 2010.

[129] Article 6 of Appendix I, SCC Arbitration Rules 2023, 2017 and 2010.

[130] Article 2(2) of Appendix V, ICC Arbitration Rules 2021, 2017 and 2012.

[131] Article 7(5), ICDR Arbitration Rules 2021; Article 6(5), ICDR Arbitration Rules 2014; Article 37(5), ICDR Arbitration Rules 2009 and 2006.

[132] Article 14 of Schedule 4, HKIAC Arbitration Rules 2024; Article 18 of Schedule 4, HKIAC Arbitration Rules 2018; Article 20 of Schedule 4, HKIAC Arbitration Rules 2013.

[133] Article 9.4, LCIA Arbitration Rules 2020 and 2014.

[134] Article 10 of Schedule 1, SIAC Arbitration Rules 2016; Article 7 of Schedule 1, SIAC Arbitration Rules 2013 and 2010.

[135] Article 1(2) of Appendix II, SCC Arbitration Rules 2023, 2017 and 2010.

[136] Article 10 of Schedule 4, HKIAC Arbitration Rules 2024.

2.4.2 *Procedural Timetable*

Considering the function of the emergency arbitrator mechanism, efficiency is essential. A procedural timetable "may even incorporate their suggestions as to the schedule and other aspects of the proceedings—may help the emergency arbitrator accomplish his mission."[137] The ICC established the rules that a procedural timetable shall be created as soon as possible, usually within two days, after the transmission of a case to an emergency arbitrator.[138] The ICDR has a similar provision by asking an emergency arbitrator to establish "a schedule for consideration of the application for emergency relief"[139] within two business days after appointment. The SIAC sets the same requirement for a schedule for the consideration of an application for emergency relief within two days[140] in its Arbitration Rules 2016. In the SIAC Arbitration Rules 2013 and 2010, the time limit was also two business days.[141] There is no similar provision concerning the procedural timetable in the HKIAC, the LCIA or the SCC arbitration rules.

2.4.3 *Procedural Fairness*

Procedural fairness in international commercial arbitration may include "the right to be heard and the right to equal treatment—with both rights being qualified by a high degree of deference to the parties' procedural autonomy and the arbitrators' procedural discretion".[142] Sometimes, urgency, which is the key in the emergency arbitrator proceedings, and procedural fairness, which is the general requirement of dispute resolution, may conflict with each other.[143] The appointed emergency arbitrator is responsible for balancing these two values in while conducting the proceedings.

In the ICC arbitration rules, an emergency arbitrator is required to act "fairly and impartially", and "each party has a reasonable opportunity to present its case".[144] The ICDR asks an emergency arbitrator to provide "a reasonable opportunity to all parties to be heard and may provide for proceedings by telephone, video, written

---

[137] Fabio G. Santacroce (2015), The emergency arbitrator: a full-fledged arbitrator rendering an enforceable decision?, 31 *Arbitration International* 287.

[138] Article 5(1) of Appendix V, ICC Arbitration Rules 2021, 2017 and 2012.

[139] Article 7(3), ICDR Arbitration Rules 2021; Article 6(3), ICDR Arbitration Rules 2014; Article 37(4), ICDR Arbitration Rules 2009 and 2006.

[140] Article 7 of Schedule 1, SIAC Arbitration Rules 2016.

[141] Article 5 of Schedule 1, SIAC Arbitration Rules 2013 and 2010.

[142] Gary B. Born (2021), *International Commercial Arbitration*, Kluwer Law International, p. 2327.

[143] Fabio G. Santacroce (2015), The emergency arbitrator: a full-fledged arbitrator rendering an enforceable decision?, 31 *Arbitration International* 287.

[144] Article 5(2) of Appendix V, ICC Arbitration Rules 2021, 2017 and 2012.

submissions, or other suitable means, as alternatives to an in-person hearing".[145] The HKIAC similarly gives all parties reasonable opportunities to be heard, taking into account the urgent nature of the emergency arbitrator proceedings.[146] The SIAC provides a reasonable chance for all parties to be heard, but such proceedings, like by telephone, video conference, or written submissions are alternatives to hearings in person.[147] The SCC refers to the due process of the emergency arbitrator proceedings in the article addressing the conduct of arbitration. An SCC emergency arbitrator shall act in "an impartial, practical and expeditious manner", by "giving each party an equal and reasonable opportunity to present its case".[148]

The LCIA does not force an emergency arbitrator to hold hearings, neither in person nor by telephone.[149] An emergency arbitrator can decide based purely on available documentation.[150] Unlike the five other arbitral institutions, the LCIA is the only arbitration center allowing for *ex parte* interim measures by an emergency arbitrator. The provisions read as follows: "[t]he Emergency Arbitrator may conduct the emergency proceedings in any manner determined by the Emergency Arbitrator to be appropriate in the circumstances, taking account of the nature of such emergency proceedings, the need to afford to each party, if possible, an opportunity to be consulted on the claim for emergency relief (whether or not it avails itself of such opportunity)."[151] Based on the above provisions of the LCIA concerning the emergency arbitrator proceedings, in some circumstances, an emergency arbitrator could decide on the application of interim measures without consulting the other party. It is still unknown whether the *ex parte* interim measures can bring more enforcement difficulties or not. However, the "recognition or enforcement of an award is generally refused where the resisting party was denied an opportunity to be heard".[152]

2.4.4 Discretion of an Emergency Arbitrator

Generally, an emergency arbitrator in all institutional rules enjoys broad discretion in deciding the issuance of interim measures. The ICC gives an emergency arbitrator

[145] Article 7(3), ICDR Arbitration Rules 2021; Article 6(3), ICDR Arbitration Rules 2014; Article 37(4), ICDR Arbitration Rules 2009 and 2006.

[146] Article 10 of Schedule 4, HKIAC Arbitration Rules 2024 and 2018; Article 11 of Schedule 4, HKIAC Arbitration Rules 2013.

[147] Article 7 of Schedule 1, SIAC Arbitration Rules 2016; Article 5 of Schedule 1, SIAC Arbitration Rules 2013 and 2010.

[148] Article 7 of Appendix II, Article 23(2), SCC Arbitration Rules 2017; Article 7 of Appendix II, Article 19(2), SCC Arbitration Rules 2010.

[149] Article 9.7, LCIA Arbitration Rules 2020 and 2014.

[150] Article 9.7, LCIA Arbitration Rules 2020 and 2014.

[151] Article 9.7, LCIA Arbitration Rules 2020 and 2014.

[152] Fabio G. Santacroce (2015), The emergency arbitrator: a full-fledged arbitrator rendering an enforceable decision?, 31 *Arbitration International* 286; Article V(1)(b), the New York Convention.

broad discretion by stating that an "emergency arbitrator shall conduct the proceedings in the manner which the emergency arbitrator considers to be appropriate, taking into account the nature and the urgency of the Application".[153] The ICDR stipulates that an "emergency arbitrator shall have the power to order or award any interim or conservatory measures that the emergency arbitrator deems necessary".[154] The HKIAC also states that an emergency arbitrator "may conduct such proceedings in such a manner as the Emergency Arbitrator considers appropriate".[155] The LCIA has a similar regulation as the ICC and the HKIAC arbitration rules.[156] The SIAC allows an emergency arbitrator to rule on the requested interim measures he or she deems necessary.[157] The SCC makes it available for an emergency arbitrator to conduct the proceedings, if appropriate, "in an impartial, practical and expeditious manner"[158] with consideration for the urgency inherent in emergency arbitrator proceedings.

It seems that those arbitral institutions tend not to specify a particular substantive standard for an emergency arbitrator to decide on the application of interim measures in the rules regulating the interim measures by an arbitral tribunal. However, the HKIAC is the only institution that has a specific article stipulating the standards for issuing interim measures for both arbitral tribunals and emergency arbitrators. When deciding on the interim measures requested by the applicant, the following elements may be taken into account: "(a) harm not adequately reparable by an award of damages is likely to result if the measure is not ordered, and such harm substantially outweighs the harm that is likely to result to the party against whom the measure is directed if the measures is granted; and (b) there is a reasonable possibility that the requesting party will succeed on the merits of the claim. The determination on this possibility shall not affect the discretion of the arbitral tribunal in making any subsequent determination".[159]

This provision in the HKIAC arbitration rules is identical to the provision in the UNCITRAL Model Law on International Commercial Arbitration (1985), with amendments as adopted in 2006. Article 17 A of the UNCITRAL Model Law 2006 reads that the party needs to satisfy the following elements for an interim measure "(a) [h]arm not adequately reparable by an award of damages is likely to result if the measure is not ordered, and such harm substantially outweighs the harm that is likely to result to the party against whom the measure is directed if the measure is granted; and (b) [t]here is a reasonable possibility that the requesting party will succeed on

[153] Article 5(2) of Appendix V, ICC Arbitration Rules 2021, 2017 and 2012.

[154] Article 7(4), ICDR Arbitration Rules 2021; Article 6(4), ICDR Arbitration Rules 2014; Article 37(5), ICDR Arbitration Rules 2009 and 2006.

[155] Article 10 of Schedule 4, HKIAC Arbitration Rules 2024 and 2018; Article 11 of Schedule 4, HKIAC Arbitration Rules 2013.

[156] Article 9.7, LCIA Arbitration Rules 2020 and 2014.

[157] Article 8 of Schedule 1, SIAC Arbitration Rules 2016; Article 5 of Schedule 1, SIAC Arbitration Rules 2013 and 2010.

[158] Article 23(2), Article 7 of Appendix II, SCC Arbitration Rules 2023 and 2017; Article 19(2), Article 7 of Appendix II, SCC Arbitration Rules 2010.

[159] Article 23.4, HKIAC Arbitration Rules 2024, 2018 and 2013.

the merits of the claim. The determination on this possibility shall not affect the discretion of the arbitral tribunal in making any subsequent determination".[160]

2.5 Decision of an Emergency Arbitrator

The decision, or in other words, the interim measures granted by an emergency arbitrator, is the final stage of the emergency arbitrator proceedings. This section discusses the limited time period for an emergency arbitrator to render a decision, the content of the decision, and the binding effect of the decision in the chosen arbitral institutional rules.

2.5.1 Time Limit for Deciding on Interim Measures

Every institution tries to restrict the period for an emergency arbitrator to decide on an application and make it as short as possible. As a result, the decision-making period in emergency arbitration is very short. The ICC sets a 15-day period from the date of submitting the files to an emergency arbitrator to decide whether the interim measures are granted or not.[161] The President of the ICC has the power to extend the time limit when necessary.[162] The HKIAC Arbitration Rules 2018 limits the period to 14 days,[163] while its Arbitration Rules 2013 granted a 15-day period as the ICC does.[164] The decision of an HKIAC emergency arbitrator may be made "even if in the meantime the file has been transmitted to the arbitral tribunal".[165] The LCIA stipulates that an emergency arbitrator shall make the decision as soon as possible, but within 14 days after the appointment.[166] The deadline can be extended only in exceptional situations or under an agreement by all parties.[167] The SIAC Arbitration Rules 2016 also takes 14 days as the period for the emergency arbitrator proceedings, and the period can be extended only in exceptional circumstances.[168] In previous versions of the arbitration rules in 2013 and 2010, the SIAC did not make the period clear in the provisions. The SCC specifies a very intensive schedule, allowing

---

[160] Article 17 A, UNCITRAL Model Law in International Commercial Arbitration (1985), with amendments as adopted in 2006, para.1, available at https://uncitral.un.org/en/texts/arbitration/modellaw/commercial_arbitration (1 June 2024).

[161] Article 6(4) of Appendix V, ICC Arbitration Rules 2021, 2017 and 2012.

[162] Article 6(4) of Appendix V, ICC Arbitration Rules 2021, 2017 and 2012.

[163] Article 12 of Schedule 4, HKIAC Arbitration Rules 2024, 2018.

[164] Article 12 of Schedule 4, HKIAC Arbitration Rules 2013.

[165] Article 13 of Schedule 4, HKIAC Arbitration Rules 2013.

[166] Article 9.8, LCIA Arbitration Rules 2020 and 2014.

[167] Article 9.8, LCIA Arbitration Rules 2020 and 2014.

[168] Article 8 of Schedule 1, SIAC Arbitration Rules 2016.

only five days for an emergency arbitrator to make a decision after the referral of a case.[169] The Board of the SCC can extend the time limit upon the request from an emergency arbitrator or when necessary.[170] The ICDR does not give a specific time limit for an emergency arbitrator to rule on the application of interim measures. However, "it is implicit from the nature of the relief sought, and the terms of the provisions overall, that an emergency arbitrator is obliged to issue his or her decision in the shortest time possible".[171]

2.5.2 Content of the Decision

The ICDR, the HKIAC, the LCIA, the SIAC, and the SCC do not specify the form of the decision made by an emergency arbitrator, meaning the interim measures can be in the form of an award or an order.[172] Only the ICC stipulates that "the emergency arbitrator's decision shall take the form of an order".[173]

Generally speaking, all institutions seldom limit the types and content of the interim measures that an emergency arbitrator can issue. Regarding the categories of interim measures that an emergency arbitrator can grant, there is no specific restriction under the ICC arbitration rules. The ICDR gives an emergency arbitrator the power to grant "any interim or conservatory measures that the emergency arbitrator deems necessary, including injunctive relief and measures for the protection or conservation of property".[174] The HKIAC allows any interim measures that are considered necessary or appropriate to be granted by an emergency arbitrator.[175] The LCIA also does not provide for any limitations regarding the interim measures that can be granted by an emergency arbitrator. An emergency arbitrator can grant any interim measures that an arbitral tribunal could make under the arbitration agreement and, additionally, can "make any order adjourning the consideration of all or

---

[169] Article 8(1) of Appendix II, SCC Arbitration Rules 2023, 2017 and 2010.

[170] Article 8(1) of Appendix II, SCC Arbitration Rules 2023, 2017 and 2010.

[171] G. Smith (2015), The Emergence of Emergency Arbitrations, Dec. *Arbitrator & Mediator Journal* 10, available at http://www.gordonsmithlegal.com.au/resources/Emergency%20Arbitrations%20(12082016).pdf (16 June 2020)..

[172] Article 7(4), ICDR Arbitration Rules 2021; Article 6(4), ICDR Arbitration Rules 2014; Article 37(5), ICDR Arbitration Rules 2009 and 2006; Article 12 of Schedule 4, HKIAC Arbitration Rules 2024, 2018 and 2013; Article 9.8, LCIA Arbitration Rules 2020 and 2014; Article 8 of Schedule 1, SIAC Arbitration Rules 2016, 2013 and 2010; Article 37(3), Article 8(1) of Appendix II, SCC Arbitration Rules 2023 and 2017; Article 32(3), Article 8(1) of Appendix II, SCC Arbitration Rules 2010.

[173] Article 29, Article 5(1) of Appendix V, ICC Arbitration Rules 2021, 2017 and 2012.

[174] Article 7(4), ICDR Arbitration Rules 2021; Article 6(4), ICDR Arbitration Rules 2014; Article 37(5), ICDR Arbitration Rules 2009 and 2006.

[175] Article 17 of Schedule 4, HKIAC Arbitration Rules 2024; Article 16 of Schedule 4, Article 23(2), HKIAC Arbitration Rules 2018 and 2013.

any part of the claim for emergency relief to the proceedings conducted by the Arbitral Tribunal(when formed)".[176] In Article 25 of the LCIA Arbitration Rules 2020 and 2014, the available interim measures include "(i) to order any respondent party to claim or cross-claim to provide security for all or part of the amount in dispute, by way of deposit or bank guarantee or in any other manner; (ii) to order the preservation, storage, sale or other disposal of any documents, goods, samples, property, site or thing under the control of any party and relating to the subject matter of the arbitration; and (iii) to order on a provisional basis, subject to a final decision in an award, any relief which the Arbitral Tribunal would have power to grant in an award, including the payment of money or the disposition of property as between any parties".[177] The SIAC provides the possibility for any interim measures to be made by an emergency arbitrator when necessary.[178] The SCC refers to the types of possible interim measures that an emergency arbitrator can grant as being similar to the powers of an arbitral tribunal, meaning that an emergency arbitrator may grant any interim measures when appropriate.[179]

As expected, the six leading arbitral institutions ask an emergency arbitrator to give reasons,[180] or at least summary reasons,[181] for the interim measures granted in the decision. Additionally, the ICC also asks for the decision issued by an emergency arbitrator to be in writing,[182] dated and signed by the emergency arbitrator.[183] The SCC also requires an emergency arbitrator to state the seat of the emergency arbitrator proceedings in the decision.[184]

---

[176] Article 9.8, LCIA Arbitration Rules 2020 and 2014.

[177] Article 25(1), LCIA Arbitration Rules 2020 and 2014.

[178] Article 8 of Schedule 1, SIAC Arbitration Rules 2016; Article 6 of Schedule 1, SIAC Arbitration Rules 2013 and 2010.

[179] Article 37(1), Article 1(2) of Appendix II, SCC Arbitration Rules 2023 and 2017; Article 32(1), Article 1(2) of Appendix II, SCC Arbitration Rules 2010.

[180] Article 6(3) of Appendix V, ICC Arbitration Rules 2021, 2017 and 2012; Article 7(4), ICDR Arbitration Rules 2021; Article 6(4), ICDR Arbitration Rules 2014; Article 37(5), ICDR Arbitration Rules 2009 and 2006; Article 9.9, LCIA Arbitration Rules 2014; Article 6 of Schedule 1, SIAC Arbitration Rules 2013 and 2010; Article 8(2) of Appendix II, SCC Arbitration Rules 2023, 2017 and 2010.

[181] Article 14(b) of Schedule 4, HKIAC Arbitration Rules 2013; Article 8 of Schedule 1, SIAC Arbitration Rules 2016.

[182] Article 6(3) of Appendix V, ICC Arbitration Rules 2021, 2017 and 2012; Article 15 of Schedule 4, HKIAC Arbitration Rules 2024; Article 14(a)(b)(c) of Schedule 4, HKIAC Arbitration Rules 2018 and 2013; Article 9.9, LCIA Arbitration Rules 2014; Article 8 of Schedule 1, SIAC Arbitration Rules 2016; Article 6 of Schedule 1, SIAC Arbitration Rules 2013 and 2010; Article 8(2) of Appendix II, SCC Arbitration Rules 2023, 2017 and 2010.

[183] Article 6(3) of Appendix V, ICC Arbitration Rules 2021, 2017 and 2012; Article 15 of Schedule 4, HKIAC Arbitration Rules 2024; Article 14(a)(b)(c) of Schedule 4, HKIAC Arbitration Rules 2018 and 2013; Article 8(2) of Appendix II, SCC Arbitration Rules 2023, 2017 and 2010.

[184] Article 8(2) of Appendix II, SCC Arbitration Rules 2023, 2017 and 2010.

2.5.3 *Binding Effect of Interim Measures Granted by an Emergency Arbitrator*

In all the six institutions, the decision made by an emergency arbitrator is binding upon the parties to the emergency arbitrator proceedings. Parties are also required to comply with such a decision.[185] The ICDR takes a step further in its Arbitration Rules 2021 and 2014 by providing that "[a]ny interim award or order shall have the same effect" as an interim measure granted by an arbitral tribunal, "shall be binding on the parties when rendered", and "[t]he parties shall undertake to comply with such an interim award or order without delay",[186] while such provisions do not exist in the ICDR Arbitration Rules 2009 and 2006. The HKIAC has very similar provisions regarding the binding effect of the decision granted by an emergency arbitrator, as the ICDR Arbitration Rules 2014.[187] The LCIA also considers that the decision of an emergency arbitrator has the same effect as the awards made by an arbitral tribunal,[188] read as "[e]very award (including reasons for such award) shall be final and binding on the parties", and the parties need to comply with it without delay. Additionally, "the parties also waive irrevocably their right to any form of appeal, review or recourse to any state court or other legal authority, insofar as such waiver shall not be prohibited under any applicable law".[189] The SIAC has adopted a comparable approach as the LCIA.[190] The SIAC also provides that the decision of an emergency arbitrator "as to such matter is final and not subject to appeal, review or recourse".[191]

The binding effect of the decision may be revoked if the following circumstances occur. The ICC provides four situations in this regard: (a) termination of the emergency arbitrator proceedings; (b) acceptance of a challenge against the appointed emergency arbitrator; (c) the issuance of a final arbitral award, unless ruled otherwise; or (d) the withdrawal of all claims or termination of the whole arbitration.[192] There is no comparable provision in the ICDR and the LCIA arbitration rules. The HKIAC has a different approach to these circumstances: (a) when an emergency arbitrator or a tribunal decides so; (b) a final award has been rendered, unless the tribunal decides otherwise explicitly; (c) there is a withdrawal of all claims or termination of the arbitration; or (d) if a tribunal cannot be constituted within 90 days which can be

---

[185] Article 29(2), ICC Arbitration Rules 2021, 2017 and 2012; Article 9(3) of Appendix II, SCC Arbitration Rules 2023, 2017 and 2010.

[186] Article 7(4), ICDR Arbitration Rules 2021; Article 6(4), ICDR Arbitration Rules 2014.

[187] Article 17 of Schedule 4, HKIAC Arbitration Rules 2024; Article 16 of Schedule 4, HKIAC Arbitration Rules 2018 and 2013.

[188] Article 9.9 & 26.8, LCIA Arbitration Rules 2020 and 2014.

[189] Article 26.8, LCIA Arbitration Rules 2020 and 2014.

[190] Article 12 of Schedule 1, SIAC Arbitration Rules 2016; Article 9 of Schedule 1, SIAC Arbitration Rules 2013 and 2010.

[191] Article 14 of Schedule 1, SIAC Arbitration Rules 2016; Article 11 of Schedule 1, SIAC Arbitration Rules 2013 and 2010 ("final and not subject to appeal").

[192] Article 6 of Appendix V, ICC Arbitration Rules 2021, 2017 and 2012.

extended by the HKIAC, after the decision of the emergency arbitrator.[193] The SIAC only revokes the binding effect of the decision by an emergency arbitrator when a tribunal is not formed within 90 days, or after the publication of a final award, or the withdrawal of the claims.[194] The SCC takes a different approach by stating that the order or award by an emergency arbitrator will cease to be binding when (a) the emergency arbitrator or a tribunal makes such a decision; (b) the determination of a final award; (c) the arbitration cannot start within 30 days after such decision; or (d) the case is not transmitted to a tribunal in 90 days after the interim measures are made.[195]

Due to the temporary nature of interim measures, the decision of an emergency arbitrator can be changed either by the emergency arbitrator himself or herself or by an arbitral tribunal afterward. The ICC expressly states that a tribunal is not bound by the order made by an emergency arbitrator in terms of any question, issue, or dispute in the order.[196] An arbitral tribunal can "modify, terminate or annul the order or any modification thereto" issued by the emergency arbitrator.[197] The ICC also allows the emergency arbitrator to "modify, terminate or annul" the order based on a reasonable request by parties before the submitting it to a tribunal.[198] The ICDR grants both emergency arbitrators and arbitral tribunals the power to change the decision in the same case. An emergency arbitrator may "modify or vacate the interim award or order".[199] An arbitral tribunal may "reconsider, modify, or vacate the interim award or order".[200] An emergency arbitrator and constituted arbitral tribunals under the HKIAC Arbitration Rules 2013 can modify, suspend or terminate the interim measures based on a reasoned request by parties.[201] However, in the HKIAC Arbitration Rules 2024 and 2018, an arbitral tribunal can modify, suspend or terminate an interim measure on its own initiative.[202] The LCIA Arbitration Rules 2014 provides that "[a]ny order or award of the Emergency Arbitrator (apart from any order adjourning to the Arbitral Tribunal, when formed, any part of the claim for emergency relief) may be confirmed, varied, discharged or revoked, in whole or in part, by order or award made by the Arbitral Tribunal upon application by any party or upon its own initiative".[203] In the latest version of rules, the LCIA

---

193 Article 18 of Schedule 4, HKIAC Arbitration Rules 2024; Article 17 of Schedule 4, HKIAC Arbitration Rules 2018; Article 19 of Schedule 4, HKIAC Arbitration Rules 2013.

194 Article 10 of Schedule 1, SIAC Arbitration Rules 2016, 2013, and 2010.

195 Article 9(4) of Appendix II, SCC Arbitration Rules 2023, 2017 and 2010.

196 Article 29(3), ICC Arbitration Rules 2021, 2017 and 2012.

197 Article 29(3), ICC Arbitration Rules 2021, 2017 and 2012.

198 Article 6(8) of Appendix V, ICC Arbitration Rules 2021, 2017 and 2012.

199 Article 7(4), ICDR Arbitration Rules 2021; Article 6(4), ICDR Arbitration Rules 2014; Article 37(5) (with extra "good cause shown"), ICDR Arbitration Rules 2009 and 2006.

200 Article 7(5), ICDR Arbitration Rules 2021; Article 6(5), ICDR Arbitration Rules 2014; Article 37(6), ICDR Arbitration Rules 2009 and 2006.

201 Article 18 of Schedule 4, HKIAC Arbitration Rules 2013.

202 Article 23.5 & Article 11 of Schedule 4, HKIAC Arbitration Rules 2024 and 2018.

203 Article 9.11, LCIA Arbitration Rules 2014.

adds Article 9.12 regarding an emergency arbitrator's right to change the decision upon application by any party or upon its own decision.[204] The SIAC states that an emergency arbitrator may "modify or vacate the preliminary order, the interim order or Award for good cause",[205] and a tribunal may "reconsider, modify or vacate any interim order or Award issued by the Emergency Arbitrator including a ruling on his own jurisdiction".[206] Additionally, a tribunal is not bound by the reasoning given in the interim measures issued by an emergency arbitrator.[207] The SCC agrees that an emergency arbitrator can "amend or revoke" the interim measures at the reasonable request of the parties.[208] Also, an arbitral tribunal "is not bound by the decision(s) and reasons" by the emergency arbitrator.[209]

2.6 Cost of the Emergency Arbitrator Proceedings

The cost of the emergency arbitrator proceedings varies depending upon the arbitration center chosen and it changes over time. Under the ICC Arbitration Rules 2017, the applicant must pay 40,000 USD, including 10,000 USD for ICC administrative fees and 30,000 USD for the expenses related to an emergency arbitrator.[210] The ICC also reserves the right to increase the amount during the proceedings.[211] The proportion that must be borne will be decided by an emergency arbitrator in the final order.[212] The ICDR does not regulate a fixed amount of costs for the emergency arbitrator proceedings. There are no administrative fees charged by the ICDR, and the expenses for an emergency arbitrator are determined "on a time basis at the emergency arbitrator's hourly rate".[213] An emergency arbitrator has the same power as an arbitral tribunal to address the allocation of costs.[214] The median cost of the emergency arbitration under the HKIAC is 57,507 USD, and the mean cost is 54,909

[204] Article 9.12, LCIA Arbitration Rules 2020.

[205] Article 8 of Schedule 1, SIAC Arbitration Rules 2016; Article 6 of Schedule 1, SIAC Arbitration Rules 2013 and 2010.

[206] Article 10 of Schedule 1, SIAC Arbitration Rules 2016; Article 7 of Schedule 1, SIAC Arbitration Rules 2013 and 2010.

[207] Article 10 of Schedule 1, SIAC Arbitration Rules 2016; Article 7 of Schedule 1, SIAC Arbitration Rules 2013 and 2010.

[208] Article 9(2) of Appendix II, SCC Arbitration Rules 2023, 2017 and 2010.

[209] Article 9(5) of Appendix II, SCC Arbitration Rules 2023, 2017 and 2010.

[210] Article 7(1) of Appendix V, ICC Arbitration Rules 2021, 2017 and 2012.

[211] Article 7(2) of Appendix V, ICC Arbitration Rules 2021, 2017 and 2012.

[212] Article 7(3) of Appendix V, ICC Arbitration Rules 2021, 2017 and 2012.

[213] G. Smith (2015), The Emergence of Emergency Arbitrations, Dec. *Arbitrator & Mediator Journal* 12, available at http://www.gordonsmithlegal.com.au/resources/Emergency%20Arbitrations%20(12082016).pdf (16 June 2020)..

[214] Article 7(8), ICDR Arbitration Rules 2021; Article 6(8), ICDR Arbitration Rules 2014; Article 37(9), ICDR Arbitration Rules 2009 and 2006.

USD.[215] When applying for the appointment of an emergency arbitrator under the HKIAC Arbitration Rules 2024, an Application Deposit of 250,000 HKD (approximately 32,000 USD) must be paid on the date of application, including the administrative fees of 45,000 HKD (approximately 5,700 USD), and a maximum amount of fees and emergency arbitrator expenses in the amount of 205,000 HKD (approximately 26,000 USD).[216] The total fee of an emergency arbitrator will normally not exceed 200,000 HKD (25,700 USD) unless agreed by both parties or determined by the HKIAC in exceptional circumstances.[217] The HKIAC also grants the power to an emergency arbitrator to decide on the allocation.[218] The LCIA Arbitration Rules 2020 requires the applicant to pay a non-refundable application fee of 10,000 GBP (approximately 12,700 USD).[219] The emergency arbitrator's fee is 25,000 GBP (approximately 32,000 USD),[220] which will be decided by the tribunal regarding the proportions borne by each party,[221] and it is non-refundable as long as the LCIA appoints an emergency arbitrator. The costs has been increased compared to the LCIA Arbitration Rules 2014 which numbers were 8,000 GBP and 20,000 GBP respectively.[222] The SIAC Arbitration Rules 2016 charges Singapore parties 5,350 SGD (approximately 4,000 USD) and overseas parties 5,000 SGD (approximately 3,600 USD) for a non-refundable administrative fee for emergency arbitrator applications.[223] The deposit of the emergency arbitrator fees and expenses is fixed at 30,000 SGD (approximately 22,000 USD), and the emergency arbitrator fees are fixed at 25,000 SGD (approximately 18,000 USD).[224] The non-refundable challenge fee is 8,560 SGD (approximately 6,200 USD) for domestic parties and 8,000 SGD (approximately 5,800 USD) for overseas parties.[225] The SIAC Arbitration Rules 2013 charges the same amount of money for the administrative fees. For the emergency arbitrator expenses, it shall be capped at 20% of a sole arbitrator maximum fee calculated based on the sum in dispute, and shall not be less than 20,000 SGD

215 HKIAC, HKIAC Average Costs and Duration, available at http://www.hkiac.org/content/costs-duration (1 June 2024).

216 HKIAC, the 2024 Schedule of Fees, available at https://hkiac.org/content/2024-schedule-fees (1 June 2024).

217 Article 5 of Schedule 4, HKIAC Arbitration Rules 2024 and 2018; HKIAC, the 2024 Schedule of Fees, available at https://hkiac.org/content/2024-schedule-fees (1 June 2024).

218 Article 16 of Schedule 4, HKIAC Arbitration Rules 2024; Article 15 of Schedule 4, HKIAC Arbitration Rules 2018 and 2013.

219 LCIA, Schedule of LCIA Arbitration Cost (2023), available at https://www.lcia.org/Dispute_Resolution_Services/schedule-of-arbitration-costs-2023.aspx (25 May 2024).

220 LCIA, Schedule of LCIA Arbitration Cost (2023), available at https://www.lcia.org/Dispute_Resolution_Services/schedule-of-arbitration-costs-2023.aspx (25 May 2024).

221 Article 9.10, LCIA Arbitration Rules 2014.

222 LCIA, Schedule of LCIA Arbitration Cost (2014), available at https://www.lcia.org/Dispute_Resolution_Services/schedule-of-costs-lcia-arbitration.aspx (25 May 2024).

223 Schedule of Fees, SIAC Arbitration Rules 2016.

224 Schedule of Fees, SIAC Arbitration Rules 2016.

225 Schedule of Fees, SIAC Arbitration Rules 2016.

(approximately 14,000 USD).[226] The deposit is required to cover the emergency arbitrator fees after the application.[227] Concerning the SIAC Arbitration Rules 2010, the expense for an emergency arbitrator shall be capped at 20% of a sole arbitrator maximum fee calculated based on the sum in dispute calculated.[228] The administration fee is lower, at 3,210 SGD (approximately 2,300 USD) for Singapore parties and 3,000 SGD (approximately 2,200 USD) for overseas parties.[229] The costs under the SIAC emergency arbitrator provisions will "initially be apportioned" by the emergency arbitrator, and finally, be determined by the arbitral tribunal.[230] For the cost of the emergency arbitrator proceedings under the SCC arbitration rules, the applicant is expected to pay the cost of the emergency arbitrator proceedings.[231] In the SCC Arbitration Rules 2023 and 2017, the application fee is 4,000 EUR (approximately 4,400 USD), and the fee of an emergency arbitrator amounts to 16,000 EUR (approximately 17,600 USD) and other reasonable costs.[232] The Board of the SCC can decide to increase the cost above. An emergency arbitrator shall apportion the costs at the request of the parties.[233] Under the SCC Arbitration Rules 2010, the application fee for the emergency arbitrator proceedings is 3,000 EUR (approximately 3,300 USD), and the fee for an emergency arbitrator is 12,000 EUR (approximately 13,200 USD).[234] A tribunal has the power to decide on the proportion of the cost by asking a party in a final award.[235]

2.7 Alternative Solutions for Interim Measures Before the Constitution of an Arbitral Tribunal

In addition to the emergency arbitrator mechanism, there are mainly three other alternatives for parties who need interim measures before the formation of an arbitral tribunal, including interim measures issued by a state court, the ICC Pre-Arbitral Referee Procedural and expedited arbitration.

[226] Schedule of Fees, SIAC Arbitration Rules 2013.

[227] Schedule of Fees, SIAC Arbitration Rules 2013.

[228] Schedule of Fees, SIAC Arbitration Rules 2010.

[229] Schedule of Fees, SIAC Arbitration Rules 2010.

[230] Article 13 of Schedule 1, SIAC Arbitration Rules 2016; Article 10 of Schedule 1, SIAC Arbitration Rules 2013 and 2010.

[231] Article 10(1) of Appendix II, SCC Arbitration Rules 2023, 2017 and 2010.

[232] Article 10(2) of Appendix II, SCC Arbitration Rules 2023, 2017.

[233] Article 10(5) of Appendix II, SCC Arbitration Rules 2023, 2017.

[234] Article 10(2) of Appendix II, SCC Arbitration Rules 2010.

[235] Article 10(5) of Appendix II, SCC Arbitration Rules 2010.

2.7.1 Interim Measures Issued by a State Court

As discussed before, all the six arbitral institutions allow for the concurrent jurisdiction of state courts regarding interim measures before the constitution of an arbitral tribunal in support of the arbitral proceedings. Furthermore the need for interim measures before the formation of an arbitral tribunal in ad hoc arbitrations, when parties need interim measures against third parties or a particular type of interim measures that are not available under the chosen institutional rules, the possibility of interim measures from a state court is essential and significant. The purpose of interim measures "is not to encroach on the procedural powers of the arbitrators but to reinforce them, and to render more effective the decision at which the arbitrators will ultimately arrive on the substance of the dispute".[236]

2.7.2 ICC Pre-arbitral Referee Procedure

The Pre-Arbitral Referee Procedure provides for a possibility for parties who need interim measures before the formal arbitration proceedings. In order to start the ICC Pre-Arbitral Referee Procedure, parties have to submit a written agreement for such a procedure either as part of their existing agreement or after a dispute arises.[237] Although the date this was enforced could be traced back to 1990, the ICC Pre-Arbitral Referee Procedure has been rarely used for its opt-in nature.[238] It took over ten years until the Pre-Arbitral Referee Procedure was applied in two cases.[239]

2.7.3 Expedited Arbitration

Expedited arbitration is another alternative way for parties to apply for interim measures. The ICC Arbitration Rules 2021 and 2017, the ICDR Arbitration Rules 2021 and 2014, the HKIAC Arbitration 2013, 2018, and 2024, the LCIA Arbitration Rules 2020 and 2014, the SIAC Arbitration Rule 2010, 2013, and 2016, all

---

[236] Gary B. Born (2021), *International Commercial Arbitration*, Kluwer Law International, p. 2712; *Front Carriers Ltd v. Atl. & Orient Shipping Corp.* [2006] SGHC 127 (High Court of Singapore, 2006); *NCC Int'l AB v. Alliance Concrete Singapore Pte Ltd* [2008] SGCA 5 (Singapore Court of Appeal, 2008); *Pathak v. Tourism Transport Ltd* [2002] 3 NZLR 681 (Auckland High Court, 2002); *Sensation Yachts Ltd v. Darby Maritime Ltd, No. CIV 2005-404-1908* (Auckland High Court 2005); *The "Lady Muriel" v. Transorient Shipping Ltd.* [1995] HKCA 615 (Hong Kong Court of Appeal, 1995).

[237] ICC, Pre-Arbitral Referee, available at https://iccwbo.org/dispute-resolution-services/pre-arbitral-referee/(25 May 2024).

[238] Gary B. Born (2021), *International Commercial Arbitration*, Kluwer Law International, p. 2632.

[239] Emmanuel Gaillard & Philippe Pinsolle (2004), The ICC Pre-Arbitral Referee: First Practical Experience, 10 *Arbitration International* 14.

provide for an expedited procedure.[240] The SCC separates the expedited procedure into another set of rules—Rules for Expedited Arbitrations 2010, 2017 and 2023 at the same time the SCC Arbitration Rules 2010, 2017 and 2023.

The application for expedited arbitration is not without conditions. For example, in the LCIA Arbitration Rules 2014, when facing "exceptional urgency", a party could apply for the expedited formation of an arbitral tribunal according to the arbitration rules and an arbitration agreement.[241] Under the ICC Arbitration Rules 2017, the expedited arbitration will automatically apply when the disputed amount is under 2 million USD, unless the parties expressly opt out in the agreement,[242] which has been increased to 3 million USD for disputes applying the ICC Arbitration Rules 2021.[243] Moreover, the application of expedited arbitration poses problems in different aspects. There is no consensus regarding the framework in expedited arbitration.[244] Arbitral institutions adopt various approaches in the application of expedited arbitration. There is also a maximum applied to the disputed amount that cannot be exceeded in a case according to most institutions.[245] Additionally, especially in recent years, the enforceability of awards granted in expedited arbitration has been questioned constantly.[246]

2.8 Concluding Remarks

According to the above systematic comparison of the ICC, the ICDR, the HKIAC, the LCIA, the SIAC, and the SCC arbitration rules, in all of their versions since the introduction of the emergency arbitrator mechanism, it is clear that they all share "a

[240] Article 30, ICC Arbitration Rules 2017; Article E, ICDR Arbitration Rules 2014; Article 42, HKIAC Arbitration Rules 2024 and 2018; Article 41, HKIAC Arbitration Rules 2013; Article 9A, LCIA Arbitration Rules 2014; Article 5, SIAC Arbitration Rules 2016, 2013, and 2010.

[241] Article 9.1, LCIA Arbitration Rules 2020 and 2014.

[242] Article 1(2) of Appendix VI, ICC Arbitration Rules 2017; Michael Bühler & Pierre Heitzmann (2017), The 2017 ICC Expedited Rules: From Softball to Hardball?, 34 *Journal of International Arbitration* 122.

[243] Article 1(2) of Appendix VI, ICC Arbitration Rules 2021.

[244] Lisa Allenden, Expedited Arbitration: Paris v. Stockholm: Full Steam Ahead, available at http://arbitrationblog.practicallaw.com/expedited-arbitration-paris-v-stockholm-full-steam-ahead/ (16 June 2020).

[245] Article 1(2) of Appendix VI, ICC Arbitration Rules 2021 and 2017; Article 1(4), ICDR Arbitration Rules 2021 and 2014; Article 42.1, HKIAC Arbitration Rules 2024 and 2018; Article 5.1(a), SIAC Arbitration Rules 2016.

[246] See in *AQZ v. ARA* [2015] SGHC 49 (High Court, Supreme Court of Singapore, 2015); *Nobles Resources Pte. Ltd. v. Shanghai Good Credit International Trade Co., Ltd.* (来宝资源国际私人有限公司与上海信泰国际贸易有限公司申请承认和执行外国仲裁裁决案, [2016]沪01协外认1号), available at http://wenshu.court.gov.cn/website/wenshu/181107ANFZ0BXSK4/index.html?docId=3977ca869daa4df39c87a7e0016e1525 (16 June 2020).

common, general procedural framework"[247] for the emergency arbitrator proceedings, despite various unique characteristics depending on the arbitral institution in question. The common ground of the emergency arbitrator proceedings will be the subject of the research in the following chapters concerning the enforceability of the decision granted by an emergency arbitrator. The differences among the institutional arbitration rules will be addressed if necessary.

[247] Fabio G. Santacroce (2015), The emergency arbitrator: a full-fledged arbitrator rendering an enforceable decision?, 31 *Arbitration International* 285.

Chapter 3
Essential Requirements to Enforce Interim Measures Granted by an Emergency Arbitrator

Both international conventions and the legislation of the jurisdictions provide grounds for the refusal to enforce foreign arbitral awards in international commercial arbitration. This chapter presents an overall discussion of the requirements for the recognition and enforcement of arbitral awards, with a particular focus on the interim measures granted by an emergency arbitrator. The discussion starts with the requirements for the enforcement of arbitral awards according to international conventions (Sect. 3.1), followed by the requirements for the enforcement of arbitral awards in the legislation of selected jurisdictions regarding international commercial arbitration (Sect. 3.2). At the end of this chapter, necessary legal requirements that need to be complied for enforceability are summarized (Sect. 3.3).

3.1 Requirements for the Enforcement of Interim Measures Granted by an Emergency Arbitrator in International Conventions

So far, there is no convention providing rules governing the enforcement of interim measures granted internationally either by emergency arbitrators or by arbitral tribunals. Hence, it is only possible to turn to the regulations providing for the recognition and enforcement of arbitral awards to see whether the interim measures granted by an emergency arbitrator can satisfy the requirements under the current enforcement regime.

Notwithstanding the increasing popularity of international commercial arbitration as a method of dispute resolution in the business community, the enforcement of foreign arbitral awards has been problematic for a long time. The ICC, which

J. Zhang, *The Enforceability of the Interim Measures Granted by an Emergency Arbitrator in International Commercial Arbitration*,
https://doi.org/10.1007/978-981-97-6536-2_3

was established in 1919,[1] has played a primary and central role in the promotion of a common legal framework for international commercial arbitration.[2] The introduction of the Protocol on Arbitration Clauses 1923 and the Convention on the Execution of Foreign Arbitral Awards 1927 improved the "chaotic condition".[3] Due to the inadequacies of the previous treaties, the New York Convention 1958 was adopted as a binding legal instrument for a better situation in the recognition and enforcement of foreign arbitral awards. The New York Convention 1958 was proven successful, and it was even seen as the most successful convention in the history of private international law.[4] Apart from the international level, regional treaties also try to enhance the development of international arbitration, for example, the European Convention on International Commercial Arbitration 1961, the Inter-American Convention on International Commercial Arbitration 1975 and other regional conventions involving international commercial arbitration.

3.1.1 Protocol on Arbitration Clauses 1923 (the Geneva Protocol of 1923)

The Protocol on Arbitration Clauses was signed at Geneva on September 24, 1923 and was administrated by the League of Nations.[5] The central concern of the Geneva Protocol of 1923 was the recognition and enforcement of specific arbitral agreements and arbitral awards in the jurisdiction where they were issued.[6] Although the provisions in this treaty were imperfect, the Geneva Protocol of 1923 nevertheless "planted the seeds"[7] for several fundamental principles in international commercial arbitration.

---

[1] ICC, History, available at https://iccwbo.org/about-icc-2/our-mission-history-and-values/ (1 June 2024).

[2] Gary B. Born (2021), *International Commercial Arbitration*, Kluwer Law International, p. 62; Marike R. P. Paulsson (2016), *The 1958 New York Convention in Action, Kluwer Law International*, p. 3; Stephen M. Schwebel (1996), A Celebration of the United Nations New York Convention on the Recognition and Enforcement of Foreign Arbitral Awards, 12 *Arbitration International* 85.

[3] Ernest G. Lorenzen (1935), Commercial Arbitration—Enforcement of Foreign Awards, 45 *Yale Law Journal* 63.

[4] Albert van den Berg, Introductory Note, Convention on the Recognition and Enforcement of Foreign Arbitral Awards, available at http://legal.un.org/avl/ha/crefaa/crefaa.html (1 June 2024).

[5] Protocol on Arbitration Clauses 1923, available at https://treaties.un.org/Pages/LONViewDetails.aspx?src=LON&id=548&chapter=30&clang=_en (1 June 2024).

[6] Adriana Braghetta (2013), The Framework of the International Arbitration System: the Challenge Derived from the Improper Conduct of Judicial Courts, in Albert van den Berg, International Arbitration: The Coming of a New Age?, 17 *ICCA Congress Series* 434; Emmanuel Gaillard & John Savage (1999), *Fouchard Gaillard Goldman on International Commercial Arbitration*, Kluwer Law International, p. 121; Leonard V. Quigley (1961), Accession by the United States to the United Nations Convention on the Recognition and Enforcement of Foreign Arbitral Awards, 70 *Yale Law Journal* 1054.

[7] Gary B. Born (2021), *International Commercial Arbitration*, Kluwer Law International, p. 63.

Firstly, this protocol admitted the presumptive validity of arbitral agreements.[8] As stated in Article 1, the contracting parties needed to recognize "the validity of an agreement whether relating to existing or future differences between parties subject respectively to the jurisdiction of different Contracting State".[9] Secondly, the principle of party autonomy was also recognized in this treaty. Article 2 in the protocol regulated that "[t]he arbitral procedure, including the constitution of the arbitral tribunal, shall be governed by the will of the parties and by the law of the country in whose territory the arbitration takes place".[10] Thirdly, the Geneva Protocol of 1923 created a more favorable environment for international arbitration, providing that the contracting parties should "agree to facilitate all steps in the procedure which require to be taken in their own territories, in accordance with the provisions of their law governing arbitral procedure applicable to existing differences".[11]

Even though the adoption of the Geneva Protocol of 1923 marked a huge step forward towards the uniformity of international arbitration, the severe criticism that followed could not be ignored. Since the treaty itself was not self-executing, therefore, supplementary domestic legislation was necessary. The Geneva Protocol of 1923 did not deal with the recognition and enforcement of foreign arbitral awards, which was a huge concern of the arbitration community. It was considered to be the reason that various jurisdictions had not ratified this treaty at that time.[12] Article 3 urged the contracting states to ensure "the execution by its authorities and in accordance with the provisions of its national laws of arbitral awards made in its own territory under the preceding articles".[13] In other words, the Geneva Protocol of 1923 only limited the enforcement of arbitral awards made in the territory of the origin, but not the "foreign" arbitral awards.[14] The need to expand the enforceability of arbitral awards rather than limiting the scope to only domestic arbitral awards led to the following introduction of the Convention on the Execution of Foreign Arbitral Awards 1927.[15]

[8] Gary B. Born (2021), *International Commercial Arbitration*, Kluwer Law International, p. 63.

[9] Article 1, The Geneva Protocol of 1923.

[10] Article 2, The Geneva Protocol of 1923.

[11] Article 2, The Geneva Protocol of 1923.

[12] Adriana Braghetta (2013), The Framework of the International Arbitration System: the Challenge Derived from the Improper Conduct of Judicial Courts, in Albert van den Berg, International Arbitration: The Coming of a New Age?, 17 *ICCA Congress Series* 435.

[13] Article 3, The Geneva Protocol of 1923.

[14] Gary B. Born (2021), *International Commercial Arbitration*, Kluwer Law International, p. 63.

[15] Gary B. Born (2021), *International Commercial Arbitration*, Kluwer Law International, p. 64.

3.1.2 Convention on the Execution of Foreign Arbitral Awards 1927 (the Geneva Convention of 1927)

The Convention on the Execution of Foreign Arbitral Awards was signed at Geneva on 26 September 1927 and was administrated by the League of Nations.[16] Unlike the predecessor, i.e., the Geneva Protocol of 1923, this convention extended the enforceability of arbitral awards to include international commercial arbitration. Any arbitral awards granted in the territory of one of the contracting parties based on an arbitral agreement covered by the Geneva Protocol of 1923 should be recognized as binding and enforceable under the auspices of the Geneva Convention of 1927.[17]

Concerning the requirements for the enforcement of those arbitral awards, the Geneva Convention of 1927 did provide for some rules. First of all, there should be a valid arbitration agreement based on the applicable law.[18] Second, the dispute between parties should be arbitrable under the law of the jurisdiction where the award was sought to be relied upon.[19] Meanwhile, and third, the arbitral proceedings, including the constitution of an arbitral tribunal, should conform with the law governing the arbitral procedure.[20] Fourth, the award needed to be final at the seat of arbitration, without being subject to appeal.[21] Additionally, the recognition and enforcement of arbitral awards could "not be contrary to the public policy or to the principles of the law of the country in which it is sought to be relied upon".[22] Furthermore, if it could be proven that "the award has been annulled in the country in which it was made",[23] or "the party against whom it is sought to use the award was not given notice of the arbitration proceedings in sufficient time to enable him to present his case",[24] or "being under a legal incapacity, he was not properly represented",[25] or the award was not falling within the arbitral agreement,[26] the relevant state courts could refuse to recognize and enforce the award.

Not surprisingly, the Geneva Convention of 1927 was not satisfactory due to its intrinsic flaws. Firstly, the field of application was limited, as in the Geneva Protocol of 1923. The parties had to be "subject to the jurisdiction of one of the High Contracting Parties", and the arbitral awards should be made "in a territory of one of the High Contracting Parties".[27] A more modern approach is to consider that

[16] Convention on the Execution of Foreign Arbitral Awards 1927, available at https://treaties.un.org/Pages/LONViewDetails.aspx?src=LON&id=549&chapter=30&clang=_en (1 June 2024).

[17] Article 1, The Geneva Convention of 1927.

[18] Article 1 (a), The Geneva Convention of 1927.

[19] Article 1 (b), The Geneva Convention of 1927.

[20] Article 1 (c), The Geneva Convention of 1927.

[21] Article 1 (d), The Geneva Convention of 1927.

[22] Article 1 (e), The Geneva Convention of 1927.

[23] Article 2 (a), The Geneva Convention of 1927.

[24] Article 2 (b), The Geneva Convention of 1927.

[25] Article 2 (b), The Geneva Convention of 1927.

[26] Article 2 (c), The Geneva Convention of 1927.

[27] Article 1, The Geneva Convention of 1927.

arbitral awards granted in contracting states and non-contacting states are alike.[28] Additionally, the burden of proof for the enforcement was placed on the enforcing party, who had to prove that all the criteria required in the convention were fulfilled.[29] The other party against the enforcement would "need only rebut one of the various tests to be successful".[30] It is considered that the convention "eased the path of the defaulting defendant and the partial tribunal" by doing so.[31] Lastly, there was a possible "double exequatur" requirement contained in the interpretation of the provisions regarding the recognition and enforcement of arbitral awards, which could be the main problem. Article 1 (d) of the Geneva Convention of 1927 required the proof of "finality" for arbitral awards to be enforced, which would lead to this "double exequatur" requirement. It meant that an arbitral award would only be recognized and enforced under the Geneva Convention of 1927 if this award had been recognized by the state courts of the seat of arbitration.[32] To achieve this, the enforcing party always needed "some form of confirmatory order or permission" from state courts in the jurisdiction where the arbitral awards were granted.[33] The "double exequatur" requirement created extra difficulty and unpredictability in establishing the "finality" of arbitral awards under the Geneva Convention of 1927.[34]

---

[28] Albert van den Berg (1981), *The New York Arbitration Convention of 1958: Towards a Uniform Judicial Interpretation*, Kluwer Law and Taxation Publishers, p. 12.

[29] Article 1 (a), The Geneva Convention of 1927; Gary B. Born (2021), *International Commercial Arbitration*, Kluwer Law International, p. 64; Leonard V. Quigley (1961), Accession by the United States to the United Nations Convention on the Recognition and Enforcement of Foreign Arbitral Awards, 70 *Yale Law Journal* 1055; Albert van den Berg (1981), *The New York Arbitration Convention of 1958: Towards a Uniform Judicial Interpretation*, Kluwer Law and Taxation Publishers, p. 7.

[30] A. Jason Mirabito (1975), The United Nations Convention on the Recognition and Enforcement of Foreign Arbitral Awards: The First Four Years, 5 *Georgia Journal of International and Comparative Law* 478.

[31] Leonard V. Quigley (1961), Accession by the United States to the United Nations Convention on the Recognition and Enforcement of Foreign Arbitral Awards, 70 *Yale Law Journal* 1055.

[32] Samuel Pisar (1959), The United Nations Convention on Foreign Arbitral Awards, 33 *Southern California Law Review* 21; Emmanuel Gaillard & John Savage (1999), *Fouchard Gaillard Goldman on International Commercial Arbitration*, Kluwer Law International, p. 122.

[33] Stefan Michael Kröll, Julian D. M. Lew & Loukas A. Mistelis (2003), *Comparative International Commercial Arbitration*, Kluwer Law International, p. 20.

[34] Gary B. Born (2021), *International Commercial Arbitration*, Kluwer Law International, p. 65; Marike R. P. Paulsson (2016), *The 1958 New York Convention in Action, Kluwer Law International*, p. 4.

Although they "turned out to have little impact on international judicial life",[35] as "the first practical realization",[36] these two conventions still represented "undoubtedly an improvement in comparison with the previous situation"[37] and a significant effort towards the harmonization of international commercial arbitration. They have inspired arbitral legislation in several jurisdictions, including France, the United Kingdom and the United States.[38] The inadequacies of the Geneva Protocol of 1923 and the Geneva Convention of 1927 motivated the introduction of the United Nations Convention on Recognition and Enforcement of Foreign Arbitral Awards 1958 (the New York Convention 1958).

3.1.3 Convention on Recognition and Enforcement of Foreign Arbitral Awards (The New York Convention) 1958

The Convention on the Recognition and Enforcement of Foreign Arbitral Awards (New York Convention) 1958[39] is a cornerstone of international arbitration. It is "by far the most significant contemporary legislative instrument relating to international commercial arbitration".[40] Although it is a remarkably short treaty with only 16 articles, it has become the foundation of the prosperity of international arbitration and a "rampart of the security of international contracts".[41] The two focuses of the New York Convention 1958 of ensuring that the arbitral agreement is respected and guaranteeing that the arbitral awards are recognized and enforced appropriately are served very well.

The journey to the introduction of this new convention was described as "a remarkable *valse hésitation*", meaning "two steps forward, two steps backward, and miraculously, at the eleventh hour, three steps forward".[42] With the observation that the framework established under the Geneva Convention of 1927 "no longer corresponded to the requirements of international trade" and, considering the fact that

---

[35] Samuel Pisar (1959), The United Nations Convention on Foreign Arbitral Awards, 33 *Southern California Law Review* 14.

[36] A. Jason Mirabito (1975), The United Nations Convention on the Recognition and Enforcement of Foreign Arbitral Awards: The First Four Years, 5 *Georgia Journal of International and Comparative Law* 478.

[37] Albert van den Berg (1981), *The New York Arbitration Convention of 1958: Towards a Uniform Judicial Interpretation*, Kluwer Law and Taxation Publishers, p. 7.

[38] Gary B. Born (2021), *International Commercial Arbitration*, Kluwer Law International, p. 66.

[39] Convention on the Recognition and Enforcement of Foreign Arbitral Awards 1958, available at https://uncitral.un.org/en/texts/arbitration/conventions/foreign_arbitral_awards (1 June 2024).

[40] Gary B. Born (2021), *International Commercial Arbitration*, Kluwer Law International, p. 99.

[41] Marike R. P. Paulsson (2016), *The 1958 New York Convention in Action, Kluwer Law International*, p. 1.

[42] Marike R. P. Paulsson (2016), *The 1958 New York Convention in Action, Kluwer Law International*, p. 5.

"the enforcement of only those awards that are strictly in accordance with the rules of procedure laid down in the law of the country where the arbitration took place", the ICC believed that "there could be no progress without full recognition of the conception of international awards".[43] Those concerns led to the proposal raised by the ICC in 1953.

The original ICC proposal establishing a framework for international commercial arbitration isolated from arbitration laws of jurisdictions was seen as "unacceptable" by most states back then.[44] The proposal was submitted to the United Nation's Economic and Social Council (ECOSOC), which revised the ICC draft to be the "Draft Convention on the Recognition and Enforcement of Foreign Arbitral Awards".[45] The change from the denationalization preferred by the ICC to the approach adopted by the ECOSOC was "less ambitious",[46] rejecting the a-national arbitration mode, but insisting on the root being in local arbitration laws. These two drafts were presented at the conference held from 20 May to 10 June 1958, in New York with representatives from 45 states.[47] Nowadays, there are 164 parties under the New York Convention 1958,[48] which "perhaps could lay claim to be the most effective instance of international legislation in the entire history of commercial law".[49]

The requirements needed for recognition and enforcement under the New York Convention 1958 are reflected in Article V, which is "the heart of the Convention".[50] According to Article V (1), the recognition and enforcement of specific arbitral

---

[43] ICC, Report and Preliminary Draft Convention adopted by the Committee on International Commercial Arbitration at its meeting of 13 March 1953, 9 ICC International Court of Arbitration Bulletin 1998, p. 32, available at http://library.iccwbo.org/content/dr/COMMISSION_REPORTS/CR_0011.htm?l1=Bulletins&l2=ICC+International+Court+of+Arbitration+Bulletin+Vol.+9%2FNo.1+-+Eng (16 June 2020).

[44] Albert van den Berg (1981), *The New York Arbitration Convention of 1958: Towards a Uniform Judicial Interpretation*, Kluwer Law and Taxation Publishers, p. 7.

[45] ECOSOC, Report of the Committee on the Enforcement of International Arbitral Awards, 1955, para. 17, available at http://newyorkconvention1958.org/index.php?lvl=notice_display&id=3423&opac_view=6 (16 June 2020).

[46] Gary B. Born (2021), *International Commercial Arbitration*, Kluwer Law International, p. 100.

[47] Gary B. Born (2021), *International Commercial Arbitration*, Kluwer Law International, p. 100; Stefan Michael Kröll, Julian D. M. Lew & Loukas A. Mistelis (2003), *Comparative International Commercial Arbitration*, Kluwer Law International, p. 21; Pieter Sanders (1999), The History of the New York Convention, in Albert van den Berg, Improving the Efficiency of Arbitration Agreements and Awards: 40 Years of Application of the New York Convention, 9 *ICCA Congress Series* 11–12; Albert van den Berg (1981), *The New York Arbitration Convention of 1958: Towards a Uniform Judicial Interpretation*, Kluwer Law and Taxation Publishers, p. 8.

[48] UNCITRAL, Status: Convention on the Recognition and Enforcement of Foreign Arbitral Awards (New York, 1958) (the "New York Convention"), available at https://treaties.un.org/Pages/ViewDetails.aspx?src=TREATY&mtdsg_no=XXII-1&chapter=22&clang=_en (1 June 2024).

[49] Michael Mustill (1989), Arbitration: History and Background, 6 *Journal of International Arbitration* 49.

[50] Pieter Sanders (1999), The History of the New York Convention, in Albert van den Berg, Improving the Efficiency of Arbitration Agreements and Awards: 40 Years of Application of the New York Convention, 9 *ICCA Congress Series* 13.

awards may be refused only if the party resisting the enforcement proves that: (a) the parties to the arbitration agreement were under an incapacity, or the agreement is not valid according to the applicable law[51]; (b) there was no proper notice given of the appointment of the arbitrators or the arbitration proceedings, or such party could not present in the procedure[52]; (c) the arbitral award is not within or beyond the terms of the submission to arbitration[53]; (d) the composition of the arbitral tribunal was not in conformity with the arbitral agreement[54]; or (e) the award has not been binding or been set aside or suspended by a competent authority at the seat of arbitration.[55] Article V (2) regulates two other situations which may lead to the refusal of the recognition and enforcement of arbitral awards by a state court on its own initiative, i.e., the dispute being not capable of settlement by arbitration under the law of that jurisdiction where the enforcement is sought,[56] or the recognition or enforcement would be contrary to the public policy of that jurisdiction where the enforcement is sought.[57]

The Geneva Protocol of 1923 and the Geneva Convention of 1927 "shall cease to have effect between Contracting States on their becoming bound and to the extent that they become bound, by this Convention".[58] It is to be noticed that the provisions in the New York Convention 1958 will not affect the validity of other international conventions regarding the similar issues regulated.[59] That is to say, if one arbitral award cannot be enforced under the New York Convention 1958, the party can try elsewhere, relying upon another applicable convention.

3.1.4 Other International Conventions

There are other major regional conventions in addition to the international conventions addressed above. A brief, but not exhaustive, introduction is given below in order to provide a bigger picture of the requirements for the recognition and enforcement of arbitral awards on a global scale.

[51] Article V (1) (a), the New York Convention 1958.
[52] Article V (1) (b), the New York Convention 1958.
[53] Article V (1) (c), the New York Convention 1958.
[54] Article V (1) (d), the New York Convention 1958.
[55] Article V (1) (e), the New York Convention 1958.
[56] Article V (2) (a), the New York Convention 1958.
[57] Article V (2) (a), the New York Convention 1958.
[58] Article VII (2), the New York Convention 1958.
[59] Article VII (1), the New York Convention 1958.

The European Convention on International Commercial Arbitration 1961[60] is "one of the world's most important regional commercial arbitration treaties".[61] This convention was drafted by the United Nations Economic Commission for Europe during the cold war time, aimed to deal with the common problems of arbitral procedures among European countries, especially for East and West Europe.[62] The convention "was the first international instrument to treat international commercial arbitration as a whole",[63] with provisions directly governing the stages of arbitral proceedings. The provisions do not, however, cover the recognition and enforcement of arbitral awards, leaving those issues to be dealt by other conventions, including the New York Convention 1958.

In practice, the European Convention on International Commercial Arbitration 1961 "never really achieved real international recognition."[64] The influence of this convention "has not been substantial",[65] because the limited numbers of contracting parties are all members of the New York Convention 1958, and the latter convention adopts a proper regime of recognition and enforcement for foreign arbitral awards. However, this convention's efforts on international arbitration doctrines are highly significant, such as the competence-competence principle and party autonomy.[66] As time passes, the European Convention on International Commercial Arbitration 1961 is "currently somewhat dated"[67] and new adjustments are needed.

The European Convention Providing a Uniform Law on Arbitration 1966[68] was signed by Austria and Belgium. Belgium is the only one of the two signatories to ratify the convention. This convention was designed by the Council of Europe to provide a uniform national and international arbitration law and a "more effective settlement of private law disputes by arbitration in international relations".[69] Unfortunately, it

---

[60] European Convention on International Commercial Arbitration, Geneva, 21 April 1961, United Nations Treaty Series, vol. 484, p. 349, available at https://treaties.un.org/Pages/ViewDetails.aspx?src=TREATY&mtdsg_no=XXII-2&chapter=22&clang=_en (1 June 2024).

[61] Gary B. Born (2021), *International Commercial Arbitration*, Kluwer Law International, p. 120.

[62] Alan Redfern, Martin Hunter, Nigel Blackaby & Constantine Partasides (2004), *Law and Practice of International Commercial Arbitration*, Sweet & Maxwell, p. 460.

[63] Emmanuel Gaillard & John Savage (1999), *Fouchard Gaillard Goldman on International Commercial Arbitration*, Kluwer Law International, p. 140.

[64] Stefan Michael Kröll, Julian D. M. Lew & Loukas A. Mistelis (2003), *Comparative International Commercial Arbitration*, Kluwer Law International, p. 23.

[65] Gary B. Born (2015), *International Arbitration: Law and Practice*, Kluwer Law International, p. 41.

[66] Gary B. Born (2021), *International Commercial Arbitration*, Kluwer Law International, p. 121; see also Article IV & Annex, the European Convention on International Commercial Arbitration 1961.

[67] Gary B. Born (2021), *International Commercial Arbitration*, Kluwer Law International, p. 121.

[68] European Convention Providing a Uniform Law on Arbitration 1966, available at https://rm.coe.int/CoERMPublicCommonSearchServices/DisplayDCTMContent?documentId=090000168006ff61 (1 June 2024).

[69] John Gaffney (2017), Should the European Union Regulate Commercial Arbitration?, 33 *Arbitration International* 85.

has never come into force[70] and "is unlikely to do so".[71] Article 29 of this uniform law regulates that a competent authority "shall refuse the application if the award or its enforcement is contrary to *ordre public* or if the dispute was not capable of settlement by arbitration".[72]

The Convention on the Settlement by Arbitration of Civil Law Disputes Arising out of Economic, Scientific and Technical Co-operation Relationships 1972[73] was prepared under the auspices of the Council for Mutual Economic Assistance (CMEA) and signed in Moscow.[74] During the existence of the Soviet Union, this convention did have a substantial effect in Eastern and Central Europe with the contracting states, including Bulgaria, Czechoslovakia, German Democratic Republic, Hungary, Mongolia, Poland, Romania, and Union of Soviet Socialist Republics.[75] However, currently it "no longer has any real purpose" after the demise of the Soviet Union.[76] Article V stipulates that the judicial authority of the enforcing state may refuse the recognition and enforcement of arbitral awards only if a) such awards violated the rules of competence; b) the arbitral procedure was not equal and fair to all parties; and c) the awards had been set aside or suspended by the state courts at the seat of arbitration.[77]

The Inter-American Convention on International Commercial Arbitration 1975,[78] also known as the Panama Convention, was signed at the conclusion of the Inter-American Specialized Conference on Private International Law in Panama,[79] which is "a landmark development in commercial arbitration in the Western Hemisphere".[80] Historically, in Latin America, there was "a traditional hostility towards international

[70] Stefan Michael Kröll, Julian D. M. Lew & Loukas A. Mistelis (2003), *Comparative International Commercial Arbitration*, Kluwer Law International, p 23.

[71] Emmanuel Gaillard & John Savage (1999), *Fouchard Gaillard Goldman on International Commercial Arbitration*, Kluwer Law International, p 145.

[72] Article 29 of Annex I, European Convention Providing a Uniform Law on Arbitration 1966.

[73] Convention on the Settlement by Arbitration of Civil Law Disputes Arising out of Economic, Scientific and Technical Co-operation Relationships 1972, available at https://treaties.un.org/Pages/showDetails.aspx?objid=080000028011 0b20&clang=_en (1 June 2024).

[74] Emmanuel Gaillard & John Savage (1999), *Fouchard Gaillard Goldman on International Commercial Arbitration*, Kluwer Law International, p 145.

[75] Stefan Michael Kröll, Julian D. M. Lew & Loukas A. Mistelis (2003), *Comparative International Commercial Arbitration*, Kluwer Law International, p. 23.

[76] Stefan Michael Kröll, Julian D. M. Lew & Loukas A. Mistelis (2003), *Comparative International Commercial Arbitration*, Kluwer Law International, p. 23.

[77] Article V, Convention on the Settlement by Arbitration of Civil Law Disputes Arising out of Economic, Scientific and Technical Co-operation Relationships 1972, available at https://treaties.un.org/Pages/showDetails.aspx?objid=080000028011 0b20&clang=_en (1 June 2024).

[78] Inter-American Convention on International Commercial Arbitration 1975, available at https://treaties.un.org/doc/Publication/UNTS/Volume%201438/volume-1438-I-24384-English.pdf (1 June 2024).

[79] Charles Robert Norberg (1978), General Introduction to Inter-American Commercial Arbitration, in Pieter Sanders, 3 *Yearbook Commercial Arbitration* 1.

[80] Committee on Arbitration of the Association of the Bar of the City of New York, The Inter-American Convention on International Commercial Arbitration, 9 University of Miami Inter-American Law Review 1977, p. 43, available at https://repository.law.miami.edu/cgi/viewcontent.cgi?referer=https://www.google.com.hk/&httpsredir=1&article=2022&context=umialr (1 June 2024).

arbitration".[81] Although in 1975, the New York Convention 1958 had been ratified by many states all over the world, "it had barely been adopted within Latin America".[82] In this case, the Inter-American Convention on International Commercial Arbitration 1975 "addressed the growing need for a measure of consistency and uniformity in the recognition and enforcement of arbitral awards in Latin America".[83]

Article 5 of the Inter-American Convention on International Commercial Arbitration 1975 regulates the grounds on which state courts may refuse the recognition and enforcement of arbitral awards, which is "almost a replica"[84] of the Article V in the New York Convention 1958. There is "no substantive difference" between the two conventions, which demonstrate a "pro-enforcement bias".[85] The "precedents under one are generally applicable to the other".[86] However, the Inter-American Convention on International Commercial Arbitration 1975 "does not contain provisions regarding its field of application, the referral by a court to arbitration, and the conditions to be fulfilled by the party seeking enforcement of the award".[87]

According to the House Report by the Judiciary Committee of the United States, "[t]he New York Convention and the Inter-American Convention are intended to achieve the same results, and their key provisions adopt the same standards, phrased in the legal style appropriate for each organization. It is the Committee's expectation, given that fact and the parallel legislation under the Federal Arbitration Act that would be applied to the Conventions, that courts in the United States would achieve a general uniformity of results under the two conventions".[88]

The Arab Convention on Commercial Arbitration (Amman Convention) 1987[89] was signed during the Fifth Session of the Council of Arab Ministers of Justice in

[81] Emmanuel Gaillard & John Savage (1999), *Fouchard Gaillard Goldman on International Commercial Arbitration*, Kluwer Law International, p. 146.

[82] Christian Leathley & Florencia Villaggi (2017), Chapter 25: The Panama Convention in the United States: Chapter 3 of the FAA, in Laurence Shore, Tai-Heng Cheng, Jenelle E. Chiusa, Lawrence Schaner & Mara V. J. Senn, *International Arbitration in the United States*, Kluwer Law International, p. 600.

[83] *Energy Transport, Ltd. and PT Cabot Indonesia v. M.V. San Sebastian, her freights etc. in rem, Oilmar Co. Ltd.*, 348 F. Supp. 2d 186, 198 (United States District Court, S.D. New York 2004).

[84] Committee on Arbitration of the Association of the Bar of the City of New York (1977), The Inter-American Convention on International Commercial Arbitration, 9 *University of Miami Inter-American Law Review* 45, available at https://repository.law.miami.edu/cgi/viewcontent.cgi?referer=https://www.google.com.hk/&httpsredir=1&article=2022&context=umialr (1 June 2024).

[85] *Corporación Mexicana de Mantenimiento Integral, S. de R.L. de C.V. v. Pemex Exploración y Producción*, 832 F. 3d 92, 105 (United States Court of Appeals, Second Circuit, 2016).

[86] *Corporacion Mexicana de Mantenimiento Integral, S. de R.L. de C.V. v. Pemex-Exploracion y Produccion*, 962 F. Supp. 2d 642, 654 (United States District Court, S.D. New York, 2013).

[87] Albert van den Berg (1989), The New York Convention 1958 and Panama Convention 1975: Redundancy or Compatibility?, 5 *Arbitration International* 229.

[88] Thomas Hale (2015), *Between Interests and Law: The Politics of Transnational Commercial Disputes*, Cambridge University Press, p. 225; *DRC, INC. v. Republic of Honduras*, 774 F. Supp. 2d 66, 71 (Unites States District Court, District of Columbia 2011).

[89] Mahir Jalili (1990), Amman Arab Convention on Commercial Arbitration, 7 *Journal of International Arbitration*, the English version of the convention is available at pp. 146–152 of this

Jordan in order to build "unified Arab Rules on commercial arbitrations".[90] Article 35 provides the only reason for the supreme courts of each contracting party to refuse the recognition and enforcement of an arbitral award, which is the enforcement of the arbitral award being contrary to public policy.[91]

Admittedly, the conventions listed above are not exhaustive, but the provisions laid down in those conventions point to the fact that they, more or less, share a similar approach as in the New York Convention 1958. That is to say, in order for an arbitral award to be enforced, it is necessary that a) the concerned arbitration agreement is valid with capable signing parties; b) the arbitral proceedings are fair to all parties; c) the award is within the submission to arbitration; d) the composition of a tribunal and the procedure is in conformity with the agreement or with the *lex arbitri*; e) the award is still binding; f) the dispute is subject to arbitration; and g) the enforcement will not lead to a conflict with public policy.

3.2 Requirements for the Enforcement of Interim Measures Granted by an Emergency Arbitrator in Selected Jurisdictions

Although the emergency arbitrator mechanism for issuing interim measures was only introduced nearly 15 years ago by the ICDR, the interim measures in either domestic or international commercial arbitration are not new. Different jurisdictions adopt a distinctive approach to dealing with interim measures in arbitration. The legislation "plays a significant role in the availability of provisional relief".[92] Usually, the arbitral bodies will not grant interim measures unless the applicable law governing the arbitral proceedings allows them to do so.[93] In this chapter, three representative jurisdictions, Singapore, Mainland China, and the United States, having different views towards the emergency arbitrator mechanism are examined to provide a systematic comparison of the statutory law and legal practice.

Some jurisdictions take a more open and positive view of recent developments in international commercial arbitration, especially related to the emergency arbitrator mechanism. These jurisdictions include Hong Kong, Singapore, the Netherlands, and New Zealand. The legislation in these jurisdictions acknowledges the application of interim measures granted by an emergency arbitrator implicitly or explicitly. The friendly view towards the emergency arbitrator mechanism may relate to the

---

article. The English version of the Arab Convention on Commercial Arbitration (Amman Convention) 1987 is also available at http://www.arbitrations.ru/userfiles/file/Law/Treaty/Arab%20convention%20on%20commercial%20arbitration%20eng_rus.pdf (1 June 2024).

[90] Stefan Michael Kröll, Julian D. M. Lew & Loukas A. Mistelis (2003), *Comparative International Commercial Arbitration*, Kluwer Law International, p. 24.

[91] Article 35, Arab Convention on Commercial Arbitration (Amman Convention) 1987.

[92] Gary B. Born (2021), *International Commercial Arbitration*, Kluwer Law International, p. 2610.

[93] Gary B. Born (2021), *International Commercial Arbitration*, Kluwer Law International, p. 2610.

trading tradition in these jurisdictions. Singapore ranked in first position in the Global Competitiveness Report 2019 by the World Economic Forum, Hong Kong took the third position, the Netherlands followed Hong Kong ranked in the fourth position, and New Zealand was the nineteenth out of 141 economies.[94] Singapore will be examined here in a detailed analysis below as a representative of those jurisdictions. The legislation of Hong Kong, the Netherlands and New Zeeland is also addressed as supporting documents.

The power to grant interim measures was historically attributed to state courts. With the continuous development of international commercial arbitration, most jurisdictions eliminated this restriction, meaning that state courts are not the only forum to grant interim measures. However, until today, there are some jurisdictions that still limit an arbitrator's power to issue interim measures. One of the arguments is that the coercive powers of arbitrators to enforce interim measures are lacking.[95] Another argument is the possibility to "endanger state jurisdiction and high ideals of impartial justice".[96] The jurisdictions not allowing arbitral bodies to grant interim measures in international commercial arbitration include the Czech Republic,[97] Finland,[98] Mainland China,[99] and Thailand.[100] Obviously, in those jurisdictions, there are significant barriers to the application of the emergency arbitrator mechanism. In this chapter, Mainland China is examined as the representative of the jurisdictions which are against the emergency arbitrator mechanism, based on the influence of the that jurisdiction in international commerce and trade. While Mainland China and Hong Kong belong to one sovereign state, i.e., the People's Republic of China, it will be more likely to see the possible development of the emergency arbitrator mechanism in future Chinese arbitration laws. The interaction between these two jurisdictions is also addressed.

In addition to these two categories of jurisdictions which have a definite opinion on the emergency arbitrator mechanism, one category of jurisdiction remains, which has no clear and no definite answer to the question of the enforceability of the interim measures issued by an emergency arbitrator. The United States is examined as a representative of this category. Although the emergency arbitrator mechanism in

---

[94] World Economic Forum, The Global Competitiveness Report 2019, available at http://www3.weforum.org/docs/WEF_TheGlobalCompetitivenessReport2019.pdf (1 June 2024).

[95] Ali Yesilirmak (2005), *Provisional Measures in International Commercial Arbitration*, Kluwer Law International, p. 35.

[96] Ali Yesilirmak (2005), *Provisional Measures in International Commercial Arbitration*, Kluwer Law International, p. 35, & 64.

[97] Section 22, Act of the Czech Republic No. 216/1994 Sb. on arbitration proceedings and on enforcement of arbitration awards, available at https://is.muni.cz/el/1422/jaro2008/SOC026/um/216-1994_EN.pdf (1 June 2024).

[98] Section 5 & 51, Finland Arbitration Act 754/2015, available at https://www.finlex.fi/fi/laki/kaannokset/1992/en19920967.pdf (1 June 2024).

[99] Article 28 & 46, Arbitration Law of the People's Republic of China 2017, translation available at http://en.pkulaw.cn/display.aspx?cgid=83c8fbd6da8a6eb8bdfb&lib=law (1 June 2024).

[100] Section 16, Thailand Arbitration Act B.E. 2545/2002, available at https://arbitrationlaw.com/sites/default/files/free_pdfs/Thailand%20Arbitration%20Act.pdf (1 June 2024).

international commercial arbitration was first introduced by the ICDR, which is based in the United States, the question of whether the interim measures rendered by an emergency arbitrator are enforceable cannot be answered with certainty. The debate whether the interim measures provided by an arbitral tribunal should be recognized and enforced is still ongoing. Moreover, the access to the case law as well as the incidence of cases are further considerations that led to choosing the United States as a representative.

3.2.1 Jurisdictions Supporting the Emergency Arbitrator Mechanism

In this section, Hong Kong, Singapore, the Netherlands, and New Zealand, all positively supporting the enforceability of the interim measures granted by the emergency arbitrator, will be discussed. Among the jurisdictions explored, notably, more attention will be paid to Singapore. The current law concerning the emergency arbitrator mechanism in Singapore will be analyzed, including the development of the legal reform in support of international arbitration in Singapore, the statutory regulation concerning the emergency arbitrator mechanism, and the case law in Singapore related to the emergency arbitrator mechanism the other jurisdictions will be introduced briefly to support the application of the emergency arbitrator mechanism.

3.2.1.1 Current Legal Framework Concerning the Emergency Arbitrator Mechanism in Singapore

Being situated in South-East Asia, Singapore's "geographical location and trade links have paved the way for it to market itself as an arbitration hub in Asia".[101] In the 2018 International Arbitration Survey: The Evolution of International Arbitration, Singapore was ranked as the third most preferred seat for arbitration in the world following London and Paris.[102] Additionally, there was a noticeable increase in the parties who selected the SIAC seated in Singapore over the HKIAC during the last

[101] Ramesh Selvaraj & Tan Kai Liang (2016), International Arbitration in Singapore, in Stephan Balthasar, I*nternational Commercial Arbitration: International Conventions, Country Reports and Comparative Analysis*, C. H. Beck·Hart·Nomos, p. 541.

[102] Queen Mary University of London and White & Case LLP, 2018 International Arbitration Survey: The Evolution of International Arbitration, p. 9, available at http://www.arbitration.qmul.ac.uk/media/arbitration/docs/2018-International-Arbitration-Survey---The-Evolution-of-International-Arbitration-(2).PDF (1 June 2024).

three years.[103] "Singapore has established itself as a leading centre for the provision of legal services in general and an innovative centre for dispute resolution in particular."[104] The current success can be attributed to the following factors: "infrastructure, the use of English as the lingua franca, transparency, the rule of law and a respected judiciary".[105]

After its independence in 1965, the continuous economic growth in Singapore was blocked by its worst recession during the 1980s.[106] In order to recover from this recession, the Economic Committee, established by the government, suggested the establishment of an arbitration center in Singapore with a view to improving legal services.[107] Subsequently, in 1986, Singapore acceded to the New York Convention on the Recognition and Enforcement of Foreign Arbitral Awards 1958.[108] The SIAC was established in 1991, and thereafter became the most well-known arbitration center in Singapore.[109] Since then, the need for a more international and arbitration-friendly legal framework became evident.[110] The Singapore Arbitration Act of 1953 mainly originated in the English Arbitration Act of 1950, governing mostly domestic arbitration.[111] It was amended from time to time, and was replaced by the Arbitration Act 2001.[112] However, the provisions of the Arbitration Act for

---

[103] Queen Mary University of London and White & Case LLP, 2018 International Arbitration Survey: The Evolution of International Arbitration, p. 13, available at http://www.arbitration.qmul.ac.uk/media/arbitration/docs/2018-International-Arbitration-Survey---The-Evolution-of-International-Arbitration-(2).PDF (1 June 2024).

[104] Sundaresh Menon (2014), *Arbitration in Singapore: A Practical Guide*, Sweet & Maxwell, p. vii.

[105] Leng Sun Chan (2018), Making Arbitration Work in Singapore, in Anselmo Reyes & Weixia Gu, *The Developing World of Arbitration: A Comparable Study of Arbitration Reform in the Asia Pacific*, Hart Publishing, p. 143.

[106] Charles Lim (2011), The Development Life Cycle of International Arbitration Legislation—Singapore IAA Case Study, 7 *Asian International Arbitration Journal* 2.

[107] Charles Lim (2011), The Development Life Cycle of International Arbitration Legislation—Singapore IAA Case Study, 7 *Asian International Arbitration Journal* 2.

[108] UNCITRAL, Status: Convention on the Recognition and Enforcement of Foreign Arbitral Awards (New York, 1958) (the "New York Convention"), available at https://treaties.un.org/Pages/ViewDetails.aspx?src=TREATY&mtdsg_no=XXII-1&chapter=22&clang=_en (1 June 2024).

[109] Jan K. Schäfer (1999), Borrowing and Cross-Fertilising Arbitration Laws—A Comparative Overview of the Development of Hong Kong and Singapore Legislation for International Commercial Arbitration, 16 *Journal of International Arbitration* 55.

[110] Lawrence Boo & Charles Lim (1995), Overview of the International Arbitration Act and Subsidiary Legislation in Singapore, 12 *Journal of International Arbitration* 75.

[111] David Howell, Leigh Duthie & Mark Lim (2002), International Arbitration in Singapore—Opting out of the UNCITRAL Model Law, 19 *Journal of International Arbitration* 39; Charles Lim (2011), The Development Life Cycle of International Arbitration Legislation—Singapore IAA Case Study, 7 *Asian International Arbitration Journal* 4.

[112] Leng Sun Chan (2002), Developments in Arbitration Laws, 14 *Singapore Academy of Law Journal* 49.

domestic arbitration were not satisfactory for international arbitration.[113] In 1994, the International Arbitration Act (Cap. 143A) was enacted and was published later in a revised 2002 edition.[114]

The purpose of the International Arbitration Act (Cap. 143A) is to make provisions for the proceedings of international commercial arbitration according to the UNCITRAL Model Law 1985 and to give effect to the New York Convention 1958 and other related matters.[115] The considerations of the Singapore legislators adopting the UNCITRAL Model Law 1985 were as follows. Firstly, the UNCITRAL Model Law 1985 was a standard of "an internationally accepted framework for international commercial arbitrations".[116] Furthermore, the approach taken by the UNCITRAL Model Law 1985 was attractive to legal practitioners in arbitration. Lastly, the introduction of the UNCITRAL Model Law 1985 would "promote Singapore's role as a growing centre for international legal services and international arbitrations".[117] Singapore tries to be innovative in legal reforms by following the latest trends in international commercial arbitration. For example, a Civil Law (Amendment) Bill 2016 came into force on 1 March 2017, to allow third-party funding in arbitration proceedings.[118] Third-party funding is a financing method to allow an entity that is not a party in a dispute to cover another party's costs.[119] On 26 June 2019, the Singapore Ministry of Law published proposals to amend the current International Arbitration Act (Cap. 143A), including a default nomination procedure for arbitrators in multi-party arbitrations and provisions for parties to opt in to an appellate

[113] Legislative History, Arbitration Act of the Statutes of the Republic of Singapore (Cap. 10) 2016, available at https://sso.agc.gov.sg/Act/AA2001?ValidDate=20160801&ProvIds=xv-#xv- (1 June 2024).

[114] Legislative History, International Arbitration Act of the Statutes of the Republic of Singapore (Cap. 143A), available at https://sso.agc.gov.sg/Act/IAA1994#xv- (1 June 2024).

[115] Preamble, International Arbitration Act of the Statutes of the Republic of Singapore (Cap. 143A), available at https://sso.agc.gov.sg/Act/IAA1994 (1 June 2024); see also Philip Jeyaretnam & Lawrence Teh (2014), Domestic and International Arbitration Framework in Singapore, in Sundaresh Menon, *Arbitration in Singapore: A Practical Guide*, Sweet & Maxwell, p. 102.

[116] Peng Kee Ho (1994), International Arbitration Bill, 63 *Official Report—Parliamentary Debates (Hansard)* Column: 627, available at https://sprs.parl.gov.sg/search/topic?reportid=027_19941031_S0004_T0010 (16 June 2020); see also Ronald Wong (2012), Interim Relief in Aid of International Commercial Arbitration—A Critique on the International Arbitration Act, 24 *Singapore Academy of Law Journal* 517.

[117] Peng Kee Ho (1994), International Arbitration Bill, 63 *Official Report—Parliamentary Debates (Hansard)* Column: 627, available at https://sprs.parl.gov.sg/search/topic?reportid=027_19941031_S0004_T0010 (16 June 2020), see also Hsu Locknie (1994), The Adoption of the UNCITRAL Model Law on International Commercial Arbitration in Singapore, 2 *Singapore Journal of Legal Studies* 391; Mahdev Mohan (2010), The New International Arbitration (Amendment) Bill: A Broader Framework for Interim Relief or Just a Tune-Up, 22 *Singapore Academy of Law Journal* 302; Ronald Wong (2012), Interim Relief in Aid of International Commercial Arbitration—A Critique on the International Arbitration Act, 24 *Singapore Academy of Law Journal* 517.

[118] Civil Law (Third-Party Funding) Regulations 2017, available at https://sso.agc.gov.sg/SL-Supp/S68-2017/Published/20170224?DocDate=20170224 (1 June 2024).

[119] Lisa Bench Nieuwveld & Victoria Shannon Sahani (2016), *Third-Party Funding in International Arbitration*, Kluwer Law International, Section 1.01.

procedure on questions of law when there are of general public importance and there is serious doubt in relation to arbitral awards.[120] Such "state-of-the-art" legal legislation for international commercial arbitration[121] has become "a turning point in the modernisation of the arbitration laws of Singapore, making the law of Singapore compliant with international standards".[122]

There have been two main amendments to the International Arbitration Act (Cap. 143A) regarding the issuance of interim measures in international arbitration. One was the 2010 amendment to allow Singapore courts to order interim measures in aid of international arbitration outside of Singapore's territory.[123] For example, in the case of *Maldives Airports Co Ltd and another v. GMR Malé International Airport Pte Ltd,* the Singapore Court of Appeals held that it had the jurisdiction to grant an injunction against the Republic of Maldives.[124] The Singapore government believed that such an amendment was in line with the latest development of international commercial arbitration.[125] The other one is the 2012 amendment to include the emergency arbitrator in the interpretation of the arbitral tribunal and to recognize the interim measures granted by the emergency arbitrator.[126] The clear legislative support for the emergency arbitrator mechanism means that the emergency arbitrator would be able to "exercise the full range of powers available to the tribunal",[127] embracing the current trend and innovation in the international commercial arbitration community.

---

[120] Morrison & Foerster LLP, Singapore Considers Amendments to Its International Arbitration Act, available at https://www.lexology.com/library/detail.aspx?g=2f8a6fb4-76b7-46ba-8258-91931f4a8156 (1 June 2024).

[121] Jan K. Schäfer (1999), Borrowing and Cross-Fertilising Arbitration Laws—A Comparative Overview of the Development of Hong Kong and Singapore Legislation for International Commercial Arbitration, 16 *Journal of International Arbitration* 71.

[122] Leng Sun Chan (2018), Making Arbitration Work in Singapore, in Anselmo Reyes & Weixia Gu, *The Developing World of Arbitration: A Comparable Study of Arbitration Reform in the Asia Pacific*, Hart Publishing, p. 144.

[123] Robert Merkin & Johanna Hjalmarsson (2016), *Singapore Arbitration Legislation: annotated,* Informa Law from Routledge, p. 1; K Shanmugam (2009), International Arbitration (Amendment) Bill, 86 *Official Report—Parliamentary Debates (Hansard)* Column: 1627, available at https://sprs.parl.gov.sg/search/topic?reportid=020_20091019_S0004_T0002 (16 June 2020).

[124] *Maldives Airports Co Ltd and another v. GMR Malé International Airport Pte Ltd* [2013] SGCA 16 (Court of Appeal of Singapore, 2013), available at https://www.uncitral.org/docs/clout/SGP/SGP_130213_FT.pdf (1 June 2024).

[125] Ronald Wong (2012), Interim Relief in Aid of International Commercial Arbitration—A Critique on the International Arbitration Act, 24 *Singapore Academy of Law Journal* 523.

[126] K Shanmugam (2009), International Arbitration (Amendment) Bill, 86 *Official Report—Parliamentary Debates (Hansard)* 66, available at https://sprs.parl.gov.sg/search/topic?reportid=024_20120409_S0003_T0004 (16 June 2020).

[127] K Shanmugam (2009), International Arbitration (Amendment) Bill, 86 *Official Report—Parliamentary Debates (Hansard)* 67, available at https://sprs.parl.gov.sg/search/topic?reportid=024_20120409_S0003_T0004 (16 June 2020).

Concerning the regulation for the emergency arbitrator mechanism, Singapore is "the first jurisdiction globally"[128] to enforce the interim measures by an emergency arbitrator. Although the focus of this subsection is the International Arbitration Act (Cap. 143A), it is noted that the regulation regarding the emergency arbitrator mechanism is identical to the Arbitration Act (Cap. 10).[129]

The International Arbitration Act (Cap. 143A), when interpreting the terms under the legislation, stipulates that "arbitral tribunal" refers to "a sole arbitration or a panel of arbitrators or a permanent arbitral institution, and includes an emergency arbitrator appointed pursuant to the rules of arbitration agreed to or adopted by the parties including the rules of arbitration of an institution or organisation".[130] Although adopting the UNCITRAL Model Law 1985, the scope of "arbitral tribunal" in the Singapore International Arbitration Act (Cap. 143A) is extended to include an emergency arbitrator.[131] The UNCITRAL Model Law 1985 states that "arbitral tribunal" means "a sole arbitrator or a panel of arbitrators".[132] An arbitral tribunal, including an emergency arbitrator, has a wide range of power to grant interim measures under Section 12(1) of the International Arbitration Act (Cap. 143A). The list for the available interim measures is neither exhaustive nor mandatory. Parties can always choose to exclude particular types of interim measures following the principle of party autonomy.[133] Section 12(6) delimitates the powers of an arbitral tribunal, including the powers of an emergency arbitrator. Decisions made by an emergency arbitrator in the context of the above interpretation are "enforceable in the same manner as if they were orders made by a court".[134] Therefore, any interim relief issued by an emergency arbitrator would have the same legal status as the interim measures granted by an arbitral tribunal and are enforceable in the same manner as if made by local

---

[128] SIAC, The Emergency Arbitrator and Expedited Procedure in SIAC: A New Direction for Arbitration in Asia, available at http://www.siac.org.sg/2013-09-18-01-57-20/2013-09-22-00-27-02/articles/420-the-emergency-arbitrator-and-expedited-procedure-in-siac-a-new-direction-for-arbitration-in-asia (16 June 2020).

[129] Section 2(1) of Part I, Arbitration Act of the Statutes of the Republic of Singapore (Cap. 10) 2016, available at https://sso.agc.gov.sg/Act/AA2001?ValidDate=20160801&ProvIds=legis#legis (1 June 2024).

[130] Section 2(1) of Part II, International Arbitration Act of the Statutes of the Republic of Singapore (Cap. 143A) 2012, available at https://sso.agc.gov.sg/Act/IAA1994 (1 June 2024).

[131] Robert Merkin & Johanna Hjalmarsson (2016), *Singapore Arbitration Legislation: annotated,* Informa Law from Routledge, p. 11.

[132] Article 2(b), UNCITRAL Model Law 1985, available at https://uncitral.un.org/sites/uncitral.un.org/files/media-documents/uncitral/en/06-54671_ebook.pdf (1 June 2024).

[133] Alastair Henderson & Vikas Mahendra (2014), Interlocutory Applications (Interim Measures), in Sundaresh Menon, *Arbitration in Singapore: A Practical Guide*, Sweet & Maxwell, p. 302; Robert Merkin & Johanna Hjalmarsson (2016), *Singapore Arbitration Legislation: annotated,* Informa Law from Routledge, p. 58; Tat, Lim, Arbitration Procedures and Practice in Singapore: overview, 2017, available at https://uk.practicallaw.thomsonreuters.com/3-381-2028?transitionType=Default&contextData=(sc.Default)&firstPage=true&bhcp=1#co_anchor_a382816 (1 June 2024).

[134] Section 12(6) of Part II, International Arbitration Act of the Statutes of the Republic of Singapore (Cap. 143A) 2012, available at https://sso.agc.gov.sg/Act/IAA1994 (1 June 2024).

courts in Singapore.[135] A failure to comply with emergency decisions can be seen as contempt of court accordingly.[136]

3.2.1.2 Case Law

As Singapore is a common law oriented legal order, the case law deals with various aspects of interim measures in arbitration, along with the amendments of the International Arbitration Act (Cap. 143A). However, currently, cases involving emergency arbitration are relatively scarce: *Star Engineering Pte Ltd v. Pollisum Engineering Pte Ltd and Great Eastern General Insurance Ltd, CVG v. CVH, AQZ v. ARA*, and *The Bank of East Asia Ltd v. Quah Su-Ling.*

In *Star Engineering Pte Ltd v. Pollisum Engineering Pte Ltd and Great Eastern General Insurance Ltd,*[137] the High Court ruled in favor of keep both parties in arbitration. When considering the urgency in the present case, the Court did not agree that such circumstances entitle unilaterally disapply the arbitration agreement and bring the case straightforward to court, since the chosen institution SIAC provides the opportunity of the emergency arbitrator which is a widely used mechanism. Further, an order granted by an emergency arbitrator "would have been as good as an order of court".[138] As stated by the Court, the applicant "could have obtained the same result through engaging an emergency arbitrator and it did not even try to do so".[139]

In *CVG v. CVH,*[140] the defendant applied to the High Court for setting aside an award made by an ICDR emergency arbitrator. In principle, the Court confirmed that the term "foreign award" in the International Arbitration Act of Singapore "includes foreign interim awards made by an emergency arbitrator and thus, the [a]ward may be

---

[135] Alastair Henderson & Vikas Mahendra (2014), Interlocutory Applications (Interim Measures), in Sundaresh Menon, *Arbitration in Singapore: A Practical Guide*, Sweet & Maxwell, p. 304; Joongi Kim (2014), International Arbitration in East Asia: From Emulation to Innovation, 4 *Arbitration Brief* 23; Francis Xavier & Tng Sheng Rong (2014), Role of the Court, in Sundaresh Menon, *Arbitration in Singapore: A Practical Guide*, Sweet & Maxwell, p. 55.

[136] Robert Merkin & Johanna Hjalmarsson (2016), *Singapore Arbitration Legislation: annotated,* Informa Law from Routledge, p. 59.

[137] *Star Engineering Pte Ltd v. Pollisum Engineering Pte Ltd and Great Eastern General Insurance Ltd* [2024] SGHC 137 (High Court, Supreme Court of Singapore, 2024), available at https://www.singaporelawwatch.sg/Portals/0/Docs/Judgments/2024/[2024]%20SGHC%20137.pdf (25 May 2024).

[138] *Star Engineering Pte Ltd v. Pollisum Engineering Pte Ltd and Great Eastern General Insurance Ltd* [2024] SGHC 137 (High Court, Supreme Court of Singapore, 2024), p. 18, available at https://www.singaporelawwatch.sg/Portals/0/Docs/Judgments/2024/[2024]%20SGHC%20137.pdf (25 May 2024).

[139] *Star Engineering Pte Ltd v. Pollisum Engineering Pte Ltd and Great Eastern General Insurance Ltd* [2024] SGHC 137 (High Court, Supreme Court of Singapore, 2024), p. 23, available at https://www.singaporelawwatch.sg/Portals/0/Docs/Judgments/2024/[2024]%20SGHC%20137.pdf (25 May 2024).

[140] *CVG v. CVH* [2022] SGHC 249 (High Court, Supreme Court of Singapore, 2022), available at https://www.singaporelawwatch.sg/Portals/0/Docs/Judgments/2022/2022%20SGHC%20249.pdf (25 May 2024).

enforced in Singapore".[141] Firstly, the definition of "arbitral awards" means a decision given by an arbitral tribunal under the IAA. In the view of the High Court, an arbitral tribunal should be interpreted to include emergency arbitrators, which is consistent with the Section 2(1) of the IAA as a whole. Secondly, the IAA was amended in 2012 to include emergency arbitrators and interim measures granted. The purpose of the amendments in 2012 "speak to an intention to make the IAA applicable to all awards, including foreign interim awards by emergency arbitrators".[142] Additionally, the purposive interpretation of arbitral awards led to the conclusion that those awards should include awards issued by emergency arbitrators. However, the High Court refused to enforce such an award in the current case since it found that defendant was not able to present its case in the emergency arbitration proceedings.

In *AQZ v. ARA*,[143] AQZ, the Plaintiff, was a mining and commodity trading company in Singapore, and ARA, the Defendant, was a subsidiary of an Indian trading and shipping conglomerate. AQZ and ARA initiated negotiations regarding the possibility of two separate sales contracts. On 7 December 2009, two parties concluded the first contract for the shipment of Indonesian non-coking coal in January 2010. However, shortly after the first shipment in January 2010, AQZ claimed that the second contract for another shipment never came into effect. Since both parties failed to solve the dispute amicably, the Defendant submitted a Notice of Arbitration to the SIAC on 20 March 2013. On the next day, ARA further submitted the application for an Expedited Procedure under the SIAC Arbitration Rules 2010. AQZ was not satisfied with the award and challenged it before the High Court of Singapore on 11 June 2014.

One of the main issues was whether the composition of the arbitral tribunal and the Expedited Procedure applied in the dispute was in accordance with the arbitration agreement or not. The High Court referred to the regulation of the emergency arbitrator mechanism in the ICC Arbitration Rules 2012 which contained an expression that "[t]he Emergency Arbitrator Provisions shall not apply if the arbitration agreement under the Rules was concluded before the date on which the Rules came into force".[144] However, there was no comparable exclusion under the SIAC Arbitration Rules 2010, which means that the adoption of the Expedited Procedure in the present case did not override the parties' agreement. In conclusion, the arbitration agreement and the contract for the second shipment were valid and the SIAC Arbitration Rules 2010 was applicable. Therefore, the High Court of Singapore had no ground to set aside the arbitral award.

[141] *CVG v. CVH* [2022] SGHC 249 (High Court, Supreme Court of Singapore, 2022), p. 2, available at https://www.singaporelawwatch.sg/Portals/0/Docs/Judgments/2022/2022%20SGHC%20249.pdf (25 May 2024).

[142] *CVG v. CVH* [2022] SGHC 249 (High Court, Supreme Court of Singapore, 2022), p. 10, available at https://www.singaporelawwatch.sg/Portals/0/Docs/Judgments/2022/2022%20SGHC%20249.pdf (25 May 2024).

[143] *AQZ v. ARA* [2015] SGHC 49 (High Court, Supreme Court of Singapore, 2015), available at https://www.singaporelawwatch.sg/Portals/0/Docs/Judgments/[2015]%20SGHC%2049.pdf (16 June 2020).

[144] Article 29 (6) (a), ICC Arbitration Rules 2012.

In *The Bank of East Asia Ltd v. Quah Su-Ling* case,[145] the Plaintiff was a commercial bank, and the Defendant was the representative of IPCO International Ltd. The Plaintiff granted the Defendant a share margin facility in January and March 2013. A share margin facility[146] allowed the Defendant to purchase shares with the credit provided by the Plaintiff. However, the Defendant failed to complete the payment despite these two notices. As a consequence, the Plaintiff applied for a summary judgment, while the Defendant applied for a stay of these proceedings in response.

In the Court of First Instance, a summary judgment was granted as requested by the Plaintiff, urging the Defendant to fulfill the payment obligation and related default interest from 3 December 2013, until the date of full payment. The Defendant appealed the decisions by the assistant registrar to the High Court of Singapore. When examining the facts, the High Court of Singapore discovered that the Defendant caused the problematic financial situation, and she had no defense to the Plaintiff's claim. Interactive Brokers LLC applied and obtained an interim award from an emergency arbitrator on 11 February 2014, in Singapore, to freeze the Defendant's assets. The emergency award was to remain in force until a final arbitral award. The High Court held that such a valid and enforceable interim award, which was in force, could not constitute an acceptable excuse for the stay of proceedings in the current case.

3.2.1.3 Other Jurisdictions Supporting the Emergency Arbitrator Mechanism

Hong Kong, with the full name of Hong Kong Special Administrative Region of the People's Republic of China, maintains its common law legal system since the handover from the United Kingdom on July 1, 1997, after more than 150 years of colonial rule.[147] As "a world-class international commercial and business center and the financial capital of Asia" today,[148] Hong Kong is one of the global "premier venues for international arbitration",[149] and "one of the most popular seats for arbitration in the world".[150] Due to its unique status in the Asia–Pacific region, as well

[145] *The Bank of East Asia Ltd v. Quah Su-Ling* [2014] SGHC 52 (High Court, Supreme Court of Singapore, 2014), available at https://www.singaporelawwatch.sg/Portals/0/Docs/Judgments/[2014]%20SGHC%2052.pdf (16 June 2020).

[146] A share margin facility can be understood as a loan facility secured by shares to manage investments provided by banks. For example, see https://www.hsbcprivatebank.com/en/bank/margin-trading-facilities (1 June 2024).

[147] Lewis Dean (2016), *The Interpretation and Uniformity of the UNCITRAL Model Law on International Commercial Arbitration: Australia, Hong Kong and Singapore*, Kluwer Law International, pp. 62–63.

[148] Michael Moser & Chiann Bao (2017), *A Guide to the HKIAC Arbitration Rules*, Oxford University Press, p. 1.

[149] Michael Moser & Chiann Bao (2017), *A Guide to the HKIAC Arbitration Rules*, Oxford University Press, p. 1.

[150] Amy Lo (2016), International Arbitration in Hong Kong, in Stephan Balthasar, I*nternational Commercial Arbitration: International Conventions, Country Reports and Comparative Analysis*, C. H. Beck·Hart·Nomos, p. 409.

as inside China, Hong Kong adopted an arbitration-friendly approach. Although Hong Kong ranked in third position of the preferred arbitration seats in the 2015 International Arbitration Survey, conducted jointly by the Queen Mary University of London and White & Case LLP,[151] it switched place with Singapore, being in the fourth position in the 2018 International Arbitration Survey.[152]

The Hong Kong Arbitration Ordinance (Cap. 609) states that an emergency arbitrator is appointed under arbitration rules and agreed by parties to deal with the applications for emergency relief before the constitution of an arbitral tribunal.[153] In the newly added sections concerning the third-party funding of arbitration in 2017, the interpretation of the law provides some clarifications for the emergency arbitrator mechanism. The scope of arbitration under the Arbitration Ordinance (Cap. 609) includes the "proceedings before an emergency arbitrator".[154] "Arbitration body" includes an emergency arbitrator.[155] The Arbitration Ordinance (Cap. 609) also regulates the types of interim measures that can be issued by the emergency arbitrator. In order to guarantee proper enforcement, the interim measures shall fall into at least one of the following non-exhaustive categories. Firstly, the interim measures are used to "maintain or restore the *status quo* pending the determination of the dispute concerned".[156] Secondly, the actions taken can "prevent, or refrain from taking action that is likely to cause, current or imminent harm or prejudice to the arbitral process itself".[157] Thirdly, the interim measures "provide a means of preserving assets out of which a subsequent award made by an arbitral tribunal may be satisfied".[158] Fourthly, in the interim measures, the relevant evidence and material to solve the dispute is preserved.[159] Fifthly, the applied interim measures are to "give security in connection

---

151 Queen Mary University of London and White & Case LLP, 2015 International Arbitration Survey: Improvements and Innovations in International Arbitration, p. 12, available at http://www.arbitration.qmul.ac.uk/media/arbitration/docs/2015_International_Arbitration_Survey.pdf (1 June 2024).

152 Queen Mary University of London and White & Case LLP, 2018 International Arbitration Survey: The Evolution of International Arbitration, p. 9, available at http://www.arbitration.qmul.ac.uk/media/arbitration/docs/2018-International-Arbitration-Survey---The-Evolution-of-International-Arbitration-(2).PDF (1 June 2024).

153 Section 22A, Arbitration Ordinance (Cap. 609) 2015, available at https://www.elegislation.gov.hk/hk/cap609 (1 June 2024).

154 Section 98F, arbitration, (b), Arbitration Ordinance (Cap. 609) 2015, available at https://www.elegislation.gov.hk/hk/cap609 (1 June 2024).

155 Section 98F, arbitration body, (b), Arbitration Ordinance (Cap. 609) 2015, available at https://www.elegislation.gov.hk/hk/cap609 (1 June 2024).

156 Section 22B (2)(a), Arbitration Ordinance (Cap. 609) 2015, available at https://www.elegislation.gov.hk/hk/cap609 (1 June 2024).

157 Section 22B (2)(b), Arbitration Ordinance (Cap. 609) 2015, available at https://www.elegislation.gov.hk/hk/cap609 (1 June 2024).

158 Section 22B (2)(c), Arbitration Ordinance (Cap. 609) 2015, available at https://www.elegislation.gov.hk/hk/cap609 (1 June 2024).

159 Section 22B (2)(d), Arbitration Ordinance (Cap. 609) 2015, available at https://www.elegislation.gov.hk/hk/cap609 (1 June 2024).

with anything to be done"[160] in relation to the previous four purposes. Lastly, the interim measures are related to the "security for the costs of the arbitration".[161] In respect of the enforcement of the interim measures granted by the emergency arbitrator in state courts, the Arbitration Ordinance (Cap. 609) gives a clear answer. It states that "[a]ny emergency relief granted, whether in or outside Hong Kong, by an emergency arbitrator under the relevant arbitration rules is enforceable in the same manner as an order or direction of the Court that has the same effect, but only with the leave of the Court".[162]

There are a few cases have been dealt with issues regarding the enforceability of interim measures granted by an emergency arbitrator, but not directly. In general, similar to the practices in Singapore, Hong Kong courts accepted the enforceability of interim measures granted by an emergency arbitrator with some exceptions regarding arbitration agreements, due process, and public policy. In *GD v. HY*,[163] the Court refused to enforce an interim measure made by an emergency arbitrator based on the determination that the relevant arbitration agreement was not valid.

New Zealand adopted the UNCITRAL Model Law 2006 in 2007[164] and amended its Arbitration Act in 2016 to include the emergency arbitrator mechanism. The judiciary has been aware of and sensitive to the UNCITRAL's purpose of promoting international harmonization. Thus, the state courts of New Zealand usually interpret the Arbitration Act on an international basis.[165] The Arbitration Act was enacted initially in 1996 and has been amended eight times so far.[166] In Arbitration Amendment Act 2016, Section 2 was amended with "arbitral tribunal" means "a sole arbitrator, a panel of arbitrators, or an arbitral institution", and "any emergency arbitrator appointed under the arbitration agreement that the parties have entered into", or "the arbitration rules of any institution or organisation that the parties have adopted".[167]

[160] Section 22B (2)(e), Arbitration Ordinance (Cap. 609) 2015, available at https://www.elegislation.gov.hk/hk/cap609 (1 June 2024).

[161] Section 22B (2)(f), Arbitration Ordinance (Cap. 609) 2015, available at https://www.elegislation.gov.hk/hk/cap609 (1 June 2024).

[162] Section 22B (1), Arbitration Ordinance (Cap. 609) 2015, available at https://www.elegislation.gov.hk/hk/cap609 (1 June 2024).

[163] *GD v. HY*, [2021] HKCFI 3900 (High Court of the Hong Kong Special Administrative Region, Court of First Instance Court of First Instance, 2021).

[164] UNCITRAL, Status: UNCITRAL Model Law on International Commercial Arbitration (1985), with amendments as adopted in 2006, available at https://uncitral.un.org/en/texts/arbitration/modellaw/commercial_arbitration/status (1 June 2024).

[165] Daniel Kalderimis (2016), New Zealand, *The Asia–Pacific Arbitration Review* 84, available at https://www.chapmantripp.com/Publication%20PDFs/The%20Asia-Pacific%20Arbitration%20Review%202016.pdf (16 June 2020).

[166] Versions and amendments, New Zealand Arbitration Act 1996, available at http://www.legislation.govt.nz/act/public/1996/0099/latest/versions.aspx (1 June 2024).

[167] Article 4, Section 2 amended (Interpretation), Arbitration Amendment Act 2016, available at http://www.legislation.govt.nz/act/public/2016/0053/latest/DLM6943708.html (1 June 2024).

The emergency arbitrator mechanism has not been widely used in New Zealand, and there is no reported case law so far in this respect.[168]

In general, Dutch law treats arbitration as a "full alternative" to court proceedings, at both the national and international level.[169] The legislator managed to limit the courts' involvement in arbitration but increased the support from state courts at the same time[170] in the newly amended Dutch Code of Civil Procedure in 2015.[171] It provides that the parties are authorized to appoint a separate arbitral tribunal for the purpose of granting interim measures on request, irrespective of whether arbitral proceedings are pending.[172] Additionally, unless the arbitral tribunal has a different opinion, the interim measures granted shall be regarded as an enforceable arbitral award.[173] In light of the above articles, Dutch law implies the possibility to recognize and enforce the interim measures by the emergency arbitrator.[174] Although the specific provisions in the Dutch Code of Civil Procedure are originally for the summary arbitral procedure, it seems to fit the emergency arbitrator mechanism as well.[175]

3.2.2 *Jurisdictions Refusing the Emergency Arbitrator Mechanism*

The prevention of the use of interim measures rendered by arbitral bodies based on legislation has been removed in most of the jurisdictions. However, some jurisdictions continue to take the traditional approach that exclusively empowers state courts to

[168] Kalderimis, Daniel & Yesberg, Kate, Recent Amendments to New Zealand's Arbitrating Act, available at http://arbitrationblog.kluwerarbitration.com/2016/11/28/recent-amendments-to-new-zealands-arbitration-act/#_ftn1 (1 June 2024).

[169] Karyl Nairn & Patrick Heneghan (2015), *Arbitration World: Jurisdictional and Institutional Comparisons*, Sweet & Maxwell, p. 699.

[170] Karyl Nairn & Patrick Heneghan (2015), *Arbitration World: Jurisdictional and Institutional Comparisons*, Sweet & Maxwell, p. 699.

[171] The Dutch Arbitration Act, Dutch Code of Civil Procedure 2015, available at http://www.dutchcivillaw.com/legislation/civilprocedure044.htm (1 June 2024).

[172] Article 1043b (2), Dutch Code of Civil Procedure 2015; Fabio G. Santacroce (2015), The Emergency Arbitrator: A Full-fledged Arbitrator Rendering an Enforceable Decision?, 31 *Arbitration International* 309.

[173] Article 1043b (4), Dutch Code of Civil Procedure 2015.

[174] J. Van Haersolte-Van Hof (2014), Revision of the Dutch Arbitration Act: Making the Netherlands an Even Better Place for Arbitration, 31 *Journal of International Arbitration* 430; Fabio G. Santacroce (2015), The Emergency Arbitrator: A Full-Fledged Arbitrator Rendering An Enforceable Decision?, 31 *Arbitration International* 309.

[175] Stephan Köll (2012), The Non-Enforceability of Decisions Rendered in Summary Arbitral Proceedings Pursuant to the NAI Rules under the New York Convention, 23 *American Review of International Arbitration* 75–102.

issue interim measures.[176] In this section, the current legal practice concerning the emergency arbitrator mechanism in Mainland China will be discussed, including the arbitration laws and the recent development of institutional arbitration rules. Furthermore, this chapter analyzes the interaction between Mainland China and Hong Kong, relating to the interim measures in arbitration, which may anticipate possible future developments. Finally, the legislation in the jurisdictions refusing to enforce the interim measures granted by an emergency arbitrator other than Mainland China is provided as additional material.

3.2.2.1 Current Legal Practice Concerning the Emergency Arbitrator Mechanism in Mainland China

Historically speaking, in ancient China, parties preferred to resolve disputes amicably, influenced by Confucian philosophy,[177] which emphasizes harmony and conflict avoidance.[178] Litigation was considered a negative result of failing to maintain social harmony.[179] Compared to litigation, other dispute resolutions were used more often, in particular conciliation, which continues to be an essential method used to solve disputes nowadays.[180] However, as Mainland China started to move away from a planned economy towards a liberal market, following the "reforms and opening up (改革开放)" process in 1978, the massive growth of international trade led to "a dynamic development of dispute resolution mechanisms".[181]

In the current legislation in Mainland China, there is no expression for "international arbitration". Instead, "foreign-related arbitration (涉外仲裁)" is the term used in both the Arbitration Law of the People's Republic of China (中华人民共和国仲裁法) and the Civil Procedure Law of the People's Republic of China (中华人民共和国民事诉讼法).[182] Foreign-related arbitration is a type of arbitration for foreign-related civil cases. "Foreign-related civil cases(涉外民事案件)" that can be resolved through arbitration refer to cases that fall into at least one of the following categories: (a) "[e]ither party or both parties are foreigners, stateless persons, foreign

[176] Gary B. Born (2015), *International Arbitration: Law and Practice*, Kluwer Law International, Section 11.01[A].

[177] Clarisse von Wunschheim (2014), *Enforcement of Commercial Arbitral Awards in China*, Sweet & Maxwell, p. 29.

[178] Kun Fan (2013), *Arbitration in China: A Legal and Cultural Analysis*, Hart Publishing, p. 3.

[179] Feinerman, James V., The History and Development of China's Dispute Resolution System in Hunter, Chris, Dispute Resolution in China—A Practical Guide to Litigation & Arbitration in China, Asia Law & Practice, 1995, p. 7; Clarisse von Wunschheim (2014), *Enforcement of Commercial Arbitral Awards in China*, Sweet & Maxwell, p. 30.

[180] Clarisse von Wunschheim (2014), *Enforcement of Commercial Arbitral Awards in China*, Sweet & Maxwell, p. 30.

[181] Kun Fan (2013), *Arbitration in China: A Legal and Cultural Analysis*, Hart Publishing, p. 3.

[182] Qi Xiong & Yong Shang (2016), International Arbitration in China (People's Republic), in Stephan Balthasar, I*nternational Commercial Arbitration: International Conventions, Country Reports and Comparative Analysis*, C. H. Beck·Hart·Nomos, pp. 267–268.

enterprises or organizations"[183]; (b) "[t]he habitual residence of either party or both parties is located outside the territory of the People's Republic of China"[184]; (c) "[t]he subject matter is outside the territory of the People's Republic of China"[185]; (d)"[t]he legal fact that leads to the establishment, change or termination of a civil relationship occurs outside the territory of the People's Republic of China"[186]; and (e) "[a]ny other circumstance under which a case may be determined as a foreign-related civil case".[187]

Before the enactment of the Arbitration Law in 1995, domestic and foreign-related arbitration applied to two separate legal frameworks.[188] There is no comprehensive and systematic legislation regarding domestic arbitration. The framework of foreign-related arbitration was rooted in the Protocol for General Conditions of Delivery of Goods between China and the Soviet Union established in 1950, which states that the disputes arising from a contract should be resolved in arbitration.[189] The legal implementation of the protocol from the Soviet Union was less perfect and unsuccessful, which caused the need to establish an international arbitral system to deal with such disputes, to replace the existing administrative arbitral bodies being used at the time.[190] The current Arbitration Law of the People's Republic of China came into force on September 1, 1995 with the latest amendments in 2017, which is "a historical milestone in the development of arbitration in China".[191]

There are two statutes relating to arbitration in Mainland China: The Arbitration Law of the People's Republic of China and the Civil Procedure Law of the People's Republic of China. Mainland China is a civil law jurisdiction with Chinese characteristics, which means that case law is not a primary source of law. However, since 2011, the Supreme People's Court of China started issuing guiding case decisions in order to provide more legal certainty throughout the country.[192]

---

[183] Article 520(1), Interpretation of the Supreme People's Court on the Application of the Civil Procedure Law of the People's Republic of China 2022 (最高人民法院关于适用《中华人民共和国民事诉讼法》的解释, 法释[2022]11号).

[184] Article 520(2), Interpretation of the Supreme People's Court on the Application of the Civil Procedure Law of the People's Republic of China 2022 (最高人民法院关于适用《中华人民共和国民事诉讼法》的解释, 法释[2022]11号).

[185] Article 520(3), Interpretation of the Supreme People's Court on the Application of the Civil Procedure Law of the People's Republic of China 2022 (最高人民法院关于适用《中华人民共和国民事诉讼法》的解释, 法释[2022]11号).

[186] Article 520(4), Interpretation of the Supreme People's Court on the Application of the Civil Procedure Law of the People's Republic of China 2022 (最高人民法院关于适用《中华人民共和国民事诉讼法》的解释, 法释[2022]11号).

[187] Article 520(5), Interpretation of the Supreme People's Court on the Application of the Civil Procedure Law of the People's Republic of China 2022 (最高人民法院关于适用《中华人民共和国民事诉讼法》的解释, 法释[2022]11号).

[188] Kun Fan (2013), *Arbitration in China: A Legal and Cultural Analysis*, Hart Publishing, p. 17.

[189] Kun Fan (2013), *Arbitration in China: A Legal and Cultural Analysis*, Hart Publishing, p. 18.

[190] Tao, Jingzhou, Arbitration Law and Practice in China, Kluwer Law International, 2008, p. 4.

[191] Kun Fan (2013), *Arbitration in China: A Legal and Cultural Analysis*, Hart Publishing, p. 20.

[192] The Supreme People's Court of the People's Republic of China, Guiding Cases, available at http://www.court.gov.cn/fabu-gengduo-77.html (16 June 2020).

The authorized bodies that can render the interim measures in arbitration in Mainland China exclude arbitral tribunals and emergency arbitrators. The only legal body that has such power is the people's court. Article 272 of the Civil Procedure Law provides that the application of interim measures in a foreign-related arbitration shall be submitted to the "intermediate people's court at the place of domicile of the respondent or at the place where the respondent's property is located". Similarly, Article 68 of the Arbitration Law provides that the application for the preservation of evidence in a foreign-related arbitration needs to be submitted to the "intermediate people's court in the place where the evidence is located".

Regarding the available types of interim measures, the Arbitration Law gives a precise range. Article 28 of the Arbitration Law regulates the "property preservation" in arbitration when it becomes "impossible or difficult for the party to implement the award due to an act of the other party or other causes". Article 46 of the Arbitration Law provides the possibility for the preservation of evidence in cases where the evidence may be "destroyed or lost or difficult to obtain at a later time". Based on these two provisions, it follows that "property preservation" and "preservation of evidence" are currently the only two possible reasons to issue interim measures under the Arbitration Law.[193]

Additionally, under urgent circumstances, when "the lawful rights and interests of an interested party will be irreparably damaged"[194] without the requested interim measures, the involved party has the right to apply for a "preservation" before the commencement of litigation or arbitration. The people's court is required to "issue a ruling within 48 h",[195] and the granted interim measures shall be "executed immediately".[196] If the applicant fails to bring a suit to a court or fails to request arbitration within 30 days after the issuance of the interim measures, then the interim measures will be removed by the court.[197]

Another unique feature of interim measures in Mainland China is that the application from a party can only be submitted by the international arbitral institutions of the People's Republic of China[198] and not by individuals themselves. Moreover, the international arbitral institutions that are based outside the jurisdiction of Mainland China cannot apply for interim measures in arbitration on behalf of a party. According to Article 66 of the Arbitration Law, "[f]oreign-related arbitration commission may be organized and established by the China Chamber of International Commerce". This

---

[193] Fan Yang (2016), *Foreign-related Arbitration in China: Commentary and Cases*, Cambridge University Press, p. 157.

[194] Article 104, Civil Procedure Law of the People's Republic of China 2023, translation available at http://en.pkulaw.cn/display.aspx?id=e55237a87e2e1d04bdfb&lib=law (1 June 2024).

[195] Article 104, Civil Procedure Law of the People's Republic of China 2023, translation available at http://en.pkulaw.cn/display.aspx?id=e55237a87e2e1d04bdfb&lib=law (1 June 2024).

[196] Article 104, Civil Procedure Law of the People's Republic of China 2023, translation available at http://en.pkulaw.cn/display.aspx?id=e55237a87e2e1d04bdfb&lib=law (1 June 2024).

[197] Article 104, Civil Procedure Law of the People's Republic of China 2023, translation available at http://en.pkulaw.cn/display.aspx?id=e55237a87e2e1d04bdfb&lib=law (1 June 2024).

[198] Article 289, Civil Procedure Law of the People's Republic of China 2023, translation available at http://en.pkulaw.cn/display.aspx?id=e55237a87e2e1d04bdfb&lib=law (1 June 2024).

makes clear that applications submitted by the ICC, the ICDR, or other international arbitration institutions, will not be accepted in the proceedings.

In the Arrangement between the Mainland and the Macau SAR on Reciprocal Recognition and Enforcement of Arbitration Awards by the Supreme People's Court (最高人民法院关于内地与澳门特别行政区相互认可和执行仲裁裁决的安排) enacted in 2008, Article 11 states "[a] court may, before or after accepting an application for admitting and enforcing an arbitration award, take protective measures against the property of the party against whom the application is filed in accordance with the legal provisions of the locality of the court if the application requires to do so".[199] There is no comparable provision in the Arrangements of the Supreme People's Court on the Mutual Enforcement of Arbitral Awards between the Mainland and the Hong Kong Special Administrative Region (最高人民法院关于内地与香港特别行政区相互执行仲裁裁决的安排) of 2000. The new Arrangement Concerning Mutual Assistance in Court-ordered Interim Measures in Aid of Arbitral Proceedings by the Courts of the Mainland and of the Hong Kong Special Administrative Region (最高人民法院、香港特别行政区政府关于内地与香港特别行政区法院就仲裁程序相互协助保全的安排) 2019 brings a new era. In the case of *Ocean Eleven Shipping Corporation v. Lao Kaiyuan Mining Sole Co. Ltd*,[200] which was an arbitral case administrated by the HKIAC in 2016, the request for the preservation of property was granted by the people's court in the Mainland according to Article 28 of the Arbitration Law. Yet, given that case law rulings are not binding for future court decisions in Mainland China, it cannot be foreseen whether similar interim measures would be granted in the future or not. It nevertheless gives a positive signal for future possibilities.

3.2.2.2 Institutional Arbitration Rules Concerning the Emergency Arbitrator Mechanism in Mainland China

An arbitral institution is also referred to as an "arbitration commission (仲裁委员会)" in the Arbitration Law. The establishment of an arbitration commission differs from the commonly-known arbitral institution, as it is formed by relevant departments from within central or local municipal governments and by the chambers of

[199] Article 11, Arrangement between the Mainland and the Macau Special Administrative Region on Reciprocal Recognition and Enforcement of Arbitration Awards 2007 (最高人民法院关于内地与澳门特别行政区相互认可和执行仲裁裁决的安排), translation available at is https://pkulaw.com/en_law/48ef3f989a7b54d0bdfb.html (16 June 2020).

[200] *Ocean Eleven Shipping Corporation v. Lao Kaiyuan Mining Sole Co. Ltd.* (海洋十一航运公司与老挝开元矿业有限公司仲裁程序案件、申请保全案件民事诉讼保全裁定书案 [鄂72财保427号],武汉海事法院), available at http://www.pkulaw.cn/case/pfnl_1970324876955896.html?keywords=%E6%B5%B7%E6%B4%8B%E5%8D%81%E4%B8%80%E8%88%AA%E8%BF%90%E5%85%AC%E5%8F%B8%E4%B8%8E%E8%80%81%E6%8C%9D%E5%BC%80%E5%85%83%E7%9F%BF%E4%B8%9A%E6%9C%89%E9%99%90%E5%85%AC%E5%8F%B8%E4%BB%B2%E8%A3%81%E7%A8%8B%E5%BA%8F%E6%A1%88%E4%BB%B6&match=Exact (16 June 2020).

commerce.[201] The arbitral commissions are independent of administrative organs, and there is no subordinate relationship between them.[202] Nowadays, as the modernization of international commercial arbitration continues to develop in Mainland China, "arbitral institutions" and "arbitration commissions" are used interchangeably on most occasions.[203]

Before the Circular of the General Office of the State Council Regarding Some Problems Which Need to Be Clarified for the Implementation of the Arbitration Law of the People's Republic of China (国务院办公厅关于贯彻实施《中华人民共和国仲裁法》需要明确的几个问题的通知) in 1996, the China International Economic and Trade Arbitration Commission (CIETAC) and China Maritime Arbitration Commission (CMAC) were the only two arbitral institutions that could administer foreign-related arbitration cases in Mainland China. After 1996, various arbitration commissions, including the Beijing Arbitration Commission (BAC), were empowered to accept the application of international commercial disputes.

In order to provide more services that meet international standards, the arbitral institutions in China amended their rules to follow the latest developments and innovations in the international commercial arbitration community, especially with regard to the emergency arbitrator mechanism. Four arbitral institutions based in Mainland China introduced the emergency arbitrator mechanism in their arbitration rules. They are the Beijing International Arbitration Center (北京仲裁委员会)(BAC), the China International Economic and Trade Arbitration Commission (中国国际经济贸易仲裁委员会)(CIETAC), the China Maritime Arbitration Commission (中国海事仲裁委员会)(CMAC), and China (Shanghai) Pilot Free Trade Zone Court of Arbitration (中国(上海)自由贸易试验区仲裁院).

The Beijing International Arbitration Center (BAC) was established in 1995 as a permanent arbitral institution dealing with "contractual and property-related disputes among equal parties including natural persons, legal persons, and other organizations in an independent, impartial and efficient manner".[204] The BAC is the only local arbitral institution that meets international standards.[205] In the BAC Arbitration Rules 2015 and 2022, it reads that "[b]efore the constitution of the Arbitral Tribunal…, any party that wishes to apply for interim measures may submit a written application to the BAC for the appointment of an emergency arbitrator in accordance with the applicable law".[206] The BAC administrated the first emergency arbitration case in Mainland

---

[201] Article 10, Arbitration Law of the People's Republic of China 2017, translation available at http://en.pkulaw.cn/display.aspx?cgid=83c8fbd6da8a6eb8bdfb&lib=law (16 June 2020).

[202] Article 14, Arbitration Law of the People's Republic of China 2017, translation available at http://en.pkulaw.cn/display.aspx?cgid=83c8fbd6da8a6eb8bdfb&lib=law (16 June 2020).

[203] Qi Xiong & Yong Shang (2016), International Arbitration in China (People's Republic), in Stephan Balthasar, *International Commercial Arbitration: International Conventions, Country Reports and Comparative Analysis*, C. H. Beck·Hart·Nomos, p. 270.

[204] BAC, Beijing Arbitration Commission, available at http://www.bjac.org.cn/english/page/gybh/introduce_index.html (1 June 2024).

[205] BAC, Beijing Arbitration Commission, available at http://www.bjac.org.cn/english/page/gybh/introduce_index.html (1 June 2024).

[206] Article 63, BAC Arbitration Rules 2022 and 2015.

China in late 2017. The interim measure ordered by the emergency arbitrator, in that case, has already been enforced by the High Court of Hong Kong in 2018.

The China International Economic and Trade Arbitration Commission (CIETAC) is "one of the major permanent arbitration institutions in the world".[207] The CIETAC was founded in 1956 under the name Foreign Trade Arbitration Commission (对外贸易仲裁委员会) under the China Council for the Promotion of International Trade (中国国际贸易促进委员会). In 1980, it was renamed the Foreign Economic and Trade Arbitration Commission (对外经济贸易仲裁委员会). Since 1988, with the State Council's Official Reply Concerning the Renaming of the Arbitration Commission as the China International Economic and Trade Arbitration Commission and Amendment of Its Arbitration Rules (国务院关于将对外经济贸易仲裁委员会改名为中国国际仲裁委员会和修订仲裁规则的批复), the current name, CIETAC, is used.[208] After 60 years of development, the CIETAC, as the "earliest and largest arbitration institution",[209] is in the leading position among Chinese arbitration institutions and willing to make continuous efforts to promote international commercial arbitration in Mainland China. The CIETAC amended its arbitration rules in 2015, including a separate appendix dealing with the emergency arbitrator mechanism. In Article 23.2 of the CIETAC Arbitration Rules 2024 and 2015, it provides that "[i]n accordance with the applicable law or the agreement of the parties, a party may apply to the Arbitration Court for emergency relief according to the CIETAC Emergency Arbitrator Procedures (Appendix III)".[210] "The emergency arbitrator may decide to order or award necessary or appropriate emergency measures. The decision of the emergency arbitrator shall be binding upon both parties".[211] The CIETAC administered its first emergency arbitration case in late 2018, which is not published, since it is still in ongoing arbitral proceedings.

The China Maritime Arbitration Commission (CMAC) was established in 1959 under the China Council for the Promotion of International Trade.[212] The primary duty of the CMAC is to resolve domestic and international disputes involving maritime elements as a permanent arbitral institution.[213] In the latest version of the CMAC Arbitration Rules 2021, it provides that "[i]n accordance with the applicable law or the agreement of the parties, a party may apply to the Arbitration Court for emergency relief" according to the CMAC Emergency Arbitrator Procedures

---

207 CIETAC, Introduction, available at http://cn.cietac.org/index.php?m=Page&a=index&id=34&l=en (1 June 2024).

208 CIETAC, Introduction, available at http://cn.cietac.org/index.php?m=Page&a=index&id=34&l=en (1 June 2024); Karyl Nairn & Patrick Heneghan (2015), *Arbitration World: Jurisdictional and Institutional Comparisons*, Sweet & Maxwell, p. 45.

209 CIETAC, Introduction, available at http://cn.cietac.org/index.php?m=Page&a=index&id=34&l=en (1 June 2024).

210 Article 23.2, CIETAC Arbitration Rules 2024 and 2015.

211 Article 23.2, CIETAC Arbitration Rules 2024 and 2015.

212 CMAC, Introduction, available at http://www.cmac.org.cn/?page_id=283&lang=en (16 June 2020).

213 CMAC, Introduction, available at http://www.cmac.org.cn/?page_id=283&lang=en (16 June 2020).

(Appendix III).[214] The emergency arbitrator has the power to grant necessary or appropriate emergency measures in the form of an order or an award. The decision of the emergency arbitrator is binding upon both parties.

The China (Shanghai) Pilot Free Trade Zone Court of Arbitration was founded by Shanghai International Economic and Trade Arbitration Commission (SHIAC) in 2013. The purpose is to provide efficient and effective arbitral services in line with international standards in the dispute resolution system of the free trade zone.[215] In 2014, the China (Shanghai) Pilot Free Trade Zone Court of Arbitration announced its first arbitration rules. Article 21 of China (Shanghai) Pilot Free Trade Zone Arbitration Rules 2015 provides that any party that intends to apply for interim measures before the constitution of an arbitral tribunal can apply for an emergency tribunal by a written application.[216] SHIAC will decide whether to nominate an emergency arbitrator accordingly.

3.2.2.3 Interaction Between Mainland China and Hong Kong SAR Related to Interim Measures in Arbitration

A groundbreaking agreement of the interim measures in arbitration between Mainland China and Hong Kong was signed on 2 April 2019, which is the Arrangement Concerning Mutual Assistance in Court-ordered Interim Measures in Aid of Arbitral Proceedings by the Courts of the Mainland and of the Hong Kong Special Administrative Region (最高人民法院、香港特别行政区政府关于内地与香港特别行政区法院就仲裁程序相互协助保全的安排) 2019.[217] Both parties must yet determine the time at which the agreement will come into effect.[218] In general, the provisions in this Agreement will not prejudice any rights relating to the arbitral tribunals or parties of Mainland China or of Hong Kong, which fall under the laws of these two jurisdictions.[219]

---

[214] Article 27 & Appendix III, CMAC Arbitration Rules 2021 and 2018.

[215] SHIAC, FTZ Court of Arbitration, available at https://www.shiac.org/pc/Trade?moduleCode=introduction (1 June 2024).

[216] Article 21, The China (Shanghai) Pilot Free Trade Zone Arbitration Rules 2015, available at http://www.shiac.org/upload_files/file/2016/20160228221941_9298.pdf (16 June 2020).

[217] Arrangement Concerning Mutual Assistance in Court-ordered Interim Measures in Aid of Arbitral Proceedings by the Courts of the Mainland and of the Hong Kong Special Administrative Region 2019 (最高人民法院、香港特别行政区政府关于内地与香港特别行政区法院就仲裁程序相互协助保全的安排), the English version is available at https://www.doj.gov.hk/pdf/2019/arbitration_interim_e.pdf (1 June 2024).

[218] Article 13, Arrangement Concerning Mutual Assistance in Court-ordered Interim Measures in Aid of Arbitral Proceedings by the Courts of the Mainland and of the Hong Kong Special Administrative Region 2019 (最高人民法院、香港特别行政区政府关于内地与香港特别行政区法院就仲裁程序相互协助保全的安排), the English version is available at https://www.doj.gov.hk/pdf/2019/arbitration_interim_e.pdf (1 June 2024).

[219] Article 11, Arrangement Concerning Mutual Assistance in Court-ordered Interim Measures in Aid of Arbitral Proceedings by the Courts of the Mainland and of the Hong Kong Special Administrative Region 2019 (最高人民法院、香港特别行政区政府关于内地与香港特别行政

The scope of the interim measures covered in the Agreement includes almost all the possible types regulated by the arbitration laws in Mainland China, including property preservation, evidence preservation, and conduct preservation; and those regulated by the Hong Kong Arbitration Ordinance (Cap. 609), including injunctions, interim measures maintaining or restoring the status quo pending the final decision of the dispute, taking actions that would prevent possible current or imminent harm or prejudice to the arbitral proceedings, the preservation of assets, and preservation of relevant and material evidence.[220] The arbitral proceedings subject to the Arrangement are limited to the arbitral proceedings administrated by listed institutions and seated in Mainland China or Hong Kong.[221]

For the arbitral proceedings seated in Mainland China, a party may apply for the interim measures to the High Court of Hong Kong under the Arbitration Ordinance and the High Court Ordinance (Cap. 609) before the issuance of a final award by a competent arbitral tribunal.[222] For the arbitral proceedings seated in Hong Kong, a party may seek interim measures from the intermediate people's court linked to the residence of the party against which the application is made or to the intermediate people's court where the property or evidence is located. The decision is then based on the Civil Procedure Law of the People's Republic of China, the Arbitration Law of the People's Republic of China and relevant judicial interpretations before a final award is made.[223] For the application to the intermediate people's court, a request for interim measures shall be presided over by the institutions listed in the Arrangement.[224]

区法院就仲裁程序相互协助保全的安排), the English version is available at https://www.doj.gov.hk/pdf/2019/arbitration_interim_e.pdf (1 June 2024).

220 Article 1, Arrangement Concerning Mutual Assistance in Court-ordered Interim Measures in Aid of Arbitral Proceedings by the Courts of the Mainland and of the Hong Kong Special Administrative Region 2019 (最高人民法院、香港特别行政区政府关于内地与香港特别行政区法院就仲裁程序相互协助保全的安排), the English version is available at https://www.doj.gov.hk/pdf/2019/arbitration_interim_e.pdf (1 June 2024).

221 Article 2, Arrangement Concerning Mutual Assistance in Court-ordered Interim Measures in Aid of Arbitral Proceedings by the Courts of the Mainland and of the Hong Kong Special Administrative Region 2019 (最高人民法院、香港特别行政区政府关于内地与香港特别行政区法院就仲裁程序相互协助保全的安排), the English version is available at https://www.doj.gov.hk/pdf/2019/arbitration_interim_e.pdf (1 June 2024).

222 Article 6, Arrangement Concerning Mutual Assistance in Court-ordered Interim Measures in Aid of Arbitral Proceedings by the Courts of the Mainland and of the Hong Kong Special Administrative Region 2019 (最高人民法院、香港特别行政区政府关于内地与香港特别行政区法院就仲裁程序相互协助保全的安排), the English version is available at https://www.doj.gov.hk/pdf/2019/arbitration_interim_e.pdf (1 June 2024).

223 Article 3, Arrangement Concerning Mutual Assistance in Court-ordered Interim Measures in Aid of Arbitral Proceedings by the Courts of the Mainland and of the Hong Kong Special Administrative Region 2019 (最高人民法院、香港特别行政区政府关于内地与香港特别行政区法院就仲裁程序相互协助保全的安排), the English version is available at https://www.doj.gov.hk/pdf/2019/arbitration_interim_e.pdf (1 June 2024).

224 Article 3, Arrangement Concerning Mutual Assistance in Court-ordered Interim Measures in Aid of Arbitral Proceedings by the Courts of the Mainland and of the Hong Kong Special Administrative Region 2019 (最高人民法院、香港特别行政区政府关于内地与香港特别行政区法院

Without any doubt, the latest Arrangement is a big step forward in Chinese legal history regarding interim measures in arbitration. It will provide parties with an alternative to arbitrate in Mainland China for interim measures from courts, and "enhance Hong Kong's attractiveness as a seat for China-related international arbitrations" as a unique jurisdiction.[225] This Agreement also gives a significant advantage to Hong Kong regarding the competition between preferred arbitral seats in Asia–Pacific region and around the world under the "One Country, Two Systems (一国两制)" principle, by making it the only jurisdiction outside Mainland China with a link to the interim measures presided over by courts in Mainland China. However, there is still no legal regime for the recognition and enforcement of interim measures granted by other authorities than the local courts between Mainland China and Hong Kong. Furthermore, this Arrangement does not apply to ad hoc arbitration.

3.2.2.4 Other Jurisdictions Refusing the Emergency Arbitrator Mechanism

In addition to Mainland China, there are other jurisdictions that also prohibit arbitral bodies, including arbitral tribunals and emergency arbitrators from issuing interim measures. These jurisdictions include the Czech Republic, Finland, and Thailand. The power in these jurisdictions is exclusively reserved for state courts in respect of arbitration.[226]

The Czech Republic allows the state court to order interim measures at the request of the parties if there is a clear chance that the enforcement of an arbitral award will be endangered.[227] The Finland Arbitration Act is silent on whether the arbitral bodies can render interim measures or not,[228] which only provides that a state court can issue interim measures before or during the arbitral proceedings with the existence of an arbitration agreement.[229] Thailand only allows parties to apply for the interim

就仲裁程序相互协助保全的安排), the English version is available at https://www.doj.gov.hk/pdf/2019/arbitration_interim_e.pdf (1 June 2024).

[225] Peter Yuen, Helen H. Shi, Damien McDonald, Olga Boltenko & Matthew Townsend, Hong Kong and Mainland China Agree upon Bilateral Arrangement Regarding Interim Measures for Arbitration, 2019, available at http://arbitrationblog.kluwerarbitration.com/2019/04/02/hong-kong-and-mainland-china-agree-upon-bilateral-arrangement-regarding-interim-measures-for-arbitration/ (1 June 2024).

[226] Gary B. Born (2015), *International Arbitration: Cases and Materials*, Kluwer Law International, p. 872.

[227] Section 22, Act of the Czech Republic No. 216/1994 Sb. on arbitration proceedings and on enforcement of arbitration awards, available at https://is.muni.cz/el/1422/jaro2008/SOC026/um/216-1994_EN.pdf (1 June 2024).

[228] Karyl Nairn & Patrick Heneghan (2015), *Arbitration World: Jurisdictional and Institutional Comparisons*, Sweet & Maxwell, p. 510.

[229] Section 51, Finland Arbitration Act 754/2015, available at https://www.finlex.fi/fi/laki/kaannokset/1992/en19920967.pdf (1 June 2024).

measures to a competent state court, either before or during the arbitral proceedings.[230] Although Thailand adopted the UNCITRAL Model Law 1985 in 2002,[231] the Thai arbitration law does not follow the direction to give arbitrators the power to grant necessary interim measures.

Based on the discussion above, it seems that the enforceability of the interim measures granted by an emergency arbitrator is not possible in the jurisdictions mentioned in this section. In the case of Mainland China, the regulating court proceedings are quite fast and efficient in terms of granting interim measures. However, time may not be a significant concern for the future adoption of the emergency arbitrator mechanisms; as such, it is still unclear whether these jurisdictions will abandon the current framework in favor of emergency arbitrator mechanisms.

3.2.3 Jurisdictions Having Undetermined Views Towards the Emergency Arbitrator Mechanism

Unlike the jurisdictions which have clear attitudes towards the emergency arbitrator mechanism, most other jurisdictions have an undetermined view towards the application of the emergency arbitrator mechanism. The current practice concerning the emergency arbitrator mechanism in the United States acts as a representative in this section, including the arbitration laws and related case law. The laws in jurisdictions other than the United States which show uncertain attitudes will provide supporting materials.

3.2.3.1 Current Practice Concerning the Emergency Arbitrator Mechanism in the United States

Arbitration, as a more private dispute resolution compared to judicial proceedings, is very popular and widely accepted in the United States.[232] Through a series of cases, *M/S Bremen v. Zapata Off-Shore Co.,*[233] *Scherk v. Alberto-Culver Co.,*[234] *Mitsubishi Motors Corp. v. Soler Chrysler-Plymouth, Inc.,*[235] and *Vimar Seguros y*

---

230 Section 16, Thailand Arbitration Act B.E. 2545/2002, available at https://arbitrationlaw.com/sites/default/files/free_pdfs/Thailand%20Arbitration%20Act.pdf (1 June 2024).

231 UNCITRAL, Status: UNCITRAL Model Law on International Commercial Arbitration (1985), with amendments as adopted in 2006, available at https://uncitral.un.org/en/texts/arbitration/modellaw/commercial_arbitration/status (1 June 2024).

232 Tilman Niedermaier (2016), International Arbitration in the U.S., in Stephan Balthasar, *International Commercial Arbitration: International Conventions, Country Reports and Comparative Analysis*, C. H. Beck·Hart·Nomos, p. 661.

233 *M/S Bremen v. Zapata Off-Shore Co.*, 407 U.S.1 (Supreme Court of the United States, 1972).

234 *Scherk v. Alberto-Culver Co.*, 417 U.S. 506 (Supreme Court of the United States, 1974).

235 *Mitsubishi Motors Corp. v. Soler Chrysler-Plymouth, Inc.*, 473 U.S. 614 (Supreme Court of the United States, 1985).

Reasequros, S.A. v. M/V Sky Reefer,[236] it has been established that favoring arbitral dispute resolution is an "emphatic federal policy"[237] and "that federal policy applies with special force in the field of international commerce" in the United States.[238]

Due to the federal system of the United States, the governing statutory laws of arbitration include both federal statutes and state statutes.[239] The Federal Arbitration Act (FAA) was first enacted in 1925 and was later codified in Title 9 of the United States Code. The United States ratified the New York Convention on the Recognition and Enforcement of Foreign Arbitral Awards 1958 in 1970 in Chapter 2 of the FAA.[240] The FAA dominates the arbitration laws in the United States, and the legislation of each state is "usually relevant only where the FAA is silent and only to the extent that the state statutes are not inconsistent with it".[241] The Supreme Court of the United States considers that Section 2 of the FAA "is substantive federal law"[242] applying in state courts, including "all international transactions and virtually every commercial transaction".[243] Each state, including the District of Columbia, has its statutes concerning arbitration. Some states adopted the Uniform Arbitration Act (UAA), which was drafted by the Uniform Law Commission in order to bring "clarity and stability to critical areas of state statutory law".[244] Some states, including California, Connecticut, Florida, Georgia, Illinois, Louisiana, Oregon, and Texas, have adopted the UNCITRAL Model Law on International Arbitration 1985 (with amendments as adopted in 2006).[245]

[236] *Vimar Seguros y Reaseguros, S.A. v. M/V Sky Reefer*, 515 U.S. 528 (Supreme Court of the United States, 1995).

[237] *Mitsubishi Motors Corp. v. Soler Chrysler-Plymouth, Inc.*, 473 U.S. 614, 632 (Supreme Court of the United States, 1985).

[238] *Mitsubishi Motors Corp. v. Soler Chrysler-Plymouth, Inc.*, 473 U.S. 614, 631 (Supreme Court of the United States, 1985).

[239] Karyl Nairn & Patrick Heneghan (2015), *Arbitration World: Jurisdictional and Institutional Comparisons*, Sweet & Maxwell, p. 1019.

[240] Louis Del Duca & Nancy A. Welsh (2017), Interpretation and Application of the New York Convention in the United States, in George A. Bermann, *Recognition and Enforcement of Foreign Arbitral Awards: The Interpretation and Application of the New York Convention by National Courts*, Springer International Publishing AG, p. 996; Tilman Niedermaier (2016), International Arbitration in the U.S., in Stephan Balthasar, *International Commercial Arbitration: International Conventions, Country Reports and Comparative Analysis*, C. H. Beck·Hart·Nomos, p. 662.

[241] Karyl Nairn & Patrick Heneghan (2015), *Arbitration World: Jurisdictional and Institutional Comparisons*, Sweet & Maxwell, p. 1019.

[242] Karyl Nairn & Patrick Heneghan (2015), *Arbitration World: Jurisdictional and Institutional Comparisons*, Sweet & Maxwell, p. 1019; see also *Allied-Bruce Terminix Companies, Inc. v. Dobson*, 513 U.S. 265 (Supreme Court of the United States, 1995).

[243] Karyl Nairn & Patrick Heneghan (2015), *Arbitration World: Jurisdictional and Institutional Comparisons*, Sweet & Maxwell, p. 1019.

[244] Uniform Law Commission, Overview, available at https://www.uniformlaws.org/aboutulc/overview (1 June 2024).

[245] UNCITRAL, Status: UNCITRAL Model Law on International Commercial Arbitration (1985), with amendments as adopted in 2006, available at https://uncitral.un.org/en/texts/arbitration/modellaw/commercial_arbitration/status (1 June 2024); Karyl Nairn & Patrick Heneghan (2015), *Arbitration World: Jurisdictional and Institutional Comparisons*, Sweet & Maxwell, p. 1019.

The FAA is silent on the issue of whether an arbitral tribunal or an emergency arbitrator has the power to grant interim measures in aid of arbitral proceedings.[246] According to the FAA, the courts in the United States may vacate an arbitral award upon the request of an arbitral party if the arbitrators have exceeded powers, or imperfectly executed the powers failing to issue "a mutual, final, and definite award".[247] The finality requirement regarding the enforceability of an arbitral award "finds its origin in judicial precedent interpreting the FAA, policy considerations, and the language of the FAA itself."[248]

The Uniform Arbitration Act (UAA) is a model law developed by the National Conference of Commissioners on Uniform State Law. The revised version, the UAA 2000, is "more comprehensive than the FAA" and more in the style of the UNCITRAL Model Law 1985.[249] The goal of the UAA 2000 was to provide "state legislatures with a more up-to-date statute to resolve disputes through arbitration".[250] The UAA 2000 provides for two stages to grant interim measures: the period before the constitution of an arbitral tribunal and the period after the appointment of arbitrators. For the first stage, state courts can issue emergency relief to protect the effectiveness of arbitral proceedings.[251] For the second stage, the appointed arbitrators have the authority to grant interim measures that are necessary to protect the effectiveness of arbitration and to promote a fair and expeditious resolution of the dispute.[252] Once an arbitral tribunal is constituted, parties can turn to state courts for interim measures "only if the matter is urgent and the arbitrator is not able to act timely or the arbitrator cannot provide an adequate remedy".[253]

The Restatement of the Law (Third) of the U.S. Law of International Commercial and Investor-State Arbitration 2019 was drafted by the American Law Institute. The American Law Institute is an organization that consists of judges, scholars and legal

---

[246] Gary B. Born (2021), *International Commercial Arbitration*, Kluwer Law International, p. 2615; Karyl Nairn & Patrick Heneghan (2015), *Arbitration World: Jurisdictional and Institutional Comparisons*, Sweet & Maxwell, p. 1032.

[247] Section 10 (a)(4), Federal Arbitration Act, United States Code Annotated 2002.

[248] William G. Bassler (2016), The Enforceability of Emergency Awards in the United States: or when interim means final, 32 *Arbitration International* 6.

[249] Edward Brunet, Richard E. Speidel, Jean R. Sternlight & Stephen J. Ware (2006), *Arbitration Law in America: A Critical Assessment*, Cambridge University Press, p. 56.

[250] Edward Brunet, Richard E. Speidel, Jean R. Sternlight & Stephen J. Ware (2006), *Arbitration Law in America: A Critical Assessment*, Cambridge University Press, note 103.

[251] Section 8 (a), Uniform Arbitration Act 2000, available at https://www.uniformlaws.org/viewdocument/final-act-2?CommunityKey=a0ad71d6-085f-4648-857a-e9e893ae2736&tab=librarydocuments (1 June 2024).

[252] Section 8 (b)(1), Uniform Arbitration Act 2000, available at https://www.uniformlaws.org/viewdocument/final-act-2?CommunityKey=a0ad71d6-085f-4648-857a-e9e893ae2736&tab=librarydocuments (1 June 2024).

[253] Section 8 (b)(2), Uniform Arbitration Act 2000, available at https://www.uniformlaws.org/viewdocument/final-act-2?CommunityKey=a0ad71d6-085f-4648-857a-e9e893ae2736&tab=librarydocuments (1 June 2024).

practitioners. The Restatement of the Law is "primarily addressed to courts".[254] Although the content of the restatement is not binding, it is "usually useful to and persuasive to courts in offering guidance, particularly in contested or unsettled areas of law".[255] In the approved final draft of the Restatement of the Law (Third) of the U.S. Law of International Commercial and Investor-State Arbitration 2019,[256] Section 1(a) states that an arbitral award is a decision that sets forth the "final and binding determination" of claims, "regardless of whether that decision resolves the entire dispute before the tribunal". Concerning the interim measures granted by an emergency arbitrator, they are "prima facie treated the same as interim measures granted by a tribunal".[257] In other words, "a presumption attaches that they are awards".[258]

With regard to the state statutes, there is no regulation directly on the application of the emergency arbitrator mechanism. Half of the 50 states, including Alaska,[259] Arizona,[260] Arkansas,[261] California,[262] Colorado,[263] Connecticut,[264] Florida,[265] Georgia,[266] Hawaii,[267] Illinois,[268] Louisiana,[269] Michigan,[270] Minnesota,[271]

---

254 American Law Institute, Frequently Asked Questions, available at https://www.ali.org/publications/frequently-asked-questions/ (1 June 2024).

255 Tai-Heng Cheng & Julia Peck, Arbitration Procedures and Practice in the United States: Overview, available at https://uk.practicallaw.thomsonreuters.com/0-502-1714?transitionType=Default&contextData=(sc.Default)&firstPage=true&bhcp=1 (16 June 2020).

256 The American Law Institute, Restatement of The U.S. Law of International Commercial and Investor-State Arbitration Is Approved, available at https://www.ali.org/news/articles/restatement-us-law-international-commercial-and-investorstate-arbitration-approved/ (1 June 2024).

257 Comment on Section 1(a), Restatement of the U.S Law of International Commercial and Investor-State Arbitration 2019, available at https://www.ali.org/projects/show/international-commercial-arbitration/ (16 June 2020).

258 Comment on Section 1(a), Restatement of the U.S Law of International Commercial and Investor-State Arbitration 2019, available at https://www.ali.org/projects/show/international-commercial-arbitration/ (16 June 2020).

259 Section 09.43.350, West's Alaska Statutes Annotated 2004.

260 Section 12-3008, Arizona Revised Statutes Annotated 2011.

261 Section 16-108-205 & 16-108-208, West's Arkansas Code Annotated 2011.

262 Section 1297.171 & 1297.91, West's Annotated California Codes 1988.

263 Section 13-22-208, West's Colorado Revised Statutes Annotated 2004.

264 Section 50a-109 & 50a-117, Connecticut General Statutes Annotated 1989.

265 Section 684.001 & 684.0018, West's Florida Statutes Annotated 2010.

266 Section 9-9-30 & 9-9-38, West's Code of Georgia Annotated 2012.

267 Section 658A-8, West's Hawaii Revised Statutes Annotated 2001.

268 Section 30/5-15 & 30/15-10, West's Smith-Hurd Illinois Complied Statutes Annotated 1998.

269 Section 4249 & 4257, West's Louisiana Statutes Annotated 2006.

270 Section 691.1688, Michigan Complied Law Annotated 2013.

271 Section 572B.08, Minnesota Statutes Annotated 2011.

Nevada,[272] New Jersey,[273] New Mexico,[274] North Carolina,[275] North Dakota,[276] Oregon,[277] Ohio,[278] Oklahoma,[279] Texas,[280] Utah,[281] Washington,[282] West Virginia,[283] and the District of Columbia[284] have empowered arbitrators to grant interim measures if necessary.

Generally, the authority for an arbitral tribunal to issue interim measures has been recognized unless parties agree otherwise.[285] It is "black-letter law" in the United States that if the interim measures granted by arbitrators "finally and definitely disposes of at least one separate independent claim",[286] such interim measures can be confirmed even if the entire dispute has not been settled yet.[287] However, currently, there are no statutes either at the federal level or state level regulating the application of the emergency arbitrator mechanism directly.

3.2.3.2 Case Law

As a common law country, case law has a significant impact in the United States. The FAA was enacted in 1925 and is considered "old, incomplete, and fragmented"[288] in regulating international commercial arbitration, especially in terms of the emergency arbitrator mechanism, which was only introduced in 2006. Case law, instead, can act as a gap-filler between the black-letter law and the current legal practice. The court decisions "eventually establish broad legal deference to arbitral jurisdiction in international matters, and lead to a merger of the domestic and international case law".[289] The interpretation of arbitration laws by the state courts in the United States

[272] Section 38.222, West's Nevada Revised Statutes Annotated 2001.

[273] Section 2A: 23B-8, New Jersey Statutes Annotated 1987.

[274] Section 44-7A-9, West's New Mexico Statutes Annotated 2001.

[275] Section 1-567.47, West's North Carolina General Statues Annotated 2017.

[276] Section 32-29. 3-08, West's North Dakota Century Code Annotated 2003.

[277] Section 36.470 & 36.486, West's Oregon Revised Statutes Annotated 1993.

[278] Section 2712.14, Baldwin's Ohio Revised Code Annotated 1991.

[279] Section 1859, Oklahoma Statutes Annotated 2006.

[280] Section 172.083, Vernon's Texas Statutes and Codes Annotated 1997.

[281] Section 78B-11-109, West's Utah Code Annotated 2008.

[282] Section 7.05.100, West's Revised Code of Washington Annotated 2015.

[283] Section 55-10-10, West's Annotated Code of West Virginia 2015.

[284] Section 16-4408, West's District of Columbia Code Annotated 2008.

[285] Gary B. Born (2021), *International Commercial Arbitration*, Kluwer Law International, p. 2615.

[286] *Metallgesellschaft A.G. v. M/V Capitan Constante*, 790 F. 2d 280, 283 (United States Court of Appeals, Second Circuit, 1986).

[287] William G. Bassler (2016), The Enforceability of Emergency Awards in the United States: or when interim means final, 32 *Arbitration International* 7.

[288] Edward Brunet, Richard E. Speidel, Jean R. Sternlight & Stephen J. Ware (2006), *Arbitration Law in America: A Critical Assessment*, Cambridge University Press, p. 202.

[289] Thomas E. Carbonneau (2014), *The Law and Practice of Arbitration*, Juris Publishing, Inc., pp. 613–614.

is of "paramount importance for the understanding of U.S. arbitration law".[290] As indicated in the judgment of *Allied-Bruce Terminix Companies., Inc. v. Dobson* case, the courts have "abandoned all pretense of ascertaining congressional intent with respect to the Federal Arbitration Act, building instead, case by case, an edifice of its own creation".[291] The following section will introduce the existing cases in the United States concerning the emergency arbitrator mechanism.

For courts tend not to recognize and enforce the interim measures granted by an emergency arbitrator often referred to two cases, i.e., *Chinmax Medical Systems Inc., v. Alere San Diego, Inc.*,[292] and *Al Raha Group for Technical Services v. PKL Services, Inc.*[293] They are an examples to show that certain U.S. courts refused to treat the interim measures given by the emergency arbitrator as a final arbitral award, and it has been described as "the poster child for the unenforceability of decisions by emergency arbitrator".[294]

In *Chinmax Medical Systems Inc., v. Alere San Diego, Inc.*,[295] the Plaintiff was a Chinese company, being the exclusive distributor of the medical devices provided by Alere since 2001. Alere is a Delaware cooperation. They entered into a distribution contract for five years. On 1 April 2007, Chinmax and Alere agreed on a new one-year contract, which would run until 31 March 2008. This new contract contained a two-year renewal clause and an automatic renewal for another two years until 31 March 2012. The optional renewal would be automatic unless one party provided notice 19 days before the expiration of the original contract. The new agreement granted Chinmax the right to register new products in China. However, Alere declared that it would register new products. As a result, Chinmax requested compensation for giving up its contractual rights and asked to be the service agent of Alere continuously. Both parties set sales targets every year. Alere's representatives stated that they would not renew the agreement if Chinmax could not meet at least 90% of the 2009 sales target. Chinmax exceeded the 2009 sales target, but, nevertheless, Alere informed Chinmax that the agreement would not be renewed on 5 January 2010. Alere also claimed Chinmax breached the contract by not making payments on time.

An arbitration agreement was contained in the contract, stating that all the disputes arising from or relating to the contract should be finally resolved by arbitration under the ICDR with a panel of three arbitrators. On 13 October 2010, Chinmax filed a

---

[290] Tilman Niedermaier (2016), International Arbitration in the U.S., in Stephan Balthasar, *International Commercial Arbitration: International Conventions, Country Reports and Comparative Analysis*, C. H. Beck·Hart·Nomos, p. 663.

[291] *Allied-Bruce Terminix Companies, Inc. v. Dobson*, 513 U.S. 265, 283 (Supreme Court of the United States, 1995).

[292] *Chinmax Medical Systems Inc., v. Alere San Diego, Inc.*, No. 10cv2467 WQH (NLS), 2011 WL 2135350 (United States District Court, S.D. California, 2011).

[293] *Al Raha Group for Technical Services v. PKL Services, Inc.*, Civil Action. No. 1:18-cv-04194-AT, 2019 WL 4267765 (United States District Court, N.D. Georgia, 2019).

[294] William G. Bassler (2016), The Enforceability of Emergency Awards in the United States: or when interim means final, 32 *Arbitration International* 13.

[295] *Chinmax Medical Systems Inc., v. Alere San Diego, Inc.*, No. 10cv2467 WQH (NLS), 2011 WL 2135350 (United States District Court, S.D. California, 2011).

request for arbitration to the ICDR. On 15 October 2010, Alere applied for the emergency arbitrator mechanism. On 23 November 2010, the emergency arbitrator rendered an interim award accordingly. In the interim award, Chinmax was required to deliver the original license and copies of all applications of the products from Alere, not to initiate any communications with any Chinese governmental agencies and customs officials concerning the registration related to the dispute and to provide all the bank accounts and balances. On 1 December 2010, Chinmax initiated the suit with the United States District Court for the Southern District of California to vacate the interim measures by the ICDR emergency arbitrator.

As it was shown in the case of *Pacific Reinsurance Management Corp. v. Ohio Reinsurance Corp.*, "judicial review of non-final arbitration awards should be indulged, if at all, only in the most extreme cases".[296] Firstly, the Court considered that the disputed interim award issued was "in order to facilitate any consideration by the full panel of conservancy"[297] and it would "remain in effect pending view of the full arbitration tribunal".[298] Additionally, since this interim award was to facilitate a decision by an arbitral tribunal, the emergency arbitrator did not intend for it to be final. Therefore, the Court concluded that the interim award was not final and was not subject to judicial review.[299]

In *Al Raha Group for Technical Services v. PKL Services, Inc.*,[300] the Petitioner was a Saudi Arabian corporation, and the Respondent was an American corporation. The Petitioner applied to the Court to confirm an arbitral award. However, the Court refused to confirm the award on the ground that it was an interim placeholder pending the constitution of a full arbitral tribunal. Since the present arbitral award was governed by the New York Convention 1958, the Court admitted that district courts have original jurisdiction over any action or proceeding failing under the Convention, but they "lack authority to confirm arbitral awards that are not final awards".[301]

[296] *Pacific Reinsurance Management Corp. v. Ohio Reinsurance Corp.*, 935 F. 2d 1019, 1022 (United States Court of Appeals, Ninth Circuit, 1991).

[297] *Chinmax Medical Systems Inc., v. Alere San Diego, Inc.*, No. 10cv2467 WQH (NLS), 2011 WL 2135350, 4 (United States District Court, S.D. California, 2011).

[298] *Chinmax Medical Systems Inc., v. Alere San Diego, Inc.*, No. 10cv2467 WQH (NLS), 2011 WL 2135350, 4 (United States District Court, S.D. California, 2011).

[299] *Chinmax Medical Systems Inc., v. Alere San Diego, Inc.*, No. 10cv2467 WQH (NLS), 2011 WL 2135350, 5 (United States District Court, S.D. California, 2011); *Publicis Communication and Publicis S.A. v. True North Communications Inc.*, 206 F. 3d 725 (United States Court of Appeals, Seventh Circuit, 2000).

[300] *Al Raha Group for Technical Services v. PKL Services, Inc.*, Civil Action. No. 1:18-cv-04194-AT, 2019 WL 4267765 (United States District Court, N.D. Georgia, 2019).

[301] *Al Raha Group for Technical Services v. PKL Services, Inc.*, Civil Action. No. 1:18-cv-04194-AT, 2019 WL 4267765, 2 (United States District Court, N.D. Georgia, 2019); Banco de Seguros del Estado v. Mut. Marine Offices, Inc., 230 F. Supp. 2d 362, 368 (United States District Court, S.D. New York, 2002).

In the instant case, the Court determined that the decision of the emergency arbitrator was not final, because it "did not finally and definitely dispose of any independent claim".[302] In the award, the emergency arbitrator clarified that it "was to prevent the termination… of the contract between the parties pending constitution of the full arbitral tribunal that will be appointed to hear the case on the merits".[303] The Court stated that based on such expression, the award is "on its face and in its substance" an interim award only intended to pause the circumstances to wait for the constitution of an arbitral tribunal with a full capacity. Hence, the Court held it did not have subject-matter jurisdiction over the case to confirm the arbitral award.

For courts tend to recognize and enforce the interim measures granted by an emergency arbitrator often referred to the following cases, i.e., *Yahoo! Inc. v. Microsoft Corporation*[304] which has been the "most prominent case so far"[305] to deal with the application of the emergency arbitrator mechanism, *Sharp Corporation and Sharp Electronics Corporation v. Hisense USA Corporation and Hisense International (Hong Kong) America Investment Co. Ltd.,*[306] *T-Mobile USA Inc. v. Verity Wireless Inc.,*[307] *Thrivest Specialty Funding, LLC v. William E. White,*[308] *Rocky Mountain Biologicals, Inc., and Skyway Purified Solutions, Inc. v. Microbix Biosystems, Inc., and Irvine Scientific Sales Company, Inc.,*[309] *James Gold, et al. v. Michael Maurer,*[310] and *Smart Technologies ULC v. Rapt Touch Ireland Ltd, et al.*[311]

In *Yahoo! Inc. v. Microsoft Corporation,*[312] Yahoo and Microsoft entered into a contract to merge their search engines Panama and Bing Ads systems in 2009 to have a better position in international competition with Google. According to the

---

[302] *Al Raha Group for Technical Services v. PKL Services, Inc.*, Civil Action. No. 1:18-cv-04194-AT, 2019 WL 4267765, 3 (United States District Court, N.D. Georgia, 2019).

[303] *Al Raha Group for Technical Services v. PKL Services, Inc.*, Civil Action. No. 1:18-cv-04194-AT, 2019 WL 4267765, 3 (United States District Court, N.D. Georgia, 2019).

[304] *Yahoo! Inc. v. Microsoft Corporation*, 983 F. Supp. 2d 310 (United States District Court, S.D. New York, 2013).

[305] William G. Bassler (2016), The Enforceability of Emergency Awards in the United States: or when interim means final, 32 *Arbitration International* 13.

[306] *Sharp Corporation and Sharp Electronics Corporation v. Hisense USA Corporation and Hisense International (Hong Kong) America Investment Co. Ltd.*, Civil Action No. 17-1648 (JEB), 2017WL5449805 (United States District Court, District of Columbia, 2017).

[307] *T-Mobile USA Inc. v. Verity Wireless Inc.*, No. 2:21-cv-00733-RAJ-BAT, 2021 WL 4295845 (United States District Court, W.D. Washington, 2021).

[308] *Thrivest Specialty Funding, LLC v. William E. White*, 2019 WL 6124955 (United States District Court, E.D. Pennsylvania).

[309] *Rocky Mountain Biologicals, Inc., and Skyway Purified Solutions, Inc. v. Microbix Biosystems, Inc., and Irvine Scientific Sales Company, Inc.*, 986 F. Supp. 2d. 1187 (United States District Court, D. Montana, Missoula Division, 2013).

[310] *James Gold, et al. v. Michael Maurer*, 251 F. Supp. 3d 127 (United States District Court, District of Columbia, 2017).

[311] *Smart Technologies ULC v. Rapt Touch Ireland Ltd, et al.*, 197 F. Supp. 3d 1204 (United States District Court, N.D. California, 2016).

[312] *Yahoo! Inc. v. Microsoft Corporation*, 983 F. Supp. 2d 310 (United States District Court, S.D. New York, 2013).

contract, Yahoo was required to transfer the search services from Panama to Bing Ads in 16 individual geographic markets. The transition had two main divided stages, "Demand" and "Ramp" phases. In 14 markets, the process was completed successfully on time. However, the remaining two transitions in Taiwan and Hong Kong were disputed in the present case. According to the initial contract, the migration in Taiwan and Hong Kong should have been completed by 2011. Subsequently, both parties agreed to extend the period to the end of October 2013. In mid-September 2013, the Ramp phrase of the Taiwan and Hong Kong transitions was prepared and ready. On 20 September 2013, Yahoo suddenly informed Microsoft that the transition would not be finished until early 2014, because of the concern about the future development of Microsoft with an upcoming new Chief Executive Officer in 2014. Microsoft claimed on the same day that Yahoo's conduct was a breach of their previous agreement.

Microsoft applied for the emergency arbitrator mechanism on 26 September 2013, based on their arbitration agreement under the AAA. The AAA emergency arbitrator rendered an interim award on 14 October 2013, after a careful examination of both the written and oral submissions. The interim award restrained Yahoo from "continuing any pause in transitioning",[313] and urged Yahoo to perform the contractual obligation by 28 October 2013, for the Taiwan transition, and 11 November 2013, for the Hong Kong transition, using all efforts.

Yahoo brought a suit to the United States District Court for the Southern District of New York requesting the Court to vacate the interim measure made by the emergency arbitrator on 15 October 2013. Yahoo argued that the award would not only lead to an interim result, but a final one, since the migration in Taiwan and Hong Kong would be irreversible. This consequence would lead to a result contradicting the purpose of the emergency arbitrator mechanism. The Court opposed this opinion, holding that the language in the contract "empowered an Emergency Arbitrator to grant non-monetary relief necessary to restore the *status quo*".[314] The performance, according to the contractual obligations, was essential for the restoration, as the emergency arbitrator correctly addressed the matter within his authority, even though the interim award was final in essence. The Court also pointed out that the decision by the emergency arbitrator was "based on significant evidence showing that it was critical that the Ramp phase immediately follows the Demand phase, including affidavits, dozens of exhibits, and the testimony of ten witnesses".[315] With the relevant consideration, the emergency arbitrator "(1) found that there was a likelihood of irreparable harm, as to Microsoft; (2) found the balance of hardships was in favor of Microsoft; and (3) considered the likelihood of Microsoft's success on the merits".[316] Therefore, the decision made by the emergency arbitrator was appropriate.

---

[313] *Yahoo! Inc. v. Microsoft Corporation*, 983 F. Supp. 2d 310, 316 (United States District Court, S.D. New York, 2013).

[314] *Yahoo! Inc. v. Microsoft Corporation*, 983 F. Supp. 2d 310, 318 (United States District Court, S.D. New York, 2013).

[315] *Yahoo! Inc. v. Microsoft Corporation*, 983 F. Supp. 2d 310, 319 (United States District Court, S.D. New York, 2013).

[316] *Yahoo! Inc. v. Microsoft Corporation*, 983 F. Supp. 2d 310, 319 (United States District Court, S.D. New York, 2013).

Yahoo further argued that the emergency arbitrator did not finally resolve all the issues. In this case, the award could not be subject to judicial review or be confirmed by a court. However, the Court refused the argument, stating that "the equitable relief awarded is final, and the Emergency Arbitrator neither exceeded his authority nor manifestly disregarded the law in awarding such relief".[317] If "an arbitral award of equitable relief based upon a finding of irreparable harm is to have any meaning at all, the parties must be capable of enforcing or vacating it at the time it is made".[318] Consequently, the Court refused to vacate the interim measure requested by Yahoo but confirmed the award by the emergency arbitrator based on the above reasoning.

In *Sharp Corporation and Sharp Electronics Corporation v. Hisense USA Corporation and Hisense International (Hong Kong) America Investment Co. Ltd.,*[319] a Japanese electronics company, Sharp, and a Chinese manufacturer, Hisense, entered into a trademark-licensing agreement in July 2015. This agreement intended to allow Hisense to "manufacture, assemble, promote, market, distribute, [and] sell"[320] the televisions from Sharp. Regarding the dispute resolution, both parties agreed that the SIAC would be the administrative institution for arbitration. Sharp terminated the contract with Hisense on 17 April 2017, based on its observation that Hisense did not perform its obligations sufficiently according to the contract. On 24 April 2017, Hisense initiated a request for arbitration in the SIAC and sought interim relief from an emergency arbitrator to reinstate the contract before the constitution of an arbitral tribunal. On 9 May 2017, an interim award was granted by the appointed emergency arbitrator from the SIAC. This interim award prohibited Sharp from disparaging Hisense, disrupting Hisense' business, and approaching Hisense's business associates or other third parties[321] pending the final resolution of the dispute.

Sharp claimed that such an interim award is a "one-sided Gag Order",[322] violating the public policy of the United States regarding the freedom of speech and the right to petition the government. On 15 August 2017, Sharp filed a complaint in the United States District Court of Columbia against Hisense and intended to seek a declaration from the Court that the interim award issued by the emergency arbitrator was not

---

[317] *Yahoo! Inc. v. Microsoft Corporation*, 983 F. Supp. 2d 310, 320 (United States District Court, S.D. New York, 2013).

[318] *Yahoo! Inc. v. Microsoft Corporation*, 983 F. Supp. 2d 310, 320 (United States District Court, S.D. New York, 2013); *Southern Seas Navigation Limited of Monrovia v. Petroleos Mexicanos of Mexico City*, 606 F. Supp. 692, 694 (United States District Court, S.D. New York, 1985).

[319] *Sharp Corporation and Sharp Electronics Corporation v. Hisense USA Corporation and Hisense International (Hong Kong) America Investment Co. Ltd.*, Civil Action No. 17-1648 (JEB), 2017WL5449805 (United States District Court, District of Columbia, 2017).

[320] *Sharp Corporation and Sharp Electronics Corporation v. Hisense USA Corporation and Hisense International (Hong Kong) America Investment Co. Ltd.*, Civil Action No. 17-1648 (JEB), 2017WL5449805, 2 (United States District Court, District of Columbia, 2017).

[321] *Sharp Corporation and Sharp Electronics Corporation v. Hisense USA Corporation and Hisense International (Hong Kong) America Investment Co. Ltd.*, Civil Action No. 17-1648 (JEB), 2017WL5449805, 3 (United States District Court, District of Columbia, 2017).

[322] *Sharp Corporation and Sharp Electronics Corporation v. Hisense USA Corporation and Hisense International (Hong Kong) America Investment Co. Ltd.*, Civil Action No. 17-1648 (JEB), 2017WL5449805, 3 (United States District Court, District of Columbia, 2017).

recognizable or enforceable in the United States. Firstly, the Court examined its jurisdiction. The recognition and enforcement of foreign arbitral awards are governed by the New York Convention 1958. In the context of the United States, the New York Convention 1958 has been ratified and enacted in the second chapter of the FAA in 1970.[323] The purpose of the New York Convention 1958 and its implementing legislation is to "encourage the recognition and enforcement of commercial arbitration agreements in international contracts".[324] According to the provisions of the New York Convention 1958, the jurisdictions fall into two categories of primary and secondary courts. The primary courts refer to the courts where the award is issued, and the secondary courts refer to the other courts in the contracting states of the New York Convention 1958. Although the primary courts enjoy broader authority compared to the secondary courts, the secondary courts have the discretion to decide on whether they would enforce the award or not.[325] In the present case, the Court is a secondary jurisdiction, having the power to decide whether the interim measures can be enforceable in the United States, which is "a permissible goal in a secondary jurisdiction".[326] Additionally, the Court raised an issue according to the SIAC Arbitration Rules 2016. Article 12 of the Schedule 1 of SIAC Arbitration 2016 provides that "[t]he parties also irrevocably waive their rights to any form of appeal, review or recourse to any State court or other judicial authority" with respect to the interim measures granted by an emergency arbitrator. The Court found that such wording in the arbitration rules appeared to preclude the complaint submitted against the decision by the emergency arbitrator in the present case. However, Hisense failed to raise the issue in its written submission, which led the Court to skip elaborating on this possible argument. Secondly, the Court went through the merits of the dispute, which was whether the interim measure rendered by the SIAC emergency arbitrator had violated U.S. public policy and whether the interim measure could be enforceable in the United States. Article V (2)(b) of the New York Convention 1958 gives the possibility for the state courts to refuse the recognition and enforcement of foreign arbitral awards if the "recognition or enforcement of the award would be contrary to the public policy of that country". However, state courts have been cautious about exercising this power based on this article. The reason was that "the public-policy defense is to be construed narrowly to be applied only where enforcement would

[323] Christopher R. Drahozal (2012), New York Convention and the American Federal System, The Symposium, *Journal of Dispute Resolution* 103.

[324] *TermoRio S.A.E.S.P. v. Electranta S.P.*, 487 F. 3d 928, 933 (United States Court of Appeals, District of Columbia Circuit, 2007).

[325] *TermoRio S.A.E.S.P. v. Electranta S.P.*, 487 F. 3d 928, 935 (United States Court of Appeals, District of Columbia Circuit, 2007); *Gulf Petri Trading Co., Inc. v. Nigerian Nat'l Petroleum Corp.*, 512 F. 3d 742, 747 (United States Courts of Appeals, Fifth Circuit, 2008).

[326] *Sharp Corporation and Sharp Electronics Corporation v. Hisense USA Corporation and Hisense International (Hong Kong) America Investment Co. Ltd.*, Civil Action No. 17-1648 (JEB), 2017WL5449805, 5 (United States District Court, District of Columbia, 2017).

violate the forum state's most basic notions of morality and justice".[327] The public policy argument needs to be sufficient to take priority over a policy favoring the recognition and enforcement of the international arbitral awards.[328] The Sharp's claim was made based on the public policy right to freedom of speech enshrined in the First Amendment of the Constitution of the United States. However, as the Court correctly pointed out, the involvement of governmental action, which is an essential element in the violation of the freedom of speech, was not found in this case. Furthermore, "the mere confirmation of a private arbitration award by a district court is insufficient state action to trigger the application".[329] Finally, the Judge concluded that the interim award made by the SIAC emergency arbitrator did not violate public policy in the United States. By entering into the agreement that included a choice of arbitration center and arbitration rules, Sharp was willing to be bound by the restrictions contained in the SIAC Arbitration Rules. In the SIAC Arbitration Rules 2016, it provides that "[t]he Emergency Arbitrator shall have the power to order or award any interim relief that he deems necessary".[330] Consequently, the interim award by the emergency arbitrator of the SIAC was binding and enforceable in the United States.

Regarding the court's jurisdiction to confirm an interim award made by an emergency arbitrator, in *T-Mobile USA Inc. v. Verity Wireless Inc.*,[331] the Court concluded that the interim order by an emergency arbitrator was final subject to confirmation, based on the consideration that "whether it provides temporary equitable relief that must be confirmed when granted to ensure that a final award may be meaningful—not whether the arbitrator who entered it was appointed on an emergency or permanent basis".[332] The judgment in *Thrivest Specialty Funding, LLC v. William E. White* adopted a similar reasoning,[333] because the relevant interim award was an interim order "calculated to preserve assets or performance needed to make a potential final award meaningful".[334] In *Rocky Mountain Biologicals, Inc., and Skyway Purified Solutions, Inc. v. Microbix Biosystems, Inc., and Irvine Scientific Sales Company,*

---

327 *TermoRio S.A.E.S.P. v. Electranta S.P.*, 487 F. 3d 928, 935 (United States Court of Appeals, District of Columbia Circuit, 2007); *Karaha Bodas Co. L.L.C. v. Perusahaan Pertambangan Minyak Dan Gas Bumi Negara*, 364 F. 3d 274, 305–306 (United States Court of Appeals, Fifth Circuit, 2004).

328 *Ministry of Def. & Support for the Armed Forces of the Islamic Republic of Iran v. Cubic Def. System, Inc.*, 665 F. 3d 1091, 1098 (United States Court of Appeals, Ninth Circuit, 2011).

329 *Davis v. Prudential Securities, Inc.*, 59 F. 3d 1186, 1192 (United States Court of Appeals, Eleventh Circuit, 1995).

330 Article 8 of Schedule 1, SIAC Arbitration Rules 2016.

331 *T-Mobile USA Inc. v. Verity Wireless Inc.*, No. 2:21-cv-00733-RAJ-BAT, 2021 WL 4,295,845 (United States District Court, W.D. Washington, 2021).

332 *T-Mobile USA Inc. v. Verity Wireless Inc.*, No. 2:21-cv-00733-RAJ-BAT, 2021 WL 4295845, 5 (United States District Court, W.D. Washington, 2021).

333 *Thrivest Specialty Funding, LLC v. William E. White*, 2019 WL 6124955 (United States District Court, E.D. Pennsylvania).

334 *Thrivest Specialty Funding, LLC v. William E. White*, 2019 WL 6124955, 1 (United States District Court, E.D. Pennsylvania); *Pacific Reinsurance Management Corp. v. Ohio Reinsurance Corp.*, 935 F. 2d 1019, 1023 (United States Court of Appeals, Ninth Circuit, 1991).

Inc.,[335] the Court agreed with the emergency arbitrator's opinion and upheld the Emergency Arbitration Order. An arbitration agreement "must be enforced notwithstanding the presence of other persons who are parties to the underlying dispute but not to the arbitration agreement".[336] The request to vacate the order rendered by the emergency arbitrator was, therefore, denied.

Regarding the possibility to seek interim measures from the emergency arbitrator mechanism, several U.S. courts referred to such an opportunity in arbitration. In *James Gold, et al. v. Michael Maurer*,[337] when analyzing the necessity to grant such an order, the Court pointed out correctly that there was an expedited procedure under the selected arbitration rules, namely the emergency arbitrator mechanism, to deal with the request. The Plaintiffs did not use their best efforts to seek interim measures by applying for the emergency arbitrator mechanism, which would only have taken one business day for the appointment. In the case of *Smart Technologies ULC v. Rapt Touch Ireland Ltd, et al.*,[338] while determining whether the Court was the proper forum to seek the interim measure, the Court ruled that there was an arbitration agreement allowing the parties to seek interim measures either from an arbitral tribunal or an emergency arbitrator. The procedure for the emergency arbitrator mechanism is fast and fair enough to provide parties with a neutral and impartial result. Additionally, the emergency arbitrator mechanism can offer procedures that are not available in courts but that can facilitate the arbitration procedure, such as the use of video conferencing. The only reason that the Plaintiff had was that a court would be more likely to offer the interim measures they were asking for. Therefore "it would not be a good reason for a federal court to get involved in a dispute whose merits both parties agree should be arbitrated".[339] The Court declined to exercise the judicial power to issue the interim measures requested by the Plaintiff.

3.2.3.3 Other Jurisdictions Showing Undetermined Views Regarding the Emergency Arbitrator Mechanism

The situation in the jurisdictions that generally allow an arbitral tribunal to grant interim measures but that do not expressly regulate the power of an emergency

[335] *Rocky Mountain Biologicals, Inc., and Skyway Purified Solutions, Inc. v. Microbix Biosystems, Inc., and Irvine Scientific Sales Company, Inc.*, 986 F. Supp. 2d. 1187 (United States District Court, D. Montana, Missoula Division, 2013).

[336] *Rocky Mountain Biologicals, Inc., and Skyway Purified Solutions, Inc. v. Microbix Biosystems, Inc., and Irvine Scientific Sales Company, Inc.*, 986 F. Supp. 2d. 1187, 1196 (United States District Court, D. Montana, Missoula Division, 2013); see also *Moses H. Cone Memorial Hosp v. Mercury Construction Corp.*, 460 U.S. 1, 20 (Supreme Court of the United States, 1983).

[337] *James Gold, et al. v. Michael Maurer*, 251 F. Supp. 3d 127 (United States District Court, District of Columbia, 2017).

[338] *Smart Technologies ULC v. Rapt Touch Ireland Ltd, et al.*, 197 F. Supp. 3d 1204 (United States District Court, N.D. California, 2016).

[339] *Smart Technologies ULC v. Rapt Touch Ireland Ltd, et al.*, 197 F. Supp. 3d 1204, 1206 (United States District Court, N.D. California, 2016).

arbitrator, is uncertain and controversial regarding the enforceability of the interim measures in emergency arbitration. The following section provides two examples of the recent practice concerning the emergency arbitrator mechanism.

In the British *Gerald Metals S.A. v. Timis & Ors* case,[340] Gerald Metals applied to the LCIA emergency arbitrator mechanism for interim measures. The application was rejected. According to the English Arbitration Act 1996, a state court has powers it may exercise in support of arbitral proceedings.[341] The court should act only when arbitral bodies have no power or are unable to render interim measures effectively.[342] Therefore, in the present case, the English High Court held that the refusal of the application was because the "LCIA was not persuaded that the application was so urgent that it needed to be decided before the arbitral tribunal".[343] Based on the facts and the applicable law, the case was dismissed by the Court.

In the Australian case, *Kaspersky Lab UK Ltd v. Hemisphere Technologies Pty Ltd,*[344] after determining that the Defendant's representatives had mistaken the test they had to satisfy before the emergency arbitrator, the Supreme Court New South Wales issued a short-term injunction to "maintain the *status quo* and to enable it to return to the Emergency Arbitrator".[345] The intention behind issuing the interim measure preserving the *status quo* was to allow the emergency arbitration to take place in the correct manner.

From the indicated practice, generally, the state courts in this category of jurisdictions have a positive attitude towards interim measures granted by the emergency arbitrator in the arbitral proceedings. Due to the discretion of different courts and a lack of statutes, legal uncertainty in relation to the enforceability of the interim measures rendered by an emergency arbitrator occurs from case to case. According to the above laws and practice, the essential elements to determine whether the interim measures granted by an emergency arbitrator can be enforced or not are focused on the power of the emergency arbitrator or the status of the emergency arbitrator, and "finality" of the interim measures.

---

[340] *Gerald Metals S.A. v. Timis & Ors*, No: HC-2016-002321, [2016] EWHC 2327 (CH) (High Court of Justice Chancery Division Commercial Court, 2016).

[341] Section 44, English Arbitration Act 1996, available at http://www.legislation.gov.uk/ukpga/1996/23/contents (1 June 2024).

[342] Section 44(5), English Arbitration Act 1996, available at http://www.legislation.gov.uk/ukpga/1996/23/contents (1 June 2024).

[343] *Gerald Metals S.A. v. Timis & Ors*, No: HC-2016-002321, [2016] EWHC 2327 (CH), para. 56 (High Court of Justice Chancery Division Commercial Court, 2016).

[344] *Kaspersky Lab UK Ltd v. Hemisphere Technologies Pty Ltd*, No. 2016/257298, [2016] NSWSC 1476 (Supreme Court New South Wales, 2016).

[345] *Kaspersky Lab UK Ltd v. Hemisphere Technologies Pty Ltd*, No. 2016/257298, [2016] NSWSC 1476, para. 26 (Supreme Court New South Wales, 2016).

3.3 Potential Barriers to the Enforcement of Interim Measures Granted by an Emergency Arbitrator

According to the above systematic comparison of current laws and practice in the application of the emergency arbitrator mechanism in different international conventions and jurisdictions, it was seen that, due to the various legal backgrounds and developments, the attitudes vary significantly. Fundamental principles, including due process, fair and equal treatment of parties, and other important aspects, arising from international treaties, have been respected in all these jurisdictions when dealing with the emergency arbitrator mechanism. However, they differ in the enforceability of interim measures made by an emergency arbitrator.

Some key elements affecting the enforceability of the interim measures granted by the emergency arbitrator are the status of the emergency arbitrator itself and the status of the interim measures that were granted. For recognition and enforcement, several conditions need to be satisfied, which are in common under international conventions and various jurisdictions.[346] Those conditions include that a) the decision-maker is an arbitrator; b) the issuance of interim measures, including the arbitrability of the subject matter, the jurisdiction of an emergency arbitrator over the claims, procedural fairness, and proper legal criteria, should be legitimate procedurally and substantively; and c) the decision needs to be binding on parties, and the recognition and enforcement of such a decision will not be contrary to public policy, which will be examined respectively in Chaps. 4, 5, and 6 to see whether the interim measures made by an emergency arbitrator can satisfy these prerequisites for enforceability.

It must be mentioned that there is no good or bad approach regarding the different legal approaches to the emergency arbitrator mechanism among the discussed jurisdictions, as long as a certain approach can meet the needs of parties in arbitration in that jurisdiction. On the other hand, the discussion also shows that the different approaches taken by jurisdictions can lead to conflicts, especially in international commercial arbitration when various jurisdictions may be involved in just one single dispute. This chapter intended to provide a comprehensive introduction to and discussion of the current situation and gave a background for a further consideration of a more unified practice in international commercial arbitration in Chap. 7.

---

[346] Gary B. Born (2021), *International Commercial Arbitration*, Kluwer Law International, p. 3760.

Chapter 4
Legal Status of an Emergency Arbitrator

Given the fact that the emergency arbitrator mechanism was introduced after most national arbitration laws and international conventions were drafted,[1] the legal status of an emergency arbitrator remains controversial and unsolved. It seems that the idea of the emergency arbitrator mechanism "has run ahead of the regulatory environment".[2] However, the status of an emergency arbitrator is crucial to determine the enforceability of the issued interim measures. This chapter aims to provide a theoretical background for the legal status of an emergency arbitrator. It starts with the legal status of an arbitrator, along with different legal theories (Sect. 4.1), and then addresses the question that whether an emergency arbitrator can be treated as a fully-fledged arbitrator (Sect. 4.2).

4.1 Legal Status of an Arbitrator

In order to determine whether an emergency arbitrator acts as a regular arbitrator, it is necessary to revert to examining the legal status of an arbitrator. However, "only rarely do arbitration laws define what an arbitrator or, more in general, arbitration is".[3] This subject causes "a measure of continuing uncertainty about the legal and conceptual basis"[4] for the arbitrators. This section firstly gives the current theories regarding the legal status of an arbitrator. Then, it addresses the source of authority of an arbitrator with the doctrine of party autonomy and the law governing arbitration.

[1] Jason Fry (2013), The Emergency Arbitrator—Flawed Fashion or Sensible Solution?, 7 *Dispute Resolution International* 187.

[2] Jason Fry (2013), The Emergency Arbitrator—Flawed Fashion or Sensible Solution?, 7 *Dispute Resolution International* 196.

[3] Fabio G. Santacroce (2015), The Emergency Arbitrator: A Full-Fledged Arbitrator Rendering An Enforceable Decision?, 31 *Arbitration International* 291.

[4] Gary B. Born (2021), *International Commercial Arbitration*, Kluwer Law International, p. 2107.

J. Zhang, *The Enforceability of the Interim Measures Granted by an Emergency Arbitrator in International Commercial Arbitration*,
https://doi.org/10.1007/978-981-97-6536-2_4

Finally, the key legal features of an arbitrator will be summarized for the following analysis of the legal status of an emergency arbitrator.

4.1.1 Different Theories Regarding the Legal Status of an Arbitrator

In the broadest sense, the determination of the legal status of an arbitrator can extend to all aspects of arbitral proceedings.[5] However, the status of an arbitrator "is not covered in any depth by the traditional sources of international arbitration law".[6] The position of an arbitrator is in accordance with the legal status of arbitration. This subsection examines four theories regarding the legal nature of arbitration to provide a theoretical background for the following discussion.

Essentially, "arbitration is an institution where individuals adjudicate privately on disputes and claims formulated by the parties" based on an arbitration agreement under relevant laws.[7] Regarding the nature of arbitration, there are generally four theories,[8] i.e., the jurisdictional theory, the contractual theory, the mixed theory, and the autonomous theory. No single theory has gained universal support,[9] and little academic agreement has been reached.[10] This debate is even called the "battle of theories".[11] Although it is suggested that the controversy surrounding the issue is

---

[5] Emmanuel Gaillard & John Savage (1999), *Fouchard Gaillard Goldman on International Commercial Arbitration*, Kluwer Law International, p. 557.

[6] Emmanuel Gaillard & John Savage (1999), *Fouchard Gaillard Goldman on International Commercial Arbitration*, Kluwer Law International, p. 557.

[7] Adam Samuel (1989), *Jurisdictional Problems in International Commercial Arbitration: A Study of Belgian, Dutch, English, French, Swedish, Swiss, US, and West German Law*, Schulthess Polygraphischer Verlag, p. 74.

[8] Gary B. Born (2021), *International Commercial Arbitration*, Kluwer Law International, p. 239; Stefan Michael Kröll, Julian D.M. Lew & Loukas A. Mistelis (2003), *Comparative International Commercial Arbitration*, Kluwer Law International, p. 72; Adam Samuel (1989), *Jurisdictional Problems in International Commercial Arbitration: A Study of Belgian, Dutch, English, French, Swedish, Swiss, US, and West German Law*, Schulthess Polygraphischer Verlag, p. 32.

[9] Stefan Michael Kröll, Julian D.M. Lew & Loukas A. Mistelis (2003), *Comparative International Commercial Arbitration*, Kluwer Law International, p. 72; Andrea Marco Steingruber (2009), Notion, Nature and Extent of Consent in International Arbitration, *PhD thesis of the Queen Mary University of London*, p. 72.

[10] Gary B. Born (2021), *International Commercial Arbitration*, Kluwer Law International, p. 239; Nadia Ramzy Salama (2015), Nature, Extent, and Role of Parties' Autonomy in the Making of International Commercial Arbitration Agreements, *PhD thesis of The University of Manchester*, p. 64.

[11] Mauro Rubino-Sammartano (2014), *International Arbitration: Law and Practice*, Juris, p. 11.

more or less an academic "tempest in a teapot",[12] the discussion can still bring light to a thorough understanding of arbitration and the emergency arbitrator mechanism.

The jurisdictional theory recognizes that "arbitration is essentially adjudicative, involving the exercise of independent, impartial decision-making by the arbitrators".[13] According to this theory, an arbitrator is considered as a "private judge",[14] acting in "a judicial temperament".[15] Initially, the discussion of the legal nature of arbitration was raised in a French case *Marquis de Santa Cristina et al. v. Princesse del Drago et al.*[16] The Paris Court of Appeal concluded that "a foreign arbitration award [is] equal or equivalent to a foreign judgment, highlighting the jurisdictional character of the award".[17] In the early twentieth century, French scholars demonstrated that the "activity performed by the arbitrators was that of judging",[18] and "the arbitral award was not a contract but rather a judgment".[19] They believed that, starting from once arbitrators are appointed, an arbitration agreement was "completely irrelevant",[20] as long as the arbitrators acted within the scope of the agreement. The jurisdictional

---

[12] Thomas E. Carbonneau (2003), *Cases and Materials on the Law and Practice of Arbitration*, Juris Publishing, p. 740; Stefan Michael Kröll, Julian D.M. Lew & Loukas A. Mistelis (2003), *Comparative International Commercial Arbitration*, Kluwer Law International, pp. 72–73.

[13] Gary B. Born (2021), *International Commercial Arbitration*, Kluwer Law International, p. 240; Nadia Ramzy Salama (2015), Nature, Extent, and Role of Parties' Autonomy in the Making of International Commercial Arbitration Agreements, *PhD thesis of The University of Manchester*, p. 64.

[14] Gary B. Born (2021), *International Commercial Arbitration*, Kluwer Law International, p. 240; Emmanuel Gaillard & John Savage (1999), *Fouchard Gaillard Goldman on International Commercial Arbitration*, Kluwer Law International, p. 586; see also Menno Aden (2015), Wrong Answers to Wrong Questions? A New Approach to Judicial Review of International Arbitral Awards, 12 *Revista Brasileira de Arbitragem* 63; Charles Jarrosson (1987), *La notion d'arbitrage*, Libr. générale de droit et de jurisprudence p. 101; Johannes Trappe (1998), The Arbitration Proceedings: Fundamental Principles and Rights of the Parties, 15 *Journal of International Arbitration* 96.

[15] Paul Eric Mason (2011), The Arbitrator as Mediator, and Mediator as Arbitrator, 28 *Journal of International Arbitration* 543.

[16] *Marquis de Santa Cristina et al. v. Princesse del Drago et al.*, 29 *Journal du Droit International Privé et de la Jurisprudence Comparée* 314 (Court of Appeal Paris, 1901); Mauro Rubino-Sammartano (2014), *International Arbitration: Law and Practice*, Juris, p. 11; Andrea Marco Steingruber (2009), Notion, Nature and Extent of Consent in International Arbitration, *PhD thesis of the Queen Mary University of London*, p. 73.

[17] Stefan Michael Kröll, Julian D.M. Lew & Loukas A. Mistelis (2003), *Comparative International Commercial Arbitration*, Kluwer Law International, p. 76.

[18] Andrea Marco Steingruber (2009), Notion, Nature and Extent of Consent in International Arbitration, *PhD thesis of the Queen Mary University of London*, p. 73; see also Armand Lainé (1899), De l'Execution en France des Sentences Arbitrales Entrangeres, 26 *Journal du Droit International Privé et de la Jurisprudence Comparée* 650–653.

[19] Andrea Marco Steingruber (2009), Notion, Nature and Extent of Consent in International Arbitration, *PhD thesis of the Queen Mary University of London*, p. 73; see also Armand Lainé (1899), De l'Execution en France des Sentences Arbitrales Entrangeres, 26 *Journal du Droit International Privé et de la Jurisprudence Comparée* 650–653.

[20] Andrea Marco Steingruber (2009), Notion, Nature and Extent of Consent in International Arbitration, *PhD thesis of the Queen Mary University of London*, p. 73; see also Antoine Pillet (1924), *Traité pratique de droit international privé*, Imprimerie J. Allier, p. 537.

theory highly values the importance of domestic laws, especially the *lex arbitri*, while putting more limits on party autonomy than the other theories.[21] In practice, the jurisdictional theory can be seen "in countries where arbitration institutions are attached to the national chambers of commerce and retain a close connection with the state",[22] for example, in Mainland China.[23] Such a theory can also be reflected in the requirement of the independence and impartiality of arbitrators and the due process in arbitral proceedings.

The contractual theory indicates that arbitration "has its origin in and depends, for its existence and continuity on the parties' agreement".[24] It is believed that an arbitration agreement creates the existence of arbitration and "the precise truth is that it is only the performance of the mandate that the parties have entrusted to the arbitrators; it is even, to put precisely, only an agreement to which the parties have bound themselves by the hands of the latter (the arbitrators)".[25] There are two types of contractual theories. The first considers that an arbitral award is a contract, which is concluded by "arbitrators as agents for the parties".[26] By doing so, the French *Roses v. Moller et Cie*[27] judgment put forward the ratio of the contractual theory. The Cour de Cassation held that "arbitral awards that are based on an arbitration agreement constitute a unit with it and share with its contractual nature".[28] However, this approach was challenged by the other version of the contractual theory. In the

[21] Gary B. Born (2021), *International Commercial Arbitration*, Kluwer Law International, p. 240; Frederick A Mann (1986), Lex Facit Arbitrum, 2 *Arbitration International* 244.

[22] Stefan Michael Kröll, Julian D.M. Lew & Loukas A. Mistelis (2003), *Comparative International Commercial Arbitration*, Kluwer Law International, pp. 76–77.

[23] Stefan Michael Kröll, Julian D.M. Lew & Loukas A. Mistelis (2003), *Comparative International Commercial Arbitration*, Kluwer Law International, p. 77.

[24] Stefan Michael Kröll, Julian D.M. Lew & Loukas A. Mistelis (2003), *Comparative International Commercial Arbitration*, Kluwer Law International, p. 77; see also Emmanuel Gaillard & John Savage (1999), *Fouchard Gaillard Goldman on International Commercial Arbitration*, Kluwer Law International, p. 29; Giorgio Balladore Pallieri (1935), L'arbitrage privé dans les rapports internationaux, 51 *Recueil des Cours* 316.

[25] Gary B. Born (2021), *International Commercial Arbitration*, Kluwer Law International, p. 240; Adam Samuel (1989), *Jurisdictional Problems in International Commercial Arbitration: A Study of Belgian, Dutch, English, French, Swedish, Swiss, US, and West German Law*, Schulthess Polygraphischer Verlag, p. 34.

[26] Adam Samuel (1989), *Jurisdictional Problems in International Commercial Arbitration: A Study of Belgian, Dutch, English, French, Swedish, Swiss, US, and West German Law*, Schulthess Polygraphischer Verlag, p. 34.

[27] *Roses v. Moller et Cie*, I Dalloz 25 (1938) (Cour de cassation, 1937), available in French at https://gallica.bnf.fr/ark:/12148/bpt6k5810054r/f34.image (1 June 2024).

[28] Mauro Rubino-Sammartano (2014), *International Arbitration: Law and Practice*, Juris, p. 61; Adam Samuel (1989), *Jurisdictional Problems in International Commercial Arbitration: A Study of Belgian, Dutch, English, French, Swedish, Swiss, US, and West German Law*, Schulthess Polygraphischer Verlag, p. 36.

other approach, the idea of the arbitrators as agents was abandoned.[29] Nevertheless, scholars supporting the second approach argued that "arbitration is still essentially private and/or contractual in nature, belonging to the law of obligations rather than that of civil procedure".[30] The contractual theory disregards the influence of national laws in the existing international commercial arbitration practice. Instead, it emphasizes "an illustration of freedom of contract and an almost unlimited party autonomy, *i.e.*, a private justice system".[31] According to this theory, "[a]n arbitrator is not dispensing justice by delegation of any state",[32] but "carries the jurisdictional authority of no particular state".[33]

Unsurprisingly, in addition to the jurisdictional and contractual theories, there is a mixed theory combining both elements of the contractual and jurisdictional nature.[34] By adopting the "dual nature" of arbitration, the mixed theory claims that "[a]n arbitration is from one perspective an exercise of private order—it is formed by private agreement, and the particular shape it takes is a result of conscious private choice",[35] meanwhile, "from another angle, it is an exercise in adjudication—resulting in an award that the force of the state makes obligatory on the litigants in much the same way as the judgment of a public tribunal".[36] The argument supporting the mixed theory dates back to 1952. It is argued that the practice of arbitration could not go beyond legal systems, that is to say, there have to be some laws that "determine the validity of submission to arbitration and the enforceability of the award".[37] Furthermore, it is also admitted that arbitration originated from parties' contracts, and the governing law depends primarily on the agreement.[38] Therefore, the contractual and

---

[29] Adam Samuel (1989), *Jurisdictional Problems in International Commercial Arbitration: A Study of Belgian, Dutch, English, French, Swedish, Swiss, US, and West German Law*, Schulthess Polygraphischer Verlag, p. 44.

[30] Adam Samuel (1989), *Jurisdictional Problems in International Commercial Arbitration: A Study of Belgian, Dutch, English, French, Swedish, Swiss, US, and West German Law*, Schulthess Polygraphischer Verlag, p. 40; Andrea Marco Steingruber (2009), Notion, Nature and Extent of Consent in International Arbitration, *PhD thesis of the Queen Mary University of London*, p. 76.

[31] Stefan Michael Kröll, Julian D.M. Lew & Loukas A. Mistelis (2003), *Comparative International Commercial Arbitration*, Kluwer Law International, p. 78.

[32] Georgios Petrochilos (2004), *Procedural Law in International Arbitration*, Oxford University Press on Demand, p. 25.

[33] Georgios Petrochilos (2004), *Procedural Law in International Arbitration*, Oxford University Press on Demand, p. 25.

[34] Gary B. Born (2021), *International Commercial Arbitration*, Kluwer Law International, p. 241; Kenneth S Carlston (1952), Theory of the Arbitration Process, 17 *Law and Contemporary Problems* 635.

[35] Alan Scott Rau (2005), The Culture of American Arbitration and the Lessons of ADR, 40 *Texas International Law Journal* 451.

[36] Alan Scott Rau (2005), The Culture of American Arbitration and the Lessons of ADR, 40 *Texas International Law Journal* 451.

[37] George Sauser-Hall (1952), L'arbitrage en droit international privé, 44-I *Annuaire de l'Institut de droit international* 469.

[38] George Sauser-Hall (1952), L'arbitrage en droit international privé, 44-I *Annuaire de l'Institut de droit international* 469.

jurisdictional elements are "indissolubly intertwined".[39] In practice, both contractual and jurisdictional elements are found in international commercial arbitration, and "a hybrid system exists de facto",[40] for example, in the "cohabitation"[41] of the New York Convention 1958 with the jurisdictional approach and in French law with the contractual approach.[42] The influence brought by the mixed theory is that it acknowledges "the strong, though not overwhelming connection"[43] between arbitration and the seat of arbitration.[44]

The autonomous theory, which was developed in 1965, is the most recent theory addressing the legal nature of arbitration. It states that the status of arbitration is "neither contractual, nor jurisdictional, nor hybrid, but autonomous".[45] The autonomous theory puts the focus on the structure of arbitration in its "social and economic context".[46] International commercial arbitration is favored by parties, because it can be "tailored for their particular needs".[47] In this regard, the emphasis needs to be on the use and purpose of arbitration and the fulfilment of parties' expectations.[48] The main argument for the autonomous theory is a distinctive element of arbitration: the user-oriented perspective, which is supported by a fundamental principle of arbitration, i.e. the party autonomy.[49] Compared to the mixed theory, the autonomous theory does not put much emphasis on the seat of arbitration and the *lex arbitri*. On

---

[39] George Sauser-Hall (1957), L'arbitrage en droit international privé, 47-II *Annuaire de l'Institut de droit international* 399.

[40] Stefan Michael Kröll, Julian D.M. Lew & Loukas A. Mistelis (2003), *Comparative International Commercial Arbitration*, Kluwer Law International, p. 80; Andrea Marco Steingruber (2009), Notion, Nature and Extent of Consent in International Arbitration, *PhD thesis of the Queen Mary University of London*, p. 79.

[41] Stefan Michael Kröll, Julian D.M. Lew & Loukas A. Mistelis (2003), *Comparative International Commercial Arbitration*, Kluwer Law International, p. 80.

[42] Andrea Marco Steingruber (2009), Notion, Nature and Extent of Consent in International Arbitration, *PhD thesis of the Queen Mary University of London*, p. 79.

[43] Stefan Michael Kröll, Julian D.M. Lew & Loukas A. Mistelis (2003), *Comparative International Commercial Arbitration*, Kluwer Law International, p. 80.

[44] Julian D. M. Lew (1978), *Applicable Law in International Commercial Arbitration*, Oceana Publications, para. 77.

[45] J. Rubellin-Devichi & Jean Vincent (1965), *L'arbitrage: Nature juridique; Droit interne et droit international privé*. Librairie générale de droit et de jurisprudence, p. 365.

[46] Andrea Marco Steingruber (2009), Notion, Nature and Extent of Consent in International Arbitration, *PhD thesis of the Queen Mary University of London*, p. 79; Adam Samuel (1989), *Jurisdictional Problems in International Commercial Arbitration: A Study of Belgian, Dutch, English, French, Swedish, Swiss, US, and West German Law*, Schulthess Polygraphischer Verlag, p. 67.

[47] Stefan Michael Kröll, Julian D.M. Lew & Loukas A. Mistelis (2003), *Comparative International Commercial Arbitration*, Kluwer Law International, p. 81.

[48] Nadia Ramzy Salama (2015), Nature, Extent, and Role of Parties' Autonomy in the Making of International Commercial Arbitration Agreements, *PhD thesis of The University of Manchester*, p. 66; see also J. Rubellin-Devichi & Jean Vincent (1965), *L'arbitrage: Nature juridique; Droit interne et droit international privé*. Librairie générale de droit et de jurisprudence, p. 18.

[49] Andrea Marco Steingruber (2009), Notion, Nature and Extent of Consent in International Arbitration, *PhD thesis of the Queen Mary University of London*, p. 82.

the contrary, it is "the intellectual foundation"[50] for the delocalization of arbitration and unlimited party autonomy.[51]

Admittedly, all four theories on the legal status of arbitration have elements that are "accurate and, in an abstract manner, useful".[52] However, they "ignore or at least do not fully accord with what happens in the real world of international commercial arbitration".[53] Maybe the discussion will never lead to a generally accepted answer to the legal status of arbitration, but the theories clarify the basic elements contained in the status of arbitration. In order to address the question, the other aspects, such as the social and economic role, must be considered. After all, "[w]hat do they know of arbitration who only arbitration know"?[54]

4.1.2 Source of an Arbitrator's Authority

The authority of an arbitrator is derived from an agreement by the parties and the relevant laws.[55] The hierarchy depends on different theories explaining the legal status of arbitration. To determine the legal status of an arbitrator, and thereby to determine the legal status of the emergency arbitrator, this subsection focuses on the source of authority on two grounds: the contractual ground, the doctrine of party autonomy, and the jurisdictional ground, the law governing arbitration.

4.1.2.1 The Contractual Ground—The Doctrine of Party Autonomy

Party autonomy enables parties to agree on the scope of rights and obligations, and how to resolve their disputes freely without intervention by judges.[56] It is not only essential to international trade as "a central principle of all aspects of private

---

[50] Levi Onyeisi Wilson Odoe (2014), Party Autonomy and Enforceability of Arbitration Agreement and Awards as the Basis of Arbitration, *PhD thesis of University of Leicester*, p. 66.

[51] Stefan Michael Kröll, Julian D.M. Lew & Loukas A. Mistelis (2003), *Comparative International Commercial Arbitration*, Kluwer Law International, p. 81.

[52] Gary B. Born (2021), *International Commercial Arbitration*, Kluwer Law International, p. 242.

[53] Stefan Michael Kröll, Julian D.M. Lew & Loukas A. Mistelis (2003), *Comparative International Commercial Arbitration*, Kluwer Law International, p. 73.

[54] Adam Samuel (1989), *Jurisdictional Problems in International Commercial Arbitration: A Study of Belgian, Dutch, English, French, Swedish, Swiss, US, and West German Law*, Schulthess Polygraphischer Verlag, p. 74.

[55] Sigvard Jarvin (1986), The Sources and Limits of the Arbitrator's Powers, 2 *Arbitration International* 140.

[56] Nadia Ramzy Salama (2015), Nature, Extent, and Role of Parties' Autonomy in the Making of International Commercial Arbitration Agreements, *PhD thesis of The University of Manchester*, p. 70.

international law",[57] but also one of the fundamental principles that "forms the basis and runs through most aspects of modern international arbitration".[58] Party autonomy gives "the underpinning for the power of the arbitrators"[59] in dispute settlement. Meanwhile, arbitrators' authority is limited to the scope of such an agreement.

Party autonomy has "particular significance" in international arbitration,[60] ensuring parties' freedom to arbitrate, to choose procedural and substantive laws, and all the other aspects of arbitral proceedings.[61] Substantial party autonomy enables parties to choose and decide on an arbitration process, which is "particularly important in international commercial arbitration because parties do not want to be subject to the jurisdiction of the other party's court system".[62] Party autonomy can be identified as either within a limited scope or in a more general way. In this book, party autonomy is used as "the autonomy of the parties to decide on all aspects of an international arbitration procedure, subject only to certain mandatory law",[63] instead of the autonomy to decide only on applicable laws.[64] This doctrine has been recognized by various international conventions as follows. Article V (1)(a) of the New York Convention 1958 guarantees party autonomy by providing it as "the primary rule"[65] on the grounds of refusing the recognition and enforcement of an award. Specifically, when an arbitration agreement is invalid under the law chosen by the parties, recognition and enforcement can be refused by state courts.[66] Article IV of the European Convention on International Commercial Arbitration 1960 precisely allows parties to an arbitration agreement to lay down the arbitral institution, the arbitration proceedings, the appointment of arbitrators, the place of arbitration, and the procedure to be followed by the arbitrators.[67] Article VII provides that the parties

[57] Celia Wasserstein Fassberg (2004), Lex Mercatoria—Hoist with Its Own Petard?, 5 *Chicago Journal of International Law* 77.

[58] Thomas H. Webster & Michael Bühler (2014), *Handbook of ICC Arbitration: Commentary, Precedents, Materials*, Sweet & Maxwell, p. 15.

[59] Margaret L. Moses (2017), *The Principles and Practice of International Commercial Arbitration*, Cambridge University Press, p. 2.

[60] Gary B. Born (2021), *International Commercial Arbitration*, Kluwer Law International, p. 82; Interim Award ICC Case No. 7929, XXV *Yearbook Commercial Arbitration* 317.

[61] Alan Redfern, Martin Hunter, Nigel Blackaby & Constantine Partasides (2004), *Law and Practice of International Commercial Arbitration*, Sweet & Maxwell, p. 315.

[62] Margaret L. Moses (2017), *The Principles and Practice of International Commercial Arbitration*, Cambridge University Press, p. 1.

[63] Karl-Heinz Bockstiegel (2010), The Role of Party Autonomy in International Commercial Arbitration, *American Arbitration Association Handbook on International Arbitration and ADR*, Juris, p. 67.

[64] Rachel Engle (2002), Party Autonomy in International Arbitration: Where Uniformity Gives Way to Predictability, 15 *The Transnational Lawyer* 335; Alan Redfern & J. Martin Hunter (2015), et al., *Redfern and Hunter on International Arbitration*, Oxford University Press, p. 187.

[65] Albert van den Berg (2008), The New York Convention of 1958: An Overview, in Emmanuel Gaillard & Domenico Di Pietro, *Enforcement of Arbitration Agreements and International Awards: The New York Convention in Practice*, Cameron May, p. 57.

[66] Article V (1)(a), the New York Convention 1958.

[67] Article IV (1), the European Convention on International Commercial Arbitration 1961.

"shall be free to determine, by agreement, the law to be applied by the arbitrators to the substance of the dispute".[68] Article 42 of the Convention on the Settlement of Investment Disputes between States and Nationals of Other States (the ICSID Convention) 1965[69] provides that the tribunal "shall decide a dispute in accordance with such rules of law as may be agreed by the parties".[70] Article 19 of the UNCITRAL Model Law 2006 states that "parties are free to agree on the procedure to be followed by the arbitral tribunal in conducting the proceedings".[71] Article 28 further regulates that an arbitral tribunal shall "decide the dispute in accordance with such rules of law as are chosen by the parties as applicable to the substance of the dispute".[72]

Unlimited party autonomy "echoes the fundamental substantive principle of freedom of contract",[73] indicating that "international arbitration is non-national and therefore, parties in a private contractual dispute should be free to select every element of their agreement"[74] without judicial intervention.[75] Such a perspective leads to a controversial theory of delocalization, which will be introduced later in this chapter.

An absolute right is, however, a myth. Criticism of the doctrine of party autonomy is not rare.[76] It is argued that arbitration shall not enjoy primacy over the law,[77] and no alternative dispute resolutions can have more power than state courts.[78] Meanwhile, arbitration is not a legal process in "an unregulated vacuum".[79] Various domestic legislation and case law regulate certain limitations in important aspects of the doctrine of party autonomy. Generally, the limitation of party autonomy is in the requirement of mandatory rules and public policy, which cannot be excluded in a contract. In the *American Diagnostica v. Gradipore* case, the Supreme Court of New

[68] Article VII (1), the European Convention on International Commercial Arbitration 1961.

[69] Convention on the Settlement of Investment Disputes between States and Nationals of Other States 1965, available at https://icsid.worldbank.org/en/Documents/icsiddocs/ICSID%20Convention%20English.pdf (1 June 2024).

[70] Article 42 (1), the ICSID Convention 1965.

[71] Article 19 (1), the UNCITRAL Model Law 2006.

[72] Article 28 (1), the UNCITRAL Model Law 2006.

[73] Friedrich K. Juenger (2000), Conflict of Laws, Comparative Law and Civil Law: The Lex Mercatoria and Private International Law, 60 *Louisiana Law Review* 1141.

[74] Rachel Engle (2002), Party Autonomy in International Arbitration: Where Uniformity Gives Way to Predictability, 15 *The Transnational Lawyer* 335.

[75] Jay R. Sever (1991), Comment, The Relaxation of Inarbitrability and Public Policy Checks on U.S. and Foreign Arbitration: Arbitration Out of Control?, 65 *Tulane Law Review* 1689.

[76] Marta Pertegás & Brooke Adele Marshall (2014), Party Autonomy and Its Limits: Convergence through the New Hague Principles on Choice of Law in International Commercial Contracts, 39 *Brooklyn Journal of International Law* 976.

[77] Jay R. Sever (1991), Comment, The Relaxation of Inarbitrability and Public Policy Checks on U.S. and Foreign Arbitration: Arbitration Out of Control?, 65 *Tulane Law Review* 1694.

[78] Jay R. Sever (1991), Comment, The Relaxation of Inarbitrability and Public Policy Checks on U.S. and Foreign Arbitration: Arbitration Out of Control?, 65 *Tulane Law Review* 1697.

[79] Franz Schwarz (2010), Limits of Party Autonomy in International Commercial Arbitration, in Christina Knahr, Christian Koller, Walter Rechberger & August Reinisch (eds), *Investment and Commercial Arbitration—Similarities and Divergences*, Eleven International Publishing, p. 73.

South Wales in Australia held that "[i]n principle, party autonomy does not mean complete freedom to exclude a system of law, or particular elements of a system of law, from the relationship between the parties".[80] Another example is the *Vita Food Products Inc. Unus Shipping Company Limited* case,[81] in which the Privy Council held that the choice by the parties should be "*bona fide* and legal".[82] Additionally, for the judicial supervision, recognition, and enforcement of arbitral awards, the assistance of state courts is inevitable.[83] The agreement reached by parties will be futile if it cannot be subsequently enforced by state courts.[84]

Certain limitations are also regulated in these legal documents. Article V of the New York Convention 1958 limits party autonomy by regulating the grounds to refuse the recognition and enforcement of arbitral awards. If a competent authority in one state finds that "[t]he subject matter of the difference is not capable of settlement by arbitration under the law of that country",[85] or the arbitral awards "would be contrary to the public policy of that country",[86] it can refuse to recognize and enforce such an award. Article VI of the European Convention on International Commercial Arbitration 1960 grants the power to the contracting states to examine the validity of arbitration agreements under the applicable law.[87] When an arbitration agreement is not valid under the applicable law, the contracting states can refuse recognition and enforcement.[88] Article 34 of the UNCITRAL Model Law 2006 provides that an arbitral award can be set aside by state courts if the "agreement is not valid under the law to which the parties have subjected it"[89] and if the composition of a tribunal or an arbitral procedure agreed by the parties is not accordance with the content of the UNCITRAL Model Law 2006 from which the parties cannot derogate.[90] Meanwhile, the state court can also refuse the arbitral award if "the subject-matter of the dispute is not capable of settlement by arbitration under the law of this State"[91] or "the award is in conflict with the public policy of this State".[92] Article 36 provides the grounds

---

[80] *American Diagnostica v. Gradipore*, 44 N.S.W.L.R. 312, 328 (Supreme Court of New South Wales, 1998).

[81] *Vita Food Products Inc. Unus Shipping Company. Limited*, [1939] UKPC 7 (Judicial Committee of the Privy Council, 1939).

[82] *Vita Food Products Inc. Unus Shipping Company. Limited*, [1939] UKPC 7, para.12 (Judicial Committee of the Privy Council, 1939).

[83] Levi Onyeisi Wilson Odoe (2014), Party Autonomy and Enforceability of Arbitration Agreement and Awards as the Basis of Arbitration, *PhD thesis of University of Leicester*, p. 78.

[84] Mia Louise Livingstone (2008), Party Autonomy in International Commercial Arbitration: Popular Fallacy or Proven Fact?, *25 Journal of International Arbitration* 531.

[85] Article V (2)(a), the New York Convention 1958.

[86] Article V (2)(b), the New York Convention 1958.

[87] Article VI (2), the European Convention on International Commercial Arbitration 1961.

[88] Article VI (2) & Article IX (1) (a), the European Convention on International Commercial Arbitration 1961.

[89] Article 34 (2)(a)(i), the UNCITRAL Model Law 2006.

[90] Article 34 (2)(a)(iv), the UNCITRAL Model Law 2006.

[91] Article 34 (2)(b)(i), the UNCITRAL Model Law 2006.

[92] Article 34 (2)(b)(ii), the UNCITRAL Model Law 2006.

to refuse recognition and enforcement. The state courts can deny the application of recognition and enforcement when "the said agreement is not valid under the law to which the parties have subjected it".[93] The state courts can also refuse the recognition and enforcement of arbitral awards based on arbitrability[94] and the public policy of that state.[95] The limitation of party autonomy is clear in the ICSID Convention 1965. The parties "may not deviate from the provisions of the ICSID Convention itself and may modify the procedural provisions of the Convention only where this is expressly authorized".[96]

The doctrine of party autonomy indicates that parties are the best candidates to access and decide on the procedure of arbitration which most suits their interests.[97] Based on this, parties can agree on the customization of arbitral procedures,[98] for example, the seat of arbitration, the language of arbitration, and the applicable law. It is the agreement between parties that vests authority in an arbitrator to settle disputes. That is to say, "the authority of an arbitrator stems from a contract".[99] Party autonomy plays a central role in determining an arbitrator's authority. Therefore, the legal status of an arbitrator certainly includes a significant contractual element.

4.1.2.2 The Jurisdictional Ground—The Law Governing Arbitration

An arbitrator may exercise the authority conferred upon him/her by the parties and also with the additional power conferred upon him/her by the *lex arbitri*.[100] National laws are not the only source that governs the fundamental question of arbitrability, but they are also the source of various forms of arbitral conduct. Although the doctrine of party autonomy is predominant in international commercial arbitration, dispute resolution "does not exist in a legal vacuum".[101] International commercial arbitration is based on the consent of parties and "it has binding effect only by virtue of complex

---

[93] Article 36 (1)(a)(i), the UNCITRAL Model Law 2006.

[94] Article 36 (1)(b)(i), the UNCITRAL Model Law 2006.

[95] Article 36 (1)(b)(ii), the UNCITRAL Model Law 2006.

[96] Stephan Wittich (2010), The Limits of Party Autonomy in Investment Arbitration, in Christina Knahr, Christian Koller, Walter Rechberger & August Reinisch (eds), *Investment and Commercial Arbitration—Similarities and Divergences*, Eleven International Publishing, p. 58.

[97] Franz Schwarz (2010), Limits of Party Autonomy in International Commercial Arbitration, in Christina Knahr, Christian Koller, Walter Rechberger & August Reinisch (eds), *Investment and Commercial Arbitration—Similarities and Divergences*, Eleven International Publishing, p. 75.

[98] Franz Schwarz (2010), Limits of Party Autonomy in International Commercial Arbitration, in Christina Knahr, Christian Koller, Walter Rechberger & August Reinisch (eds), *Investment and Commercial Arbitration—Similarities and Divergences*, Eleven International Publishing, p. 75.

[99] Fabio G. Santacroce (2015), The Emergency Arbitrator: A Full-Fledged Arbitrator Rendering An Enforceable Decision?, 31 *Arbitration International* 291.

[100] Alan Redfern & J. Martin Hunter (2015), et al., *Redfern and Hunter on International Arbitration*, Oxford University Press, p. 18.

[101] Margaret L. Moses (2017), *The Principles and Practice of International Commercial Arbitration*, Cambridge University Press, p. 63.

framework of national and international law".[102] The law applicable to the arbitration agreement, the law applicable to the contract, the law applicable to the arbitration, other applicable laws or guidelines of arbitration (soft law), and the law governing the recognition and enforcement of awards are included in this framework of national and international law.[103] Generally, domestic laws regulate the behavior of an arbitrator in two ways.[104] One way is to decide the validity of an arbitration agreement and the arbitrability of the subject matter. The other way is by regulating the mandatory rules of arbitral procedures. Meanwhile, arbitrators need to make "every effort to make sure that the award is enforceable at law".[105] These issues are all linked to the law of the seat of arbitration.

Law Governing Arbitral Proceedings

The jurisdictional source of an arbitrator's power, including the division of powers between arbitrators and judges to render interim measures,[106] is commonly referred to as the *lex arbitri*. When parties choose the seat of arbitration in a particular location, their intention generally is that "the arbitration is conducted within the framework of the law of arbitration of (that location)".[107] In this case, the *lex arbitri* is "almost always the law of the place of arbitration".[108] Parties can always choose another legal system to govern arbitral proceedings. The *lex arbitri* "provides a mandatory legal framework applicable to the conduct of the arbitral proceedings, and to the form, notification, correction, and annulment of an arbitral award".[109] Every state decides for itself on the laws governing arbitral proceedings, including the mandatory laws. However, the *lex arbitri* is not purely procedural law.[110]

At the early stage of arbitration, the *lex arbitri* is relevant in order to determine the validity of an arbitration agreement and the arbitrability of a certain dispute under

---

[102] Gary B. Born (2001), *International Commercial Arbitration: Commentary and Materials*, Kluwer Law International, p. 3.

[103] Alan Redfern & J. Martin Hunter (2015), et al., *Redfern and Hunter on International Arbitration*, Oxford University Press, p. 157.

[104] Sigvard Jarvin (1986), The Sources and Limits of the Arbitrator's Powers, 2 *Arbitration International* 149.

[105] Article 42, ICC Arbitration Rules 2017; Margaret L. Moses (2017), *The Principles and Practice of International Commercial Arbitration*, Cambridge University Press, p. 88.

[106] Raymond J. Werbicki (2010), Arbitral Interim Measures: Fact or Fiction?, in *American Arbitration Association Handbook on International Arbitration and ADR*, Juris Publishing, p. 95.

[107] Jeffrey Waincymer (2012), *Procedure and Evidence in International Arbitration*, Kluwer Law International, p. 67; Claude Reymond (1992), Where Is an Arbitral Award Made?, 108 *Law Quarterly Review* 3.

[108] Margaret L. Moses (2017), *The Principles and Practice of International Commercial Arbitration*, Cambridge University Press, p. 73.

[109] Gary B. Born (2021), *International Commercial Arbitration*, Kluwer Law International, p. 371.

[110] Alan Redfern & J. Martin Hunter (2015), et al., *Redfern and Hunter on International Arbitration*, Oxford University Press, p. 175.

domestic laws. Generally, there are two types of arbitration agreements serving a similar purpose. One is an arbitration clause in a contract for future disputes and the other one is a submission agreement for existing disputes.[111] An arbitration agreement between parties is the primary representation of party autonomy and "a basic source of the powers of the arbitral tribunal".[112] Meanwhile, an arbitration agreement also establishes an obligation for the parties and the jurisdiction of arbitrators.[113] The governing law is significant to an arbitration agreement, since the different laws may affect the validity, the arbitrability and the interpretation of a particular arbitration agreement,[114] which may extend or limit the scope of party autonomy.

The doctrine of separability demonstrates "the arbitration clause in a main contract as a separate contract, independent and distinct from the main contract".[115] Although an arbitration clause is a part of a contract, due to the doctrine of separability, the governing law of the arbitration agreement may not be the same as the applicable law of the contract. Most likely, if parties do not choose a specific law governing their arbitration agreement, the applicable law would either be the *lex arbitri* or the law governing the substance.[116] The law governing the substance is another important issue in international commercial arbitration, which, however, is not the main focus and will not be discussed in depth in this book.

During arbitral proceedings, the *lex arbitri* plays an essential role in regulating the conduct of arbitrators. The *lex arbitri* normally gives broad guidance to the arbitrators and parties in both internal and external procedural issues. Internal issues concern the conduct of arbitral proceedings. There is one distinction that needs to be made, especially in this book, between the procedural law governing arbitration and the procedures in arbitral proceedings. The latter can be "adopted consensually by the parties (subject to any mandatory provisions of the *lex arbitri*) to govern the conduct of the arbitration".[117] In most jurisdictions, internal issues only cover general requirements of arbitral proceedings, for example, independence and impartiality of arbitrators, the requirement of fairness and due process. In some jurisdictions, internal

---

[111] Emmanuel Gaillard & John Savage (1999), *Fouchard Gaillard Goldman on International Commercial Arbitration*, Kluwer Law International, p. 193.

[112] Alan Redfern & J. Martin Hunter (2015), et al., *Redfern and Hunter on International Arbitration*, Oxford University Press, p. 17.

[113] Julian Lew (1999), The Law Applicable to the Form and Substance of the Arbitration Clause, 9 *ICCA Congress Series* 114.

[114] Marc Blessing (1998), The law applicable to the arbitration clause, *ICC Congress Series No. 9, Improving the Efficiency of Arbitration Agreements and Awards: 40 Years of Application of the New York Convention*, Kluwer Law International, pp. 169–171.

[115] Stefan Michael Kröll, Julian D.M. Lew & Loukas A. Mistelis (2003), *Comparative International Commercial Arbitration*, Kluwer Law International, p. 102; Adam Samuel, Separability of Arbitration Clauses-Some Awkward Questions about the Law on Contracts, Conflict of Laws and the Administration of Justice, p. 1, available at http://www.adamsamuel.com/separabi.pdf (16 June 2020).

[116] Margaret L. Moses (2017), *The Principles and Practice of International Commercial Arbitration*, Cambridge University Press, p. 74.

[117] *Cargill International SA v. Peabody Australia Mining Ltd*, [2010] NSWSC 887 (New South Wales Supreme Court, 210), para. 84.

issues can be more specific; for example, requirement for the language used, and time limits.

External procedural issues deal with the relationship between arbitral proceedings and state courts in that seat of arbitration. These issues[118] may relate to the determination of an arbitrator's jurisdiction, the challenge of arbitrators, judicial assistance in interim measures, evidence, and the judicial review of arbitral awards. Most jurisdictions regulate those external arbitral procedural issues differently. For example, some jurisdictions grant exclusive power to state courts to issue interim measures. The diversity of the *lex arbitri* implies a "unique, and sometimes critical"[119] role of the seat of arbitration.

Lastly, at the final stage of arbitration, an arbitral award may be set aside due to a violation of mandatory laws and public policy. For example, the New York Convention 1958 stipulates that recognition and enforcement may be refused if "[t]he composition of the arbitral authority or the arbitral procedure was not in accordance with the agreement of the parties, or failing such agreement, was not in accordance with the law of the country where the arbitration took place".[120] The reason for the refusal of recognition and enforcement can also because the arbitral award "would be contrary to the public policy of that country".[121]

There is a possibility for parties to choose a different foreign procedural law to govern arbitration, regardless of the seat of the arbitration. In this situation, the foreign procedural law "will not ordinarily supplant, but rather operate within, the arbitration legislation of the arbitral seat, which remains mandatorily applicable".[122]

Theory of Delocalization

In the 1960s, the theory of delocalization was advocated in international arbitration.[123] Delocalization refers to "stateless", "floating", or "a-national" arbitration.[124] This theory argues that there should be no seat in international arbitration and that international arbitration should be detached from the state of origin.[125] The primary

---

[118] Gary B. Born (2021), *International Commercial Arbitration*, Kluwer Law International, p. 1652.

[119] Gary B. Born (2021), *International Commercial Arbitration*, Kluwer Law International, p. 1653.

[120] Article V (1)(d), the New York Convention 1958.

[121] Article V (2)(b), the New York Convention 1958.

[122] Gary B. Born (2021), *International Commercial Arbitration*, Kluwer Law International, p. 1727.

[123] Renata Brazil-David (2011), Harmonization and Delocalization of International Commercial Arbitration, 28 *Journal of International Arbitration* 454.

[124] Margaret L. Moses (2017), *The Principles and Practice of International Commercial Arbitration*, Cambridge University Press, p. 64; Hans Smit (1989), A-national Arbitration, 63 *Tulane Law Review*.

[125] Renata Brazil-David (2011), Harmonization and Delocalization of International Commercial Arbitration, 28 *Journal of International Arbitration* 454; Alexander J. Belohlavek (2013), Importance of the Seat of Arbitration in International Arbitration: Delocalization and Denationalization of Arbitration as an Outdated Myth, 31 *ASA Bulletin* 269; Margaret L. Moses (2017), *The Principles and Practice of International Commercial Arbitration*, Cambridge University Press, p. 64.

concern of delocalization is the observation that parties who choose a particular state as the seat of arbitration may do so for convenience or neutrality and not with the intention of being bound by the local arbitration laws.[126] In that case, the local authority may "impede the effectiveness of the arbitration proceedings"[127] and the "hopes for a more open and more universal system of international arbitration would be disappointed".[128]

The supporting practice of delocalization comes from case law in France and the United States. French courts have been known for their "traditionally liberal, or laissez faire" approach.[129] One of the first cases to uphold the theory of delocalization was *General National Maritime Transport Company v. Société Gotaverken Arendal A.B.*[130] in 1980. The Paris Court of Appeal ruled that, in view of the very clear Article 11 of the ICC Rules 1975,[131] which reflected full acceptance of party autonomy, the place of arbitration was chosen only to guarantee neutrality, was not significant and that the choice could not be regarded as an implicit expression, even "subsidiary"[132] to apply the French procedural law.[133]

In 1996, the landmark[134] U.S. case *Chromalloy Aeroservices v. The Arab Republic Egypt*[135] followed the trend of delocalization of international arbitration by upholding

[126] Pippa Read (1999), Delocalization of International Commercial Arbitration: Its Relevance in the New Millennium, 10 *American Review of International Arbitration* 177.

[127] Margaret L. Moses (2017), *The Principles and Practice of International Commercial Arbitration*, Cambridge University Press, p. 64.

[128] Jan Paulsson (1983), Delocalization of International Commercial Arbitration: When and Why It Matters, 32 *International and Comparative Law Quarterly* 55.

[129] Renata Brazil-David (2011), Harmonization and Delocalization of International Commercial Arbitration, 28 *Journal of International Arbitration* 455.

[130] *General National Maritime Transport Company v. Société Gotaverken Arendal A.B.*, 20 I.L.M. 884 (Paris Court of Appeal, 1980), available at http://newyorkconvention1958.org/index.php?lvl=notice_display&id=111 (1 June 2024); Jan Paulsson (1981), Arbitration Unbound: Award Detached from the Law of Its Country of Origin, 30 *International and Comparative Law Quarterly* 385.

[131] Article 11 of the ICC Arbitration Rules 1975: "[t]he rules governing the proceedings before the arbitrator shall be those resulting from these Rules and, where these Rules are silent, any rules which the parties (or, failing them, the arbitrator) may settle, and a whether or not reference is thereby made to a municipal procedural law to be applied to the arbitration".

[132] Jan Paulsson (1981), Arbitration Unbound: Award Detached from the Law of Its Country of Origin, 30 *International and Comparative Law Quarterly* 386.

[133] *General National Maritime Transport Company v. Société Gotaverken Arendal A.B*, 20 I.L.M. 884, 885–886 (Paris Court of Appeal, 1980), available at http://newyorkconvention1958.org/index.php?lvl=notice_display&id=111 (1 June 2024); Jan Paulsson (1981), Arbitration Unbound: Award Detached from the Law of Its Country of Origin, 30 *International and Comparative Law Quarterly* 386; Renata Brazil-David (2011), Harmonization and Delocalization of International Commercial Arbitration, 28 *Journal of International Arbitration* 454; Pippa Read (1999), Delocalization of International Commercial Arbitration: Its Relevance in the New Millennium, 10 *American Review of International Arbitration* 186.

[134] Renata Brazil-David (2011), Harmonization and Delocalization of International Commercial Arbitration, 28 *Journal of International Arbitration* 461.

[135] *Chromalloy Aeroservices v. The Arab Republic Egypt*, 939 F. Supp. 907 (United State District Court, District of Columbia, 1996).

the validity of a foreign arbitral award which had been rejected by the Egyptian Court of Appeal based on Article V (1)(e) and Article VII of the New York Convention 1958.[136] It was the first time that the United States courts addressed the delocalization issue.[137] With "competing presumptions" under the U.S. law favoring both foreign judgments and arbitral awards, the United States District Court of Columbia chose to support the arbitral award in this case.[138] However, later cases in the United States did not follow this approach. In *Baker Marine (Nig.) Ltd v. Chevron (Nig.) Ltd and Chevron Corp., Inc.,*[139] and *Martin I. Spier v. Calzaturificio Tecnica S.p.A.,*[140] both the Second Circuit Court and the District Court of New York distinguished the facts and emphasized that the decision in *Chromalloy Aeroservices v. the Arab Republic Egypt* was a "special case".[141] Academic criticism indicates that the *Chromalloy* decision increases the unpredictability and legal uncertainty of international arbitration, which is not a desirable result.[142]

In the past years, Belgium adopted a very high level of delocalization in the Act of March 27, 1985 supplementing the Belgian Judicial Code.[143] In the Act of 1985, Article 1717 (4) of the Belgian Judicial Code provides that the "Belgian courts can take cognizance of an application to set aside only if at least one of the parties to the dispute decided in the arbitral award is either a physical person having Belgian nationality or residing in Belgium or a legal person formed in Belgium or having a branch or some seat of operation in Belgium",[144] meaning "Belgian law offered no possibilities to apply to set aside the award in Belgium unless a party had Belgian

[136] *Chromalloy Aeroservices v. The Arab Republic Egypt*, 939 F. Supp. 907, 914 (United State District Court, District of Columbia, 1996).

[137] Stephen T. Ostrowski & Shany Yuval (1998), Chromalloy: United States Law and International Arbitration at the Crossroads, 73 *New York University Law Review* 1653.

[138] Stephen T. Ostrowski & Shany Yuval (1998), Chromalloy: United States Law and International Arbitration at the Crossroads, 73 *New York University Law Review* 1653.

[139] *Baker Marine (Nig.) Ltd v. Chevron (Nig.) Ltd and Chevron Corp., Inc.*, 191 F. 3d 194 (United States Court of Appeals, Second Circuit, 1999).

[140] *Martin I. Spier v. Calzaturificio Tecnica S.p.A.*, 71 F. Supp. 2d 279 (United States District Court, S.D. New York, 1999).

[141] *Martin I. Spier v. Calzaturificio Tecnica S.p.A.*, 71 F. Supp. 2d 279, 288 (United States District Court, S.D. New York, 1999).

[142] Carbonneau, Thomas E., Carbonneau on International Arbitration: Collected Essays, Juris Publishing, 2011, pp. 329–330; Thomas E. Carbonneau (2003), *Cases and Materials on the Law and Practice of Arbitration*, Juris Publishing, pp. 831–834; Ray Y. Chan (1999), The Enforceability of Annulled Foreign Arbitral Awards in the United States: A Critique of Chromalloy, 17 *Boston University International Law Journal*; Marc J Goldstein (2014), Annulled Awards in the US Courts: How Primary Is" Primary Jurisdiction"?, 25 *American Review of International Arbitration*; Philipp Wahl (1999), Enforcement of Foreign Arbitral Awards Set Aside in their Country of Origin: The Chromalloy Case Revisited, 16 *Journal of International Arbitration* 140.

[143] Alexander J. Belohlavek (2013), Importance of the Seat of Arbitration in International Arbitration: Delocalization and Denationalization of Arbitration as an Outdated Myth, 31 *ASA Bulletin* 269.

[144] Article 1717(4), the Belgian Judicial Code 1985, available at https://www.ejustice.just.fgov.be/cgi_loi/arch_a.pl (1 June 2024).

nationality or resided in Belgium".[145] However, instead of the original intent of increasing the arbitration practice in Belgium, the provision seemed to deter and discourage parties from choosing Belgium as the seat of arbitration.[146]

Consequently, Belgium amended the provisions in 1998 providing that "[t]he parties may, by an explicit declaration in the arbitration agreement or by a later agreement, exclude any application for the setting aside of an arbitral award, in case none of them is a physical person of Belgian nationality or a physical person having his normal residence in Belgium or a legal person having its main seat or a branch office in Belgium".[147] The Belgian experience suggests that "parties are not very interested in completely delocalized arbitrations, and that they prefer having the possibility of court supervision at the place of arbitration".[148]

It should also be noted that new types of arbitration may restart the debate on delocalization, such as online arbitration and sports arbitration.[149] However, in the current stage of international commercial arbitration, the *lex arbitri* still plays a significant and central role in arbitral proceedings; "even ardent proponents of 'a-national' or 'delocalized' arbitrations regard the possibility of a delocalized award as exceptional".[150] Nevertheless, arbitrators always try to comply with the mandatory rules of the seat of arbitration.[151]

---

[145] Alan Redfern, Martin Hunter, Nigel Blackaby & Constantine Partasides (2004), *Law and Practice of International Commercial Arbitration*, Sweet & Maxwell, p. 329; see also Bernard Hanotiau & Guy Block (1999), The Law of 19 May 1988 amending Belgian Arbitration Legislation, 15 *Arbitration International* 97.

[146] Alan Redfern & J. Martin Hunter (2015), et al., *Redfern and Hunter on International Arbitration*, Oxford University Press, p. 183; see also Hossein Abedian (2011), Judicial Review of Arbitral Awards in International Arbitration: A Case of an Efficient System of Judicial Review, 28 *Journal of International Arbitration* 600; Alexander J. Belohlavek (2013), Importance of the Seat of Arbitration in International Arbitration: Delocalization and Denationalization of Arbitration as an Outdated Myth, 31 *ASA Bulletin* 270.

[147] Article 1717(4), the Belgian Judicial Code 1998, available at https://www.ejustice.just.fgov.be/cgi_loi/arch_a.pl?=&sql=(text+contains+(%27%27))&language=fr&rech=1&tri=dd+AS+RANK&numero=1&table_name=loi&F=&cn=1967101006&caller=archive&fromtab=loi&la=F&ver_arch=003 (1 June 2024).

[148] Margaret L. Moses (2017), *The Principles and Practice of International Commercial Arbitration*, Cambridge University Press, p. 65.

[149] See more in Bas van Zelst (2018), The End of Justice(s): Perspectives and Thoughts on Automation in Dispute Resolution, Inaugural Lecture at Maastricht University, available at https://pdfs.semanticscholar.org/a321/e1245440c3786790303aa0e21e6740ddc930.pdf (1 June 2024).

[150] Gary B. Born (2021), *International Commercial Arbitration*, Kluwer Law International, p. 1719.

[151] Georgios Petrochilos (2004), *Procedural Law in International Arbitration*, Oxford University Press on Demand, p. 169.

Jurisdictional Status of an Arbitrator

The *lex arbitri* plays a "vitally-important"[152] role in international commercial arbitration, providing "a mandatory, essentially territorial legal framework for international arbitral proceedings"[153] comparable to that of the *lex fori*. Although arbitration is a private dispute resolution method, it provides for the settlement of disputes with the possibility of enforcement. It is stated that "an arbitrator's right to deal with the adjudication of the dispute exists only to the extent that various states will recognize the validity of the arbitration and assist in the enforceability of arbitral award".[154] Ultimately, a decision made by arbitrators is binding and has the same effect as a judgment from state courts.[155] The judicial character of arbitration differs from other mechanisms,[156] for example, conciliation and mediation.

The *lex arbitri*, to some extent, limits the power conferred on an arbitrator by the parties with various mandatory rules and public policy, but meanwhile it provides for the legitimacy of arbitration. With the previous discussion in this part concerning the law governing arbitration, it points to the nature of an arbitrator having a jurisdictional element.

4.1.3 Definition of an Arbitrator

Various definitions of an arbitrator can be drawn upon considering the different views and theories within international arbitration. Nevertheless, a common core is widely accepted.[157] Arbitration is "a process by which parties consensually submit a dispute to a non-governmental decision-maker, selected by or for the parties, who renders a binding decision finally resolving the dispute in accordance with neutral, adjudicative procedures affording the parties an opportunity to be heard".[158] An arbitrator is that decision maker.

The authority of an arbitrator consists of party autonomy, which includes a contractual element and an adjudicatory function within a certain jurisdiction. A proper

---

[152] Gary B. Born (2021), *International Commercial Arbitration*, Kluwer Law International, p. 1657; *Star Shipping AG v. China National Foreign Trade Transportation Corp* (The Star Texas), 2 Lloyd's Rep. 445, 452 (Court of Appeal, Civil Division, 1993).

[153] Gary B. Born (2021), *International Commercial Arbitration*, Kluwer Law International, p. 1659.

[154] Bernard G. Poznanzki (1987), The Nature and Extent of an Arbitrator's Power in International Commercial Arbitration, 4 *Journal of International Arbitration* 71.

[155] Emmanuel Gaillard & John Savage (1999), *Fouchard Gaillard Goldman on International Commercial Arbitration*, Kluwer Law International, p. 12.

[156] Emmanuel Gaillard & John Savage (1999), *Fouchard Gaillard Goldman on International Commercial Arbitration*, Kluwer Law International, p. 12.

[157] Gary B. Born (2021), *International Commercial Arbitration*, Kluwer Law International, p. 318.

[158] Gary B. Born (2021), *International Commercial Arbitration*, Kluwer Law International, p. 318; Kah Cheong Lye, Chuan Tat Yeo & William Miller (2011), Legal Status of the Emergency Arbitrator under the SIAC 2010 Rules, 23 *Singapore Academy of Law Journal* 103.

functioning arbitrator is subject to these two connected elements at the same time.[159] In the following section, the legal status of an emergency arbitrator will be examined based on this observation.

4.2 Legal Status of an Emergency Arbitrator

Regardless of the jurisdictions that support the emergency arbitrator mechanism, under most national arbitration laws and all international conventions or instruments, there is no provision elaborating on the legal status of the emergency arbitrator. This situation makes the legal status of the emergency arbitrator controversial. This part of the book aims to determine the status of the emergency arbitrator by comparing and analyzing its contractual and jurisdictional nature.

4.2.1 Contractual Nature of an Emergency Arbitrator

The contractual characteristic of an emergency arbitrator is easier to identify compared to its jurisdictional features. Parties are free to agree to opt out the emergency arbitrator provisions[160] included in the arbitral rules according to party autonomy. The agreement by the parties is the foundation for the conduct of an emergency arbitrator.

The case *Société Nationale des Pétroles du Congo et République du Congo v. Total Fina Elf E&P Congo*[161] is usually used as a supportive argument for the contractual nature of an emergency arbitrator. This case was the first case before a state court that was related to the ICC Pre-Arbitral Referee Procedure 1990. The ICC Pre-Arbitral Referee Procedure is intended for applications for interim measures, which have a similar function as the emergency arbitrator mechanism but they have a different legal status. On September 10, 2001, Société Nationale des Pétroles du Congo and the Republic of Congo, together with Total Fina Elf E&P Congo, entered into a contract. In that contract, Total Fina Elf E&P Congo would "refinance debts owed by the Republic of Congo in exchange for a certain quantity of crude oil".[162] There

[159] Fabio G. Santacroce (2015), The Emergency Arbitrator: A Full-Fledged Arbitrator Rendering An Enforceable Decision?, 31 *Arbitration International* 292.

[160] Article 29(6)(b), ICC Arbitration Rules 2017; Article 9.14; LCIA Arbitration Rules 2014.

[161] *Société Nationale des Pétroles du Congo et République du Congo v. Total Fina Elf E&P Congo* (Court of Appeal Paris, 2003), *Revue de l'Arbitrage*, pp. 1296–1299, English translation of the judgment and the referee's decision can be found in Emmanuel Gaillard & Philippe Pinsolle (2004), The ICC Pre-Arbitral Referee: First Practical Experience, 20 *Arbitration International*.

[162] Emmanuel Gaillard (2003), First Court Decision on Pre-Arbitral Referee, 229 New York Law Journal, available at https://www.shearman.com/~/media/Files/NewsInsights/Publications/2003/06/First-Court-Decision-on-PreArbitral-Referee/Files/Download-PDF-First-Court-Decision-on-PreArbitral__/FileAttachment/IA_060503.pdf (16 June 2020).

was an article in that contract providing that "[e]ach party may request interim or conservatory measures in application of the Pre-arbitral Referee Procedure Rules of the International Chamber of Commerce, the referee, acting under the said Rules, having exclusive jurisdiction to take such measures".[163] On December 26, 2001, Total Fina Elf E&P Congo submitted a request for interim measures asking the Republic of Congo to perform the contractual obligations. The referee was appointed on January 10, 2002. On February 6, 2002, the referee issued an order favoring Total Fina Elf E&P Congo. After the order was made, the Republic of Congo (the Claimant) initiated an appeal for annulment before the Court of Appeal in Paris. The Claimant declared that such an order could amount to an arbitral award which could be set aside by the French courts. On the other hand, Total Fina Elf E&P Congo (the Respondent) claimed that the order rendered by the referee was not regarded as an arbitral award and, therefore, could not be annulled by the courts. On April 29, 2003, the Paris Court of Appeal ruled that the appeal for the annulment of the order of the pre-arbitral referee was inadmissible.[164] The Paris Court of Appeal considered the first and key issue to be decided was whether the referee under the ICC Pre-Arbitral Referee Procedure could constitute an arbitrator, which was the foundation of determining whether this order could constitute an arbitral award or not.

The ruling explained that "the contractual rather than jurisdictional nature"[165] of the referee was based on two grounds. Firstly, the Paris Court of Appeal noticed that, in the ICC Rules for a Pre-Arbitral Referee Procedure 1990, "the word 'arbitration' and reference to the third person as an 'arbitrator' had been carefully avoided",[166] which indicated that the procedure was not a part of the arbitration.[167] Secondly, due to "the binding nature of the order derived solely from the parties' agreement",[168]

---

[163] Emmanuel Gaillard & Philippe Pinsolle (2004), The ICC Pre-Arbitral Referee: First Practical Experience, 20 *Arbitration International* 27.

[164] Emmanuel Gaillard & Philippe Pinsolle (2004), The ICC Pre-Arbitral Referee: First Practical Experience, 20 *Arbitration International* 37; Emmanuel Gaillard (2003), First Court Decision on Pre-Arbitral Referee, 229 New York Law Journal, available at https://www.shearman.com/~/media/Files/NewsInsights/Publications/2003/06/First-Court-Decision-on-PreArbitral-Referee/Files/Download-PDF-First-Court-Decision-on-PreArbitral__/FileAttachment/IA_060503.pdf (16 June 2020).

[165] Diana Paraguacuto-Maheo & Christine Lecuyer-Thieffry (2016), Emergency Arbitrator: A New Player in The Field-The French Perspective, 40 *Fordham International Law Journal* 764.

[166] Baruch Baigel (2014), The Emergency Arbitrator Procedure under the 2012 ICC Rules: A Juridical Analysis, 31 *Journal of International Arbitration* 4.

[167] Kah Cheong Lye, Chuan Tat Yeo & William Miller (2011), Legal Status of the Emergency Arbitrator under the SIAC 2010 Rules, 23 *Singapore Academy of Law Journal* 115.

[168] Emmanuel Gaillard & Philippe Pinsolle (2004), The ICC Pre-Arbitral Referee: First Practical Experience, 20 *Arbitration International* 22.

the Paris Court of Appeal held that the order was the result of "a contractual mechanism"[169] and "had no more binding effect than that of a contractual provision".[170] Consequently, the Court concluded that the referee was not acting as a proper arbitrator. Therefore, his decision was not qualified to be set aside by state courts. However, the ruling in *Société Nationale des Pétroles du Congo and République du Congo v. Total Fina Elf E&P Congo* case has been criticized for several reasons.[171] Firstly, the reasoning was "overly formalistic".[172] The use of wording in the ICC Pre-Arbitral Referee Procedure 1990 cannot be the decisive factor in drawing the conclusion. It is for the courts "to characterize an order despite the improper determination given by the parties or the arbitral tribunal".[173] Secondly, arbitration is based on arbitration agreements and has a contractual nature. The reason that the referee's decision was derived from the parties' agreement cannot be considered to be a satisfying argument.[174] Additionally, the analysis of the case is not fully applicable to the discussion regarding the legal status of the emergency arbitrator, considering the significant differences between the ICC Pre-Arbitral Referee Procedure 1990 and the emergency arbitrator mechanism. The differences can be seen in the jurisdictional status of an emergency arbitrator, which will be discussed in the following section. Nevertheless, the case does provide insights into the contractual basis of these two mechanisms for interim measures.

4.2.2 Jurisdictional Nature of an Emergency Arbitrator

The contractual nature of an emergency arbitrator is almost undisputed. The key controversial issue is the jurisdictional element in the legal status of an emergency

[169] Emmanuel Gaillard & Philippe Pinsolle (2004), The ICC Pre-Arbitral Referee: First Practical Experience, 20 *Arbitration International* 22.

[170] Emmanuel Gaillard (2003), First Court Decision on Pre-Arbitral Referee, 229 New York Law Journal, available at https://www.shearman.com/~/media/Files/NewsInsights/Publications/2003/06/First-Court-Decision-on-PreArbitral-Referee/Files/Download-PDF-First-Court-Decision-on-PreArbitral__/FileAttachment/IA_060503.pdf (16 June 2020).

[171] Ali Yesilirmak (2005), *Provisional Measures in International Commercial Arbitration*, Kluwer Law International, p. 145.

[172] Diana Paraguacuto-Maheo & Christine Lecuyer-Thieffry (2016), Emergency Arbitrator: A New Player in The Field-The French Perspective, 40 *Fordham International Law Journal* 765.

[173] Christine Lécuyer-Thieffry (2003), First Court Ruling on the ICC Pre-Arbitral Referee Procedure, 20 *Journal of International Arbitration* 603.

[174] Emmanuel Gaillard & Philippe Pinsolle (2004), The ICC Pre-Arbitral Referee: First Practical Experience, 20 *Arbitration International* 22; see also Baruch Baigel (2014), The Emergency Arbitrator Procedure under the 2012 ICC Rules: A Juridical Analysis, 31 *Journal of International Arbitration* 6; Kah Cheong Lye, Chuan Tat Yeo & William Miller (2011), Legal Status of the Emergency Arbitrator under the SIAC 2010 Rules, 23 *Singapore Academy of Law Journal* 116; Diana Paraguacuto-Maheo & Christine Lecuyer-Thieffry (2016), Emergency Arbitrator: A New Player in The Field-The French Perspective, 40 *Fordham International Law Journal* 766.

arbitrator. Generally, under the emergency arbitrator mechanism in arbitral institutions, the authority of an emergency arbitrator is similar to the authority of a regular arbitrator in determining its jurisdiction, conducting arbitral proceedings and granting interim measures.[175]

4.2.2.1 Jurisdiction of an Emergency Arbitrator

In the six arbitral institutional rules examined in this book in Chap. 2, all the emergency arbitrator provisions expressly regulate that the emergency arbitrator has the power to rule on his or her own jurisdiction, excluding the SCC arbitration rules.[176] Such a regulation is consistent with one of the fundamental principles of arbitration: the principle of competence-competence.

The principle of competence-competence provides that "arbitrators are competent to determine their own competence—that is, they are empowered to decide [on] their own jurisdiction to hear and determine the dispute before them".[177] The principle of competence-competence originated in Germany, which "was historically understood as recognizing an arbitral tribunal's jurisdiction to finally decide questions regarding its own jurisdiction, without the possibility of subsequent judicial review".[178] The modern competence-competence principle recognizes the power of an arbitrator to determine his or her jurisdiction, but such a ruling is subject to judicial review, either at the time of pronouncement or at the final stage of enforcement.[179] For example, in the UNCITRAL Model Law 2006, Article 16 states that an "arbitral tribunal may rule on its own jurisdiction, including any objections with respect to the existence or validity of the arbitration agreement".[180] The principle of competence-competence "must be rather grounded in the jurisdictional nature of an arbitrator's mandate".[181] The jurisdictional nature of competence-competence was confirmed in

---

175 Grant Hanessian (2014), Emergency Arbitrator, in Lawrence W. Newman & Richard D. Hill, *The Leading Arbitrators' Guide to International Arbitration*, Juris Publishing, p. 349.

176 Raja Bose & Ian Meredith (2012), Emergency Arbitration Procedures: A Comparative Analysis, 5 *International Arbitration Law Review* 190.

177 Margaret L. Moses (2017), *The Principles and Practice of International Commercial Arbitration*, Cambridge University Press, p. 96; Gary B. Born (2021), *International Commercial Arbitration*, Kluwer Law International, p. 1141; see also Lawrence Collins (2012), et al., *Dicey, Morris and Collins on the Conflict of Laws*, Sweet & Maxwell, p. 835; Thomas E. Carbonneau (2003), *Cases and Materials on the Law and Practice of Arbitration*, Juris Publishing, p. 21; Alan Redfern & J. Martin Hunter (2015), et al., *Redfern and Hunter on International Arbitration*, Oxford University Press, p. 340.

178 Gary B. Born (2021), *International Commercial Arbitration*, Kluwer Law International, p. 1143; Schlosser, Peter, Das Recht der internationalen privaten Schiedsgerichtsbarkeit, Mohr Siebeck, 1989, para. 553–554.

179 Thomas E. Carbonneau (2003), *Cases and Materials on the Law and Practice of Arbitration*, Juris Publishing, p. 21.

180 Article 16(1), UNCITRAL Model Law 2006.

181 Fabio G. Santacroce (2015), The Emergency Arbitrator: A Full-Fledged Arbitrator Rendering An Enforceable Decision?, 31 *Arbitration International* 294.

the *Texaco Overseas Petroleum Company, California Asiatic Oil Company v. The Government of the Libyan Arab Republic* case.[182] It is emphasized that the principle of competence-competence is "in harmony with both the jurisdictional aspect and the contractual aspect of arbitration"[183] and "derived from the jurisdictional nature of the arbitration".[184] The same principle can be found in arbitration laws, arbitration rules, and case law with regard to the emergency arbitrator mechanism.

In Hong Kong arbitration law, by adopting the UNCITRAL Model Law 2006, an arbitral tribunal can rule on its own jurisdiction.[185] Moreover, by recognizing an emergency arbitrator as an arbitrator,[186] an emergency arbitrator then has the same power. Singapore included an emergency arbitrator in the interpretation of an arbitral tribunal[187] which has the power to determine its own jurisdiction.[188] Under the Dutch Code of Civil Procedure, with the amendments of 2015, an arbitral tribunal, including an emergency arbitrator,[189] shall have the power to decide on its own jurisdiction.[190]

In the ICC Arbitration Rules 2017, an emergency arbitrator "shall determine whether the Application is admissible"[191] and "whether the emergency arbitrator has jurisdiction to order Emergency Measures".[192] The ICDR clearly includes the emergency arbitrator provisions directly within the power of a tribunal, which includes the authority to rule on the jurisdiction issue.[193] The HKIAC stipulates that an "emergency arbitrator shall have the power to rule on objections that the emergency arbitrator has no jurisdiction, including any objections with respect to the existence, validity or scope of the arbitration clause or of the separate arbitration agreement".[194] The LCIA states that Article 23, which states that "[t]he Arbitral Tribunal shall have the power to rule upon its own jurisdiction and authority including any objections

---

[182] *Texaco Overseas Petroleum Company, California Asiatic Oil Company v. The Government of the Libyan Arab Republic (1979)*, IV Yearbook Commercial Arbitration 177–187 (Award by Dupuy, René-Jean, 1977).

[183] *Texaco Overseas Petroleum Company, California Asiatic Oil Company v. The Government of the Libyan Arab Republic (1979)*, IV Yearbook Commercial Arbitration 179 (Award by Dupuy, René-Jean, 1977).

[184] *Texaco Overseas Petroleum Company, California Asiatic Oil Company v. The Government of the Libyan Arab Republic (1979)*, 53 *International Law Reports* 407.

[185] Section 34, Arbitration Ordinance (Cap. 609) 2015, available at https://www.elegislation.gov.hk/hk/cap609 (1 June 2024).

[186] Section 98F, arbitration, (b), Arbitration Ordinance (Cap. 609) 2015, available at https://www.elegislation.gov.hk/hk/cap609 (1 June 2024).

[187] Section 2(1) of Part II, International Arbitration Act of the Statutes of the Republic of Singapore (Cap. 143A) 2012, available at https://sso.agc.gov.sg/Act/IAA1994 (1 June 2024).

[188] Article 16 of First Schedule, International Arbitration Act of the Statutes of the Republic of Singapore (Cap. 143A) 2012, available at https://sso.agc.gov.sg/Act/IAA1994 (1 June 2024).

[189] Article 1043b(2), Dutch Code of Civil Procedure 2015.

[190] Article 1052(1), Dutch Code of Civil Procedure 2015.

[191] Article 6(2) of Appendix V, ICC Arbitration Rules 2021.

[192] Article 6(2) of Appendix V, ICC Arbitration Rules 2021.

[193] Article 7(3), ICDR Arbitration Rules 2021.

[194] Article 10 of Schedule 4, HKIAC Arbitration Rules 2024.

to the initial or continuing existence, validity, effectiveness or scope of the Arbitration Agreement",[195] shall also apply to the emergency arbitrator mechanism.[196] The SIAC Arbitration Rules 2016 provides that an emergency arbitrator shall have the power vested in a regular tribunal, including authority to rule on the jurisdiction.[197] It is noticed that the SCC does not specify the principle of competence-competence in its arbitration rules. Instead, it states that "[a]n Emergency Arbitrator shall not be appointed if the SCC manifestly lacks jurisdiction over the dispute". When looking into the cases managed by the SCC, an emergency arbitrator's ruling included this principle. In the SCC emergency arbitration case 139/2010,[198] the Respondent declared that the appointed emergency arbitrator lacked jurisdiction over the dispute. The reasoning by the emergency arbitrator started with the premise that the emergency arbitrator "could only conduct a *prima facie* assessment",[199] without touching upon the merits of the dispute, since the SCC arbitration rules in the agreement signed by both parties contained the emergency arbitrator provisions. Subsequently, the emergency arbitrator claimed to have jurisdiction based on a valid arbitration agreement under the SCC arbitration rules. Accordingly, the emergency arbitrator concluded that he had "*prima facie* jurisdiction".[200]

The principle of competence-competence applies "even where the arbitration agreement is defective, its source may not be found in the contractual basis of arbitration".[201] An example is another SCC emergency arbitration case 070/2011.[202] When dealing with the jurisdiction issue, the emergency arbitrator, in this case, noticed that the arbitration agreement in the contract was, in fact, defective. The arbitration agreement read that all disputes were to be "resolved exclusively by the International Arbitration Court in Stockholm, Sweden".[203] Nevertheless, the emergency arbitrator

---

[195] Article 23.1, LCIA Arbitration Rules 2020.

[196] Article 9.14, LCIA Arbitration Rules 2020.

[197] Article 7 of Schedule 1, SIAC Arbitration Rules 2016.

[198] Johan Lundstedt, SCC Practice: Emergency Arbitrator Decisions, 1 January 2010 -31 December 2013, p. 6, available at https://sccarbitrationinstitute.se/sites/default/files/2022-11/scc-practice-2010-2013-emergency-arbitrator_final.pdf (1 June 2024).

[199] Johan Lundstedt, SCC Practice: Emergency Arbitrator Decisions, 1 January 2010 -31 December 2013, p. 7, available at https://sccarbitrationinstitute.se/sites/default/files/2022-11/scc-practice-2010-2013-emergency-arbitrator_final.pdf (1 June 2024).

[200] Johan Lundstedt, SCC Practice: Emergency Arbitrator Decisions, 1 January 2010 -31 December 2013, p. 7, available at https://sccarbitrationinstitute.se/sites/default/files/2022-11/scc-practice-2010-2013-emergency-arbitrator_final.pdf (1 June 2024).

[201] Fabio G. Santacroce (2015), The Emergency Arbitrator: A Full-Fledged Arbitrator Rendering An Enforceable Decision?, 31 *Arbitration International* 294; see also Emmanuel Gaillard & John Savage (1999), *Fouchard Gaillard Goldman on International Commercial Arbitration*, Kluwer Law International, p. 658.

[202] Johan Lundstedt, SCC Practice: Emergency Arbitrator Decisions, 1 January 2010 -31 December 2013, p. 12, available at https://sccarbitrationinstitute.se/sites/default/files/2022-11/scc-practice-2010-2013-emergency-arbitrator_final.pdf (1 June 2024).

[203] Johan Lundstedt, SCC Practice: Emergency Arbitrator Decisions, 1 January 2010 -31 December 2013, p. 13, available at https://sccarbitrationinstitute.se/sites/default/files/2022-11/scc-practice-2010-2013-emergency-arbitrator_final.pdf (1 June 2024).

held that "the reference is clear as to indicating an institution (capital initial letters and the designation 'Court', which has the connotation of a permanent institutional framework)".[204] The only possible institution would, therefore, be the SCC. The emergency arbitrator considered "the only rational and readily available interpretation of the arbitration clause in the Contract is that the parties intended that disputes arising thereunder be referred to arbitration according to the SCC Rules".[205] Hence, the emergency arbitrator had jurisdiction over the submitted request.

Based on the above analysis on the jurisdiction of an emergency arbitrator, the application in the determination of the jurisdiction of the emergency arbitrator relies on the principle of competence-competence which addresses a jurisdictional nature. Therefore, with respect to jurisdiction, an emergency arbitrator exercises a jurisdictional function similar to a regular arbitrator.

4.2.2.2 Emergency Arbitration Proceedings

With regard to the emergency arbitration proceedings, the role and function of an emergency arbitrator are comparable to that of an arbitrator, which is to resolve the request submitted by parties in an adjudicatory manner.[206]

Impartiality requires that an arbitrator is not biased.[207] Independence calls for an arbitrator not to be bound by any relationship with the parties.[208] Acting as an adjudicator, the basic and essential requirements are impartiality and independence, which also reflect an arbitrator's jurisdictional function.[209] Such requirements have been "a defining feature of arbitration since Antiquity".[210] Basically, all modern arbitration laws and institutional rules call for the impartiality and independence of arbitrators. Meanwhile, if an arbitrator fails to fulfill these requirements, the parties are granted the opportunity to challenge such an appointment. For example, the UNCITRAL Model Law 2006 provides that "[a]n arbitrator may be challenged only

---

[204] Johan Lundstedt, SCC Practice: Emergency Arbitrator Decisions, 1 January 2010 -31 December 2013, p. 13, available at https://sccarbitrationinstitute.se/sites/default/files/2022-11/scc-practice-2010-2013-emergency-arbitrator_final.pdf (1 June 2024).

[205] Johan Lundstedt, SCC Practice: Emergency Arbitrator Decisions, 1 January 2010 -31 December 2013, p. 13, available at https://sccarbitrationinstitute.se/sites/default/files/2022-11/scc-practice-2010-2013-emergency-arbitrator_final.pdf (1 June 2024).

[206] Gary B. Born (2021), *International Commercial Arbitration*, Kluwer Law International, p. 2129.

[207] Margaret L. Moses (2017), *The Principles and Practice of International Commercial Arbitration*, Cambridge University Press, p. 141; see also Gary B. Born (2021), *International Commercial Arbitration*, Kluwer Law International, p. 2132.

[208] Margaret L. Moses (2017), *The Principles and Practice of International Commercial Arbitration*, Cambridge University Press, p. 141; see also Gary B. Born (2021), *International Commercial Arbitration*, Kluwer Law International, p. 2132.

[209] Emmanuel Gaillard & John Savage (1999), *Fouchard Gaillard Goldman on International Commercial Arbitration*, Kluwer Law International, p. 564.

[210] Gary B. Born (2021), *International Commercial Arbitration*, Kluwer Law International, p. 2132.

if circumstances exist that give rise to justifiable doubts as to his impartiality or independence, or if he does not possess qualifications agreed to by the parties".[211]

Concerning the impartiality and independence of an emergency arbitrator, the requirements are the same as for regular arbitrators. The ICC, as an institution providing for both the emergency arbitrator mechanism and the ICC Pre-Arbitral Referee Procedure, which is always used to compare its contractual nature with the legal status of the emergency arbitrator mechanism, requires the impartiality and independence of both regular arbitrators and emergency arbitrators. In the ICC Arbitration Rules 2021, Article 11 states very clearly that "[e]very arbitrator must be and remain impartial and independent of the parties involved in the arbitration".[212] Similar wording is used for the emergency arbitrator provisions in Article 2 of Appendix V: "[e]very emergency arbitrator shall be and remain impartial and independent of the parties involved in the dispute".[213] Both regular arbitrators and emergency arbitrators must "sign a statement of acceptance, availability, impartiality and independence"[214] before being appointed. The appointment of a regular arbitrator as well as an emergency arbitrator can be challenged and this challenge can be based on the lack of impartiality and independence.[215] However, there is one article in the ICC Rules for a Pre-Arbitral Referee Procedure 1990 that vaguely addresses this issue. Article 4.2 of the ICC Rules for a Pre-Arbitral Referee Procedure 1990 provides that the appointment of the referee must be made by "taking account of his technical or professional qualifications, nationality, residence, other relationships with the countries in which the parties are established or with which they are otherwise connected".[216] The different wordings used in the emergency arbitrator provisions and the ICC Pre-Arbitral Referee Procedure Rule 1990 suggest that a referee acts merely in a contractual function, but an emergency arbitrator acts in the same way as a regular arbitrator.

The seat of arbitration refers to the concept that "an arbitration is governed by the law of the place in which it is held, which is the 'seat' (or 'forum', or *locus arbitri*) of the arbitration", which is well established and widely accepted in both the theory and practice of international arbitration.[217] The seat of arbitration, or the place of arbitration,[218] connects arbitral proceedings with a certain domestic legal order.[219] The law of the seat of arbitration normally would be the law governing the arbitral procedures. In this case, the seat of arbitration is significant in conducting

[211] Article 12(2), UNCITRAL Model Law 2006.

[212] Article 11(1), ICC Arbitration Rules 2021.

[213] Article 2(4) of Appendix V, ICC Arbitration Rules 2021.

[214] Article 11(2) & Article 2(5) of Appendix V, ICC Arbitration Rules 2021.

[215] Article 14(1) & Article 3 of Appendix V, ICC Arbitration Rules 2021.

[216] Article 4.2, ICC Rules for a Pre-Arbitral Referee Procedure 1990.

[217] Alan Redfern & J. Martin Hunter (2015), et al., *Redfern and Hunter on International Arbitration*, Oxford University Press, pp. 171–172.

[218] Article 20, UNCITRAL Model Law 2006.

[219] Fabio G. Santacroce (2015), The Emergency Arbitrator: A Full-Fledged Arbitrator Rendering An Enforceable Decision?, 31 *Arbitration International* 296.

arbitration,[220] because an arbitral seat is "determinative of procedural norms, court intervention and review, and logistical realities".[221] However, a distinction needs to be made. The seat of arbitration is not necessarily the specific geographic location of a particular arbitral proceeding.[222] The English Arbitration Act 1996 expressly states that the "seat" is a juridical concept.[223] For instance, the LCIA Arbitration Rules 2020 provides that an arbitral tribunal "may hold any hearing at any convenient geographical place", and "the arbitration shall be nonetheless be treated for all purposes as an arbitration conducted at the arbitral seat and any order or award as having been made at that seat".[224]

In the same way that a regular arbitration has its seat, an emergency arbitration also has its seat. In the six institutional rules discussed in this book, excluding the ICDR, all emergency arbitrator provisions provide for rules for determining the seat. The ICC, the HKIAC and the SIAC allow the seat of emergency arbitration to be different from the seat of arbitration.[225] The determination of the seat of an emergency arbitration is regulated in a comparable way as for a regular arbitration. The ICC stipulates that the institution will fix the seat for both a regular arbitration and an emergency arbitration, unless there is an agreement between parties.[226] The SCC takes a similar approach as ICC.[227] The HKIAC provides that if there is no agreement between parties, the seat of arbitration or the seat of emergency arbitration shall be in Hong Kong.[228] For the seat of an emergency arbitration, the LCIA directly refers to its provisions concerning the seat of arbitration.[229] If an agreement is lacking, the SIAC provides that a tribunal can determine the seat of arbitration.[230] The SIAC determines that the seat of an emergency arbitration shall be Singapore if there is no agreement.[231]

The ICC Pre-Arbitral Referee Procedure does not contain any provisions regarding the seat and does not require a seat to connect the proceedings to a national legal

---

220 Stephen Bond (1990), How to draft an arbitration clause (revisited), 1 *ICC International Court of Arbitration Bulletin* 18.

221 N. Rubins (2001), The Arbitral Seat is No Fiction: A Brief Reply to Tatsuya Nakamura's Commentary, 16 *Mealey's International Arbitration Report* 27; Gary B. Born (2021), *International Commercial Arbitration*, Kluwer Law International, p. 2207; Aníbal Sabater (2010), When Arbitration Begins Without a Seat, 27 *Journal of International Arbitration* 443.

222 Gary B. Born (2021), *International Commercial Arbitration*, Kluwer Law International, p. 2207.

223 Section 3, English Arbitration Act 1996, available at http://www.legislation.gov.uk/ukpga/1996/23/contents (1 June 2024); Jeffrey Waincymer (2012), *Procedure and Evidence in International Arbitration*, Kluwer Law International, p. 169.

224 Article 16.3, LCIA Arbitration Rules 2020.

225 Article 4(1) of Appendix V, ICC Arbitration Rules 2021; Article 9 of Schedule 4, HKIAC Arbitration Rules 2024; Article 4 of Schedule 1, SIAC Arbitration Rules 2016.

226 Article 18 & Article 4(1) of Appendix V, ICC Arbitration Rules 2021.

227 Article 25 & Article 5 of Appendix II, SCC Arbitration Rules 2023.

228 Article 14.1 & Article 9 of Schedule 4, HKIAC Arbitration Rules 2024.

229 Article 9.14 & 16, LCIA Arbitration Rules 2020.

230 Article 21.1, SIAC Arbitration Rules 2016.

231 Article 4 of Schedule 1, SIAC Arbitration Rules 2016.

system.[232] The provisions regarding the seat of emergency arbitration include a jurisdictional element in the status of an emergency arbitrator.

To make arbitral awards enforceable, either domestically or internationally, states "delegate jurisdictional power"[233] to arbitrators in the form of quality standards, including a due process requirement. For example, the UNCITRAL Model Law 2006 states that "[t]he parties shall be treated with equality and each party shall be given a full opportunity of presenting his case".[234] It is always a dilemma to balance procedural fairness and efficiency, especially in the case of emergency arbitration. In an emergency arbitration, procedural fairness is guaranteed throughout the proceedings with specific consideration for the "emergency".

Firstly, procedural fairness can be seen at the beginning stage of an emergency arbitration. All parties should be notified of interim measures, either by the applicant or by the institution.[235] At least, there should be "an explanation of the steps taken in good faith to notify all parties".[236] Such a notice of proceedings is considered "as the core of due process protections".[237] In all cases, "regard must be had of the importance of the notice of proceedings to the respondent, as essential due process protection of its rights, particularly given the expeditious nature of the proceedings".[238] Secondly, during the arbitral proceedings, Article 22 of the ICC Arbitration Rules 2017 states that "[i]n all cases, the arbitral tribunal shall act fairly and impartially and endure that each party has a reasonable opportunity to present its case".[239] The wording is identical to the emergency arbitrator provisions, reading "[i]n all cases, the emergency arbitrator shall act fairly and impartially and ensure that each party has a reasonable opportunity to present its case".[240] If one party asks for a hearing in an emergency arbitration and an emergency arbitrator denies the request, this "would constitute a violation of due process".[241] A similar procedural requirement is provided by the

232 Fabio G. Santacroce (2015), The Emergency Arbitrator: A Full-Fledged Arbitrator Rendering An Enforceable Decision?, 31 *Arbitration International* 296.

233 Matti Kurkela & Santtu Turunen (2010), *Due Process in International Commercial Arbitration*, Oxford University Press, p. 201.

234 Article 18, UNCITRAL Model Law 2006.

235 Article 1(2) of Appendix V, ICC Arbitration Rules 2021; Article 9.5, LCIA Arbitration Rules 2020; Article 2(j) of Schedule 4, HKIAC Arbitration Rules 2024; Article 1(c) of Schedule 1, SIAC Arbitration Rules 2016; Article 3 of Appendix II, SCC Arbitration Rules 2023.

236 Article 7(1), ICDR Arbitration Rules 2021.

237 Patricia Shaughnessy (2010), Pre-arbitral Urgent Relief: The New SCC Emergency Arbitrator Rules, 27 *Journal of International Arbitration* 340.

238 Carlos de Los Santos Lago & Victor Bonnin (2012), Emergency Proceedings under the New ICC Rules, 13 *Spain Arbitration Review* 10.

239 Article 22, ICC Arbitration Rules 2021.

240 Article 5(2) of Appendix V, ICC Arbitration Rules 2021.

241 Herman Verbist & Erik Schfer (2015), et al., *ICC Arbitration in Practice*, Kluwer Law International, p. 169.

ICDR,[242] the HKIAC,[243] the SIAC,[244] and the SCC.[245] Regarding the possible *ex parte* interim measures under the LCIA, it "should be exceptional" that an emergency arbitrator decides on the interim measures without providing the other party with an opportunity to be heard.[246] Additionally, unless agreed by the parties, an emergency arbitrator should not serve as an arbitrator in main arbitral proceedings to ensure procedural fairness.[247] This reflects the concerns that an emergency arbitrator may be prejudiced by their involvement during emergency arbitration.[248] Finally, as it could be expected, an emergency arbitrator is required to give reasons[249] or at least summary reasons[250] for his or her decision.

4.2.2.3 Interim Measures Rendered by an Emergency Arbitrator

Two aspects need to be considered related to an arbitrator's judicial role in arbitral decisions. The decisions must be binding on the parties and must resolve a dispute.[251] The interim measure granted by an emergency arbitrator fulfills such requirements. The decision issued by an emergency arbitrator is binding, and the question whether to issue the interim measures requested or not, which is the purpose of the emergency arbitrator mechanism, can be solved with that decision.

An emergency arbitrator in all of the six arbitral institutions discussed in this book has similar authority as that vested in a regular arbitrator, not only within the arbitral proceedings but also in its relationship with state courts. According to the ICC Arbitration Rules 2021, an emergency arbitrator can conduct the emergency arbitration proceedings in the manner he or she thinks "appropriate",[252] considering the urgency of the application. The regular arbitrators under ICC can grant interim

[242] Article 7(3), ICDR Arbitration Rules 2021.

[243] Article 10 of Schedule 4, HKIAC Arbitration Rules 2024.

[244] Article 7 of Schedule 1 & Article 19.1, SIAC Arbitration Rules 2016.

[245] Article 7 of Appendix II & Article 23(2), SCC Arbitration Rules 2023.

[246] Scherer, Maxi & Richman, Lisa, et al., Arbitrating under the 2014 LCIA Rules: A User's Guide, Kluwer Law International, 2015, p. 156.

[247] Article 2(2) of Appendix V, ICC Arbitration Rues 2021; Article 7(4), ICDR Arbitration Rules 2021; Article 19 of Schedule 4, HKIAC Arbitration Rules 2024; Article 6 of Schedule 1, SIAC Arbitration Rules 2016; Article 4(4) of Appendix II, SCC Arbitration Rules 2023.

[248] Christoph Muller& Sabrina Pearson (2015), Waving the Green Flag to Emergency Arbitration under the Swiss Rules: the Sauber Saga, 33 *ASA Bulletin* 814.

[249] Article 6(3) of Appendix V, ICC Arbitration Rules 2021; Article 7(4), ICDR Arbitration Rules 2021; Article 9.9, LCIA Arbitration Rules 2020; Article 8(2) of Appendix II, SCC Arbitration Rules 2023.

[250] Article 15(b) of Schedule 4, HKIAC Arbitration Rules 2024; Article 8 of Schedule 1, SIAC Arbitration Rules 2016.

[251] Emmanuel Gaillard & John Savage (1999), *Fouchard Gaillard Goldman on International Commercial Arbitration*, Kluwer Law International, p. 12.

[252] Article 5(2) of Appendix V, ICC Arbitration Rules 2021.

measures they deem "appropriate".[253] The ICDR Arbitration Rules 2021 states that "[t]he emergency arbitrator shall have the authority vested in the arbitral tribunal"[254] and "shall have the power to order or award any interim or conservancy measures that the emergency arbitrator deems necessary".[255] The HKIAC directly points out that, under the HKIAC Arbitration Rules 2024, any interim measures granted by an emergency arbitrator shall have the same effect as the interim measures granted by a regular tribunal.[256] The LCIA also empowers an emergency arbitrator with a wide scope of authority by stating that the emergency arbitrator "may make any order or award which the Arbitral Tribunal could make under the Arbitration Agreement".[257] Such interim measures shall take the same effect as an award issued by a regular tribunal.[258] The SIAC Arbitration Rules 2016 provides that an emergency arbitrator "shall have the power to order or award any interim relief that he deems necessary"[259] and a regular tribunal may issue any interim measures it deems appropriate.[260] The SCC sets out the power of an emergency arbitrator and a regular tribunal together, as they may grant any interim measures they deem appropriate.[261]

Additionally, the relationship between an emergency arbitrator and a state court, and a regular tribunal and a state court, is similar. Under the ICC arbitration rules, in a regular arbitral tribunal, "the parties may apply to any competent judicial authority for interim or conservatory measures",[262] while for an emergency arbitrator, the ICC stipulates that the proceedings are "not intended to prevent any party from seeking urgent interim measures from a competent judicial authority at any time".[263] The HKIAC uses similar wording and adopts a similar approach[264] as the ICC. The ICDR stipulates that a request by parties for interim measures to a judicial authority is not incompatible with the agreement to arbitrate[265] and the emergency arbitrator provisions.[266] The LCIA provides that the power of a regular arbitrator and an emergency arbitrator "shall not prejudice any party's right to apply to a state or other legal authority for any interim or conservatory measures".[267] The SIAC states that "[a] request for interim relief made by a party to a judicial authority prior to the constitution of the Tribunal, or in exceptional circumstances thereafter, is

---

253 Article 28(1), ICC Arbitration Rules 2021.
254 Article 7(4), ICDR Arbitration Rules 2021.
255 Article 7(4), ICDR Arbitration Rules 2021.
256 Article 17 of Schedule 4, HKIAC Arbitration Rules 2024.
257 Article 9.8, LCIA Arbitration Rules 2020.
258 Article 9.9, LCIA Arbitration Rules 2020.
259 Article 8 of Schedule 1, SIAC Arbitration Rules 2016.
260 Article 30.1, SIAC Arbitration Rules 2016.
261 Article 37(1) & Article 1(2) of Appendix II, SCC Arbitration Rules 2023.
262 Article 28(2), ICC Arbitration Rules 2021.
263 Article 29(7), ICC Arbitration Rules 2021.
264 Article 20 of Schedule 4, HKIAC Arbitration Rules 2024.
265 Article 27(3), ICDR Arbitration Rules 2014.
266 Article 7(7), ICDR Arbitration Rules 2021.
267 Article 9.13, LCIA Arbitration Rules 2014.

not compatible with these Rules".[268] The SCC makes it clear that asking a judicial authority for interim measures is not incompatible with the power of a tribunal and an emergency arbitrator.[269]

4.2.3 Status of an Emergency Arbitrator in Issuing Interim Measures Before the Constitution of an Arbitral Tribunal

Admittedly, limits to the role of an emergency arbitrator exist. Firstly, an emergency arbitrator's jurisdiction terminates once an arbitral tribunal is constituted. Secondly, an emergency arbitrator cannot prejudge the merits of a submitted dispute. Finally, the decision of an emergency arbitrator can be revised, terminated or annulled by an arbitral tribunal. However, the function of an emergency arbitrator is purely to provide a fast-track possibility of interim measures for parties instead of going to state courts. Bearing this in mind, with both the contractual and jurisdictional elements in the emergency arbitrator mechanism, an emergency arbitrator acts in the same way as an arbitrator by issuing interim measures before the formation of an arbitral tribunal. The decision of an emergency arbitrator is seen as the same as an arbitrator's decision.

After the systematic analysis of the legal status of an emergency arbitrator, who "is a neutral person [that] determines, in a judicial manner, the issues before him in a binding decision",[270] it can be concluded that an emergency arbitrator acts as a proper arbitrator[271] with respect to issuing interim measures pending the constitution of a tribunal.[272]

4.3 Concluding Remarks

There is much academic debate regarding the initial question of the legal status of arbitration, in general, and subsequently in particular with regard to emergency arbitration. The jurisdictional theory, the contractual theory, the mixed theory, and the autonomous theory all try to establish the nature of arbitration from different

[268] Article 30.3, SIAC Arbitration Rules 2016.

[269] Article 37(5), SCC Arbitration Rules 2023.

[270] Ali Yesilirmak (2005), *Provisional Measures in International Commercial Arbitration*, Kluwer Law International, pp. 145–146.

[271] Fabio G. Santacroce (2015), The Emergency Arbitrator: A Full-Fledged Arbitrator Rendering An Enforceable Decision?, 31 *Arbitration International* 302.

[272] Christopher Boog (2018), Chapter 4, Part II: Commentary on the ICC Rules, Article 29 [Emergency arbitrator], in M Arroyo (ed), *Arbitration in Switzerland: The Practitioner's Guide*, Kluwer Law International, p. 2383.

perspectives and with different emphasis. However, there is currently no universal agreement on this issue. By examining the source of the power of an arbitrator, it can be concluded that the authority of an arbitrator is primarily conferred by the parties to the arbitration agreement, but it is limited by the law governing the arbitration. The role and function of an arbitrator suggest that both contractual and jurisdictional elements are at issue. Based on these two elements, this chapter addressed the legal status of an emergency arbitrator. By comparing the role and function of a regular arbitrator and an emergency arbitrator, with respect to the decision on interim measures, their authorities are similar and often even identical. Additionally, the emergency arbitrator mechanism adopts an opt-out approach, which reflects its contractual basis. The requirements and regulations in the emergency arbitration proceedings reflect the jurisdictional elements. Therefore, this chapter concludes, with respect to issuing interim measures pending the constitution of the tribunal, that an emergency arbitrator acts as a proper arbitrator, and a decision rendered by an emergency arbitrator must be seen as the same as an arbitrator's decision.

Chapter 5
Issuance of Interim Measures by an Emergency Arbitrator

The proceedings concerning the issuance of interim measures by an emergency arbitrator affect their enforceability. The issuance will be discussed in this chapter from both procedural and substantial perspectives, the jurisdiction of an emergency arbitrator Sect. 5.1, the categories and limitations of the interim measures granted by an emergency arbitrator Sect. 5.2, and necessary legal criteria when granting interim measures in emergency arbitration Sect. 5.3.

5.1 Jurisdiction of an Emergency Arbitrator

Jurisdictional issue can be used to question the enforceability of the interim measures issued by an emergency arbitrator. For example, in the New York Convention 1958, Article V (1) (c) gives state courts the possibility to refuse recognition and enforcement if an award "deals with a difference not contemplated by or not falling within terms of the submission to arbitration, or it contains decisions on matters beyond the scope of the submission to arbitration".[1] Compared to the concept of competence, jurisdiction is more general and abstract. Proper jurisdiction is a premise of a finding of competence,[2] while "a finding of jurisdiction does not necessarily entail competence".[3]

[1] Article V (1) (c), New York Convention 1958.

[2] Veijo Heiskanen (1994), Jurisdiction v. Competence: Revisiting a Frequently Neglected Distinction, 5 *Finnish Yearbook of International Law* 5.

[3] Gerald Fitzmaurice (1958), The Law and Procedure of the International Court of Justice, 1951–4: Questions of Jurisdiction, Competence and Procedure, 34 *British Year Book of International Law* 8–9.

J. Zhang, *The Enforceability of the Interim Measures Granted by an Emergency Arbitrator in International Commercial Arbitration*,
https://doi.org/10.1007/978-981-97-6536-2_5

5.1.1 Applicable Law on the Authority of an Emergency Arbitrator

It is natural to consider the law governing arbitral proceedings, usually the law of the seat of arbitration, to be the applicable law governing the jurisdiction issue. The issuance of interim measures by an emergency arbitrator or an arbitral tribunal is "generally classified as a matter of procedure and therefore governed primarily by the law governing the arbitration".[4] In fact, it is also a common choice in arbitration practices.[5] For example, the ICC Case No. 8786/1996 relied on the Swiss Private International Law Act, which was the arbitration law of the seat of arbitration as the applicable law for the power to issue interim measures.[6] Of course, it is also possible for parties to choose another system of law to govern the arbitral proceedings, other than the law of the seat.

Bearing in mind the fact that some jurisdictions refuse to grant the power to emergency arbitrators to issue interim measures, there is a dilemma that the choice by the parties may not be consistent with the applicable law here. In the case of a conflict arising between the applicable arbitration law and the institutional rules chosen by parties in an arbitration agreement representing party autonomy, "[i]n principle", an emergency arbitrator "would be free, and indeed obliged, to give effect to the parties' agreement".[7] The reason is that, under international conventions, for example, Article II of the New York Convention 1958, an arbitration agreement should be respected by contracting states the choice of specific institutional rules containing the emergency arbitrator mechanism as a part of the arbitration agreement by reference.[8] In this case, party autonomy prevails. However, if an emergency arbitrator issues interim measures regardless of the mandatory law of the seat of arbitration, the interim measures may be annulled by the state courts at the seat of arbitration.

---

[4] Stefan Michael Kröll, Julian D. M. Lew & Loukas A. Mistelis (2003), *Comparative International Commercial Arbitration*, Kluwer Law International, p. 588.

[5] Christopher Boog (2011), The Laws Governing Interim Measures in International Arbitration, in Franco Ferrari & Kröll, *Conflict of Laws in International Arbitration*, Sellier, p. 419; Eric A. Schwartz (1993), *The Practices and Experience of the ICC Court, in Conservatory and Provisional Measures in International Arbitration*, International Chamber of Commerce, p. 58.

[6] Interim Award in Case 8786, Extracts from ICC Awards Referring to Interim and Conservatory Measures, 11 *ICC International Court of Arbitration Bulletin* (Issue 1) 2000, p. 82.

[7] Gary B. Born (2021), *International Commercial Arbitration*, Kluwer Law International, p. 2642.

[8] Julian D.M. Lew (2000), Commentary on Interim and Conservatory Measures in ICC Arbitration Cases, 11 *ICC International Court of Arbitration Bulletin* 25.

5.1.2 Basis of the Jurisdiction of an Emergency Arbitrator to Issue Interim Measures

The authority of an emergency arbitrator to issue interim measures comes from three legal bases, i.e., relevant international conventions, applicable arbitration laws, and specific arbitration agreements.[9]

Most of the international conventions do not specify the authority of arbitrators to grant interim measures in arbitration, excluding the ICSID Convention 1965. Article 47 of the ICSID Convention stipulates that "[e]xcept as the parties otherwise agree, the Tribunal may, if it considers that the circumstances so require, recommend any provisional measures which should be taken to preserve the respective rights of either party".[10] Despite the word "recommend", this provision has been interpreted as granting arbitrators the power to order interim measures.[11]

Arbitration laws in each jurisdiction are of great importance with respect to the authority for arbitrators to issue interim measures. It is believed that "[a]n arbitrator will generally not grant provisional relief unless he or she is satisfied that the law applicable to the arbitral proceedings (typically, the arbitration legislation of the arbitral seat) allows". If the *lex arbitri* excludes such authority, the concerned state court may refuse the recognition and enforcement of the granted interim measures accordingly. The detailed analysis regarding the interim measures issued by an emergency arbitrator in various jurisdictions based on their arbitration legislation was provided in Chapter 3.

The other source of the authority for an emergency arbitrator to grant interim measures is the parties' arbitration agreement, which includes arbitral institutional rules. Usually, parties seldom state the authority of arbitrators to grant interim measures in their arbitration agreements explicitly. If parties have chosen a set of institutional rules that contain the emergency arbitrator mechanism, then the consent providing emergency arbitrators with the authority to issue interim measures can also be established. As discussed in Chap. 2, most of the world's leading arbitral institutions, including the ICC, the ICDR, the HKIAC, the LCIA, the SIAC, and the SCC, have included the emergency arbitrator provisions in their arbitral rules. If parties do not exclude the application of such provisions, an emergency arbitrator will have the authority to decide on the request.

There is one additional and very controversial issue that needs to be addressed when dealing with the authority of an emergency arbitrator in issuing interim measures, which is the *ex parte* interim measure. The Swiss Rules of International Arbitration (The Swiss Arbitration Rules) 2012 by the Swiss Chamber's Arbitration Institution expressly accords an emergency arbitrator the power to grant interim measures on an *ex parte* basis. Article 26 (3) of the Swiss Arbitration Rules 2012

---

[9] Gary B. Born (2021), *International Commercial Arbitration*, Kluwer Law International, p. 2607.

[10] Article 47, the ICSID Convention 1965.

[11] Gary B. Born (2021), *International Commercial Arbitration*, Kluwer Law International, p. 2608; Christoph H.Schreuer, Loretta Malintoppi, August Reinich & Anthony Sinclair (2009), *The ICSID Convention: a Commentary*, Cambridge University Press, p. 764–765.

provides that "[i]n exceptional circumstances, the arbitral tribunal may rule on a request for interim measures by way of a preliminary order before the request has been communicated to any other party".[12] Since, under the Swiss Arbitration Rules 2012, decisions made by an emergency arbitrator "have the same effect"[13] as the decision made by a tribunal, an emergency arbitrator equally has the power to issue *ex parte* interim measures.[14] However, the communication to other parties regarding the request of interim measures "is made at the latest together with the preliminary order", and "the other parties are immediately granted an opportunity to be heard".[15] Another institution that possibly allows an emergency arbitrator to grant the *ex parte* interim measures is the LCIA.[16] The LCIA Arbitration Rules 2020 state that "[t]he Emergency Arbitrator may conduct the emergency proceedings in any manner determined by the Emergency Arbitrator to be appropriate in the circumstances, taking account of the nature of such emergency proceedings, the need to afford to each party, if possible, an opportunity to be consulted on the claim for emergency relief (whether or not it avails itself of such opportunity)."[17]

The answer to the question of whether the *ex parte* interim measures by an emergency arbitrator are enforceable or not, is almost undisputedly negative, with very few exceptions.[18] For example, under the New York Convention 1958, it is mandatory that both parties should have a fair and equal opportunity to be heard. A violation of due process is also a ground for a refusal of the recognition and enforcement of arbitral awards.[19] The exceptions mainly exist because of the UNCITRAL Model Law 2006. Article 17 B (2) stipulates that "[t]he arbitral tribunal may grant a preliminary order provided it considers that prior disclosure of the request for the interim measure to the party against whom it is directed risks frustrating the purpose of the measure".[20] However, the content of this provision has been criticized as "ill-considered",[21] because "the right to be heard and the observance of the rules of natural justice are fundamental to arbitration".[22]

---

[12] Article 26 (3), Swiss Arbitration Rules 2012.

[13] Article 43 (8), Swiss Arbitration Rules 2012.

[14] Grant Hanessian & E. Alexandra Dosman (2016), Songs of Innocence and Experience: Ten Years of Emergency Arbitration, 27 *American Review of International Arbitration* 223.

[15] Article 26 (3), Swiss Arbitration Rules 2012.

[16] Fabio G. Santacroce (2015), The emergency arbitrator: a full-fledged arbitrator rendering an enforceable decision?, 31 *Arbitration International* 286.

[17] Article 9.7, LCIA Arbitration Rules 2020.

[18] Georg von Segesser & Christopher Boog (2013),Chapter 6: Interim Measures, in Elliott Geisinger & Nathalie Voser, *International Arbitration in Switzerland: A Handbook for Practitioners*, Kluwer Law International, p. 117.

[19] Article V (1) (B), New York Convention 1958.

[20] Article 17 B (2), UNCITRAL Model Law 2006.

[21] Gary B. Born (2021), *International Commercial Arbitration*, Kluwer Law International, p. 2696.

[22] Stefan Michael Kröll, Julian D. M. Lew & Loukas A. Mistelis (2003), *Comparative International Commercial Arbitration*, Kluwer Law International, p. 607; Albert van den Berg (1981), *The New York Arbitration Convention of 1958: Towards a Uniform Judicial Interpretation*, Kluwer Law and Taxation Publishers, p. 306.

5.1.3 Jurisdictional Conflicts with State Courts in the Case of Interim Measures

Although parties may prefer the emergency arbitrator mechanism over state courts in the issuance of interim measures in international commercial arbitration, under the emergency arbitrator mechanism, state courts have concurrent power to issue interim measures in arbitration.[23] The emergency arbitrator provisions "are not intended to prevent any party from seeking urgent interim or conservatory measures from a competent judicial authority at any time".[24] Similarly in Sect. 21 of Hong Kong Arbitration Ordinance (Cap. 609), which refers to the UNCITRAL Model Law 2006, states that "[i]t is not incompatible with an arbitration agreement for a party to request, before or during arbitral proceedings, from a court an interim measure of protection and for a court to grant such measure".[25] Consequently, it is possible that the overlapping jurisdictions of an emergency arbitrator and state courts may lead to conflicts. For example, parties may apply to a state court and an emergency arbitrator for interim measures simultaneously, or they may be refused by a state court and then they seek the interim measure from an emergency arbitrator later.[26]

It is difficult to give a definitive solution in this situation. Some practical experiences may be considered when facing these situations. In *Smart Technologies ULC v. Rapt Touch Ireland Ltd, et al.*,[27] the United States District Court for the Northern District of California held that "it would not be a good reason for a federal court to get involved in a dispute whose merits both parties agree should be arbitrated".[28] Similarly, in the well-known case, *Channel Tunnel Group Ltd. and Another v. Balfour Beatty Construction Ltd. and Others*, the House of Lords, accepting its own jurisdiction to decide on the request for interim measures, still ruled that "the duty of the court to respect the choice of tribunal which both parties have made, and not to take out of the hands of the arbitrators (or other decision-makers) a power of

---

[23] Andrea Carlevaris & José Ricardo Feris (2014), Running in the ICC Emergency Arbitrator Rules: The First Ten Cases, 25 *ICC International Court of Arbitration Bulletin* 34.

[24] Article 29 (7), ICC Arbitration Rules 2021; Article 7 (7), ICDR Arbitration Rules 2021; Article 20 of Schedule 4, HKIAC Arbitration Rules 2024; Article 9.13, LCIA Arbitration Rules 2020; Article 30.3, SIAC Arbitration Rules 2016; Article 37 (5), SCC Arbitration Rules 2023.

[25] Section 21, Arbitration Ordinance (Cap. 609) 2015, available at https://www.elegislation.gov.hk/hk/cap609 (1 June 2024). The content is identical with Article 9, UNCITRAL Model Law 2006.

[26] Georg von Segesser & Christopher Boog (2013),Chapter 6: Interim Measures, in Elliott Geisinger & Nathalie Voser, *International Arbitration in Switzerland: A Handbook for Practitioners*, Kluwer Law International, p. 127.

[27] *Smart Technologies ULC v. Rapt Touch Ireland Ltd, et al.*, 197 F. Supp. 3d 1204 (United States District Court, N.D. California, 2016). See also, *A & C Discount Pharmacy, L.L.C. d/b/a Medcore Pharmacy v. Caremark, L.L.C., et al.*, Civil Action No. 3:16-CV-0264-D, 2016 WL 3,476,970 (United States District Court, N.D. Texas, Dallas Division, 2016).

[28] *Smart Technologies ULC v. Rapt Touch Ireland Ltd, et al.*, 197 F. Supp. 3d 1204, 1206 (United States District Court, N.D. California, 2016).

decision which the parties have entrusted to them alone" prevailed in this case.[29] In the situation of a sequential use of jurisdictions regarding the interim measures, the arbitrators in ICC Case No. 5/2002 dismissed the request for interim measures, stating that "[i]f the state court orders or declines to order a measure, the parties cannot subsequently resort to the arbitral tribunal to obtain a more favorable ruling, and vice-versa" if the requests are identical in accordance with judicial efficiency and procedural economy.[30] This situation can also lead to a discussion of public policy concerns, which will be examined in Chap. 6.

5.2 Categories and Limitations of Interim Measures Granted by an Emergency Arbitrator

Generally speaking, an emergency arbitrator enjoys a wide range of discretion to grant "any interim or conservatory measures that the emergency arbitrator deems necessary"[31] or "appropriate"[32] subject to certain limitations. The limitations mainly "stem from the private, contractual nature of arbitration",[33] that is to say, the power of an emergency arbitrator is restricted to the parties who have consented to an arbitration agreement. An emergency arbitrator cannot rule on the request for interim measures involving third parties, which include commercial banks, which is a typical third party when freezing assets of one party is involved in a dispute.[34] Alternatively, an emergency arbitrator can order parties to place money in an escrow account to avoid this problem.[35]

[29] *Channel Tunnel Group Ltd. and Another v. Balfour Beatty Construction Ltd. and Others*, [1993] A.C. 334, 368 (House of Lords, 1993).

[30] *A v. Z*, Order, 2 April 2002, 21 ASA Bulletin 2003, p. 816–817.

[31] Article 7(4), ICDR Arbitration Rules 2021; Article 8 of Schedule 1, SIAC Arbitration Rules 2016.

[32] Article 23(2) & Article 10 of Schedule 4, HKIAC Arbitration Rules 2024; Article 37(1), Article 1(2) of Appendix II, SCC Arbitration Rules 2023.

[33] Maxi Scherer & Lisa Richman, et al. (2015), Ar*bitration under the 2014 LCIA Rules: A User's Guide*, Kluwer Law International, p. 263.

[34] Christopher Boog (2013), Chapter 13, Part III: Interim Measures in International Arbitration, in Manuel Arroyo, *Arbitration in Switzerland: The Practitioner's Guide, Kluwer Law International*, p. 1356; Raymond J. Werbicki (2010), Arbitral Interim Measures: Fact or Fiction?, in *American Arbitration Association Handbook on International Arbitration and ADR*, Juris Publishing, p. 95; SCC Emergency Arbitration No. 070/2011, in Johan Lundstedt, SCC Practice: Emergency Arbitrator Decisions, 1 January 2010-31 December 2013, p. 14, available at https://sccarbitrationinstitute.se/sites/default/files/2022-11/scc-practice-2010-2013-emergency-arbitrator_final.pdf (1 June 2024).

[35] Andrea Carlevaris & José Ricardo Feris (2014), Running in the ICC Emergency Arbitrator Rules: The First Ten Cases, 25 *ICC International Court of Arbitration Bulletin* 34; Raymond J. Werbicki (2010), Arbitral Interim Measures: Fact or Fiction?, in *American Arbitration Association Handbook on International Arbitration and ADR*, Juris Publishing, p. 95.

The interim measures preserving the *status quo* can be seen in various cases. In the SCC Emergency Arbitration No. 187/2010, the emergency arbitrator ordered the Respondent "not to sell, assign, transfer, pledge or otherwise dispose any of its shares"[36] in a specific company. In the SCC Emergency Arbitrations No. 2015/002, the emergency arbitrator prohibited the Respondent from any further steps to limit the business of the claimants and to declare that the newly changed legislation had no legal effect on the claimants.[37] In the SCC Emergency Arbitration No. 2016/046, the emergency arbitrator prevented the Respondent from transferring the immovable assets and authorizing any transfer regarding those assets until the final award.[38] In the SCC Emergency Arbitration No. 2016/095, the emergency arbitrator issued interim measures stopping the Respondent from enforcing or implementing the decree and from interfering with the shareholding of the claimant until the final award.[39]

The interim measures are issued to secure the enforcement of a final arbitral award to be delivered by the tribunal. In the SCC Emergency Arbitrations No. 2014/053 and No. 2014/183, the emergency arbitrator declared that the Respondent had illegally expropriated the assets owned by the requesting party.[40] In one ICC emergency arbitration, due to the concern that the Respondent failed to make certain payments and the parent company of the Respondent was in an insolvency procedure, the emergency arbitrator was asked to order the Respondent to guarantee the payments under the disputed contracts.[41]

The interim measures can be issued requiring a specific performance of obligations. In the SCC Emergency Arbitration No. 057/2013, the emergency arbitrator ordered the Respondents to fulfill the particular contractual obligations regarding

[36] SCC Emergency Arbitration No. 187/2010, in Johan Lundstedt, SCC Practice: Emergency Arbitrator Decisions, 1 January 2010-31 December 2013, p. 11, available at https://sccarbitrationinstitute.se/sites/default/files/2022-11/scc-practice-2010-2013-emergency-arbitrator_final.pdf (1 June 2024).

[37] SCC Emergency Arbitration No. 2015/002, in Anja Havedal Ipp, SCC Practice Note Emergency Arbitrator Decisions Rendered 2015–2016, p. 5, available at https://sccarbitrationinstitute.se/sites/default/files/2022-11/ea-practice-note-emergency-arbitrator-decisions-rendered-2015-2016.pdf (1 June 2024).

[38] SCC Emergency Arbitration No. 2016/046, in Anja Havedal Ipp, SCC Practice Note Emergency Arbitrator Decisions Rendered 2015–2016, p. 8, available at https://sccarbitrationinstitute.se/sites/default/files/2022-11/ea-practice-note-emergency-arbitrator-decisions-rendered-2015-2016.pdf (1 June 2024).

[39] SCC Emergency Arbitration No. 2016/095, in Anja Havedal Ipp, SCC Practice Note Emergency Arbitrator Decisions Rendered 2015–2016, p. 14, available at https://sccarbitrationinstitute.se/sites/default/files/2022-11/ea-practice-note-emergency-arbitrator-decisions-rendered-2015-2016.pdf (1 June 2024).

[40] SCC Emergency Arbitration No. 2014/053 and No. 2014/183, in Lotta Knapp, SCC Practice Emergency Arbitrator Decisions Rendered 2014, p. 9, available at https://sccarbitrationinstitute.se/sites/default/files/2022-11/scc-practice-emergency-arbitrators-2014_final.pdf (1June 2024).

[41] Andrea Carlevaris & José Ricardo Feris (2014), Running in the ICC Emergency Arbitrator Rules: The First Ten Cases, 25 *ICC International Court of Arbitration Bulletin* 34.

the removal and return of the disputed objects.[42] In the SCC Emergency Arbitrations No. 2016/30, No. 2016/31, and No. 2016/32, the emergency arbitrator urged the Respondent to resume the deliveries in the original contract as requested by the Claimants.[43] In the SCC Emergency Arbitration No. 2016/142, the emergency arbitrator urged the Respondent to deliver the product in the contract.[44] In the SCC Emergency Arbitration No. 2016/195, the emergency arbitrator permitted the request for the appointment of an expert, as indicated in the original contract.[45]

The interim measures may also be anti-suit injunctions issued by an emergency arbitrator to prevent other parties from initiating new lawsuits in courts. In two ICC emergency arbitrations, the emergency arbitrators were asked to stop the commenced court proceedings. In another ICC emergency arbitration, the request was to forbid the responding party from initiating future legal suits.[46]

The interim measures also include interim payments. One emergency arbitration case administrated by the ICC involved a request ordering the responding party to make an immediate payment with the possibility of reimbursement.[47]

Interim measures preserving evidence have not been found in current cases, while it is indeed a type of interim measure that must be taken into account.[48] Evidence is "crucial for the determination of the substantive issues",[49] but it can also be fragile. Such evidence may include witnesses, important data that could be erased, financial reports that may be modified, to name some examples.

---

[42] SCC Emergency Arbitration No. 057/2013, in Johan Lundstedt, SCC Practice: Emergency Arbitrator Decisions, 1 January 2010-31 December 2013, p. 25, available at https://sccarbitrationinstitute.se/sites/default/files/2022-11/scc-practice-2010-2013-emergency-arbitrator_final.pdf (1 June 2024).

[43] SCC Emergency Arbitration No. 2016/30, No. 2016/31, and No. 2016/32, in Anja Havedal Ipp, SCC Practice Note Emergency Arbitrator Decisions Rendered 2015–2016, p. 7, available at https://sccarbitrationinstitute.se/sites/default/files/2022-11/ea-practice-note-emergency-arbitrator-decisions-rendered-2015-2016.pdf (1 June 2024).

[44] SCC Emergency Arbitration No. 2016/142, in Anja Havedal Ipp, SCC Practice Note Emergency Arbitrator Decisions Rendered 2015–2016, p. 16, available at available at https://sccarbitrationinstitute.se/sites/default/files/2022-11/ea-practice-note-emergency-arbitrator-decisions-rendered-2015-2016.pdf (1 June 2024).

[45] SCC Emergency Arbitration No. 2016/195, in Anja Havedal Ipp, SCC Practice Note Emergency Arbitrator Decisions Rendered 2015–2016, p. 17, available at https://sccarbitrationinstitute.se/sites/default/files/2022-11/ea-practice-note-emergency-arbitrator-decisions-rendered-2015-2016.pdf (1 June 2024).

[46] Andrea Carlevaris & José Ricardo Feris (2014), Running in the ICC Emergency Arbitrator Rules: The First Ten Cases, 25 *ICC International Court of Arbitration Bulletin* 34.

[47] Andrea Carlevaris & José Ricardo Feris (2014), Running in the ICC Emergency Arbitrator Rules: The First Ten Cases, 25 *ICC International Court of Arbitration Bulletin* 34.

[48] Section 35 (1)(d) of Part 6, Arbitration Ordinance (Cap. 609) 2015, available at https://www.elegislation.gov.hk/hk/cap609 (1 June 2024).

[49] Stefan Michael Kröll, Julian D. M. Lew & Loukas A. Mistelis (2003), *Comparative International Commercial Arbitration*, Kluwer Law International, p. 595.

5.3 Legal Criteria for Granting Interim Measures by an Emergency Arbitrator

For the enforceability of the interim measures granted by an emergency arbitrator, it is crucial to guarantee that the relevant interim measures are applied in a justified way, procedurally and substantively. After addressing the jurisdiction issue of an emergency arbitrator, this part mainly focuses on the substantive legal criteria that an emergency arbitrator adopts to issue interim measures in international commercial arbitration. It starts from the current practice of emergency arbitrations in various arbitral institutions followed by the necessity to clarify the legal criteria concerning the issuance of interim measures by an emergency arbitrator and the applicable law regulating the process. The proposal for the legal criteria that must be considered by an emergency arbitrator is then provided.

5.3.1 Current Practice with Regard to Legal Criteria for Granting Interim Measures

Due to the confidentiality of international arbitration, there is a remarkable difficulty in relation to having access to cases. The number of cases that are available is limited and not exhaustive, which results in the "practical impossibility to deal 'scientifically' with interim relief" by making a thorough analysis of the experience in practice.[50] Most emergency arbitration cases that are available come from publications by arbitral institutions, for example, the ICC and the SCC. A small number of cases are available in the commentaries of practitioners in international commercial arbitration. Even though decisions by arbitrators "do not have a true precedential effect",[51] the reasoning in such decisions is considered "persuasive",[52] or at least it can serve as guidance.[53]

The ICC has published a task force report regarding the first 80 ICC emergency arbitrations, the Report of the ICC Commission on Arbitration and ADR Task Force on Emergency Arbitrator Proceedings published by the ICC in April 2019,[54] which

---

[50] José María Abascal Zamora (2007), The Art of Interim Measures, in Albert van den Berg, International Arbitration 2006: Back to Basics?, 13 *ICCA Congress Series* 751.

[51] Rolf A. Schütze (1994), The Precedential Effect of Arbitration Decisions, 11 *Journal of International Arbitration* 69.

[52] Ali Yesilirmak (2011), Interim and Conservatory Measures in ICC Arbitral Practice, 1999–2008, 22 *ICC International Court of Arbitration Bulletin* (Special Supplement) 9.

[53] Julian D.M. Lew (1982), The Case for the Publication of Arbitration Awards, in Jan C. Schultsz & Albert Jan van den Berg, *The Art of Arbitration: Essays on International Arbitration*, Kluwer Law and Taxation Publishers, p. 227.

[54] ICC, ICC Arbitration and ADR Commission Report on Emergency Arbitrator Proceedings, 2019, available at https://iccwbo.org/news-publications/arbitration-adr-rules-and-tools/emergency-arbitrator-proceedings-icc-arbitration-and-adr-commission-report/ (25 May 2024).

provides necessary information for the legal criteria adopted during the issuance of interim measures by the ICC emergency arbitrators.[55] The SCC also published almost all emergency arbitrator cases in its online practice notes. Accordingly, this book will mainly examine the practice in these two institutions, while using other materials from practitioners in international commercial arbitration as a supplementary source.

Since Article 29 of the ICC Arbitration Rules 2021, 2017 and 2012 clearly require a party to be in need of "urgent interim or conservatory measures that cannot await the constitution of an arbitral tribunal", the ICC emergency arbitrators referred to the "urgency" element in most of their decisions.[56] In the ICC emergency arbitration practice, there were two other frequently quoted criteria for granting interim measures, namely, a *prima facie* case for the requested measure and risk of irreparable harm.[57]

In the first 80 ICC emergency arbitrations, at least 31 of the emergency arbitrators took the possibility of success on the merits of the case into consideration.[58] Among the 31 cases, 25 of the emergency arbitrators only required the establishment of a *prima facie* case.[59] 40 of the first 80 ICC emergency arbitrators referred "irreparable harm", half of which did not simply interpreted this criterion in a literal sense.[60] For instance, one ICC emergency arbitrator elaborated that such "[s]tandard is not so high as to require harm that cannot be compensated by money but rather the that the harm will alter the status quo significantly and compound the damages".[61] Regarding the element of a risk of irreparable harm, the emergency arbitrators adopted a more flexible approach in one case, providing that "the applicant was entitled to relief despite the absence of such a risk, as the dispute would otherwise have worsened and granting the request would not cause irreparable harm to the responding party".[62]

---

[55] ICC, ICC Arbitration and ADR Commission Report on Emergency Arbitrator Proceedings, 2019, available at https://iccwbo.org/news-publications/arbitration-adr-rules-and-tools/emergency-arbitrator-proceedings-icc-arbitration-and-adr-commission-report/ (25 May 2024).

[56] ICC, ICC Arbitration and ADR Commission Report on Emergency Arbitrator Proceedings, 2019, p. 24, available at https://iccwbo.org/news-publications/arbitration-adr-rules-and-tools/emergency-arbitrator-proceedings-icc-arbitration-and-adr-commission-report/ (25 May 2024).

[57] Andrea Carlevaris & José Ricardo Feris (2014), Running in the ICC Emergency Arbitrator Rules: The First Ten Cases, 25 *ICC International Court of Arbitration Bulletin* 36.

[58] ICC, ICC Arbitration and ADR Commission Report on Emergency Arbitrator Proceedings, 2019, p. 25, available at https://iccwbo.org/news-publications/arbitration-adr-rules-and-tools/emergency-arbitrator-proceedings-icc-arbitration-and-adr-commission-report/ (25 May 2024).

[59] ICC, ICC Arbitration and ADR Commission Report on Emergency Arbitrator Proceedings, 2019, p. 25, available at https://iccwbo.org/news-publications/arbitration-adr-rules-and-tools/emergency-arbitrator-proceedings-icc-arbitration-and-adr-commission-report/ (25 May 2024).

[60] ICC, ICC Arbitration and ADR Commission Report on Emergency Arbitrator Proceedings, 2019, p. 26, available at https://iccwbo.org/news-publications/arbitration-adr-rules-and-tools/emergency-arbitrator-proceedings-icc-arbitration-and-adr-commission-report/ (25 May 2024).

[61] ICC, ICC Arbitration and ADR Commission Report on Emergency Arbitrator Proceedings, 2019, p. 26, available at https://iccwbo.org/news-publications/arbitration-adr-rules-and-tools/emergency-arbitrator-proceedings-icc-arbitration-and-adr-commission-report/ (25 May 2024).

[62] Andrea Carlevaris & José Ricardo Feris (2014), Running in the ICC Emergency Arbitrator Rules: The First Ten Cases, 25 *ICC International Court of Arbitration Bulletin* 36.

Other than the three most commonly applied criteria under the ICC Arbitration Rules, i.e., urgency, the likelihood of success on the merits, and irreparable harm, there are some additional ones. 19 of the first 80 ICC emergency arbitrators addressed the "no prejudgment on merits", which means they would not grant an interim measure if the request related is the same as the one on the merits.[63] 16 of the first 80 ICC emergency arbitrators referred to the "balance of equities", and 12 of them mentioned the principle of non-aggravation of a dispute. Even there is one ICC emergency arbitrator only relied on the risk of aggravation of the case to grant an interim measure.[64]

The SCC provides most of its emergency arbitrator practices in the SCC Practice Note on Emergency Arbitrator Decisions, which has been referred to by various SCC emergency arbitrators as "international best practice that any emergency arbitrator in proceedings conducted under the SCC Rules".[65] Further, an emergency arbitrator clarified that those requirements in practice are not "merely a mechanical check-list", but the foundation to build an assessment of whether the requests are "necessary and appropriate".[66]

In the 42 reported SCC emergency arbitrations, despite 6 ones without details of the proceedings, 27 of them adopted "a reasonable possibility of success on the merits" on a *prima facie* basis, 26 emergency arbitrators referred the "urgency" criterion, 28 used "the risk of irreparable harm" as guidance, and 20 considered "proportionality" of the issued interim measures.[67]

There are three SCC emergency arbitrators referred to "imminence" when examining the requirements of granting interim measures. The emergency arbitrator in the SCC Emergency Arbitration 2018/140 stated that "[t]he concept of urgency is

---

[63] ICC, ICC Arbitration and ADR Commission Report on Emergency Arbitrator Proceedings, 2019, p. 27, available at https://iccwbo.org/news-publications/arbitration-adr-rules-and-tools/emergency-arbitrator-proceedings-icc-arbitration-and-adr-commission-report/ (25 May 2024).

[64] ICC, ICC Arbitration and ADR Commission Report on Emergency Arbitrator Proceedings, 2019, p. 26, available at https://iccwbo.org/news-publications/arbitration-adr-rules-and-tools/emergency-arbitrator-proceedings-icc-arbitration-and-adr-commission-report/ (25 May 2024).

[65] Evelina T. Wahlström (2023), SCC Practice Note Emergency Arbitrator Decisions 2019–2022, 2023, p. 19, available at https://sccarbitrationinstitute.se/sites/default/files/2023-10/scc_practice-note_emergency-arbitrator-decisions-2019-2022.pdf (25 May 2024).

[66] SCC Emergency Arbitration No. 2014/053 and No. 2014/183, SCC Practice Emergency Arbitrator Decisions Rendered 2014, 2015, p. 7, available at https://sccinstitute.com/media/62020/scc-practice-emergency-arbitrators-2014_final.pdf (16 June 2020).

[67] SCC, SCC Practice Note Emergency Arbitrator Decision 2010–2013, available at https://sccarbitrationinstitute.se/sites/default/files/2022-11/scc-practice-2010-2013-emergency-arbitrator_final.pdf; SCC Practice Note Emergency Arbitrator Decision 2014, 2015, available at https://sccarbitrationinstitute.se/sites/default/files/2022-11/scc-practice-emergency-arbitrators-2014_final.pdf; SCC Practice Note Emergency Arbitrator Decision 2015–2016, 2017, available at https://sccarbitrationinstitute.se/sites/default/files/2022-11/ea-practice-note-emergency-arbitrator-decisions-rendered-2015-2016.pdf; SCC Practice Note Emergency Arbitrator Decision 2017–2018, 2020, available at https://sccarbitrationinstitute.se/sites/default/files/2022-11/scc_practise_note_dec2020.pdf; SCC Practice Note Emergency Arbitrator Decisions 2019–2022, 2023, available at https://sccarbitrationinstitute.se/sites/default/files/2023-10/scc_practice-note_emergency-arbitrator-decisions-2019-2022.pdf (25 May 2024).

interdependent on the existence of imminence of a threat: if the threat of grave harm is imminent, there is a need of urgent relief".[68] In one case, the emergency arbitrator of the SCC Emergency Arbitrator 057/2013 only relied on evident and explicit "urgency" in a conclusion describing the case as "a textbook example of a case in which a request for interim relief is justified".[69]

Other than the ICC and the SCC, the ICDR emergency arbitrators introduced four conditions when analyzing the request of an interim measure to prohibit one party from using confidential and sensitive information. The four conditions were: (a) a risk of irreparable harm which cannot be compensated by damages; (b) good prospects of success on the merits; (c) no other alternative remedy could be adequate to the same effect; and (d) any harm could be compensated by damages if the issuance was proven wrong.[70] The emergency arbitrators appointed by the SIAC tended to use "the real probability test or a good arguable case test" for issuing interim measures, together with "whether irreparable harm is likely to be caused" if the interim measures are not granted.[71]

5.3.2 *Necessity to Clarify the Legal Criteria*

Based on the comparison in Chap. 2, almost every arbitral institution empowers emergency arbitrators with broad discretion to issue interim measures. The debate between "flexibility and certainty"[72] is still ongoing in this area of law. Some submit that issuing interim measures is "at the full discretion of the arbitral tribunal".[73] By analogy, "there seems to be no reason to believe that emergency arbitrators will be less successful in using the same discretion entrusted upon them".[74] However, such an approach "is not conducive to consistency and predictability", especially when

---

[68] Evelina T. Wahlström (2020), SCC Practice Note Emergency Arbitrator Decision 2017–2018, p. 9, available at https://sccarbitrationinstitute.se/sites/default/files/2022-11/scc_practise_note_dec2020.pdf (25 May 2024).

[69] SCC, SCC Practice: Emergency Arbitrator Decisions, 2010–2013, 2014, p. 24, available at https://sccinstitute.com/media/29995/scc-practice-2010-2013-emergency-arbitrator_final.pdf (16 June 2020).

[70] Guillaume Lemenez & Paul Quigley (2008), The ICDR's Emergency Arbitrator Procedure in Action: Part I: A Look at the Empirical Data, 63 *Dispute Resolution Journal* 67.

[71] Vivekananda, N., The SIAC Emergency Arbitrator Experience, available at http://siac.org.sg/2013-09-18-01-57-20/2013-09-22-00-27-02/articles/338-the-siac-emergency-arbitrator-experience (16 June 2020).

[72] Jeffrey Waincymer (2012), *Procedure and Evidence in International Arbitration*, Kluwer Law International, p. 625.

[73] Pierre A. Karrer & Peter A. Straub (2009), *Practitioner's Handbook on International Commercial Arbitration*, Oxford Univeristy Press, para. 12.119. See also Christopher Boog (2011), The Laws Governing Interim Measures in International Arbitration, in Franco Ferrari & Kröll, *Conflict of Laws in International Arbitration*, Sellier, p. 425.

[74] Yesilirmak, Ali, Provisional Measures in International Commercial Arbitration, Kluwer Law International, 2005, p. 137.

the importance of interim measures continues to grow.[75] This book argues that, although such discretion based on a case-by-case approach is reasonable, it is still necessary to clarify the applicable legal criteria, because there is no existing universal standard for the issuance of interim measures and there are quite some differences between the practice of an emergency arbitrator and that of an arbitral tribunal. The approach suggested does not require specific rules but instead by developing general legal criteria for interim measures by an emergency arbitrator to gain better global recognition and enforcement.

5.3.2.1 No Universal Standards Applied to the Issuance of Interim Measures

Currently, "there is little guidance"[76] on the legal standards applied to the interim measures in the emergency arbitrator mechanism. Generally, arbitral institutions do not specify the detailed requirements for an emergency arbitrator to consider while issuing interim measures. The ICC states that an emergency arbitrator "shall conduct the proceedings in the manner which the emergency arbitrator considers to be appropriate, taking into account the nature and the urgency of the Application".[77] The ICDR similarly stipulates that an "emergency arbitrator shall have the power to order or award any interim or conservatory measures that the emergency arbitrator deems necessary".[78] The HKIAC makes it clear that an emergency arbitrator "may conduct such proceedings in such a manner as the emergency arbitrator considers appropriate".[79] The LCIA shares a similar view as in the ICC and the HKIAC arbitration rules.[80] The SIAC considers that an "Emergency Arbitrator shall have the power to order or award any interim relief that he deems necessary".[81] The SCC makes it available for an emergency arbitrator to grant "any interim measures it deems appropriate".[82] The words used by those institutions, such as "appropriate"

---

[75] Kaj Hobér (2007), Interim Measures by Arbitrators, in Van den Berg, Albert, International Arbitration 2006: Back to Basics?, 13 *ICCA Congress Series* 731.

[76] Kap-You (Kevin) Kim & Bhushan Satish (2018), Legal Criteria for Granting Relief in Emergency Arbitrator Proceedings: Where Are We Now and Where Do We Go from Here?, in Neil Kaplan & Michael J.Moser, *Jurisdiction, Admissibility and Choice of Law in International Arbitration: Liber Amicorum Michael Pryles*, Kluwer Law International, p. 175; Edgardo Muñoz (2015), How Urgent Shall an Emergency Be?—The Standards Required to Grant Urgent Relief by Emergency Arbitrators, 4 *Yearbook on International Arbitration* 43; Patricia Shaughnessy (2017), The Emergency Arbitrator, in Patricia Shaughnessy & Sherlin Tung, *The Powers and Duties of an Arbitrator: Liber Amicorum Pierre A. Karrer*, Kluwer Law International, p. 346; Robert Sills (2015), The Continuing Role of the Courts in the Era of the Emergency Arbitrator, in Albert van den Berg, Legitimacy: Myths, Realities, Challenges, 18 *ICCA Congress Series* 281.

[77] Article 5(2) of Appendix V, ICC Arbitration Rules 2021.

[78] Article 7(4), ICDR Arbitration Rules 2021.

[79] Article 10 of Schedule 4, HKIAC Arbitration Rules 2024.

[80] Article 9.7, LCIA Arbitration Rules 2020.

[81] Article 8 of Schedule 1, SIAC Arbitration Rules 2016.

[82] Article 37 & Article 1(2) of Appendix II, SCC Arbitration Rules 2023.

and "necessary", are vague and broad, which may cause confusion when it is applied by emergency arbitrators in practice.

Since the interim measures granted by regular arbitrators are used more frequently, and an emergency arbitrator has the same power as a regular arbitrator in issuing interim measures (see Chap. 4), it seems reasonable to seek some guidance from the requirements set for regular arbitrators in arbitral tribunals. Article 28 of the ICC Arbitration Rules 2017 stipulates that "[u]nless the parties have otherwise agreed, as soon as the file has been transmitted to it, the arbitral tribunal may, at the request of a party, order any interim or conservatory measure it deems appropriate".[83] The ICDR also does not regulate specifically by stating that "[a]t the request of any party, the arbitral tribunal may order or award any interim or conservatory measures it deems necessary, including injunctive relief and measures for the protection or conservation of property".[84] The HKIAC states similarly that "[a]t the request of either party, the arbitral tribunal may order any interim measures it deems necessary or appropriate".[85] The LCIA provides that an arbitral tribunal shall have the power to order the interim measures as the tribunal considers "appropriate".[86] The SIAC adopts the same approach stating that "[t]he Tribunal may, at the request of a party, issue an order or an Award granting an injunction or any other interim relief it deems appropriate".[87] The SCC also uses "appropriate" as the only yardstick for the consideration of the arbitral tribunal.[88] Based on these expressions, arbitral institutions "typically do not provide meaningful standards for the grant of provisional measures".[89]

By using these formulations, arbitral institutions seem to leave the issuance of interim measures at the full discretion of the emergency arbitrators. However, this book maintains that those expressions should be understood as an emergency arbitrator "will formulate and apply legal standards specifying when provisional measures will be granted".[90] Despite the wide discretion, some guidelines need to be addressed.

In addition to the above general standards adopted by arbitral institutions in granting interim measures either by an emergency arbitrator or by an arbitral tribunal, there are two exceptions. One can be found in the HKIAC, and the other one is provided by the Australian Centre for International Commercial Arbitration (ACICA).[91] Although the ACICA[92] is not among the six chosen arbitral institutions

---

[83] Article 28, ICC Arbitration Rules 2021.

[84] Article 27 (1), ICDR Arbitration Rules 2021.

[85] Article 23.2, HKIAC Arbitration Rules 2024.

[86] Article 25.1, LCIA Arbitration Rules 2020.

[87] Article 30.1, SIAC Arbitration Rules 2016.

[88] Article 37(1), SCC Arbitration Rules 2023.

[89] Gary B. Born (2021), *International Commercial Arbitration*, Kluwer Law International, p. 2649.

[90] Gary B. Born (2021), *International Commercial Arbitration*, Kluwer Law International, p. 2649.

[91] Grant Hanessian & E. Alexandra Dosman (2016), Songs of Innocence and Experience: Ten Years of Emergency Arbitration, 27 *American Review of International Arbitration* 227.

[92] ACICA, Introduction, available at https://acica.org.au/ (1 June 2024).

that are the main focus of the comparison of arbitral rules in this book (see Chap. 2), its arbitral rules will be used here as supplementary information.

The HKIAC provides two factors for an arbitral tribunal to consider, which are also applicable to the emergency arbitrator proceedings. These two facts include, but are not limited to "(a) harm not adequately reparable by an award of damages which is likely to result if the measure is not ordered, and such harm substantially outweighs the harm that is likely to result to the party against whom the measure is directed if the measures are granted; and (b) there is a reasonable possibility that the requesting party will succeed on the merits of the claim. The determination on this possibility shall not affect the discretion of the arbitral tribunal in making any subsequent determination".[93]

In the ACICA Arbitration Rules 2021, the section on the emergency arbitrator mechanism specifies that the party requesting interim measures shall satisfy "(a) irreparable harm is likely to result if the Emergency Interim Measure is not ordered; (b) such harm substantially outweighs the harm that is likely to result to the party affected by the Emergency Interim Measure if the Emergency Interim Measure is granted; and (c) there is a reasonable possibility that the requesting party will succeed on the merits, provided that any determination on this possibility shall not affect the liberty of decision of the Arbitral Tribunal in making any subsequent determination".[94] These three criteria correspond with the standards provided by the UNCITRAL Model Law on International Commercial Arbitration (1985) with amendments as adopted in 2006 (UNCITRAL Model Law 2006). Article 17 of UNCITRAL Model Law 2006 requires a party to satisfy the following elements for an interim measure "(a) [h]arm not adequately reparable by an award of damages is likely to result if the measure is not ordered, and such harm substantially outweighs the harm that is likely to result to the party against whom the measure is directed if the measure is granted; and (b) [t]here is a reasonable possibility that the requesting party will succeed on the merits of the claim. The determination on this possibility shall not affect the discretion of the arbitral tribunal in making any subsequent determination",[95] if the parties request the interim measures to "(a)[m]aintain or restore the status quo pending determination of the dispute; (b) [t]ake action that would prevent, or refrain from taking action that is likely to cause (i) current or imminent harm or (ii) prejudice to arbitral process itself; (c)[p]rovide a means of preserving assets out of which a subsequent award may be satisfied".[96] For the interim measures relating to material evidence which is critical to arbitration, the UNCITRAL Model Law empowers arbitrators to decide what they consider "appropriate".[97] However, notice needs to be given to the fact that the interim measures rendered by an emergency arbitrator and by an arbitral tribunal are not the same, due to the different timeframes, stages of the decisions and the types of interim measures available.

---

93 Article 23.4, HKIAC Arbitration Rules 2024.

94 Article 3.5 of Schedule 1, ACICA Arbitration Rules 2021.

95 Article 17 A (1), UNCITRAL Model Law 2006.

96 Article 17(2)(a)-(c), UNCITRAL Model Law 2006.

97 Article 17A (2), UNCITRAL Model Law 2006.

5.3.2.2 Differences Between Interim Measures Granted by an Emergency Arbitrator and by an Arbitral Tribunal

As discussed in Chap. 4, this book considers that an emergency arbitrator acts as a proper arbitrator, and the decision issued needs to be seen as an arbitrator's decision issuing interim measures pending the constitution of a tribunal. Nevertheless, due to the following distinction between the interim measures granted by an emergency arbitrator and those granted by an arbitral tribunal, the legal criteria applied when issuing interim measures shall be different.[98]

Firstly, the timeframes available for an emergency arbitrator and an arbitral tribunal result in a difference. An emergency arbitrator does not enjoy the "benefit of time" compared to a fully constituted tribunal.[99] The purpose of the emergency arbitrator mechanism is set up for very urgent situations where parties cannot wait for the constitution of an arbitral tribunal. Generally, the period for an emergency arbitrator to decide whether and how to grant the interim measures requested by parties is between 5 and 15 days, with a possible extension under exceptional circumstances. The period for an arbitral tribunal to decide on the requests for interim measures is much longer. Under the ICC Arbitration Rules 2021, an arbitral tribunal is granted at least six months to issue a final award.[100] Starting from the submission of a case file, an arbitral tribunal can order interim measures at the request of a party.[101] The ICDR provides for 60 days for an arbitral tribunal to deliver a final award after the closure of hearing.[102] As soon as an arbitral tribunal is constituted, interim measures can be issued by the arbitral tribunal. The LCIA does not provide a deadline for an award, but merely states that an arbitral tribunal "shall seek to make its final award as soon as reasonably possible following the last submission from the parties".[103] Based on the HKIAC Arbitration Rules 2024, an arbitral tribunal can order interim measures prior to a final award and after the constitution of a tribunal.[104] The HKIAC does not specify the timeframe for a tribunal to issue a final award.

---

[98] Kap-You (Kevin) Kim & Bhushan Satish (2018), Legal Criteria for Granting Relief in Emergency Arbitrator Proceedings: Where Are We Now and Where Do We Go from Here?, in Neil Kaplan & Michael J.Moser, *Jurisdiction, Admissibility and Choice of Law in International Arbitration: Liber Amicorum Michael Pryles*, Kluwer Law International, p. 176; Edgardo Muñoz (2015), How Urgent Shall an Emergency Be?—The Standards Required to Grant Urgent Relief by Emergency Arbitrators, 4 *Yearbook on International Arbitration* 53.

[99] Kap-You (Kevin) Kim & Bhushan Satish (2018), Legal Criteria for Granting Relief in Emergency Arbitrator Proceedings: Where Are We Now and Where Do We Go from Here?, in Neil Kaplan & Michael J.Moser, *Jurisdiction, Admissibility and Choice of Law in International Arbitration: Liber Amicorum Michael Pryles*, Kluwer Law International, p. 188.

[100] Article 31, ICC Arbitration Rules 2021.

[101] Article 28(1), ICC Arbitration Rules 2021.

[102] Article 33(1), ICDR Arbitration Rules 2021.

[103] Article 15.10, LCIA Arbitration Rules 2020.

[104] Article 23.3, HKIAC Arbitration Rules 2024.

Even in the expedited procedure, a tribunal at least can have six months to issue a final award.[105] The SIAC asks a tribunal to submit the award "not later than 45 days from the date on which the [t]ribunal declares the proceedings closed".[106] After the commencement of arbitration or the reference of the case to an arbitral tribunal, the SCC provides for six months for the arbitral tribunal to grant appropriate interim measures.[107] By comparing the duration of the proceedings, an emergency arbitrator has much less time to decide on the request of interim measures due to the nature of such proceedings. As a result, it is reasonable to expect that the substantive legal criteria for emergency arbitrators are not identical to those applied by arbitral tribunals.

Secondly, the decision-making stages are different. An emergency arbitrator cannot decide on the full picture of a dispute at such an early stage of arbitration. From the perspective of the parties, they are not in the position to access all materials and evidence effectively and accurately and to argue convincingly at this stage.[108] Furthermore, the decision made by an emergency arbitrator can be modified or even terminated by a tribunal, which implies that any facts and issues, for example, the issue of joinder,[109] discovered by the tribunal later on, will possibly have an influence on the decision about the interim measures. In this sense, the legal criteria applied to the interim measures granted by an emergency arbitrator should be less strict.

Additionally, the types of interim measures that are available may vary. For example, the Hong Kong Arbitration Ordinance (Cap. 609), which is the current effective arbitration law of Hong Kong, adopts the regulation regarding the interim measures granted by an arbitral tribunal from the UNCITRAL Model Law 2006. It reads that an arbitral tribunal can order a party to "(a) [m]aintain or restore the status quo pending determination of the dispute; (b) [t]ake action that would prevent, or refrain from taking action that is likely to cause, current or imminent harm or prejudice to the arbitral process itself; (c) [p]rovide a means of preserving assets out of which a subsequent award may be satisfied; or (d) [p]reserve evidence that may be relevant and material to the resolution of the dispute".[110] When regulating the types of interim measures which may be granted by an emergency arbitrator, in addition to these four types, the Arbitration Ordinance (Cap. 609) provides for two more

[105] Article 42.2, HKIAC Arbitration Rules 2024.

[106] Article 32.3, SIAC Arbitration Rules 2016.

[107] Article 43, SCC Arbitration Rules 2023.

[108] Kap-You (Kevin) Kim & Bhushan Satish (2018), Legal Criteria for Granting Relief in Emergency Arbitrator Proceedings: Where Are We Now and Where Do We Go from Here?, in Neil Kaplan & Michael J.Moser, *Jurisdiction, Admissibility and Choice of Law in International Arbitration: Liber Amicorum Michael Pryles*, Kluwer Law International, p. 188.

[109] The issue of joinder deals with adding non-signatories into an arbitration proceeding, see this topic in detail in Dongdoo Choi (2019), Joinder in International Commercial Arbitration, 35 *Arbitration International* 29–55.

[110] Section 35 of Part 6, Arbitration Ordinance (Cap. 609) 2015, available at https://www.elegislation.gov.hk/hk/cap609 (1 June 2024).

possibilities, namely "(e) give security in connection with anything to be done under paragraph (a), (b), (c) or (d); (f) give security for the costs of the arbitration".[111]

In light of the arguments given above, it is reasonable to believe that the standards applied to the interim measures rendered by an emergency arbitrator need to differ from the requirements applied for an arbitral tribunal, even if the distinction may be just slight. The following part starts with an analysis of the law applicable to the issuance of interim measures.

5.3.3 *Law Applicable to the Issuance of Interim Measures*

First, there is one crucial distinction that needs to be made when discussing the law applicable to the issuance of interim measures in international commercial arbitration. There are two legal issues in question. One is the law applicable to an emergency arbitrator's power to issue interim measures, and the other one is the law applicable to an emergency arbitrator's exercise of that authority. In other words, the former question deals with the limitation of the power of an emergency arbitrator, and the latter is more of "how" an emergency arbitrator can exercise such power.

Due to the organization of this book, the first question will be addressed in the next chapter when discussing the possible barriers for the recognition and enforcement of the interim measures granted by an emergency arbitrator.

Assuming that an emergency arbitrator does have the authority to provide interim measures requested by parties, either under an arbitration agreement or an applicable law,[112] the next step is to consider the law governing the legal criteria. This issue, however, has attracted little intention in the international commercial arbitration community.[113]

If parties have chosen an applicable law or have agreed on standards for the issuance of interim measures, the content of such straightforward party autonomy determines the legal criteria of the process. However, this situation is rarely witnessed

[111] Section 22B (2) of Part 3A, Arbitration Ordinance (Cap. 609) 2015, available at https://www.elegislation.gov.hk/hk/cap609 (1 June 2024).

[112] Such an arbitration agreement refers to the chosen set of institutional rules, for example, ICC Arbitration Rules 2017 containing the emergency arbitrator provisions. Regarding the applicable law, the Hong Kong Arbitration Ordinance (Cap. 609) explicitly empowers the emergency arbitrator to issue the necessary interim measures. At the same time, other jurisdictions may give such power to the emergency arbitrator implicitly.

[113] Gary B. Born (2021), *International Commercial Arbitration*, Kluwer Law International, p. 2644; Christopher Boog (2011), The Laws Governing Interim Measures in International Arbitration, in Franco Ferrari & Kröll, *Conflict of Laws in International Arbitration*, Sellier, p. 424.

in international commercial arbitration.[114] The possible exception may occur in intellectual property disputes, where parties agree to the specific requirements of interim measures in their contracts.[115]

In most cases, parties seldom choose specific rules regulating the standards of interim measures. Regarding this issue, the opinions about which law applies, arguably vary. Some emergency arbitrators adopt the requirements available from the law of the seat of arbitration, some follow "universally accepted criteria", and others take the previous institutional practice and legal commentaries into consideration.[116] This section, when examining the law governing the legal criteria, takes both an emergency arbitrator and an arbitral tribunal into consideration as the issuers of interim measures. There are four main suggested sources: the law of the seat of arbitration; the law applicable to the merits of the case; the law of the place where the enforcement is sought; and international standards.[117] After discussing these four approaches, this book proposes a combined approach.

5.3.3.1 Law Governing Arbitral Proceedings (the *Lex Arbitri*)

The law of the seat of arbitration is usually the law governing arbitral proceedings when there is no specific choice made by parties. As confirmed by continuous practice, the law governing arbitration "will have to be respected".[118] Occasionally, arbitrators may refer to the law governing arbitration, i.e., the *lex arbitri* when issuing interim measures.[119] For example, the ICC Arbitration case No. 8786 referred to the *lex arbitri* when the tribunal examined the legal criteria for possible interim measures, namely the Swiss Private International Law Act and the commentaries regarding the Swiss Arbitration Act.[120] An ICC arbitral tribunal once noted that the trend in arbitration practice is "to refer to the requirements either set by the applicable

---

[114] Gary B. Born (2021), *International Commercial Arbitration*, Kluwer Law International, p. 2650.

[115] Gary B. Born (2016), *International Arbitration and Forum Selection Agreements: Drafting and Enforcing*, Kluwer Law International, para. 12–14.

[116] Patricia Shaughnessy (2017), The Emergency Arbitrator, in Patricia Shaughnessy & Sherlin Tung, *The Powers and Duties of an Arbitrator: Liber Amicorum Pierre A. Karrer*, Kluwer Law International, p. 346.

[117] Mika Savola (2015), Interim Measures and Emergency Arbitrator Proceedings, Presentation at the 23rd Croatian Arbitration Days: Access to Arbitral Justice, p. 9, available at https://arbitration.fi/wp-content/uploads/sites/22/2016/04/23-cad-savola-interim-measures-and-emergency-arbitrator-proceedings.pdf (16 June 2020).

[118] Georgios Petrochilos (2004), *Procedural Law in International Arbitration*, Oxford University Press on Demand, p. 169.

[119] Andrea Carlevaris & José Ricardo Feris (2014), Running in the ICC Emergency Arbitrator Rules: The First Ten Cases, 25 *ICC International Court of Arbitration Bulletin* 36.

[120] Interim Award in Case 8786, Extracts from ICC Awards Referring to Interim and Conservatory Measures, 11 *ICC International Court of Arbitration Bulletin* (Issue 1) 2000, p. 81.

law or deemed appropriate by the tribunal".[121] In another case seated in Paris, when discussing the standards for the determination of a requested interim measure, the arbitral tribunal considered that "French procedural law is helpful as a pointer to and an example of the general principles to be exercised in dealing with such applications".[122] As a result, it seems necessary to compare different arbitration laws. The chosen jurisdictions are the same as those addressed in Chap. 3.

The International Arbitration Act of the Statutes of the Republic of Singapore (Cap. 143A), amended in 2012, only empowers arbitral tribunals, including emergency arbitrators,[123] issue "an interim injunction or any other interim measure" without specific legal standards.[124] Hong Kong has adopted the UNCITRAL Model Law 2006 as the main source of its arbitration law, with necessary modifications and supplements.[125] In Part 3A of the Hong Kong Arbitration Ordinance (Cap. 609) regarding the emergency arbitrator provisions, there is no specific regulation for which legal criteria should be used. For arbitral tribunals, the Hong Kong Arbitration Ordinance (Cap. 609) takes the standards set out in the UNCITRAL Model law 2006 as the conditions applicable in this scenario.[126] The Dutch Code of Civil Procedure, which was amended in 2015, also does not specify criteria.

There is no available provision governing the emergency arbitrator proceedings in the current legislation in Mainland China. Since interim measures are closely related to arbitration, although tribunals by themselves have no power to issue the interim measures requested,[127] the law does provide several requirements for the issuance of such interim measures. The Arbitration Law of the People's Republic of

---

[121] Partial Award in Case 12,040, in Ali Yesilirmak (2011), Interim and Conservatory Measures in ICC Arbitral Practice, 1999–2008, 22 *ICC International Court of Arbitration Bulletin* (Special Supplement) 9.

[122] Interim Award in Case 7544, Extracts from ICC Awards Referring to Interim and Conservatory Measures, 11 *ICC International Court of Arbitration Bulletin* (Issue 1) 2000, p. 58.

[123] Section 5.2 (1) of Part II, International Arbitration Act of the Statutes of the Republic of Singapore (Cap. 143A) 2012, available at https://sso.agc.gov.sg/Act/IAA1994 (1 June 2024).

[124] Section 12 (1)(i) of Part II, International Arbitration Act of the Statutes of the Republic of Singapore (Cap. 143A) 2012, available at https://sso.agc.gov.sg/Act/IAA1994 (1 June 2024).

[125] Section 5.4 of Part 1, Arbitration Ordinance (Cap. 609) 2015, available at https://www.elegislation.gov.hk/hk/cap609 (1 June 2024).

[126] Section 36 of Part 6, Arbitration Ordinance (Cap. 609) 2015, available at https://www.elegislation.gov.hk/hk/cap609 (1 June 2024).

[127] Article 28 of the Arbitration Law of the People's Republic of China regulates that "[i]f a party applies for property preservation, the arbitration commission shall submit the party's application to the people's court in accordance with the relevant provisions of the Civil Procedure Law". Article 68 of the Arbitration Law gives that "[i]f a party to a foreign-related arbitration applies for preservation of the evidence, the foreign-related arbitration commission shall submit his application to the intermediate people's court in the place where the evidence is located". Article 289 of the Civil Procedure Law of the People's Republic of China provides that "[When] a party applies for a preservation measure, the international arbitral institution of the People's Republic of China shall submit the party's application to the intermediate people's court at the place of domicile of the respondent or at the place where the respondent's property is located". Translation of the Arbitration Law of the People's Republic of China 2017 is available at http://en.pkulaw.cn/display.aspx?cgid=83c8fbd6da8a6eb8bdfb&lib=law (1 June 2024); translation of the Civil Procedure Law

China provides for two possible reasons that allow parties to seek interim measures regarding property preservation: "if it may become impossible or difficult for the party to implement the award due to an act of the other party or other causes"[128]; And, regarding the preservation of evidence, Article 46 of the Arbitration Law provides that "[u]nder the circumstances where the evidence may be destroyed or lost or difficult to obtain at a later time, a party may apply for preservation of the evidence".[129]

The Federal Arbitration Act (FAA) of the United States does not contain articles relating to arbitral interim measures. The Restatement of the Law (Third)—The U.S. Law of International Commercial Arbitration 2012 is also silent on granting interim measures by arbitral tribunals. On the state level, the statutes of 50 states contain various regulations. There are no regulations governing the procedures for the interim measures issued by arbitral tribunals in the states of Alabama, Mississippi, New Hampshire, New York, Rhode Island, and Wisconsin. The states of California, Connecticut, Florida, Georgia, Illinois, Louisiana, Oregon, and Texas use the UNCITRAL Model Law 1985 as the basis for the legislation, among which, Florida has also adopted the UNCITRAL Model Law 2006.[130] West's Annotated California Codes provides that "[u]nless otherwise agreed by the parties, the arbitral tribunal may, at the request of a party, order a party to take any interim measure of protection as the arbitral tribunal may consider necessary in respect of the subject matter of the dispute".[131] The statutes of Connecticut,[132] Illinois,[133] Louisiana,[134] Oregon,[135] and Texas[136] use the same criteria for the issuance of interim measures by arbitral tribunals, namely it must be "necessary". The Georgia statutes states: "[u]nless otherwise agreed by the parties, the arbitration tribunal may, at the request of a party, grant interim measures as it deems appropriate".[137] As Florida has adopted the UNCITRAL Model Law 2006 in its statutes, the conditions for arbitral tribunals are identical to those in the UNCITRAL Model Law 2006.[138] Although the legislation of Washington does not rely on the provisions in the UNCITRAL Model Law

of the People's Republic of China 2023 is available at http://en.pkulaw.cn/display.aspx?id=e55237a87e2e1d04bdfb&lib=law (1 June 2024).

[128] Article 28, the Arbitration Law of the People's Republic of China 2017, translation is available at http://en.pkulaw.cn/display.aspx?cgid=83c8fbd6da8a6eb8bdfb&lib=law (1 June 2024).

[129] Article 46, the Arbitration Law of the People's Republic of China 2017, translation is available at http://en.pkulaw.cn/display.aspx?cgid=83c8fbd6da8a6eb8bdfb&lib=law (1 June 2024).

[130] UNCITRAL, Status: UNCITRAL Model Law on International Commercial Arbitration (1985), with amendments as adopted in 2006, available at https://uncitral.un.org/en/texts/arbitration/modellaw/commercial_arbitration/status (1 June 2024).

[131] Section 1297.171, West's Annotated California Codes 1988.

[132] Section 50a-117, Connecticut General Statutes Annotated 1989.

[133] Section 30/15–10, West's Smith-Hurd Illinois Compiled Statutes Annotated 1998.

[134] Section 4257, West's Louisiana Statutes Annotated 2006.

[135] Section 36.486, West's Oregon Revised Statutes Annotated 1991.

[136] Section 172.083, Vernon's Texas Statutes and Codes Annotated 1997.

[137] Section 9-9-38(a), West's Code of Georgia Annotated 2012.

[138] Section 684.0019, West's Florida Statutes Annotated 2013.

2006, the standards in its statutes nevertheless match those provided by the UNCITRAL Model Law 2006.[139] Delaware,[140] North Carolina,[141] and Ohio[142] also use "necessary" as guidance for arbitral tribunals when granting the interim measures.

The Uniform Arbitration Act (UAA) 2000 simply provides that an arbitrator "may issue such orders for provisional remedies, including interim awards, as the arbitrator finds necessary to protect the effectiveness of the arbitration proceeding and to promote the fair and expeditious resolution of the controversy, to the same extent and under the same conditions as if the controversy were the subject of a civil action".[143] However, the federal statutes do not provide enough guidance for the conditions of interim measures that should be adopted in litigation by national judges.[144] Understandably, the United States is a common law country, in which the statutes are only a part of the law as a whole.

Traditionally, there are four prerequisites to be considered by the U.S. courts and the legislation of different states in their own civil codes, i.e.: (1) the existence of irreparable harm without the interim measures; (2) a likelihood of success in the merits; (3) a balance between the harm suffered by parties; and (4) public interest.[145] By adopting or introducing the UAA as arbitration law, the states of Alaska,[146] Arizona,[147] Arkansas,[148] Colorado,[149] Hawaii,[150] Kansas,[151] Michigan,[152] Minnesota,[153] Nevada,[154] New Jersey,[155] New Mexico,[156] North

---

[139] Section 7.05.190, West's Revised Code of Washington Annotated 2015.

[140] Section 5807, West's Delaware Code Annotated 2015. Although this is the chapter for Delaware Rapid Arbitration Act, it implies the requirement of the legislators' intention of the legal criteria for the interim measures.

[141] Section 1-567.47–(a), West's North Carolina General Statutes Annotated 2017.

[142] Section 2712.36, Baldwin's Ohio Revised Code Annotated 1991.

[143] Section 8 (b)(1), Uniform Arbitration Act 2000, available at https://www.uniformlaws.org/viewdocument/final-act-2?CommunityKey=a0ad71d6-085f-4648-857a-e9e893ae2736&tab=librarydocuments (1 June 2024).

[144] Title VII. Provisional and Final Remedies, Federal Rules of Civil Procedure for the United States District Courts, United States Code Annotated 1991.

[145] Bethany M. Bates (2011), Reconciliation after Winter: The Standard for Preliminary Injunctions in Federal Courts, 111 *Columbia Law Review* 1522; Gebreyesus Abegaz Yimer (2016), Standards for Provisional and Protective Measures in Civil Litigation: What Ethiopian Courts May Learn from US Courts, 24 *African Journal of International and Comparative Law* 335.

[146] Section 09.43.350(b) (1), West's Alaska Statutes Annotated 2004.

[147] Section 12-3008 (B) (1), Arizona Revised Statutes Annotated 2011.

[148] Section 16-108-208 (b) (1), West's Arkansas Code Annotated 2011.

[149] Section 13-22-208 (2) (a), West's Colorado Revised Statutes Annotated 2004.

[150] Section 658A-8 (b) (1), West's Hawaii Revised Statutes Annotated 2001.

[151] Section 5-430 (b) (1), West's Kansas Statutes Annotated 2018.

[152] Section 691.1688 (2) (a), Michigan Compiled Laws Annotated 2013.

[153] Section 572B.08 (b), Minnesota Statutes Annotated 2011.

[154] Section 38.222 (1) (a), West's Nevada Revised Statutes Annotated 2001.

[155] Section 2A:23B-8 (b) (1), New Jersey Statutes Annotated 2003.

[156] Section 44-7A-9 (b) (1), West's New Mexico Statutes Annotated 2001.

Dakota,[157] Oklahoma,[158] Pennsylvania,[159] Utah,[160] West Virginia,[161] and the District of Columbia[162] follow the same provision as above. Although Idaho, Indiana, Iowa, Kentucky, Maine, Maryland, Massachusetts, Missouri, Montana, Nebraska, South Carolina, South Dakota, Tennessee, Vermont, Virginia, and Wyoming have enacted the content of the UAA, their codes do not provide the standard in as much detail as in the UAA.

Based on the above overview, in most circumstances, the *lex arbitri* is either silent or only provides minimal guidance for how interim measures should be granted in arbitration. The only exception is the arbitration laws of the states that have adopted the UNCITRAL Model Law 2006. However, the UNCITRAL Model Law 2006 is not a piece of internal legislation, as such, but a set of international standards that aim to harmonize the practice in international commercial arbitration.

From another perspective, using the *lex arbitri* does not seem to be an ideal approach to determine the legal criteria for the issuance of interim measures by an emergency arbitrator. Although there is no need to characterize a specific issue as "procedural",[163] to some extent, the legal criteria discussed in this chapter are more "substantive" in nature than purely "procedural". Additionally, as indicated in practice, when parties choose a particular seat of arbitration or the law governing arbitral proceedings, they seldom expect that the same law would apply to the substantive criteria for rendering interim measures.[164]

After the discussion in this part, it can be concluded that, unless the arbitration law contains specific mandatory rules for the issuance of interim measures by an emergency arbitrator, "there is little reason to apply the law of the arbitral seat, i.e., the *lex arbitri*, to the question of prerequisites for granting interim relief".[165] However, the above discussion can also be identified as an inspiring source for the following discussion regarding proposed legal criteria for the interim measures made by emergency arbitrators.

[157] Section 32-29.3-08 (2) (a), West's North Dakota Century Code Annotated 2003.

[158] Section 1859 (B) (1), Oklahoma Statutes Annotated 2006.

[159] Section 7321.9 (b) (1), Purdon's Pennsylvania Statutes and Consolidated Statutes 2019.

[160] Section 78B-11-109 (2) (a), West's Utah Code Annotated 2008.

[161] Section 55-10-10 (b) (1), West's Annotated Code of West Virginia 2015.

[162] Section 16-4408 (b) (1), West's District of Columbia Code Annotated 2008.

[163] Georgios Petrochilos (2004), *Procedural Law in International Arbitration*, Oxford University Press on Demand, p. 169.

[164] Gary B. Born (2021), *International Commercial Arbitration*, Kluwer Law International, p. 2647.

[165] Christopher Boog (2011), The Laws Governing Interim Measures in International Arbitration, in Franco Ferrari & Kröll, *Conflict of Laws in International Arbitration*, Sellier, p. 425; Kap-You (Kevin) Kim & Bhushan Satish (2018), Legal Criteria for Granting Relief in Emergency Arbitrator Proceedings: Where Are We Now and Where Do We Go from Here?, in Neil Kaplan & Michael J.Moser, *Jurisdiction, Admissibility and Choice of Law in International Arbitration: Liber Amicorum Michael Pryles*, Kluwer Law International, p. 178.

5.3.3.2 Governing Law of the Substance (the *Lex Causae*)

Another suggestion for the law governing the legal criteria for issuing interim measures is the law applicable to the merits of cases. It refers to the law that "governs the interpretation and validity of the contract, the rights and obligations of the parties, the mode of performance, and the consequences of breaches of the contract".[166] In the ICC Arbitration case No. 8879,[167] the arbitration clause in this dispute stated that the Mexican law, which was the law governing the substance, would be the law applicable to the resolution. The tribunal, in this case, considered "it appropriate to apply Mexican substantive law to the issues addressed in this interim award".[168]

Usually, parties tend to choose a substantive national law to govern the contract in a dispute. Sometimes, when a case involves international sales of goods, then the United Nations Convention on Contracts for the International Sale of Goods 1980 (CISG) may be chosen as the governing law. The *lex mercatoria,* including the general principles of international law, the UNIDROIT Principles of International Commercial Contracts, trade usages, and other sources, could also be selected by parties to be the substantive law.[169]

However, it is not very convincing that the law governing the substance should be employed as applicable to the legal criteria of the interim measures granted by an emergency arbitrator. Firstly, there are no or at least there are limited meaningful requirements listed in general for arbitration. The possible existence of such legal criteria may be found in the civil procedure law for litigation in a specific jurisdiction. Due to the different duties of arbitrators and judges, the limitation of an arbitrator's power to issue interim measures and the fact that arbitrators lack coercive powers, the legal criteria outlined for litigation conducted by judges may not be suitable for arbitrators.[170] This is especially the case if parties choose the substantive law of a particular jurisdiction but they choose a different seat in which to arbitrate, it is less reasonable to apply the law governing the substance to be applicable to interim measures.[171] Moreover, applying the requirements of interim measures from the law

---

[166] Alan Redfern & J. Martin Hunter (2015), et al., *Redfern and Hunter on International Arbitration*, Oxford University Press, p. 185–186.

[167] Interim Award in Case 8879, Extracts from ICC Awards Referring to Interim and Conservatory Measures, 11 *ICC International Court of Arbitration Bulletin* (Issue 1) 2000, p. 84.

[168] Interim Award in Case 8879, Extracts from ICC Awards Referring to Interim and Conservatory Measures, 11 *ICC International Court of Arbitration Bulletin* (Issue 1) 2000, p. 85.

[169] Margaret L. Moses (2017), *The Principles and Practice of International Commercial Arbitration*, Cambridge University Press, p. 78–83.

[170] Christopher Boog (2011), The Laws Governing Interim Measures in International Arbitration, in Franco Ferrari & Kröll, *Conflict of Laws in International Arbitration*, Sellier, p. 426; Mika Savola (2015), Interim Measures and Emergency Arbitrator Proceedings, Presentation at the 23rd Croatian Arbitration Days: Access to Arbitral Justice, p. 9, available at https://arbitration.fi/wp-content/uploads/sites/22/2016/04/23-cad-savola-interim-measures-and-emergency-arbitrator-proceedings.pdf (16 June 2020).

[171] Steven Lim, Interim Relief in International Arbitration, available at http://www.siac.org.sg/2013-09-18-01-57-20/2013-09-22-00-27-02/articles/444-interim-relief-in-international-arbitration (16 June 2020).

governing the substance may lead to an "unattractive result" that the requests for interim measures related to different claims, for example, the claims related to tort law, contract law, intellectual property law, and other similar situations, would be governed by diverse national standards in different branches of legislation.[172]

5.3.3.3 Law of the Place Where the Enforcement is Sought (the *Lex Executions*)

In addition to the above two sources, there is another approach for the determination of the law governing the legal criteria for granting interim measures, namely, the arbitration law of the place where enforcement is sought.[173] However, as examined in the previous discussion, usually, the local arbitration laws do not specify the legal criteria. Moreover, "an international arbitrator will not necessarily be in a position to know, in any event, where the execution of an award is likely to be sought".[174] If there is more than one jurisdiction for enforcement, applying a provision from a specific jurisdiction where an interim measure is sought may lead to potential conflicts in different legal orders.

5.3.3.4 Overarching International Standards

Applying international standards is a frequently accepted approach to addressing the conditions for granting interim measures. The conditions usually refer to those included in the UNCITRAL Model Law 2006 and the UNCITRAL Arbitration Rules (as revised in 2010).[175] The UNCITRAL Model Law is an attempt by the UNCITRAL to reform, modernize and unify all stages of arbitral procedure in different states with particular characteristics and needs of international arbitration.[176] Currently, there are 125 jurisdictions in 83 states that adopt the UNCITRAL Model Law, including 48 jurisdictions that adopt the 2006 version, which has provisions on the conditions

---

[172] Gary B. Born (2021), *International Commercial Arbitration*, Kluwer Law International, p. 2647.

[173] John Beechey & Gareth Kenny (2008), How to Control the Impact of Time Running between the Occurrence of the Damage and its Full Compensation: Complementary and Alternative Remedies in Interim Relief Proceedings, in F.J.M. De Ly, & Laurent Lévy, *Interest, Auxiliary and Alternative Remedies in International Arbitration*, International Chamber of Commerce (ICC), p. 107.

[174] Yves Derains & Eric A. Schwartz (2005), *A Guide to ICC Rules of Arbitration*, Kluwer Law International, p. 385–386.

[175] Patricia Shaughnessy (2017), The Emergency Arbitrator, in Patricia Shaughnessy & Sherlin Tung, *The Powers and Duties of an Arbitrator: Liber Amicorum Pierre A. Karrer*, Kluwer Law International, p. 346.

[176] UNCITRAL, UNCITRAL Model Law on International Commercial Arbitration (1985), with amendments as adopted in 2006, available at https://uncitral.un.org/en/texts/arbitration/modellaw/commercial_arbitration (1 June 2024).

for granting interim measures.[177] The UNCITRAL Arbitration Rules "provide a comprehensive set of procedural rules upon which parties may agree for the conduct of arbitral proceedings arising out of their commercial relationship and are widely used in ad hoc arbitrations as well as administered arbitrations".[178]

Article 26 of the UNCITRAL Model Rules 2010 provides that, if parties request interim measures in order to "(a)[m]aintain or restore the status quo pending determination of the dispute; (b) [t]ake action that would prevent, or refrain from taking action that is likely to cause (i) current or imminent harm or (ii) prejudice to arbitral process itself; (c)[p]rovide a means of preserving assets out of which a subsequent award may be satisfied",[179] they shall satisfy the tribunal that "(a)[h]arm not adequately reparable by an award of damages is likely to result if the measure is not ordered, and such harm substantially outweighs the harm that is likely to result to the party against whom the measure is directed if the measure is granted; and (b) [t]here is a reasonable possibility that the requesting party will succeed on the merits of the claim. The determination on this possibility shall not affect the discretion of the arbitral tribunal in making any subsequent determination."[180] If parties ask for the interim measures regarding the preservation of evidence that may be "relevant and material to the resolution of the dispute",[181] the tribunal is not bound by the conditions stated in Article 26(3)(a) and Article 26(3)(b).[182]

It is easily observed that, regardless of the numbering, the wording in these two articles regarding the conditions for granting interim measures by arbitrators, i.e., Article 17A of UNCITRAL Model Law 2006, and Article 26 of UNCITRAL Arbitration Rules 2010, read "practically the same".[183] The provisions in the UNCITRAL Arbitration Rules 2010 are, in fact, "modelled"[184] on the provisions contained in the UNCITRAL Model Law 2006.

Despite the extensive usage of both the UNCITRAL Model Law 2006 and the UNCITRAL Arbitration Rules 2010, there is much criticism on the conditions for rendering interim measures by arbitrators. It is believed that the detailed imposition under the UNCITRAL Model Law 2006 "ignore[s] the specifics of particular

177 UNCITRAL, Status: UNCITRAL Model Law on International Commercial Arbitration (1985), with amendments as adopted in 2006, available at https://uncitral.un.org/en/texts/arbitration/modellaw/commercial_arbitration/status (1 June 2024).

178 UNCITRAL, UNCITRAL Arbitration Rules, https://uncitral.un.org/en/texts/arbitration/contractualtexts/arbitration (1 June 2024).

179 Article 26 (2) (a)-(c), UNCITRAL Arbitration Rules 2010.

180 Article 26 (3), UNCITRAL Arbitration Rules 2010.

181 Article 26 (2)(d), UNCITRAL Arbitration Rules 2010.

182 Article 26 (4), UNCITRAL Arbitration Rules 2010.

183 Christopher Boog (2011), The Laws Governing Interim Measures in International Arbitration, in Franco Ferrari & Kröll, *Conflict of Laws in International Arbitration*, Sellier, p. 428.

184 Working Group II (Arbitration and Conciliation) of United Nations Commission on International Trade Law (2009), Settlement of commercial disputes: Revision of the UNCITRAL Arbitration Rules: Note by the Secretariat, A/CN.9/WG/II/WP.154/Add.1, p. 9, available at https://documents.un.org/doc/undoc/ltd/v09/855/86/pdf/v0985586.pdf?token=TBS2qyWnzP0IytNcNP&fe=true (1 June 2024).

types of cases".[185] Therefore, introducing and prescribing specific legal criteria for granting interim measures is "unnecessary and unwise".[186] However, regulating exact requirements for granting interim measures is very difficult, because of the various circumstances of the cases and other related factors. This book does not aim at specifying any detailed rules, but it provides general and standard legal criteria for emergency arbitrators to consider in practice. Additionally, this book focuses on the special requirements of the emergency arbitrator mechanism but not arbitral tribunals in general. As a result, despite the criticism, the UNCITRAL Model Law 2006 serves as quite a good example of building international standards for granting interim measures by arbitrators.[187] The prerequisites in the UNCITRAL Model Law 2006 will be taken into consideration in the following part of this chapter.

5.3.3.5 Proposed Approach to Determine the Legal Criteria for Granting Interim Measures by an Emergency Arbitrator

By integrating the discussion in this part of the chapter, the suggested approach for the emergency arbitrator mechanism is, with respect to party autonomy and the mandatory rules of either the *lex arbitri* or the law governing the substance, to establish a set of international standards as a benchmark for recognition and enforcement.

Firstly, party autonomy must be followed. As stated in the previous chapter, party autonomy is not only the basis of modern international commercial arbitration, but it is also one of the sources of power of the emergency arbitrators. Furthermore, although there are only a few mandatory rules included in the *lex arbitri* and the law governing the substance, it is better for an emergency arbitrator to respect those mandatory provisions to avoid any chance of refusal of recognition and enforcement of the measures, due to international conventions, for example, the New York Convention 1958. Potential barriers to the enforcement of the interim measures granted by an emergency arbitrator will be discussed in the next chapter.

The overarching international standards may consist of considerations of the interim measures granted by emergency arbitrators and regulator arbitral tribunals, as well as common practices and principles of law.[188] As discussed in Chap. 2, the provisions of the emergency arbitrator mechanism in different institutional rules share "a common, general procedural framework".[189] Applying international standards guarantees the uniformity of the interim measures granted by the emergency arbitrator, thus ensuring legal certainty and the predictability of the quality and standards of

---

185 Gary B. Born (2021), *International Commercial Arbitration*, Kluwer Law International, p. 2648.

186 Gary B. Born (2021), *International Commercial Arbitration*, Kluwer Law International, p. 2648.

187 Christopher Boog (2011), The Laws Governing Interim Measures in International Arbitration, in Franco Ferrari & Kröll, *Conflict of Laws in International Arbitration*, Sellier, p. 429.

188 Gary B. Born (2021), *International Commercial Arbitration*, Kluwer Law International, p. 2647.

189 Fabio G. Santacroce (2015), The emergency arbitrator: a full-fledged arbitrator rendering an enforceable decision?, 31 *Arbitration International* 285.

the interim measures granted by the emergency arbitrator. Additionally, such international standards can be tailored to the specific needs of international commercial arbitration and "embrace a more flexible, business-oriented approach".[190]

5.3.4 *Proposed Legal Criteria for Granting Interim Measures by an Emergency Arbitrator*

Diverse standards can be observed when discussing the issuance of interim measures by either emergency arbitrators or arbitral tribunals. What is more troublesome is, even for a similar criterion, interpretations vary among practitioners using those criteria based on their own analytical framework.[191] From the above discussion regarding the emergency arbitration cases from institutions and other cases involving interim measures granted by arbitrators, there are four commonly adopted legal criteria, namely a *prima facie* jurisdiction, a good arguable case, urgency, and proportionality. In following part, the book provides its recommended interpretation and understanding regarding these criteria.

5.3.4.1 A *Prima Facie* Jurisdiction

For the jurisdiction of an arbitral tribunal when issuing interim measures, the well-settled consensus in international arbitration is that "an international tribunal may decide on provisional measures prior to establishing its jurisdiction over the dispute if it appears that there is, *prima facie*, a basis for asserting such jurisdiction".[192] Unlike a regular arbitral tribunal that can determine its own jurisdiction later in the following arbitral proceedings, an emergency arbitrator needs to establish its jurisdiction as soon as dealing with the request of interim measures. The comprehensive analysis regarding the jurisdiction issue of emergency arbitrators will be elaborated upon when discussing the grounds of refusal of recognition and enforcement in the next chapter.

[190] Christopher Boog (2011), The Laws Governing Interim Measures in International Arbitration, in Franco Ferrari & Kröll, *Conflict of Laws in International Arbitration*, Sellier, p. 428.

[191] Francisco González de Cossío (2015), Interim Measures in Arbitration: Towards a Better Injury Standard, in Albert van den Berg, Legitimacy: Myths, Realities, Challenges, 18 *ICCA Congress Series* 260.

[192] Ibrahim F.I. Shihata & Antonio R. Parra (1999), The Experience of the International Centre for Settlement of Investment Disputes, 14 *ICSID Review—Foreign Investment Law Journal* 326.

5.3.4.2 A Good Arguable Case

The expression for the second criterion can also be the *fumus boni juris*, the likelihood of success, "the adequacy of the case on the merits",[193] a reasonable possibility to succeed on the merits of a dispute, and other phrases having a similar meaning. According to the survey conducted in early 2006, over 85% of arbitrators interviewed took this condition seriously into consideration as a "fundamental prerequisite" for granting interim measures.[194] A large majority of arbitrators agreed that a claiming party for interim measures needs to show that there is a possibility of success on the merits.[195] The criterion of a good arguable case is essential in the determination of interim measures in order to make "rational and commercially-sensible decisions",[196] and to serve the purpose of interim measures. It would make little sense for an emergency arbitrator to grant an interim measure requested by one party if there is little prospect that the claiming party may prevail in a final decision made by a tribunal.

Some attention needs to be paid to the boundary between the determination of a good arguable case and prejudgment of the merits. In most cases, the interim measures requested by parties are closely connected to the merits of a dispute, resulting in a dilemma faced by arbitrators "whether granting the measure may amount to disposing of the subject matter of the dispute".[197] No prejudgment requires arbitrators to not be precluded from "ultimately deciding the arbitration in any particular manner after the parties have presented their case",[198] and not to "prejudge the outcome of the arbitration or even partially close its mind to one party's submissions or deny one party an opportunity to be heard in subsequent proceedings".[199] This requirement is reasonable because parties deserve to have a fair opportunity to present their full cases. Some even argue that such a requirement should be so strict that if arbitrators "cannot grant an interim or conservatory measure without examining the merits of the case, it may refrain from doing so, in order not to prejudge on the merits".[200]

Such a risk of prejudging the merits of disputes seems to be less in the emergency arbitrator proceedings than arbitral tribunals for three reasons. One is that an appointed emergency arbitrator, in principle, will not serve as an arbitrator after the

---

[193] Grant Hanessian & E. Alexandra Dosman (2016), Songs of Innocence and Experience: Ten Years of Emergency Arbitration, 27 *American Review of International Arbitration* 228.

[194] Kaj Hobér (2007), Interim Measures by Arbitrators, in Van den Berg, Albert, International Arbitration 2006: Back to Basics?, 13 *ICCA Congress Series* 735.

[195] Kaj Hobér (2007), Interim Measures by Arbitrators, in Van den Berg, Albert, International Arbitration 2006: Back to Basics?, 13 *ICCA Congress Series* 735.

[196] Gary B. Born (2021), *International Commercial Arbitration*, Kluwer Law International, p. 2662.

[197] José María Abascal Zamora (2007), The Art of Interim Measures, in Albert van den Berg, International Arbitration 2006: Back to Basics?, 13 *ICCA Congress Series* 751.

[198] Gary B. Born (2021), *International Commercial Arbitration*, Kluwer Law International, p. 2660.

[199] Gary B. Born (2021), *International Commercial Arbitration*, Kluwer Law International, p. 2660.

[200] Ali Yesilirmak (2000), Interim and Conservatory Measures in ICC Arbitral Practice, 11 *ICC International Court of Arbitration Bulletin* 34.

constitution of a tribunal unless agreed by parties otherwise.[201] The ICC goes one step further by regulating that "[a]n emergency arbitrator shall not act as an arbitrator in any arbitration relating to the dispute that gave rise to the Application".[202] Secondly, any decisions made by an emergency arbitrator, although binding on parties, are subject to modification, termination, and even annulment by a tribunal.[203] An arbitral tribunal, therefore, is not bound by either the reasoning or the determination of the interim measures granted by an emergency arbitrator. Additionally, an emergency arbitrator is not in the position to determine the relevant issues necessary to prejudge the merits of a case, for example, the applicable law governing the contract, or the validity of an arbitration agreement.

Bearing the requirement of no prejudgment in mind, this standard of likelihood of success on the merits must not be set at a very high level. Admittedly, the understanding regarding "a good arguable case" varies, since it is difficult to assess the circumstances without prejudging the merits of a case at an early stage like the emergency arbitrator proceedings. For example, in the SCC practice, the emergency arbitrator agreed that the Claimant had established probable cause, since the Claimant "had listed a number of alleged contract breaches by the Respondent". In contrast, the Respondent "did not file a reply to these allegations, apart from a general denial of wrongdoing".[204] An emergency arbitrator should consider both parties' claims and defenses in order to decide whether the request for the interim measure is reasonable on a *prima facie* basis. Balancing the probabilities needs to be done carefully.

5.3.4.3 Urgency

In order to be granted an interim measure, the claiming party has to prove harm or possible urgent harm caused by the other party. Urgency is also the very "basic requirement"[205] for granting interim measures, although the UNCITRAL Model Law 2006 does not refer to it directly. Two factors contained the requirement of urgency. One is that the claiming party might suffer substantial harm if the interim

---

[201] Article 7(5), ICDR Arbitration Rules 2021; Article 19 of Schedule 4, HKIAC Arbitration Rules 2024; Article 6 of Schedule 1, SIAC Arbitration Rules 2016; Article 4(4) of Appendix II, SCC Arbitration Rules 2023.

[202] Article 2(6) of Appendix V, ICC Arbitration Rules 2021.

[203] Article 29(3), ICC Arbitration Rules 2021; Article 7(5), ICDR Arbitration Rules 2021; Article 18 of Schedule 4, HKIAC Arbitration Rules 2024; Article 9.11, LCIA Arbitration Rules 2020; Article 10 of Schedule 1, SIAC Arbitration Rules 2016; Article 9(5) of Appendix II, SCC Arbitration Rules 2023.

[204] SCC Emergency Arbitration No. 187/2010, in Johan Lundstedt, SCC Practice: Emergency Arbitrator Decisions, 1 January 2010 -31 December 2013, p. 11, available at https://sccarbitrationinstitute.se/sites/default/files/2022-11/scc-practice-2010-2013-emergency-arbitrator_final.pdf (1 June 2024).

[205] Partial Award in Case 8113, Extracts from ICC Awards Referring to Interim and Conservatory Measures, 11 *ICC International Court of Arbitration Bulletin* (Issue 1) 2000, p. 67; Eric A. Schwartz (1993), *The Practices and Experience of the ICC Court, in Conservatory and Provisional Measures in International Arbitration*, International Chamber of Commerce, p. 60.

measures are not granted. The other one is that such substantial harm is so urgent that it cannot wait for the constitution of a competent arbitral tribunal. These two factors are interconnected with each other and therefore they will be analyzed together.

According to the above introduction of the case law and practice in different institutions, as well as in Article 17 of UNCITRAL Model Law 2006, the expression frequently used is "irreparable harm". However, this book suggests that, in the context of the emergency arbitrator mechanism, the expression of this criterion adopted should be "substantial harm" or "serious harm", instead of "irreparable harm". Theoretically, irreparable harm is very rare in international arbitration. It can result in, for example, the possible insolvency of a claiming party. It has been rightfully reasoned that, if the "irreparable harm" test is strictly applied, the consequence would be that most commercial disputes cannot qualify for interim measures "since an award of damages can, at least, in theory, rectify nearly all commercial loses".[206] In this regard, the "irreparable harm" should be interpreted "in an economic, not a literal, sense".[207] In the SCC emergency arbitration No. 2016/095, the emergency arbitrator stated that "irreparable harm in international law has a flexible meaning, and… the possibility of monetary compensation does not necessarily eliminate the need for interim measures".[208]

Additionally, adopting a strict "irreparable harm" test precludes achieving the purpose of interim measures. The purpose of interim measures provided by the emergency arbitrator mechanism is to protect parties' rights in a very urgent situation, pending a final award granted by a tribunal. If the legal criterion was set too high,[209] then interim measures would not be accessible. Consequently, the emergency arbitrator mechanism would be meaningless. The tribunal of the ICC Case No. 8786/1996 shared the same position that, to preserve legal rights, the measures taken must be "necessary", by quoting that "[t]his requirement is satisfied only of the delay in the adjudication of the main claim caused by the arbitral proceedings would lead to 'substantial' (but not necessarily 'irreparable' as known in common law doctrine) prejudice for the requesting party".[210]

---

[206] Stewart Abercrombie Baker & Mark David Davis (1992), *The UNCITRAL Arbitration Rules in Practice: the experience of the Iran-United States Claims Tribunal*, Kluwer Law and Taxation Publishers, p. 139–140.

[207] Stefan Michael Kröll, Julian D. M. Lew & Loukas A. Mistelis (2003), *Comparative International Commercial Arbitration*, Kluwer Law International, p. 605.

[208] SCC Emergency Arbitration No. 2016/095, in Anja Havedal Ipp, SCC Practice Note Emergency Arbitrator Decisions Rendered 2015–2016, p. 13, available at https://sccarbitrationinstitute.se/sites/default/files/2022-11/ea-practice-note-emergency-arbitrator-decisions-rendered-2015-2016.pdf (1 June 2024).

[209] David D. Caron & Lee Caplan (2013), *The UNCITRAL Arbitration Rules: A Commentary*, Oxford University Press, p. 522.

[210] Klaus Peter Berger (1993), *International Economic Arbitration*, Kluwer Law and Taxation Publishers, p. 336; Interim Award in Case 8786, Extracts from ICC Awards Referring to Interim and Conservatory Measures, 11 *ICC International Court of Arbitration Bulletin* (Issue 1) 2000, p. 83;

Based on those examinations, a more appropriate expression regarding this criterion should be that the claiming party may suffer substantial or serious harm if the applied interim measures are not granted. There is a consensus that "the granting of an interim measure generally presupposes an urgent need for interim protection".[211] In principle, if the request for interim measures can wait until a final award is granted, there is no need to grant such interim measures logically.[212] That is to say, the risk of substantial harm faced by the applicant is imminent.[213] It is worthy to note that the applicant requesting interim measures does not have to prove substantial harm would certainly occur for sure. Instead, it is enough to "establish of a sufficient risk or threat that grave or serious harm will occur"[214] if interim measures are rejected.

5.3.4.4 Proportionality

The criterion of proportionality requires that "the possible injury caused by the requested measure must not be out of proportion with the advantage which the applicant hopes to derive from".[215] When achieving a legitimate objective, an emergency arbitrator has to weigh a decision of the outcome not only for the applicant but also for the party which the interim measures are against, in other words, the allocation of risks between parties is assessed.[216] If granting interim measures may cause "significant" harm to parties other than the applicant, then the requested interim measures are unlikely to be issued by an emergency arbitrator.[217] It is even suggested that

Sergei Paushok, CJSC Golden East Company and CJSC Vostokneftegaz Company v. The Government of Mongolia (Order on Interim measures, 2008, available at http://opil.ouplaw.com.ezproxy.ub.unimaas.nl/abstract/10.1093/law:iic/351-2008.case.1/law-iic-351-2008-IIC351(2008)D.pdf (16 June 2020).

[211] Ali Yesilirmak (2011), Interim and Conservatory Measures in ICC Arbitral Practice, 1999–2008, 22 *ICC International Court of Arbitration Bulletin* (Special Supplement) 9.

[212] Julian D.M. Lew (2000), Commentary on Interim and Conservatory Measures in ICC Arbitration Cases, *11 ICC International Court of Arbitration Bulletin* (Issue 1) 27.

[213] Nathalie Voser (2007), Interim Relief in International Arbitration: The Tendency towards a More Business-Oriented Approach, 1 *Dispute Resolution International* 177.

[214] Gary B. Born (2021), *International Commercial Arbitration*, Kluwer Law International, p. 2655.

[215] Mika Savola (2015), Interim Measures and Emergency Arbitrator Proceedings, Presentation at the 23rd Croatian Arbitration Days: Access to Arbitral Justice, p. 10, available at https://arbitration.fi/wp-content/uploads/sites/22/2016/04/23-cad-savola-interim-measures-and-emergency-arbitrator-proceedings.pdf (16 June 2020).

[216] Shadat Mohmeded (2014), A Critical Analysis of Arbitral Provisional Measures in England and Wales, *PhD thesis of Brunel University*, p. 108.

[217] Anja Havedal Ipp, SCC Practice Note Emergency Arbitrator Decisions Rendered 2015–2016, p. 18, available at https://sccarbitrationinstitute.se/sites/default/files/2022-11/ea-practice-note-emergency-arbitrator-decisions-rendered-2015-2016.pdf (1 June 2024).; Anja Havedal Ipp (2017), Urgency, Irreparable Harm and Proportionality: Seven Years of SCC Emergency Proceedings, available at http://arbitrationblog.kluwerarbitration.com/2017/06/29/urgency-irreparable-harm-proportionality-seven-years-scc-emergency-proceedings/ (1 June 2024); see also Monika Feigerlová (2018), Emergency Measures of Protection in International Arbitration, 18 *International and Comparative Law Review* 166.

proportionality shall be the only standard for issuing interim measures.[218] Alternatively, this book holds that proportionality is better as one of the steps for emergency arbitrators to assess when granting interim measures.

In the SCC Emergency Arbitration No. 010/2012,[219] the emergency arbitrator in this dispute stated that both parties had established a *prima facie* case, and it was not the emergency arbitrator's position to determine which one would prevail without prejudging the merits of the dispute. Nevertheless, the findings based on the submissions and evidence provided by parties indicated that, if the interim measures requested were granted, then "that would risk exposing the Respondent (with its parent company and officers) to grave risks of severe civil and criminal sanctions under the laws".[220] In order to avoid causing conflicting legal obligations for the Respondent, especially causing the risk of criminal liability, the emergency arbitrator denied the request for interim measures applied by the Claimant, due to concern for proportionality in relation to this point. In the ICC Case No. 12361/2003, the tribunal also considered "the impact of the possible relief on the rights of the other party", and "arbitrators must endeavour to balance the relative harm to each party that may or may not flow from the granting or denial of the measures granted".[221]

The UNCITRAL Model Law 2006 also adopted this prerequisite. Article 17 stipulates that the harm suffered by the applicant of interim measures "substantially outweighs the harm that is likely to result to the party against whom the measure is directed if the measure is granted".[222] This requirement can also be understood as a "balance of interests", "balance of hardships", or "balance of convenience".[223] In this accessing process, an overall evaluation must be taken by an emergency arbitrator, with consideration for the possible undertakings or security.[224]

---

[218] Francisco González de Cossío (2015), Interim Measures in Arbitration: Towards a Better Injury Standard, in Albert van den Berg, Legitimacy: Myths, Realities, Challenges, 18 *ICCA Congress Series* 274.

[219] SCC Emergency Arbitration No. 010/2012, in Johan Lundstedt, SCC Practice: Emergency Arbitrator Decisions, 1 January 2010 -31 December 2013, p. 16, available at https://sccarbitrationinstitute.se/sites/default/files/2022-11/scc-practice-2010-2013-emergency-arbitrator_final.pdf (1 June 2024).

[220] SCC Emergency Arbitration No. 010/2012, in Johan Lundstedt, SCC Practice: Emergency Arbitrator Decisions, 1 January 2010 -31 December 2013, p. 17–19, available at https://sccarbitrationinstitute.se/sites/default/files/2022-11/scc-practice-2010-2013-emergency-arbitrator_final.pdf (1 June 2024).

[221] ICC Case 12,361, Interim Award, 22 *ICC International Court of Arbitration Bulletin* (Special Supplement) 2011, p. 62.

[222] Article 17A (1)(a), UNCITRAL Model Law 2006.

[223] Nathalie Voser (2007), Interim Relief in International Arbitration: The Tendency towards a More Business-Oriented Approach, 1 *Dispute Resolution International* 177.

[224] Stefan Michael Kröll, Julian D. M. Lew & Loukas A. Mistelis (2003), *Comparative International Commercial Arbitration*, Kluwer Law International, p. 605; Nathalie Voser (2007), Interim Relief in International Arbitration: The Tendency towards a More Business-Oriented Approach, 1 *Dispute Resolution International* 177.

5.4 Concluding Remarks

The purpose of this chapter was to provide a better understanding of the procedure for interim measures granted by an emergency arbitrator. Due to the diverse practice in issuing interim measures either by emergency arbitrators or arbitral tribunals, no harmonized set of legal criteria could be determined as being universally adopted by arbitrators. After discussing the law regulating the issuance of interim measures, the book found that, despite possible party autonomy and mandatory rules related to arbitration, international standards could serve as a better approach for international commercial arbitration. Furthermore, after an in-depth examination of the existing and accessible cases run by emergency arbitrators and arbitral tribunals, four legal criteria, which include jurisdiction, a good arguable case, urgency, and proportionality, were proposed as the international standards for emergency arbitrators to consider in granting interim measures.

Chapter 6
Recognition and Enforcement of Interim Measures Rendered by an Emergency Arbitrator

There are three elements left to be discussed when considering the recognition and enforcement of interim measures granted by an emergency arbitrator, i.e., the arbitrability of claims related to the request for interim measures Sect. 6.1; the binding nature of interim measures Sect. 6.2; and public policy concerns Sect. 6.3.

6.1 Arbitrability of Claims Related to the Request for Interim Measures

Arbitrability represents one of the issues "where the contractual and jurisdictional natures of international commercial arbitration meet head on".[1] That is to say, it "determines the point at which the exercise of contractual freedom ends, and the public mission of adjudication begins".[2]

6.1.1 Distinction Between Arbitrability, Jurisdiction and Public Policy

Arbitrability has been used in a very diverse way, which can cause confusion in its actual application. This subsection discusses the distinction between arbitrability and jurisdiction, together with the distinction between arbitrability and public policy,

[1] Stefan Michael Kröll, Julian D. M. Lew & Loukas A. Mistelis (2003), *Comparative International Commercial Arbitration*, Kluwer Law International, p. 187.

[2] Thomas E. Carbonneau & Francois Janson (1994), Cartesian Logic and Frontier Politics: French and American Concepts of Arbitrability, 2 *Tulane Journal of International and Comparative Law* 194.

J. Zhang, *The Enforceability of the Interim Measures Granted by an Emergency Arbitrator in International Commercial Arbitration*,
https://doi.org/10.1007/978-981-97-6536-2_6

to clarify the boundaries between different grounds for barriers. According to these differences, this chapter will further analyze these three concepts, i.e., arbitrability, jurisdiction and public policy separately.

The difference between jurisdiction and public policy is quite clear. The legal sources determining jurisdiction are the parties' agreement and the laws of a related jurisdiction. If an arbitral award granted by arbitrators is "in contradiction to or merely ignoring a mandatory law or public policy could subsequently be set aside or be unenforceable".[3] For the difference between arbitrability and jurisdiction, due to the different approaches taken by different jurisdictions, the meaning and the scope of arbitrability vary. Jurisdictions other than the United States choose a straightforward approach.[4] In this context, arbitrability determines which types of issues may be settled by arbitration and which issues can only and exclusively be decided by state courts.[5] However, in the United States, the concept of arbitrability as "an all-embracing criterion",[6] covers more than the above determination, but it also includes a full set of questions related to the jurisdiction of arbitrators.[7] It has been described as an "intriguing manifestation of American exceptionalism".[8] In this book, the first approach is adopted to provide a more precise understanding in the discussion of the potential obstacles to the enforcement of interim measures granted by the emergency arbitrator as a possible preliminary barrier.

Arbitrability and public policy do not necessarily mean the same thing. However, Article V (2) (a) and Article V (2) (b) of the New York Convention 1958 regulating arbitrability and public policy respectively "can be deemed to be superfluous".[9] These two criteria are "the most national, and the least international grounds for refusing enforcement of arbitral awards".[10] However, they are also exceptional on their own. Firstly, a part of the arbitrability concern can be dealt with as a procedural and threshold problem once the arbitration has commenced. At the same time, public policy requires a review of the merits of the dispute. Inarbitrability leads to the result that "the arbitral process itself cannot be used to produce a binding decision in

---

[3] Julian D.M. Lew (1987), *Contemporary Problems in International Arbitration*, Springer, p. 78.

[4] Laurence Shore (2009), Defining "Arbitrability": The United States vs. the rest of the world, *New York Law Journal*, available at https://indiacorplaw.in/wp-content/uploads/2016/08/shore-definingarbitrability.pdf (16 June 2020).

[5] Alan Redfern & J. Martin Hunter (2015), et al., *Redfern and Hunter on International Arbitration*, Oxford University Press, p. 110.

[6] Natalja Freimane (2012), Arbitrability: Problematic Issues of the Legal Term, *Master Thesis of Riga Graduate School of Law*, p. 28, available at https://sccarbitrationinstitute.se/sites/default/files/2022-11/arbitrability-problematic-issues.pdf (1 June 2024).

[7] Stefan Michael Kröll, Julian D. M. Lew & Loukas A. Mistelis (2003), *Comparative International Commercial Arbitration*, Kluwer Law International, p. 188.

[8] William W. Park (2008), Arbitral Jurisdiction in the United States: Who Decides What?, 11 *International Arbitration Law Review* 33, available at http://williamwpark.com/documents/Arbitral%20Jurisdiction%20%20IALR.pdf (16 June 2020).

[9] Karl-Heinz Böckstiegel (1987), Public Policy and Arbitrability, in Pieter Sanders, Comparative Arbitration Practice and Public Policy in Arbitration, 3 *ICCA Congress Series* 183.

[10] Gary B. Born (2011), Arbitrability and Public Policy, 5 *World Arbitration and Mediation Review* 293.

cases related to a particular subject matter",[11] regardless of the arbitral results. If the arbitral awards are contrary to public policy, the outcome would be that such arbitral decisions cannot be recognized and enforced. Additionally, the violation of public policy does not necessarily mean that the other claims in the same arbitration are not arbitrable.[12] In a French case *Société Almira Films v. Pierrel*, the Paris Court of Appeal ruled that "the impact of public policy on the arbitrability of a dispute does not cause arbitrators to be prohibited from applying mandatory rules, but only from hearing cases which, because of their subject-matter, can only be heard by courts".[13]

In general, the arbitrability issue can be divided into two classifications, i.e., subjective arbitrability and objective arbitrability, or contractual arbitrability and substantive arbitrability.[14] Subjective arbitrability (contractual arbitrability), also known as "arbitrability *ratione personae*", refers to the situation that certain parties, including individuals and entities, are entitled to enter into an arbitration agreement with proper legal capacity.[15] Further discussions regarding subjective arbitrability are beyond the scope of this book. As a result, the focus will mainly be objective arbitrability. Objective arbitrability (substantive arbitrability), also known as "arbitrability *ratione materiae*", refers to the situation that certain types of claims may be resolved by arbitration.[16] In this case, other claims can only be heard by state courts. The original basis for introducing objective arbitrability is "the distinction between claims arising from contract and claims brought pursuant to provisions of regulatory law", because the latter may contain "special safeguards and remedies and proscribe conduct for the good of society".[17] Arbitration laws of different jurisdictions determine the types of disputes and claims that are within the exclusive domain of state courts, and such a determination varies from jurisdiction to jurisdiction "reflecting the political, social and economic prerogative", as well as "its general attitude towards

---

[11] Gary B. Born (2021), *International Commercial Arbitration*, Kluwer Law International, p. 1037.

[12] Gary B. Born (2021), *International Commercial Arbitration*, Kluwer Law International, p. 1035.

[13] *Société Almira Films v. Pierrel ès qual, Revue de l'Arbitrage* (1989), 714 (Court of Appeal Paris, 1989); English translation of the judgment can be seen in Gary B. Born (2021), *International Commercial Arbitration*, Kluwer Law International, p. 1036.

[14] Thomas E. Carbonneau & Francois Janson (1994), Cartesian Logic and Frontier Politics: French and American Concepts of Arbitrability, 2 *Tulane Journal of International and Comparative Law* 195.

[15] Emmanuel Gaillard & John Savage (1999), *Fouchard Gaillard Goldman on International Commercial Arbitration*, Kluwer Law International, p. 312–313; Bernard Hanotiau & Olivier Caprasse (2008), Arbitrability, Due Process, and Public Policy Under Article V of the New York Convention, 25 *Journal of International Arbitration* 724.

[16] Natalja Freimane (2012), Arbitrability: Problematic Issues of the Legal Term, *Master Thesis of Riga Graduate School of Law*, p. 22, available at https://sccarbitrationinstitute.se/sites/default/files/2022-11/arbitrability-problematic-issues.pdf (1 June 2024); Emmanuel Gaillard & John Savage (1999), *Fouchard Gaillard Goldman on International Commercial Arbitration*, Kluwer Law International, p. 313; Daniel Gisberger & Nathalie Voser (2016), *International Arbitration: Comparative and Swiss Perspectives*, Kluwer Law International, p. 7.

[17] Thomas E. Carbonneau & Francois Janson (1994), Cartesian Logic and Frontier Politics: French and American Concepts of Arbitrability, 2 *Tulane Journal of International and Comparative Law* 196.

arbitration".[18] As international commercial arbitration has been accepted by most states, objective inarbitrability is diminishing gradually.

6.1.2 *Current Trend of Arbitrability in the Issuance of Interim Measures by an Emergency Arbitrator*

The issues regarding arbitrability and granting interim measures depends mainly on the law governing arbitration.[19] As indicated in Chap. 3, the arbitration law of Mainland China does not grant the power rendering issue interim measures to arbitrators. The only legitimate body permitted to grant interim measures is a state court, meaning the claims related to interim measures during arbitration proceedings lack arbitrability due to such exclusive jurisdiction.[20] Changes to that situation can be witnessed since 2015, when several major international arbitration centers located in Mainland China adopted the emergency arbitrator mechanism in their institutional rules.

In late 2017, the BAC administrated the first known emergency arbitration conducted in Mainland China, which was published in late 2018 and referred to as the *GKML* case.[21] The BAC is a permanent arbitral institution based in Mainland China, which introduced the emergency arbitrator mechanism in its rules in 2015. Article 63 of the BAC Arbitration Rules 2015 states that "[a]fter the acceptance of the case by the BAC [Articles 8 and 9] and before the constitution of the Arbitral Tribunal [Article 19 or Article 64], any party that wishes to apply for interim measures may submit a written application to the BAC for the appointment of an emergency arbitrator in accordance with the applicable law".[22] The *GKML* case involved a dispute concerning two investment contracts. The Claimants were companies based in Hong Kong and the Respondent included a company registered in the Cayman Islands and a Chinese national who owned assets in Hong Kong.[23] The contracts under dispute dealt with the repurchase of the Claimants' shares in Respondent's company. During the arbitration proceedings, the Claimants sought to prevent the Respondents from transferring the relevant assets. Immediately after filing the Request for Arbitration under

---

[18] Stefan Michael Kröll, Julian D. M. Lew & Loukas A. Mistelis (2003), *Comparative International Commercial Arbitration*, Kluwer Law International, p. 199.

[19] Maxi Scherer & Lisa Richman, et al. (2015), *Arbitration under the 2014 LCIA Rules: A User's Guide*, Kluwer Law International, p. 262.

[20] Dirk Otto & Omaia Elwan (2010), Article V (2), in Herbert Kronke & Patricia Nacimiento, et al., *Recognition and Enforcement of Foreign Arbitral Awards: A Global Commentary on the New York Convention*, Kluwer Law International, p. 392.

[21] Jie Xu (2018), Emergency Arbitrator Proceedings and the GKML Case, available at http://www.bjac.org.cn/news/view?id=3330 (1 June 2024).

[22] Article 63, BAC Arbitration Rules 2015.

[23] Haifeng Li (2018), First Emergency Arbitrator Proceedings in China and Enforcement in Hong Kong, available at https://globalarbitrationnews.com/first-emergency-arbitrator-proceedings-in-china-and-enforcement-in-hong-kong/ (1 June 2024).

the BAC Arbitration Rules 2015 in accordance with the contracts, the Claimants applied for an emergency arbitrator for interim measures which included (a) Asset Information Disclosure; (b) Disposal Restraint; (c) Anti-suit Injunction; and (d) No Assistance, meaning that the Respondents may not turn to any third party to take actions.[24] The BAC went through different arbitration laws in various jurisdictions and confirmed that, in the target jurisdiction, i.e., Hong Kong, the enforcement of interim measures granted by an emergency arbitrator was possible.[25] Since the assets in the primary dispute were located mainly in Hong Kong which would be the place for the enforcement after the emergency arbitration, and the Hong Kong Arbitration Ordinance (Cap. 609) expressly recognizes the enforceability of interim measures granted by an emergency arbitrator, the BAC permitted the application submitted by the Claimants regarding the emergency arbitration. The appointed emergency arbitrator assessed the facts and evidence submitted by both parties taking account of (a) likelihood of success; (b) the urgency of the case; and (c) the reasonableness of interim measures.[26] In the end, he granted the interim measure partially that the Respondents "were restrained from disposing [of] the assets specifically listed by the applicants and shall not instruct, encourage or suggest others to conduct the restricted behaviors".[27]

The interim measure issued by the emergency arbitrator in the *GKML* case was eventually enforced in Hong Kong, which is a jurisdiction that legally supports the enforceability of interim measures granted by emergency arbitrators. Although both changes in institutional cases and rules did not turn out to be a new act of arbitration law for Mainland China, hopefully, future amendments can be expected, ultimately that the recognition and enforcement of interim measures can also be achieved in the territory of Mainland China. Not only in Mainland China but also in other jurisdictions, "the current tendency to minimize the application of substantive inarbitrability, especially in the context of international arbitration, may be a necessary part of forging a modern destiny and role for arbitration".[28] "In fact, areas fundamental to the public interest and requiring exclusive judicial jurisdiction are becoming fewer

[24] Haifeng Li (2018), First Emergency Arbitrator Proceedings in China and Enforcement in Hong Kong, 2018, available at https://globalarbitrationnews.com/first-emergency-arbitrator-proceedings-in-china-and-enforcement-in-hong-kong/ (1 June 2024).

[25] Jie Xu (2018), Emergency Arbitrator Proceedings and the GKML Case, available at http://www.bjac.org.cn/news/view?id=3330 (1 June 2024).

[26] Wei Sun (2018), First Emergency Arbitrator Proceeding in Mainland China: Reflections on How to Conduct an EA Proceeding from Procedural and Substantive Perspectives, 2018, available at http://arbitrationblog.kluwerarbitration.com/2018/09/01/first-ea-proceeding-mainland-china-reflections-conduct-ea-proceeding-procedural-substantive-perspectives/ (1 June 2024).

[27] Wei Sun (2018), First Emergency Arbitrator Proceeding in Mainland China: Reflections on How to Conduct an EA Proceeding from Procedural and Substantive Perspectives, 2018, available at http://arbitrationblog.kluwerarbitration.com/2018/09/01/first-ea-proceeding-mainland-china-reflections-conduct-ea-proceeding-procedural-substantive-perspectives/ (1 June 2024).

[28] Thomas E. Carbonneau & Francois Janson (1994), Cartesian Logic and Frontier Politics: French and American Concepts of Arbitrability, 2 *Tulane Journal of International and Comparative Law* 201.

and more difficult to identify".[29] The issue that comes to arbitrability is important, but the significance should not be exaggerated.[30] After all, "arbitrability is the rule, inarbitrability the exception".[31]

6.2 Binding Nature of Interim Measures

6.2.1 Grounds for Setting Aside by State Courts at the Seat of Arbitration

In Singapore, the High Court may set aside the award if (a) the decision was induced or affected by fraud or corruption or (b) the decision is in connection with a breach of natural justice, in addition to the grounds set out in Article 34 (2) of the UNCITRAL Model Law 1985.[32] The grounds regulated in Article 34 (2) of the UNCITRAL Model Law 1985 include that (a) incapacity of a party to an arbitration agreement or the arbitration agreement is not valid under the applicable law; (b) the party that an arbitral award is against was not given proper notice or was not able to present the case; (c) an award is not within the scope of an arbitration agreement; or (d) the composition of an arbitral tribunal or arbitral proceedings were not in accordance with an arbitration agreement. These four grounds need to be proven by a claiming party.[33] The court can set aside an arbitral award if it finds the subject matter of dispute is inarbitrable or finds any conflicts between an award and public policy.[34]

Under the Hong Kong Arbitration Ordinance (Cap. 609), section 81 regulates the exclusive grounds for courts to set aside arbitral awards, which is identical to Article 34 of the UNCITRAL Model Law 2006 being ratified by Hong Kong in 2010. The courts located in Hong Kong may set aside the arbitral awards if parties can prove that (a) incapacity of a party to conclude an arbitration agreement or the agreement is not valid; (b) there was no proper notice of arbitration or the party was unable to present the case; (c) the award does not fall within the scope of the arbitration agreement; or

---

[29] Thomas E. Carbonneau & Francois Janson (1994), Cartesian Logic and Frontier Politics: French and American Concepts of Arbitrability, 2 *Tulane Journal of International and Comparative Law* 197.

[30] Alan Redfern & J. Martin Hunter (2015), et al., *Redfern and Hunter on International Arbitration*, Oxford University Press, p. 124.

[31] Bernard Hanotiau & Olivier Caprasse (2008), Arbitrability, Due Process, and Public Policy Under Article V of the New York Convention, 25 *Journal of International Arbitration* 724.

[32] Section 24 of Part II, International Arbitration Act of the Statutes of the Republic of Singapore (Cap. 143A) 2012, available at https://sso.agc.gov.sg/Act/IAA1994 (1 June 2024).

[33] Article 34(2)(a) of First Schedule, International Arbitration Act of the Statutes of the Republic of Singapore (Cap. 143A) 2012, available at https://sso.agc.gov.sg/Act/IAA1994 (1 June 2024).

[34] Article 34(2)(b) of First Schedule, International Arbitration Act of the Statutes of the Republic of Singapore (Cap. 143A) 2012, available at https://sso.agc.gov.sg/Act/IAA1994 (1 June 2024).

(d) the arbitral proceedings were not in compliance with the arbitration agreement.[35] If the subject matter of the dispute is not arbitrable according to the laws of Hong Kong, or the award is against the public policy of Hong Kong, the courts can also set aside the relevant arbitral award *ex officio*.[36]

According to Article 58 of the Arbitration Law of the People's Republic of China, the intermediate people's courts shall set aside the arbitral award if the party can prove that (a) there is no valid arbitration agreement in the present dispute; (b) an award exceeds the scope of the arbitration agreement; (c) the constitution of a tribunal or the arbitral procedure was not in conformity with the law; d) the evidence supporting an award was forged; e) the party withheld the evidence that could lead to the impartiality of arbitrators; or (f) there was misbehavior of arbitrators violating the fairness and partiality of arbitration.[37] If the state courts decide that an award is against the public interest, then the award should be set aside.[38]

Section 10 of the FAA of the United States of America gives grounds for local courts to vacate specific arbitral awards. Those grounds include that (a) the award was gained through corruption, fraud or other illegal methods; (b) corruption of arbitrators; (c) arbitrators was responsible for refusing to postpone the hearings, refusing to hear controversial evidence and materials, or any other misbehavior; (d) the arbitrator exceeded the jurisdiction or failed to execute the powers; or (e) the award wrongly affected third parties' rights.[39]

6.2.2 *Existence of the Finality Test*

Influenced by the previous conventions, especially during the drafting process of the New York Convention 1958, it was held that only "final and binding" decisions made by arbitrators could be recognized and enforced.[40] An often-cited representative of this kind of case[41] is *Resort Condominiums International Inc. v. Ray Bolwell*

[35] Section 81, Arbitration Ordinance (Cap. 609) 2015, available at https://www.elegislation.gov.hk/hk/cap609 (1 June 2024); Article 34 (2) (a), UNCITRAL Model Law 2006.

[36] Section 81, Arbitration Ordinance (Cap. 609) 2015, available at https://www.elegislation.gov.hk/hk/cap609 (1 June 2024); Article 34 (2) (b), UNCITRAL Model Law 2006.

[37] Article 58, the Arbitration Law of the People's Republic of China 2017, translation is available at http://en.pkulaw.cn/display.aspx?cgid=83c8fbd6da8a6eb8bdfb&lib=law (1 June 2024).

[38] Article 58, the Arbitration Law of the People's Republic of China 2017, translation is available at http://en.pkulaw.cn/display.aspx?cgid=83c8fbd6da8a6eb8bdfb&lib=law (1 June 2024).

[39] Section 10, Federal Arbitration Act, United States Code Annotated 2002.

[40] Article 1(d), The Geneva Convention of 1927.

[41] Ali Yesilirmak (2005), *Provisional Measures in International Commercial Arbitration*, Kluwer Law International, p. 260.

and Resort Condominiums (Australasia) Pty. Ltd. by the Supreme Court of Queensland.[42] In this case, the parties entered into a "License Agreement" for a time-sharing business in Australia, Fiji, New Zealand and Tahiti. The principle operation of this business was a contractual relationship "by way of exchange whereby a person agrees to utilise the time-sharing facilities of a resident in another country, who, in turn, has the reciprocal right to utilise the time-sharing facilities of the first person in that person's country".[43]

In the arbitration agreement, both parties consented that the American Arbitration Association (AAA) arbitration rules would apply. After the dispute, the Plaintiff applied for an interim measure in a U.S. state court, asking the Defendants to provide necessary information including audited financial statements, monies held in trust in Australia and other related information. The interim measure was granted on February 24, 1993. In the following month, the Plaintiff filed the request for interim measures to the tribunal, which issued an "Interim Arbitration Order and Award" on July 16, 1993. The Plaintiff sought the enforcement of this "Interim Arbitration Order and Award" in the Supreme Court of Queensland, which was denied in the end. The Supreme Court of Queensland stated that the interim measures in the present case were "of an interlocutory and procedural nature and in no way purport to finally resolve the disputes or any of them referred by RCI for decision or to finally resolve the legal rights of the parties".[44] Moreover, such interim measures "may be rescinded, suspended, varied or reopened by the tribunal which pronounced it, is not 'final' and binding on the parties".[45] Lacking finality, the interim measures could not constitute an award under the New York Convention 1958. Therefore, the Supreme Court of Queensland refused to recognize and enforce the interim measures made by the arbitrator.

However, it is worth pointing out that, in the New York Convention 1958 itself, there is no provision containing the word "final" literally. Only Article V (1)(e) stipulates that the recognition and the enforcement may be refused if "[t]he award has not yet become binding on the parties, or has been set aside or suspended by a

[42] *Resort Condominiums International Inc. v. Ray Bolwell and Resort Condominiums (Australasia) Pty. Ltd.*, MOT. No. 389 of 1993 (The Supreme Court of Queensland, 1993), available at https://www.queenslandjudgments.com.au/caselaw/qsc/1993/351 (1 June 2024); Australia No. 11, *Resort Condominiums International Inc. v. Ray Bolwell and Resort Condominiums, Pty. Ltd.*, Supreme Court of Queensland, 389, 29 October 1993, in Albert Jan van den Berg (1995), 20 *Yearbook Commercial Arbitration* 628–650.

[43] Australia No. 11, *Resort Condominiums International Inc. v. Ray Bolwell and Resort Condominiums, Pty. Ltd., Supreme Court of Queensland*, 389, 29 October 1993, in Albert Jan van den Berg (1995), 20 *Yearbook Commercial Arbitration* 628.

[44] *Resort Condominiums International Inc. v. Ray Bolwell and Resort Condominiums (Australasia) Pty. Ltd.*, MOT. No. 389 of 1993 (The Supreme Court of Queensland, 1993), p. 11, available at https://www.queenslandjudgments.com.au/caselaw/qsc/1993/351 (1 June 2024).

[45] *Resort Condominiums International Inc. v. Ray Bolwell and Resort Condominiums (Australasia) Pty. Ltd.*, MOT. No. 389 of 1993 (The Supreme Court of Queensland, 1993), p. 30, available at https://www.queenslandjudgments.com.au/caselaw/qsc/1993/351 (1 June 2024).

competent authority of the country in which, or under the law of which, that award was made".[46]

6.2.3 *Finality of Interim Measures*

Even if "finality" is an issue to be considered, the interim measures made by an emergency arbitrator can still be treated as "final".

The six chosen arbitral institutions, the ICDR, the HKIAC, the LCIA, the SIAC, and the SCC do not specify the form of the decision issued by an emergency arbitrator, meaning that the interim measures can be in the form of an award or an order.[47] The ICC stipulates that "the emergency arbitrator's decision shall take the form of an order".[48] By adopting a different formality requirement, the ICC avoids the interim measures granted by an emergency arbitrator to go through the scrutiny process necessary for all ICC "awards" to guarantee the effectiveness of the emergency arbitrator mechanism.[49]

Whether the interim measures can be final or not should not be determined only based on its terminology, meaning that, even if the interim measures are called orders, they could also be enforceable.[50] This approach has been confirmed by various judgments. For example, in the French case, *Braspetro Oil Services Company-Brasoil v. The Management and Implementation Authority of the Great Man-Made River Project*, the Court of Appeal confirmed that "[t]he qualification of [a decision as an] award does not depend on the terms used by the arbitrators or by the parties".[51] Therefore the present order was subject to review by the Court of Appeal. Similarly,

---

[46] Article V (1) (e), New York Convention 1958.

[47] Article 7(4), ICDR Arbitration Rules 2021; Article 12 of Schedule 4, HKIAC Arbitration Rules 2024; Article 9.8, LCIA Arbitration Rules 2020; Article 8 of Schedule 1, SIAC Arbitration Rules 2016; Article 37(3), Article 8(1) of Appendix II, SCC Arbitration Rules 2023.

[48] Article 29, Article 5(1) of Appendix V, ICC Arbitration Rules 2021.

[49] Article 34, ICC Arbitration Rules 2021; Christopher Boog (2018), Chapter 17, Part II: Commentary on the ICC Rules, Article 29 [Emergency arbitrator], in Manuel Arroyo, *Arbitration in Switzerland: The Practitioner's Guide, Kluwer Law International*, p. 2392; Philippe Cavalieros& Janet Kim (2018), Emergency Arbitrators Versus the Courts: From Concurrent Jurisdiction to Practical Considerations, 35 *Journal of International Arbitration* 279.

[50] Philippe Cavalieros& Janet Kim (2018), Emergency Arbitrators Versus the Courts: From Concurrent Jurisdiction to Practical Considerations, 35 *Journal of International Arbitration* 290; Philipp Peters& Christian Koller (2010), Chapter III: The Award and the Courts—The Notion of Arbitral Award: An Attempt to Overcome a Babylonian Confusion, in Gerold Zeiler & Irene Welser, et al., *Austrian Yearbook on International Arbitration* 152.

[51] *Braspetro Oil Services Company-Brasoil v. The Management and Implementation Authority of the Great Man-Made River Project*, Cour d' Appel [Court of Appeal], 1 July 1999, in Albert Jan van den Berg, 24 *Yearbook Commercial Arbitration* 297.

in the U.S. case, *Publicis Communication and Publicis S.A. v. True North Communications Inc.,*[52] the Plaintiff and the Defendant were two advertising companies with a joint venture. Both parties agreed to arbitrate for any disputes concerning the division in the joint venture. During the LCIA arbitration, the tribunal ordered the Plaintiff to provide tax information from 1994 to 1996. The Defendant turned to the Northern District Court of Illinois to enforce this interim order. The Plaintiff appealed the confirmation made by the Northern District Court of Illinois to the Seventh Circuit Court in this present case. The Plaintiff insisted that "an arbitral ruling can be final in every respect, but unless the document bears the word 'award' it is not final and is unenforceable".[53] The Seventh Circuit Court disagreed with the Plaintiff's position, by stating this argument was "extreme and untenable formalism".[54] The Seventh Circuit Court considered that, when discussing arbitral decisions, both the New York Convention 1958 and the applicable arbitration rules did "not bestow transcendental significance on the term", meaning that "synonyms such as decision, opinion, order, or ruling" could also be final.[55] After all, "[t]he content of a decision—not its nomenclature—determines finality".[56] Moreover, if the Defendant had to wait for all the other issues in arbitration to be resolved to enforce the interim order at hand, the interim decision would be "a meaningless waste of time".[57] Therefore, the Seventh Circuit Court concluded that the interim order issued by the tribunal was final.

Due to the fact that the interim measures granted by an emergency arbitrator only developed in recent times, there are not many courts' judgments directly addressing the finality issue in emergency measures. In the case of *Chinmax Medical Systems Inc., v. Alere San Diego, Inc.,*[58] the United States District Court of S.D. California refused to vacate the interim order granted by an ICDR emergency arbitrator, because the order was not subject to judicial review, as it was not "final and binding as all of the issues presented to the arbitrator".[59] Conversely, in *Yahoo! Inc. v. Microsoft Corporation,*[60] the United States District Court of S.D. New York stated that "[a]s

[52] *Publicis Communication and Publicis S.A. v. True North Communications Inc.*, 206 F. 3d 725 (United States Court of Appeals, Seventh Circuit, 2000).

[53] *Publicis Communication and Publicis S.A. v. True North Communications Inc.*, 206 F. 3d 725, 728 (United States Court of Appeals, Seventh Circuit, 2000).

[54] *Publicis Communication and Publicis S.A. v. True North Communications Inc.*, 206 F. 3d 725, 728 (United States Court of Appeals, Seventh Circuit, 2000).

[55] *Publicis Communication and Publicis S.A. v. True North Communications Inc.*, 206 F. 3d 725, 728 (United States Court of Appeals, Seventh Circuit, 2000).

[56] *Publicis Communication and Publicis S.A. v. True North Communications Inc.*, 206 F. 3d 725, 728 (United States Court of Appeals, Seventh Circuit, 2000).

[57] *Publicis Communication and Publicis S.A. v. True North Communications Inc.*, 206 F. 3d 725, 731 (United States Court of Appeals, Seventh Circuit, 2000).

[58] *Chinmax Medical Systems Inc., v. Alere San Diego, Inc.*, No. 10cv2467 WQH (NLS), 2011 WL 2,135,350 (United States District Court, S.D. California, 2011).

[59] *Chinmax Medical Systems Inc., v. Alere San Diego, Inc.*, No. 10cv2467 WQH (NLS), 2011 WL 2,135,350, 4 (United States District Court, S.D. California, 2011).

[60] *Yahoo! Inc. v. Microsoft Corporation*, 983 F. Supp. 2d 310 (United States District Court, S.D. New York, 2013).

long as the Arbitrator is even arguably construing or applying the contract and acting within the scope of this authority",[61] the award should be upheld. The emergency arbitrator in this case "neither exceeded his authority nor manifestly disregarded the law in awarding such relief",[62] and the concerned interim measure granted was "in essence, final".[63] In the *Blue Cross Blue Shield of Michigan v. Medimpact Healthcare Systems, Inc.* case,[64] the United States District Court Eastern District of Michigan Southern Division confirmed an interim measure granted according to the 1999 AAA Optional Rules for Emergency Measures of Protection, by quoting that "[a]n 'interim' award may be sufficiently final to warrant review in federal district court when it 'finally and definitely disposes of a separate independent claim'".[65]

Bearing in mind the Australian judgment *Resort Condominiums International Inc. v. Ray Bolwell and Resort Condominiums (Australasia) Pty. Ltd.* and, interestingly, in a more recent case *Sauber Motorsport AG v. Giedo van der Garde BV and Giedo Gijsbertus Gerrit van der Garde*,[66] the Commercial Court of the Supreme Court of Victoria decided to enforce the award made by an emergency arbitrator appointed by the Swiss Chambers' Arbitration Institution. The decision was confirmed by the Court of Appeal of the Supreme Court of Victoria, since the award did not go beyond the arbitration agreement, the subject matter was arbitrable and the enforcement would not be contrary to public policy.

Since an emergency arbitrator acts as a proper arbitrator and the decision issued needs to be seen as an arbitrator's decision with respect to issuing interim measures pending the constitution of a tribunal (see Chap. 4), the decision of an emergency arbitrator is "of the same legal nature as a tribunal-ordered interim measure".[67] It is appropriate to examine the practices in state courts concerning the interim measures also

---

[61] *United Paperworkers International Union, AFL-CIO, et al., v. Misco, Inc.*, 484 U.S. 29, 30 (Supreme Court of the United States, 1987); ReliaStar Life Insurance Company of New York v. EMC National Life Company, 564 F. 3d 81, 86 (United States Court of Appeals, Second Circuit, 2009).

[62] *Yahoo! Inc. v. Microsoft Corporation*, 983 F. Supp. 2d 310, 319 (United States District Court, S.D. New York, 2013).

[63] *Yahoo! Inc. v. Microsoft Corporation*, 983 F. Supp. 2d 310, 317 (United States District Court, S.D. New York, 2013).

[64] *Blue Cross Blue Shield of Michigan v. Medimpact Healthcare Systems, Inc.*, 2010 WL 2595340 (United States District Court, E.D. Michigan, Southern Division, 2010).

[65] *Island Creek Coal Sales Company. v. City of Gainesville, Florida*, 729 F. 2d 1046, 1049 (United States Court of Appeals, Sixth Circuit, 1984).

[66] *Sauber Motorsport AG v. Giedo van der Garde BV and Giedo Gijsbertus Gerrit van der Garde*, [2015] VSCA 37(The Supreme Court of Victoria, 2015), available at http://www8.austlii.edu.au/cgi-bin/viewdoc/au/cases/vic/VSCA/2015/37.html (1 June 2024); Australia No. 42, *Giedo van der Garde BV et al. v. Sauber Motorsport AG*, Supreme Court of Victoria, Commercial Court, 11 March 2015, Supreme Court of Victoria, Court of Appeal, 12 March 2015 and Supreme Court of Victoria, Commercial Court, Arbitration List, 27 March 2015, in Albert Jan van den Berg, 40 *Yearbook Commercial Arbitration* 372–376.

[67] Christopher Boog (2013), Chapter 4, Part II: Commentary on the ICC Rules, Article 29 [Emergency arbitrator], in Manuel Arroyo, *Arbitration in Switzerland: The Practitioner's Guide*, Kluwer Law International, p. 822.

granted by tribunals. In the case of *Southern Seas Navigation Limited of Monrovia v. Petroleos Mexicanos of Mexico City,*[68] the Plaintiff petitioned to the United States District Court of S.D. New York for the confirmation of an interim measure in arbitration. The Defendant argued that the order "was only an 'interim' and not a 'final' award".[69] The Court ruled that, if it had accepted such argument and not enforced the interim measure, the conduct of the Court "would render meaningless the arbitrators' power to grant such equitable relief".[70] The Court further reasoned that "if an arbitral award of equitable relief based upon a finding of irreparable harm is to have any meaning at all, the parties must be capable of enforcing or vacating it at the time it is made".[71] An interim measure was not "interim" as it was labeled, but rather "an end in itself, for its very purpose to clarify the parties' rights in the 'interim' period pending a final decision on the merits".[72] In order not to frustrate the interim measure with irreparable harm, the United States District Court of S.D. New York found that the present interim measure was "ripe for confirmation".[73] In the case of *Pacific Reinsurance Management Corp. v. Ohio Reinsurance Corp.*,[74] the Plaintiff and the Defendants had an agreement allowing the Plaintiff to manage reinsurance business. The Defendants were not satisfied with the service. Therefore, they brought the dispute before the United States District Court for the Central District of California. Due to the existence of an arbitration clause, the United States District Court for the Central District of California ordered both parties to resolve their dispute through arbitration. In 1988, the tribunal granted an Interim Final Order to establish an escrow account for security. The Plaintiff declared that this interim measure should not be confirmed as it was not a final award. The Ninth Circuit disagreed, providing that "if temporary equitable relief is to have any meaning, the relief must be enforceable at the time it is granted, not after an arbitrator's final decision on the merits".[75] The enforcement of such interim measures by state courts was "essential

[68] *Southern Seas Navigation Limited of Monrovia v. Petroleos Mexicanos of Mexico City*, 606 F. Supp. 692 (United States District Court, S.D. New York, 1985).

[69] *Southern Seas Navigation Limited of Monrovia v. Petroleos Mexicanos of Mexico City*, 606 F. Supp. 692, 693 (United States District Court, S.D. New York, 1985).

[70] *Southern Seas Navigation Limited of Monrovia v. Petroleos Mexicanos of Mexico City*, 606 F. Supp. 692, 694 (United States District Court, S.D. New York, 1985).

[71] *Southern Seas Navigation Limited of Monrovia v. Petroleos Mexicanos of Mexico City*, 606 F. Supp. 692, 694 (United States District Court, S.D. New York, 1985).

[72] *Southern Seas Navigation Limited of Monrovia v. Petroleos Mexicanos of Mexico City*, 606 F. Supp. 692, 694 (United States District Court, S.D. New York, 1985).

[73] *Southern Seas Navigation Limited of Monrovia v. Petroleos Mexicanos of Mexico City*, 606 F. Supp. 692, 695 (United States District Court, S.D. New York, 1985).

[74] *Pacific Reinsurance Management Corp. v. Ohio Reinsurance Corp.*, 935 F. 2d 1019(United States Court of Appeals, Ninth Circuit, 1991).

[75] Pacific Reinsurance Management Corp. v. Ohio Reinsurance Corp., 935 F. 2d 1019, 1023 (United States Court of Appeals, Ninth Circuit, 1991).

to preserve the integrity of that [arbitral] process".[76] Hence the interim measure at hand could be "reviewed for confirmation and enforcement".[77]

6.3 Public Policy Concerns

In international commercial arbitration, public policy "is never argued at all but when other points fail"[78] as "a last resort to prevent unwanted effects" by state courts.[79]

6.3.1 Clarification of the Public Policy Exception in International Commercial Arbitration

The public policy principle is one of "the oldest and most strongly established principles of private international law", which "bars the application of foreign rules of law offensive to a basic policy of the forum, despite the putative applicability of such rules under accepted choice-of-law methods".[80] Despite the fact that public policy is an important ground under both international conventions and the arbitration laws of various jurisdictions, there is no clear definition of public policy nor a complete list of the issues considered to be public policy matters. The content of public policy varies from jurisdiction to jurisdiction and from era to era,[81] and it "may continue to evolve".[82] Public policy is "a function of time and place".[83]

Basically, there are three types of public policy according to the applicable situations, i.e., domestic public policy, international public policy, and transnational public

---

[76] *Pacific Reinsurance Management Corp. v. Ohio Reinsurance Corp.*, 935 F. 2d 1019, 1023 (United States Court of Appeals, Ninth Circuit, 1991).

[77] *Pacific Reinsurance Management Corp. v. Ohio Reinsurance Corp.*, 935 F. 2d 1019, 1023 (United States Court of Appeals, Ninth Circuit, 1991).

[78] Dirk Otto & Omaia Elwan (2010), Article V (2), in Herbert Kronke & Patricia Nacimiento, et al., *Recognition and Enforcement of Foreign Arbitral Awards: A Global Commentary on the New York Convention*, Kluwer Law International, p. 365; *Richardson v. Mellish*, (1824) 2 Bingham 229, 252 (Court of Common Pleas, 1824).

[79] Dirk Otto & Omaia Elwan (2010), Article V (2), in Herbert Kronke & Patricia Nacimiento, et al., *Recognition and Enforcement of Foreign Arbitral Awards: A Global Commentary on the New York Convention*, Kluwer Law International, p. 365.

[80] Jacob Dolinger (1982), World Public Policy: Real International Public Policy in the Conflict of Law, 17 *Texas International Law Journal* 167.

[81] Dirk Otto & Omaia Elwan (2010), Article V (2), in Herbert Kronke & Patricia Nacimiento, et al., *Recognition and Enforcement of Foreign Arbitral Awards: A Global Commentary on the New York Convention*, Kluwer Law International, p. 368.

[82] Margaret Moses, Public Policy: National, International and Transnational, available at http://arbitrationblog.kluwerarbitration.com/2018/11/12/public-policy-national-international-and-transnational/ (1 June 2024).

[83] Gerhart Husserl (1938–1939), Public Policy and Ordre Public, 25 *Virginia Law Review* 42.

policy. The public policy in domestic relations "does not necessarily pertain to public policy in international relations".[84] In other words, the scope of international public policy is narrower than that of domestic public policy. "Not every breach of a mandatory rule of the host country could justify refusing recognition or enforcement of a foreign award. Such refusal is only justified where the award contravenes principles which are considered in the host country as reflecting its fundamental convictions, or as having an absolute, universal value."[85] However, international public policy is still viewed through the lens of the jurisdiction's own laws or standards for handling foreign arbitral awards.[86] On the contrary, transnational public policy, sometimes called "truly international public policy",[87] refers to those "arising out of an international consensus regarding universal standards as to norms of conduct that are generally recognized and agreed upon as unacceptable in most civilized countries".[88] It is not the public policy of any jurisdiction but rather the public policy that transcends boundaries.[89] Transnational public policy is also a controversial notion, for the fact that "international law has not been adopted as governing law by the parties to an international commercial transaction nor directly incorporated and self-executing in the system of national law".[90]

Although establishing a uniform transnational public policy will undoubtedly make sure arbitral awards can be recognized and enforced more fluently, based on the current legal regime, the refusal of recognition and enforcement still depends on every jurisdiction's attitude. For example, the public policy exception under the New York Convention 1958 provides that the competent authority in the country where recognition and enforcement are sought may refuse the enforcement if "[t]he recognition or enforcement of the award would be contrary to the public policy of that country".[91] In its official French version "the public policy of that country" is "*l'ordre public de ce pays*".

---

[84] Bernard Hanotiau & Olivier Caprasse (2008), Arbitrability, Due Process, and Public Policy Under Article V of the New York Convention, 25 *Journal of International Arbitration* 724.

[85] Emmanuel Gaillard & John Savage (1999), *Fouchard Gaillard Goldman on International Commercial Arbitration*, Kluwer Law International, p. 996.

[86] Margaret Moses, Public Policy: National, International and Transnational, available at http://arbitrationblog.kluwerarbitration.com/2018/11/12/public-policy-national-international-and-transnational/ (1 June 2024).

[87] Pierre Lalive (1987), Transnational (or Truly International) Public Policy and International Arbitration, in Pieter Sanders, Comparative Arbitration Practice and Public Policy in Arbitration, 3 *ICCA Congress Series*.

[88] Margaret Moses, Public Policy: National, International and Transnational, available at http://arbitrationblog.kluwerarbitration.com/2018/11/12/public-policy-national-international-and-transnational/ (1 June 2024).

[89] Michael Pryles (2007), Reflections on Transnational Public Policy, 24 *Journal of International Arbitration* 3.

[90] W Michael Reisman (2007), Law International Public Policy (So-called) and Arbitral Choice in International Commercial Arbitration, in Albert Jan van den Berg, International Arbitration 2006: Back to Basics?, 13 *ICCA Congress Series* 853.

[91] Article V (2) (b), New York Convention 1958.

The concept of "*ordre public* generally differs from public policy in that it is embodied by statute in the rules of civil law countries",[92] while public policy reflects the common law practice.[93] Although these two terms are commonly used interchangeably today, the scope of *ordre public* was more general than public policy.[94] French law treats *ordre public* as "a rational, integrated doctrinal element" to achieve legal certainty.[95] In the common law system, public policy acts in a more indefinite and flexible way, reflecting a set of moral and legal principles.[96]

In the Civil Procedural Law and Arbitration Law of the People's Republic of China, the comparable expression used is "public interest (社会公共利益)". Article 291 states that "[i]f a people's court holds that the enforcement of an arbitration award is contrary to the public interest, the people's court shall issue a ruling not to enforce the award".[97] A similar expression can also be found in the Arbitration Law. Article 58 of the Arbitration Law stipulates that "[i]f the people's court determines that the arbitration award violates the public interest, it shall rule to set aside the award".[98] Unfortunately, there is no clear definition in these legislations regarding what is included in the scope of "public interests".[99]

Turning to the judicial interpretation by the Supreme Court of the People's Republic of China, which is a binding legal source in Mainland China, the terminology is not identical and consistent. According to the Relevant Provisions of the Supreme People's Court on Issues concerning Application for Verification of Arbitration Cases under Judicial Review 2017 (最高人民法院关于仲裁司法审查案件报核问题的有关规定), when handling with foreign-related or Hong Kong, Macao or Taiwan related arbitration cases, any intermediate people's court decides not to revoke or enforce an arbitral award granted in Hong Kong SAR, Macao SAR, Taiwan Region, or not to recognize or enforce a foreign arbitral award, the intermediate

---

[92] Kent Murphy (1981), The Traditional View of Public Policy and *Ordre Public* in Private International Law, 11 *Georgia Journal of International and Comparative Law* 599.

[93] Kent Murphy (1981), The Traditional View of Public Policy and *Ordre Public* in Private International Law, 11 *Georgia Journal of International and Comparative Law* 591.

[94] Karl-Heinz Böckstiegel (1987), Public Policy and Arbitrability, in Pieter Sanders, Comparative Arbitration Practice and Public Policy in Arbitration, 3 *ICCA Congress Series* 179, note 2; Pierre Lalive (1987), Transnational (or Truly International) Public Policy and International Arbitration, in Pieter Sanders, Comparative Arbitration Practice and Public Policy in Arbitration, 3 *ICCA Congress Series* 261.

[95] Kent Murphy (1981), The Traditional View of Public Policy and *Ordre Public* in Private International Law, 11 *Georgia Journal of International and Comparative Law* 597.

[96] Kent Murphy (1981), The Traditional View of Public Policy and *Ordre Public* in Private International Law, 11 *Georgia Journal of International and Comparative Law* 595.

[97] Article 291, The Civil Procedure Law of the People's Republic of China 2023, translation available at http://en.pkulaw.cn/display.aspx?id=e55237a87e2e1d04bdfb&lib=law (1 June 2024).

[98] Article 58, Arbitration Law of the People's Republic of China 2017, translation available at http://en.pkulaw.cn/display.aspx?cgid=83c8fbd6da8a6eb8bdfb&lib=law (1 June 2024).

[99] See more in Cheng Bian & Yuwen Li (2019), Elements of Public Policy in the Making of the China-EU Comprehensive Agreement on Investment, in Yuwen Li, Tong Qi & Cheng Bian (eds), *China, the EU and International Investment Law: Reforming Investor-state Dispute Settlement*, Routledge, Chapter 4.

people's court should file an application for verification with the higher court. If the higher court agrees with the decision not to recognize or enforce such awards, then the higher court needs to submit the case for verification to the Supreme People's Court upon review.[100]

In these replies, the Supreme Court of the People's Republic of China did not unify the use of terminology. Public policy and public interests seem to have been used interchangeably. For example, in the Reply of the Supreme People's Court to the Request for Instructions on Non-Recognition of No. 07–11 (Tokyo) Arbitral Award of the Japan Commercial Arbitration Association 2010 (最高人民法院关于不予承认日本商事仲裁协会东京07-11号仲裁裁决一案的请示的复函), the expression adopted was "public policy", limiting the scope to the "basic legal system" and "fundamental social interests".[101] While in the Reply of the Supreme People's Court on Request for Instructions Re Application of Zhoushan Zhonghai Cereals & Oils Industry Co., Ltd. for Non-Enforcement of Arbitration Award of Hong Kong International Arbitration Centre 2009 (最高人民法院关于舟山中海粮油工业有限公司申请不予执行香港国际仲裁中心仲裁裁决一案的请示报告的复函), the expression was "social and public interests".[102] It can be assumed that there was "a shift merely in terminology rather than in actual substance"[103] in the determination of the public policy exception in the recognition and enforcement of foreign arbitral awards by Chinese courts.

One of "the most-cited"[104] clarifications of public policy is the *Parsons & Whittemore Overseas Co., Inc., v. Société Générale de l' Industrie du Papier (RAKTA)* case.[105] The Second Circuit Court of the United States held that the public policy defense "should be construed narrowly," and the refusal to enforce the foreign arbitral award may be based on "only where enforcement would violate the forum state's

---

100 Article 2, Relevant Provisions of the Supreme People's Court on Issues concerning Applications for Verification of Arbitration Cases under Judicial Review 2017 (最高人民法院关于仲裁司法审查案件报核问题的有关规定), translation is available at http://en.pkulaw.cn/display.aspx?cgid=41864b6840cb509abdfb&lib=law (1 June 2024).

101 Reply of the Supreme People's Court to the Request for Instructions on Non-Recognition of No. 07–11 (Tokyo) Arbitral Award of the Japan Commercial Arbitration Association (2010) (最高人民法院关于不予承认日本商事仲裁协会东京07-11号仲裁裁决一案的请示的复函, [2010]民四他字第32号), translation is available at http://en.pkulaw.cn/display.aspx?cgid=9c1fb82b51eb96a4bdfb&lib=law (1 June 2024).

102 Reply of the Supreme People's Court on Request for Instructions Re Application of Zhoushan Zhonghai Cereals & Oils Industry Co., Ltd. for Non-Enforcement of Arbitration Award of Hong Kong International Arbitration Centre (2009) (最高人民法院关于舟山中海粮油工业有限公司申请不予执行香港国际仲裁中心仲裁裁决一案的请示报告的复函, [2009]民四他字第2号].

103 Yongping Xiao & Zhengxin Huo (2005), Ordre Public in China's Private International Law, 53 *American Journal of Comparative Law* 657.

104 Margaret L. Moses (2017), *The Principles and Practice of International Commercial Arbitration*, Cambridge University Press, p. 243.

105 *Parsons & Whittemore Overseas Co., Inc., v. Société Générale de l' Industrie du Papier (RAKTA)*, 508 F. 2d 969 (United Startes Court of Appeals, Second Circuit, 1974).

most basic notions of morality and justice".[106] As a last resort against the recognition and enforcement of arbitral decisions, the adoption of a public policy exception needs to be used with caution, which was reflected in the restrictive approach taken by courts in most jurisdictions.

6.3.2 *Public Policy in the Emergency Arbitrator Mechanism in Practice*

Within the limited number of cases addressing the emergency arbitrator mechanism, several cases deserve to be analyzed with respect to the public policy exception in international commercial arbitration.

The first case is a U.S. case, *Sharp Corporation and Sharp Electronics Corporation v. Hisense USA Corporation and Hisense International (Hong Kong) America Investment Co. Ltd.*.[107] On 24 April 2017, Hisense initiated a request for arbitration in SIAC and sought interim relief to reinstate the contract from an emergency arbitrator. On 9 May 2017, an interim award was granted by the appointed emergency arbitrator from the SIAC. Sharp claimed that such an interim measure violated the public policy of the United States, i.e., the freedom of speech. The District Court, however, held that state courts have been cautious to exercise power based on this article. The reason is that "the public-policy defense is to be construed narrowly to be applied only where enforcement would violate the forum state's most basic notions of morality and justice".[108] The Sharp's claim was made according to the public policy of the right of freedom of speech in the First Amendment of the Constitution of the United States. However, as the Court pointed out, there is an essential element in the violation of the freedom of speech, meaning the involvement of the governmental action. Furthermore, "the mere confirmation of a private arbitration award by a district court is insufficient state action to trigger the application".[109] In the end, the District Court of Columbia concluded that the interim measure did not violate the public policy in the United States. As a reasonable person, by entering into the agreement containing the choice of arbitration center and arbitration rules, Sharp was willing to be bound by the restrictions stated in the SIAC Arbitration Rules 2016, which contained the emergency arbitrator provisions. As a result, the interim measure by the emergency arbitrator of SIAC was binding and enforceable.

[106] *Parsons & Whittemore Overseas Co., Inc., v. Société Générale de l' Industrie du Papier (RAKTA)*, 508 F. 2d 969, 974 (United States Court of Appeals, Second Circuit, 1974).

[107] *Sharp Corporation and Sharp Electronics Corporation v. Hisense USA Corporation and Hisense International (Hong Kong) America Investment Co. Ltd.*, Civil Action No. 17–1648 (JEB), 2017WL5449805 (United States District Court, District of Columbia, 2017).

[108] *TermoRio S.A.E.S.P. v. Electranta S.P.*, 487 F. 3d 928, 935 (United States Court of Appeals, District of Columbia Circuit, 2007); *Karaha Bodas Co. L.L.C. v. Perusahaan Pertambangan Minyak Dan Gas Bumi Negara*, 364 F. 3d 274, 305–306 (United States Court of Appeals, Fifth Circuit, 2004).

[109] *Davis v. Prudential Securities, Inc.*, 59 F. 3d 1186, 1192 (United States Court of Appeals, Eleventh Circuit, 1995).

The second case is a Ukrainian investment arbitration case *Jkx Oil & Gas PLC, Poltava Gas B.V. and Poltava Petroleum Company JV v. The State of Ukraine.*[110] It differs from an international commercial arbitration case. Although the discussion is provided, less guidance can be taken from this specific investment case. The three Plaintiffs in this case were involved in the production of gas in the Ukraine. The production was governed by the Energy Charter Treaty. On 28 December 2014, the Ukraine enacted "Regarding tax reform amendments to the Tax Code of Ukraine and other legislative acts", increasing the royalty payments on gas production.[111] As a result, the Plaintiffs brought the case to the SCC, considering that the increased royalty payments were a violation of rights and a breach of the investment treaty. On 14 January 2015, the appointed emergency arbitrator issued a decision No. 2015/002[112] to prohibit the Defendant from any further steps to limit the business of the Plaintiffs and to declare that the newly changed legislation had no legal effect on the Plaintiffs. Since the state of the Ukraine did not follow the interim measure voluntarily, the three Plaintiffs requested that the Ukrainian courts for recognize and enforce this emergency arbitrator decision.

On 8 June 2015, the Pechersky District Court of Kyiv City disregarded the argument relying on public policy by the state of Ukraine and granted the permission for recognition and enforcement, by stating that the interim measure "is aimed at preventing the Applicants' interests from being violated and at preventing any unavoidable effects in respect thereof and establishes no other rules except for those

---

[110] *Jkx Oil & Gas PLC, Poltava Gas B.V. and Poltava Petroleum Company JV v. The State of Ukraine*, in Oksana Kravchenko, Yaroslave Petrov & Anna Tkachova, JKX Oil & Gas PLC, Poltava Gas B.V. and Poltava Petroleum Company JV v. The State of Ukraine seeking to grant permission for enforcement of a foreign arbitral award dated 14 January 2015, issued by the Emergency Arbitrator Rudolf Dolzer under the Arbitration Rules of the Stockholm Chamber of Commerce, Supreme Specialized Court of Ukraine for Civil and Criminal Cases, No. 757/5777/15-ц, 17 May 2016; A contribution by the ITA Board of Reporters, available at http://www.kluwerarbitration.com.ezproxy.ub.unimaas.nl/document/kli-ka-16-25-005?q=%22Jkx%20oil%22 (16 June 2020); Ank A. Santens & Jaroslav Kudrna (2017), The State of Play of Enforcement of Emergency Arbitrator Decisions, 34 *Journal of International Arbitration* 7–9; Ihor Siusel & Olesya Omelyannovich (2019), Ukraine: Enforceability of Emergency Arbitral Awards (JKX Oil & Gas PLC v. Ukraine), available at https://globalarbitrationnews.com/ukraine-enforceability-of-emergency-arbitral-awards-jkx-oil-gas-plc-v-ukraine/ (1 June 2024); Ukraine No. 9, *Ministry of Justice of Ukraine v. JKX Oil Plc et al.*, Supreme Court, 24 February 2016 and Court of Appeal, Kyiv, 17 May 2016, in Albert Jan van den Berg,, 41 *Yearbook Commercial Arbitration* 581–584.

[111] *Jkx Oil & Gas PLC, Poltava Gas B.V. and Poltava Petroleum Company JV v. The State of Ukraine*, in Oksana Kravchenko, Yaroslave Petrov & Anna Tkachova, JKX Oil & Gas PLC, Poltava Gas B.V. and Poltava Petroleum Company JV v. The State of Ukraine seeking to grant permission for enforcement of a foreign arbitral award dated 14 January 2015, issued by the Emergency Arbitrator Rudolf Dolzer under the Arbitration Rules of the Stockholm Chamber of Commerce, Supreme Specialized Court of Ukraine for Civil and Criminal Cases, No. 757/5777/15-ц, 17 May 2016; A contribution by the ITA Board of Reporters, available at http://www.kluwerarbitration.com.ezproxy.ub.unimaas.nl/document/kli-ka-16-25-005?q=%22Jkx%20oil%22 (1 June 2024).

[112] SCC Emergency Arbitration No. 2015/002.

applicable in Ukraine and pertaining solely to the Applicants".[113] However, the Court of Appeal in Kyiv overruled the decision by the Pechersky District Court of Kyiv City and denied the recognition and enforcement of the interim measure granted by the emergency arbitrator based on public policy on 17 September 2015. According to the Court of Appeal in Kyiv, the public policy referred to in the New York Convention 1958, which was the governing law for recognition and enforcement, should be understood as "the fundamental principles and rules of Ukraine's legal system".[114] The enforcement of the SCC interim measure would be in violation of the Ukraine Tax Code and would affect the Ukrainian economic situation negatively.

On 24 February 2016, the Civil Chamber of the High Specialized Court of Ukraine for Civil and Criminal Matters reversed the ruling by the Court of Appeal in Kyiv, since the emergency award "would not alter Ukraine's system of taxation or replace the provisions of the Ukrainian Tax Code".[115] On 17 May 2016, the Civil Chamber of the Kyiv Court of Appeal dismissed the appeal made by the state of Ukraine, because the interim measure granted by the emergency arbitrator "in essence has nothing to do with the general rates or royalty changing procedures applicable in Ukraine".[116] On 19 September 2018, the Ukrainian Supreme Court finally refused to enforce the emergency award under the SCC arbitration rules, because of public policy which, in this case, would be "the fundamental principles of the Ukrainian tax legislation" and an improper notice of arbitration proceedings as a violation of due process.[117] Unfortunately, none of those Ukrainian courts addressed the enforceability of interim measures granted by the emergency arbitrator, specifically on the public policy ground, which was the focus of this case here. At the same time, none of the courts made any distinction between the award granted by an emergency arbitrator and an arbitral tribunal. It could be demonstrated that "on the positive side, emergency arbitrator awards can be recognized in Ukraine".[118]

---

[113] Ukraine No. 7, *JKX Oil & Gas PLC et al. v. State of Ukraine*, represented by the Ministry of Justice of Ukraine, Pechersk District Court, Kyiv City, Case No. 757/5777/15-ц, 8 June 2015, in Van den Berg, Albert Jan, 40 *Yearbook Commercial Arbitration* 2015, para. 33 in Excerpt.

[114] Ukraine No. 8, *The Ministry of Justice of Ukraine v. JKX Oil Plc et al.*, Court of Appeals of the City of Kiev, Case No. 22-ц/796/9284/2015, 17 September 2015, in Albert Jan van den Berg,, 41 *Yearbook Commercial Arbitration* 2016, Kluwer Law International, p. 580.

[115] Ukraine No. 9, *Ministry of Justice of Ukraine v. JKX Oil Plc et al.*, Supreme Court, 24 February 2016 and Court of Appeal, Kyiv, 17 May 2016, in Albert Jan van den Berg,, 41 *Yearbook Commercial Arbitration* 2016, Kluwer Law International, p. 583.

[116] Ukraine No. 9, *Ministry of Justice of Ukraine v. JKX Oil Plc et al.*, Supreme Court, 24 February 2016 and Court of Appeal, Kyiv, 17 May 2016, in Albert Jan van den Berg,, 41 *Yearbook Commercial Arbitration* 2016, Kluwer Law International, para. 76 in Excerpt.

[117] Ihor Siusel & Olesya Omelyannovich (2019), Ukraine: Enforceability of Emergency Arbitral Awards (JKX Oil & Gas PLC v. Ukraine), available at https://globalarbitrationnews.com/ukraine-enforceability-of-emergency-arbitral-awards-jkx-oil-gas-plc-v-ukraine/ (1 June 2024).

[118] Olga Hamama & Olga Sendetska (2018), Interim Meaures in Support of Arbitration in Ukraine: lessons from JKX Oil & Gas et al. v. Ukraine and the Recent Reform of Ukrainian Legislation, 34 *Arbitration International*313. See also Sai Ramani Garimella & Poomintr Sooksripaisarnkit (2019), Chapter 5: Emergency Arbitrator Awards: Addressing Enforceability Concerns Through National

Another one is a Chinese case *Hemofarm DD, MAG International Trade Holding DD & Suramu Media Ltd. v. Jinan Yongning Pharmaceutical Co., Ltd.*[119] In this case, the Supreme People's Court of the People's Republic of China refused to recognize and enforce a foreign arbitral award concerning interim measures based on the public policy under the New York Convention 1958 for the first time.[120] Although this case was not directly linked to the enforcement of interim measures granted by the emergency arbitrator, it did address the enforcement of interim measures issued by the tribunal. In 1995, Hemofarm DD, MAG International Trade Holding DD and Jinan Yongning Pharmaceutical Co., Ltd. entered into a contract for the establishment of Jinan-Hemofarm Pharmaceutical Co., Ltd. There was an arbitration agreement in the contract, stating that any disputes regarding the performance of the contract should be resolved by negotiation. If negotiation did not work, the ICC would be the arbitration institution to administer the dispute resolution under the ICC arbitration rules.

In 2000, Suramu Media Ltd. joined in the joint venture. On 6 August 2002, Yongning brought this case before Jinan Intermediate Court, asking for payments of rent and the return of related property. During this court proceeding, Yongning applied for interim measures for property preservation with some necessary security. The interim measure was granted by Jinan Intermediate Court. On 18 October 2005, the Jinan Intermediate Court supported the claims submitted by Yongning with a final judgment. During the litigation, Hemofarm, MAG and Suramu submitted the request for arbitration to the ICC. The arbitral tribunal held that the application for the interim measure granted by Jinan Intermediate Court was not legal and justified. It also led to direct substantive losses of the joint venture. The tribunal decided that Yongning should be liable for damages. The joint venture asked Jinan Intermediate Court to enforce this arbitral award in September 2007. The Jinan Intermediate Court refused to enforce the arbitral award based on public policy. According to the Notice of the Supreme People's Court on the Disposal of the Relevant Issues concerning the Foreign-Related Arbitration and Foreign Arbitral Matters by People's Courts, such a decision to refuse the recognition and enforcement of arbitral awards under the New York Convention 1958 needs to be submitted to higher courts. On 2 June 2008, the Supreme People's Court delivered a final ruling, stating that the arbitral award involving the interim measure granted by the Jinan Intermediate Court was a

Law and the New York Convention, in Katia Fach Gomez & Ana M. Lopez-Rodriguez, *60 Years of the New York Convention: Key Issues and Future Challenges*, Kluwer Law International, p. 81.

[119] *Hemofarm DD, MAG International Trade Holding DD & Suramu Media Ltd. v. Jinan Yongning Pharmaceutical Co., Ltd.*, Letter of Reply of the Supreme People's Court to a Request for Instructions on the Non-Recognition and Non-Enforcement of an Arbitration Award of the ICC International Court of Arbitration (2008) (最高人民法院关于不予承认和执行国际商会仲裁院仲裁裁决的请示的复函，[2008]民四他字第11号), translation is available at http://en.pkulaw.cn/display.aspx?cgid=445d02b47bfe3f3ebdfb&lib=law (1 June 2024).

[120] Zhao, Xiuwen (2009), Refusing Recognition and Enforcement of Foreign Arbitral Awards on the Ground of Public Policy from the Case of Yongning Corporation (从永宁公司案看公共政策作为我国法院拒绝执行外国仲裁裁决的理由), 4 *The Jurist (法学家)* 101.

violation of judicial sovereignty and against the jurisdiction of Chinese courts when the recognition and enforcement were sought in the territory of Mainland China.[121]

In another ruling concerning the applicant *Castel Electronics Pty Ltd.* requesting that the Chinese courts recognize and enforce an arbitral award, the Supreme People's Court of China stipulated specific grounds that could violate public policy in China under the New York Convention 1958. If the recognition and enforcement of an arbitral award will lead to a) violation of fundamental legal principles (违反法律基本原则); b) violation of sovereignty (侵犯国家主权); c) endangering public security (危害公共安全); d) violation of good morals (违反善良风俗), or any other situation against public order.[122] In the Letter of Reply of the Supreme People's Court on Request for Instructions on Application of ED & F (Hong Kong) Co. Ltd. for Recognition and Enforcement of the Arbitral Award of London Sugar Association 2003, the Supreme People's Court made it clear that a violation of mandatory law of China did not equal a violation of public policy under the New York Convention 1958.[123]

In summary, the public policy argument is a potential risk when parties try to enforce the interim measures granted by an emergency arbitrator. However, the power of state courts to rely on a public policy exception to refuse the recognition and enforcement of foreign arbitral decisions should be used with caution. As explained, public policy "is a very unruly horse" and "when once you get astride it you never know where it will carry you".[124]

---

[121] *Hemofarm DD, MAG International Trade Holding DD & Suramu Media Ltd. v. Jinan Yongning Pharmaceutical Co., Ltd.*, Letter of Reply of the Supreme People's Court to a Request for Instructions on the Non-Recognition and Non-Enforcement of an Arbitration Award of the ICC International Court of Arbitration (2008) (最高人民法院关于不予承认和执行国际商会仲裁院仲裁裁决的请示的复函，[2008]民四他字第11号), translation is available at http://en.pkulaw.cn/display.aspx?cgid=445d02b47bfe3f3ebdfb&lib=law (1 June 2024).

[122] Letter of Reply of the Supreme People's Court to a Request for Instructions on the Recognition and Enforcement of a Foreign Arbitration Award applied by Castel Electronics Pty Ltd. (2013) (最高人民法院关于申请人Castel Electronics Pty Ltd.申请承认和执行外国仲裁裁决一案请示的复函，[2013]民四他字第46号), original text is available at http://www.pkulaw.cn/fulltext_form.aspx?Db=chl&Gid=63a8559603999347bdfb&keyword=%e5%85%ac%e5%85%b1%e6%94%bf%e7%ad%96&EncodingName=&Search_Mode=accurate&Search_IsTitle=0 (1 June 2024).

[123] Letter of Reply of the Supreme People's Court on Request for Instructions on Application of ED & F (Hong Kong) Co. Ltd. for Recognition and Enforcement of the Arbitral Award of London Sugar Association (2003) (最高人民法院关于ED & F曼氏(香港)有限公司申请承认和执行伦敦糖业协会仲裁裁决案的复函,[2003]民四他字第3号), original text is available at http://www.pkulaw.cn/fulltext_form.aspx?Db=chl&Gid=9b28920402971a45bdfb&keyword=%e5%85%ac%e5%85%b1%e6%94%bf%e7%ad%96&EncodingName=&Search_Mode=accurate&Search_IsTitle=1 (1 June 2024).

[124] *Richardson v. Mellish*, (1824) 2 Bingham 229, 252 (Court of Common Pleas, 1824).

6.4 Concluding Remarks

Although currently there is no international convention and only a few jurisdictions addressing the recognition and enforcement of interim measures issued by an emergency arbitrator, it is still possible to understand the existing conventions, especially the New York Convention 1958, as the constitutional instruments which are intended to promote the development of international commercial arbitration and eliminate the restrictions on interim measures in general.[125] It seems that the interim measures granted by an emergency arbitrator could overcome almost all the barriers preventing them from being enforced after the assessment in this chapter. However, there are still risks in relation to treating the interim measures granted by an emergency arbitrator as enforceable arbitral awards. For example, the possibility of annulment,[126] based on local arbitration law at the seat of an emergency arbitration, may delay the fast-track proceeding, which is the original purpose of the emergency arbitrator mechanism. In the next chapter, the book will give a proposal regarding a possible way out in relation to the situation of the enforceability of interim measures granted by emergency arbitrators.

[125] Gary B. Born (2021), *International Commercial Arbitration*, Kluwer Law International, p. 2610.
[126] Jonathan Hill (2018), Is an Interim Measure of Protection Ordered by an Arbitral Tribunal an Arbitral Award?, 9 *Journal of International Dispute Settlement* 607.

Chapter 7
Harmonization of the Enforceability of Interim Measures Granted by an Emergency Arbitrator in International Commercial Arbitration

Along with the process of regionalization and globalization, international commercial arbitration has witnessed a movement towards harmonization. It is even argued that "the pursuit of harmonisation is an absolute objective as far as arbitration law is concerned".[1] Harmonization can reduce conflicts between practices by state courts located in different jurisdictions and overcome potential obstacles to guarantee the enforceability of interim measures granted by an emergency arbitrator. This chapter starts with a general introduction to the concept of legal harmonization with a focus on international commercial arbitration Sect. 7.1 and then gives an analysis regarding the conflict between harmonization and diversity in this area of law Sect. 7.2. The discussion on the necessity of harmonization regarding the enforceability of the interim measures granted by an emergency arbitrator will follow Sect. 7.3. In the end, this chapter proposes several possible ways to harmonize the enforceability of the interim measures granted by emergency arbitrators Sect. 7.4.

7.1 Harmonization in International Commercial Arbitration

There is no precise definition of harmonization. The meaning of the term depends on the context.[2] The term "harmonization" may be derived from "the music notion of harmony",[3] referring to "the combination of musical notes, so as to produce a pleasing

[1] Richard Garnett (2002), International Arbitration Law: Progress towards Harmonisation, 3 *Melbourne Journal of International Law* 409.

[2] Katherine Lynch (2003), *The Forces of Economic Globalization: Challenges to the Regime of International Commercial Arbitration*, Kluwer Law International, p. 199.

[3] David W. Leebron (1996), Claims for Harmonization: A Theoretical Framework, 27 *Canadian Business Law Journal* 67.

J. Zhang, *The Enforceability of the Interim Measures Granted by an Emergency Arbitrator in International Commercial Arbitration*,
https://doi.org/10.1007/978-981-97-6536-2_7

effect".[4] Musical harmony and the harmonization of laws may have something in common, but nevertheless they are different. In music theory, harmony represents the vertical integration of notes,[5] meaning "the simultaneous sounding of different tones or pitches".[6] Musical harmony asks for diversity, not uniformity, because "uniformity, the simultaneous sounding of two identical tones, results in a monotone or silence".[7] On the other hand, the harmonization of laws "can be loosely defined as making the regulatory requirements or governmental policies of different jurisdictions identical, or at least more similar".[8] In both ways, harmonization leads to a result that "diverse elements are combined or adapted to each other so as to form a coherent whole while retaining their individuality".[9] Harmonization itself is "a value neutral concept"[10] which depends on the nature of connected components.

Harmonization, unification and uniformity are three different but inter-linked concepts.[11] Harmonization puts more weight on "a common understanding" of concepts and principles,[12] "avoiding complete uniformity",[13] as "a collective descriptor in legal disciplines for all attempts to bring about some form of legal similarity".[14] Unification of laws aims to standardize the legislation of jurisdictions by adopting a model and uniform law across divides of different legal cultures,[15]

---

[4] Martin Boodman (1991), The Myth of Harmonization of Laws, 39 *American Journal of Comparative Law* 701.

[5] Don Michael Randel (2003), *The New Harvard Dictionary of Music*, The Belknap Press of Harvard University Press, p. 379.

[6] Martin Boodman (1991), The Myth of Harmonization of Laws, 39 *American Journal of Comparative Law* 701.

[7] Martin Boodman (1991), The Myth of Harmonization of Laws, 39 *American Journal of Comparative Law* 701.

[8] David W. Leebron (1996), Claims for Harmonization: A Theoretical Framework, 27 *Canadian Business Law Journal* 66.

[9] Martin Boodman (1991), The Myth of Harmonization of Laws, 39 *American Journal of Comparative Law* 702.

[10] Martin Boodman (1991), The Myth of Harmonization of Laws, 39 *American Journal of Comparative Law* 702.

[11] Eva J. Lohse (2011), The Meaning of Harmonisation in the Context of European Union Law—a process in need of definition, in Mads Andenas & Camilla Baasch Andersen, *Theory and Practice of Harmonisation*, Edward Elgar, p. 309.

[12] Katherine Lynch (2003), *The Forces of Economic Globalization: Challenges to the Regime of International Commercial Arbitration*, Kluwer Law International, p. 198.

[13] Eva J. Lohse (2011), The Meaning of Harmonisation in the Context of European Union Law—a process in need of definition, in Mads Andenas & Camilla Baasch Andersen, *Theory and Practice of Harmonisation*, Edward Elgar, p. 309.

[14] Camilla Baasch Andersen (2007), Defining Uniformity in Law, 12 *Uniform Law Review* 15.

[15] Camilla Baasch Andersen (2012), Uniformity and Harmonization by Case Law: The CISG and the Global Jurisconsultorium, in Morten M. Fogt, *Unification and Harmonization of International Commercial Law: Interaction or Deharmonization?*, Kluwer Law International, p. 176; Katherine Lynch (2003), *The Forces of Economic Globalization: Challenges to the Regime of International Commercial Arbitration*, Kluwer Law International, p. 198.

aiming at "the sameness of rules".[16] Uniformity refers to a part of "a larger process requiring agreement of rules" as an ultimate goal.[17] It can be said that the unification of laws is the "harmonization with a zero margin".[18] Harmonization and uniformity of laws are essential and complementary "in efforts to 'internationalize' arbitration law".[19] In recent years, the movement towards unifying laws has tilted away from uniformity, but instead it went towards a "less ambitious and yet more indeterminate notion of harmonization".[20] In this chapter, the purpose is to explore a basis for consensus in improving the enforceability of the interim measures issued by an emergency arbitrator in international commercial arbitration, but it does not require an identical set of rules and procedures for all jurisdictions. Therefore, harmonization, in a general sense, is the chosen approach in the book.

In international commercial arbitration, globalization and regionalization lead to a more harmonized framework. Geographical, legal and cultural boundaries "would disappear, paving the way for a global perception of arbitration as the prime method for settling disputes".[21] In turn, arbitration also acts as an "engine of transnational procedural law", because it goes ahead in the procedural harmonization by laying down various international instruments.[22] Harmonization in arbitration is with approached with "considerable elasticity",[23] and is an attempt to "minimize or eliminate discord" between different laws.[24] Although legal reform requires justifications of the desirability of harmonization in international commercial arbitration, since the harmonization of laws is neutral in value, such justifications "cannot be found in any attribute of harmonization" in itself.[25] The following discussion aims to find the justifications step by step.

---

[16] Bruno Zeller (2007), *CISG and the Unification of International Trade Law*, Routledge-Cavendish, p. 12.

[17] Katherine Lynch (2003), *The Forces of Economic Globalization: Challenges to the Regime of International Commercial Arbitration*, Kluwer Law International, p. 198.

[18] David W. Leebron (1996), Claims for Harmonization: A Theoretical Framework, 27 *Canadian Business Law Journal* 72.

[19] Katherine Lynch (2003), *The Forces of Economic Globalization: Challenges to the Regime of International Commercial Arbitration*, Kluwer Law International, p. 198.

[20] Katherine Lynch (2003), *The Forces of Economic Globalization: Challenges to the Regime of International Commercial Arbitration*, Kluwer Law International, p. 198.

[21] Marc Blessing (1992), Globalization (and Harmonization?) of Arbitration, 9 *Journal of International Law* 79.

[22] Thomas Pfeiffer (2014), The Contribution of Arbitration to the Harmonization of Procedural Laws in Europe, 19 *Uniform Law Review* 204–205.

[23] Jacob Ziegel (1997), Harmonization of Private Laws in Federal Systems of Government: Canada, the USA, and Australia, in Ross Cranston, *Making Commercial Law: Essays in Honour of Roy Goode*, Clarendon Press Oxford, p. 133.

[24] Sandeep Gopalan (2004), The Creation of International Commercial Law: Sovereignty Felled?, 5 *San Diego International Law Journal* 276.

[25] Martin Boodman (1991), The Myth of Harmonization of Laws, 39 *American Journal of Comparative Law* 708.

7.2 Conflict Between Harmonization and Diversity in International Commercial Arbitration

Economic globalization and regionalization lead to two conflicting approaches in international commercial arbitration.[26] One approach is harmonization to meet the needs of international transactions and the other is the maintenance of distinctive arbitration laws in different jurisdictions. The motivation to eliminate diversity among the various legal systems in international trade "has manifested itself" as long as the existence of the necessity to trade across legal and political boundaries.[27] Meanwhile, the diversity of arbitration laws also has legitimacy and value. The following discussion examines the justifications favoring more harmonization, the justifications favoring diversity in international arbitration, and the reasons why harmonization is preferred in international commercial arbitration respectively.

7.2.1 Justifications Favoring More Harmonization in International Commercial Arbitration

Despite the statement that the question is not whether harmonization in international arbitration should be strived for or not, "but only how this [is] to be achieved",[28] it is necessary to go through the justifications and arguments for why harmonization is favored.

7.2.1.1 Providing a Neutral Interface

The most common justification for harmonization in international commercial arbitration is the need to provide a neutral interface for parties to reduce transaction costs.[29] A neutral and harmonized interface ensures fairness in dispute resolution by overcoming the limitations of purely domestic arbitration laws and divisions among the various legal backgrounds of participants.

---

[26] Katherine Lynch (2003), *The Forces of Economic Globalization: Challenges to the Regime of International Commercial Arbitration*, Kluwer Law International, p. 234; Esin Örücü (2004), *The Enigma of Comparative Law: Variations on a Theme for the Twenty-First Century*, Springer Science + Business Media, p. 180.

[27] Paul B. Stephan (1999), The Futility of Unification and Harmonization in International Commercial Law, 39 *Virginia Journal of International Law* 744.

[28] Gralf-Peter Calliess & Insa Buchmann (2016), Global Commercial Law between Unity, Pluralism, and Competition: the case of the CISG, 21 *Uniform Law Review* 4.

[29] Katherine Lynch (2003), *The Forces of Economic Globalization: Challenges to the Regime of International Commercial Arbitration*, Kluwer Law International, p. 201.

Arbitration law, in one particular jurisdiction, may not be adequate to meet the demands of international commerce.[30] When drafting legal provisions, the legislators of one state decide independently how legal relations should be dealt with and what the best solutions for their jurisdictions are. Although some jurisdictions enact laws designed especially for international commercial arbitration, they are still not international regulations that would be binding in other jurisdictions as well, and they are only binding from the perspective of domestic legislators.

On the one hand, solving disputes which are essentially international with domestic tools "is to square the circle".[31] On the other hand, some mechanisms cannot always be found in domestic legal systems. For example, the emergency arbitrator mechanism has not been included in the statutory laws of most jurisdictions, while it has been widely accepted in the international commercial arbitration community. Applying only a specific arbitration law can hardly narrow the gap in the period between submitting the request for arbitration and before the constitution of an arbitral tribunal when asking for interim measures by not turning to state courts. Parties may need to apply for interim measures in various jurisdictions having different procedures. Conversely, the emergency arbitrator mechanism is introduced to bridge that gap. Here, the need for a harmonized solution is evident.

Moreover, relying on the arbitration laws by parties may cause unfairness and bias in solving disputes. Parties "may be loath to disavow reliance on their own laws",[32] because their own systems are the most familiar and comfortable legal systems to them. This could lead to a result that two or more legal systems might be involved in the resolution of one dispute. Even in the situation of an agreed seat of arbitration, the disputed assets or evidence usually will not be in that place. The involvement of multiple legal systems is inevitable in international commercial arbitration. The harmonization of arbitration laws can be a way out of this dead-end by creating a common and neutral interface.[33]

Additionally, a neutral interface overcomes divisions between various legal backgrounds. An important function of legal harmonization is to provide participants in international commercial arbitration from different jurisdictions with a platform to communicate.[34] International commercial arbitration has always been "a direct witness" of the interaction among legal cultures.[35] There are still differences,

---

[30] Sandeep Gopalan (2004), The Creation of International Commercial Law: Sovereignty Felled?, 5 *San Diego International Law Journal* 282.

[31] René David (1971), Chapter 5 The International Unification of Private Law, *Volume II The Legal Systems of the World: Their Comparison and Unification, International Encyclopedia of Comparative Law*, J.C.B. Mohr & Mouton & Oceana Publications Inc., p. 7.

[32] Sandeep Gopalan (2004), The Creation of International Commercial Law: Sovereignty Felled?, 5 *San Diego International Law Journal* 288–289.

[33] Sandeep Gopalan (2004), The Creation of International Commercial Law: Sovereignty Felled?, 5 *San Diego International Law Journal* 289.

[34] David W. Leebron (1996), Claims for Harmonization: A Theoretical Framework, 27 *Canadian Business Law Journal* 75–76.

[35] Bernardo M. Cremades (1998), Overcoming the Clash of Legal Cultures: The Role of Interactive Arbitration, 14 *Arbitration International* 160.

including legal values, core procedures and other aspects. It is necessary to create a neutral interface that provides a common framework to solve disputes in a fair and unbiased way. In this sense, it is understandable that there is "an ongoing globalization process of arbitration, also with a harmonization of its basic notions".[36] However, these "have not resulted in a completely harmonized nor uniform system" nor "a truly transnational arbitral procedure".[37] It will save considerable time and expenses if the laws governing international commercial arbitration are similar. In such a case, there would be "a level playing field" for arbitration, wherever it takes place.[38]

7.2.1.2 Providing a Predictable Legal System

The first objective of a benevolent legislator "should be predictability and stability in international commercial relations".[39] Although a total unification and harmonization, setting aside arbitration laws of different jurisdictions, i.e., delocalization, may not achieve a desirable reduction of legal uncertainty, and it may not encourage international commerce,[40] harmonization "has the evident attraction of predictability".[41] There are two aspects of the legal predictability provided by harmonization in international commercial arbitration, reducing legal risks and increasing transparency.

Harmonization reduces the legal risks arising from divergent arbitration laws. In international commercial arbitration, several different legal systems with foreign languages may be involved in one dispute. During the negotiation, it is difficult and not reasonable to expect parties to foresee all the arbitration laws at issue. Once such a dispute arises, parties have to educate themselves about the regulations in certain jurisdictions. Extra uncertainty and risks also include unfamiliarity with the arbitration environment, various interpretations by state courts regarding different definitions in arbitration and unique mandatory rules limiting party autonomy. It is often the case that many central questions of arbitration laws have not been decided yet by state courts. Or if so, such decisions by state courts may not be binding and may be disputed by scholars. Under this circumstance, parties may be taken by surprise when they realize the outcome of the law chosen by them to govern the

---

[36] Marc Blessing (1992), Globalization (and Harmonization?) of Arbitration, 9 *Journal of International Law* 88–89.

[37] Katherine Lynch (2003), *The Forces of Economic Globalization: Challenges to the Regime of International Commercial Arbitration*, Kluwer Law International, p. 31–32.

[38] Alan Redfern & J. Martin Hunter (2015), et al., *Redfern and Hunter on International Arbitration*, Oxford University Press, p. 179.

[39] Paul B. Stephan (1999), The Futility of Unification and Harmonization in International Commercial Law, 39 *Virginia Journal of International Law* 746.

[40] Paul B. Stephan (1999), The Futility of Unification and Harmonization in International Commercial Law, 39 *Virginia Journal of International Law* 747.

[41] Fernando Mantilla-Serrano & John Adam (2008), UNCITRAL Model Law: Missed Opportunities for Enhanced Uniformity, 31 *University of New South Wales Law Journal* 308.

arbitration proceedings.[42] This can lead to potential conflicts between orders made by state courts seated in different jurisdictions as well. A legal system that offers predictable consequences encourages participants in international commerce to give commitments and cooperate. That is so to say, the reduction of unpredictability and legal risks increases the transaction value.[43] However, with the current level of harmonization in international commercial arbitration, parties have a great chance to "be unpleasantly surprised by the idiosyncrasies" of different arbitration laws.[44]

Harmonization also increases transparency in international commercial arbitration. Different jurisdictions can "legitimately arrive at quite different policy choices".[45] These policy choices may include the public policy that concerns the fundamental morality and justice of one jurisdiction or merely be for the protection of local industries. In these circumstances, transparency is difficult to achieve with divergent arbitration laws and procedures, while the harmonization of general and fundamental aspects is a better choice. For example, the International Bar Association (IBA) puts forward several guidelines and rules which have been adopted by practitioners in arbitration.[46] These guidelines and rules include the IBA Guidelines on Conflicts of Interest in International Arbitration 2024[47] and the IBA Rules on the Taking of Evidence in International Arbitration 2020.[48]

7.2.1.3 Modernizing and Reforming Arbitration Laws

As presented by the UNCITRAL, "the progressive modernization and harmonization of international trade law, in reducing or removing legal obstacles to the flow of international trade, especially those affecting the developing countries, would contribute significantly to universal economic cooperation", on the basis of equality, common interest, and the rule of law, and "thereby, to peace, stability and the well-being of

[42] Ingeborg Schwenzer (2013), Who Needs a Uniform Contract Law, and Why, 58 *Villanova Law Review* 725–726.

[43] Paul B. Stephan (1999), The Futility of Unification and Harmonization in International Commercial Law, 39 *Virginia Journal of International Law* 746.

[44] Renata Brazil-David (2011), Harmonization and Delocalization of International Commercial Arbitration, 28 *Journal of International Arbitration* 454.

[45] David W. Leebron (1996), Claims for Harmonization: A Theoretical Framework, 27 *Canadian Business Law Journal* 89.

[46] Thomas Pfeiffer (2014), The Contribution of Arbitration to the Harmonization of Procedural Laws in Europe, 19 *Uniform Law Review* 212.

[47] IBA Guidelines on Conflicts of Interest in International Arbitration 2024, available at https://www.ibanet.org/resources#Practice%20Rules%20and%20Guidelines (1 June 2024).

[48] IBA Rules on the Taking of Evidence in International Arbitration 2020, available at https://www.ibanet.org/resources#Practice%20Rules%20and%20Guidelines (1 June 2024).
(1 June 2024).

all peoples",[49] and, therefore, the modernization and reform of arbitration laws are strong motivations for harmonization.[50]

Developing regions suffer from criticism concerning their arbitration laws, as they are considered legal barriers to international commerce. For example, the general reputation and formal legal structure are vital considerations when parties choose an arbitral seat in international commercial arbitration.[51] The requirements of international commercial arbitration have probably exceeded the capacity and resources of those developing regions at present. In this case, harmonization can serve as a guidance to trigger and accelerate the process of modernizing and reforming arbitration laws. Harmonization "places the world's resources at the developing world's disposal in terms of its intellectual capital, and also carries with it legitimacy afforded to it by the reputations of the world's foremost experts" at a systemic level.[52] Law reform is a complicated issue, and it can more easily be achieved once some similar provisions have been adopted at the international level.[53]

7.2.2 *Justifications Favoring Diversity in International Commercial Arbitration*

Despite the justifications for harmonization in international commercial arbitration, counterarguments favoring diversity also have serious support. Harmonization efforts may not be necessary and even "in fact are detrimental to international commerce".[54] Diversity, however, has its own and unique benefits for the sustainable development of international commercial arbitration.

[49] UNCITRAL (2009), Reports of the United Nations Commission on International Trade Law on the work of its resumed fortieth and its forty-first session, A/RES/63/120, available at https://documents.un.org/doc/undoc/gen/n08/477/99/pdf/n0847799.pdf?token=5bv7z0RYg7NEOoNnC6&fe=true (1 June 2024).

[50] Sandeep Gopalan (2004), The Creation of International Commercial Law: Sovereignty Felled?, 5 *San Diego International Law Journal* 283.

[51] Queen Mary University of London and White & Case LLP, 2018 International Arbitration Survey: The Evolution of International Arbitration, p. 10, available at http://www.arbitration.qmul.ac.uk/media/arbitration/docs/2018-International-Arbitration-Survey---The-Evolution-of-International-Arbitration.PDF (1 June 2024).

[52] Sandeep Gopalan (2004), The Creation of International Commercial Law: Sovereignty Felled?, 5 *San Diego International Law Journal* 288.

[53] Loukas Mistelis (2001), Is Harmonisation a Necessary Evil? The Future of Harmonisation and New Sources of International Trade Law, in Ian Fletcher, Lukas Mistelis & Marise Cremona (eds), *Foundations and Perspectives of International Trade Law*, Sweet & Maxwell, p. 21.

[54] Sandeep Gopalan (2004), The Creation of International Commercial Law: Sovereignty Felled?, 5 *San Diego International Law Journal* 290; Paul B. Stephan (1999), The Futility of Unification and Harmonization in International Commercial Law, 39 *Virginia Journal of International Law* 744.

7.2.2.1 Encouraging Regulatory Competition and Innovation

To some extent, "harmonization acts as an impediment to innovation"[55] and adaptation.[56] Jurisdictions continue to try to improve the legal framework and creating a friendly environment to attract participants in international commerce. Regulatory competition sometimes pushes the level of protection higher. It can be seen in the so-called "California effect".[57] The high standards of Californian environmental regulation forces other states to raise their levels of protection in order not to lose market share.[58]

Such competition acts as a motivation for further innovation of new mechanisms that can improve the international commercial arbitration regime.[59] This phenomenon can be witnessed in recent practice, including the emergency arbitrator mechanism, the expedited procedures, the development of online arbitration, the use of third-party funding, and the involvement of artificial intelligence in arbitral proceedings. The rapid development of international commercial arbitration contributes largely to competition and innovation, not only of jurisdictions but also in arbitral institutions. Legal diversity enables parties to choose between the existing available arbitration laws freely and to determine which law works best for their disputes.[60]

However, regulatory competition among different jurisdictions can sometimes be "destructive".[61] In this case, harmonization may not necessarily push jurisdictions towards a race to the top, but it prevents the emergence of the race to the bottom.[62] A famous example of the race to the bottom in regulatory competition occurred in the area of corporate law in the United States.[63] In this kind of regulatory competition, the

---

[55] Sandeep Gopalan (2004), The Creation of International Commercial Law: Sovereignty Felled?, 5 *San Diego International Law Journal* 290.

[56] Jacob Ziegel (1997), Harmonization of Private Laws in Federal Systems of Government: Canada, the USA, and Australia, in Ross Cranston, *Making Commercial Law: Essays in Honour of Roy Goode*, Clarendon Press Oxford, p. 136.

[57] Philipp Genschel & Thomas Plumper (1997), Regulatory Competition and International Cooperation, 4 *Journal of European Public Policy* 627.

[58] Stelios Andreadakis (2011), Regulatory Competition or Harmonisation: the Dilemma, the Alternatives and the Prospect of Reflexive Harmonisation, in Mads Andenas & Camila Baasch Andersen, *Theory and Practice of Harmonisation*, Edward Elgar, p. 55.

[59] Stelios Andreadakis (2011), Regulatory Competition or Harmonisation: the Dilemma, the Alternatives and the Prospect of Reflexive Harmonisation, in Mads Andenas & Camila Baasch Andersen, *Theory and Practice of Harmonisation*, Edward Elgar, p. 54.

[60] Camilla Baasch Andersen (2007), Defining Uniformity in Law, 12 *Uniform Law Review* 28.

[61] Michael G. Faure (2003), How Law and Economics May Contribute to the Harmonisation of Tort Law in Europe, in R. Zimmerman, *Grundstrukturen des Europäischen Deliktsrechts*, Nomos Verlagsgesellschaft, p. 51.

[62] William L. Cary (1974), Federalism and Corporate Law: Reflections Upon Delaware, 83 *Yale Law Journal* 705.

[63] Uriel Procaccia (1998), The Case Against Lex Mercatoria, in Jacob S. Ziegel, *New Developments in International Commercial and Consumer Law: Proceedings of the 8th Biennial Conference of the International Academy of Commercial and Consumer Law*, p. 90.

level of protection for the public has been "progressively lowered".[64] Additionally, harmonization does not make local arbitration laws disappear. As "party autonomy reigns supreme in all aspects of commercial laws",[65] the freedom to choose the governing law of arbitration is not affected. Lastly, regulatory competition may also induce "a degree of spontaneous convergence" between different legal regimes.[66] "Predictability, certainty, and stability" in international commercial arbitration are important common values shared by most jurisdictions, even though they may have different legal regulations.[67]

7.2.2.2 Retaining Legal Identities

Each jurisdiction has its own characteristics, its interests to protect and its concepts of how international commercial arbitration should be conducted in its territory.[68] The historical and cultural backgrounds strongly influence the legal systems and interpretation regarding specific regulations.[69] "Culture gives people a sense of who they are, of belonging, of how they should behave, and what they should be doing".[70] It implies that, in some sense, "each country or society has a legal culture of its own and that no two are exactly alike" in many ways.[71] Cultural diversity with unique identities makes creativity and innovation possible in each jurisdiction.[72] Cultural differences in jurisdictions "are far from irrelevant today, because neither ad hoc nor institutional rules adopted by the parties answer all procedural questions".[73] For example, the East-Asian region prefers non-confrontational dispute resolution.[74] On

---

[64] Philipp Genschel & Thomas Plumper (1997), Regulatory Competition and International Cooperation, 4 *Journal of European Public Policy* 626.

[65] Camilla Baasch Andersen (2007), Defining Uniformity in Law, 12 *Uniform Law Review* 28.

[66] Katherine Lynch (2003), *The Forces of Economic Globalization: Challenges to the Regime of International Commercial Arbitration*, Kluwer Law International, p. 291.

[67] Katherine Lynch (2003), *The Forces of Economic Globalization: Challenges to the Regime of International Commercial Arbitration*, Kluwer Law International, p. 292.

[68] Alan Redfern & J. Martin Hunter (2015), et al., *Redfern and Hunter on International Arbitration*, Oxford University Press, p. 179.

[69] Pieter Sanders (1999), *Quo Vadis Arbitration? Sixty Years of Arbitration Practice: A Comparative Study*, Kluwer Law International, p. 60.

[70] Philip Harris & Robert Moran (1991), *Managing Culture Differences*, Gulf, p. 12.

[71] Lawrence M. Friedman (1975), *The Legal System: A Social Science Perspective*, Russell Sage Foundation, p. 199.

[72] Adam Łopatka (2004), Cultural Diversity and Cultural Human Rights, in Guenther Doeker-Mach & Klaus A. Ziegert, *Law and Legal Culture in Comparative Perspective*, Franz Steiner Verlag Stuttgart, p. 216.

[73] Lara M. Pair (2002), Cross-Cultural Arbitration: Do the Differences between Cultures Still Influence International Commercial Arbitration Despite Harmonization?, 9 *ILSA Journal of International and Comparative Law* 61.

[74] Lara M. Pair (2002), Cross-Cultural Arbitration: Do the Differences between Cultures Still Influence International Commercial Arbitration Despite Harmonization?, 9 *ILSA Journal of International and Comparative Law* 68.

the contrary, the model of the U.S, style of dispute resolution has influenced its arbitration procedures to have more "judicialization" and "to be more like litigation".[75] Another argument against harmonization is the lack of representation. The "output of law is simply what the legal system produces in response to social demand".[76] It is almost impossible to reflect the demands of every jurisdiction in the harmonization of laws. Harmonization always comes with compromise.[77] The result of harmonization is probably not compatible with the social development of a particular jurisdiction.

However, "[a]ny creative activity refers to its cultural traditions but can flourish only in contact with other cultures".[78] In globalization and regionalization, some arbitration laws may not reflect the needs of modern international commerce, which may slow down or even hinder the development and involvement of these jurisdictions in international trade. Harmonization is more than a legal restriction, "as it always involves the art of judgment as well as the science of understanding".[79] Especially for international commercial arbitration, harmonization is not the only objective to achieve, but it is also a natural result of interaction between different legal cultures. International commercial arbitration is "one of the earliest examples of an attempt to adapt independent national legal systems to the relentless progress of international commerce".[80] The persistence of legal identities does not necessarily preclude harmonization and progressive evolution in relation to fundamental norms of international commercial arbitration,[81] for example, the universal recognition and enforcement of arbitral awards including interim measures granted by arbitrators.

7.2.2.3 Difficulties in Implementing Harmonization

The process of international lawmaking is time-consuming and costly,[82] not only due to the drafting and negotiation process but also because of the subsequent ratification

[75] Elena V. Helmer (2003), International Commercial Arbitration: Americanized, "Civilized," or Harmonized?, 19 *Ohio State Journal on Dispute Resolution* 36.

[76] Lawrence M. Friedman (1975), *The Legal System: A Social Science Perspective*, Russell Sage Foundation, p. 17.

[77] Camilla Baasch Andersen (2007), Defining Uniformity in Law, 12 *Uniform Law Review* 27.

[78] Adam Łopatka (2004), Cultural Diversity and Cultural Human Rights, in Guenther Doeker-Mach & Klaus A. Ziegert, *Law and Legal Culture in Comparative Perspective*, Franz Steiner Verlag Stuttgart, p. 217.

[79] Stelios Andreadakis (2011), Regulatory Competition or Harmonisation: the Dilemma, the Alternatives and the Prospect of Reflexive Harmonisation, in Mads Andenas & Camila Baasch Andersen, *Theory and Practice of Harmonisation*, Edward Elgar, p. 53; D. Murphy (2004), *The Structure of Regulatory Competition: Corporations and Public Policies in A Global Economy*, Oxford University Press, p. 254.

[80] Bernardo M. Cremades (1998), Overcoming the Clash of Legal Cultures: The Role of Interactive Arbitration, 14 *Arbitration International* 157–158.

[81] Katherine Lynch (2003), *The Forces of Economic Globalization: Challenges to the Regime of International Commercial Arbitration*, Kluwer Law International, p. 306.

[82] Sandeep Gopalan (2004), The Creation of International Commercial Law: Sovereignty Felled?, 5 *San Diego International Law Journal* 295.

by jurisdictions. This is also true for further amendments and updates when something is proven to be insufficient or even incorrect.[83] Furthermore, there is no guarantee that "harmonised law will be interpreted in a harmonised manner".[84] That is to say, even though the harmonization of laws can be agreed upon, such harmonization may not necessarily result in a harmonized effect.

It has to be noted that, "[h]armonization is not an end in itself".[85] It is equally important to ensure that "harmonization does not result in petrification".[86] Implementation of the harmonization of laws rests on the shoulders of jurisdictions. Different jurisdictions can choose the most suitable and comfortable way to execute the requirements of harmonization, which guarantees the equal participation of jurisdictions in international commercial arbitration.

7.2.3 Preference of Harmonization in International Commercial Arbitration

International commercial arbitration, as a special field of law, is benefited by the free flow of arbitral awards established by the New York Convention 1958. Reducing local legal obstacles to international trade is one of the key goals highly valued by the existing international treaties and the international commercial arbitration community. For instance, parties with an arbitration agreement do not want to encounter obscure *lex arbitri* or the laws of the potential place of enforcement.[87] These laws sometimes are not evident to parties when they draft the arbitration agreement prior to a dispute.

Harmonization can solve possible conflicts between jurisdictions and guarantee the free flow of arbitral decisions. It facilitates the resolution of commercial disputes in international transactions. Unlike absolute unification of laws, harmonization focuses on "approximating differences and setting common standards and principles across the board",[88] while preserving various elements like legal cultures of

[83] Loukas Mistelis (2001), Is Harmonisation a Necessary Evil? The Future of Harmonisation and New Sources of International Trade Law, in Ian Fletcher, Lukas Mistelis & Marise Cremona (eds), *Foundations and Perspectives of International Trade Law*, Sweet & Maxwell, p. 21.

[84] Loukas Mistelis (2001), Is Harmonisation a Necessary Evil? The Future of Harmonisation and New Sources of International Trade Law, in Ian Fletcher, Lukas Mistelis & Marise Cremona (eds), *Foundations and Perspectives of International Trade Law*, Sweet & Maxwell, p. 22.

[85] David W. Leebron (1996), Claims for Harmonization: A Theoretical Framework, 27 *Canadian Business Law Journal* 65.

[86] Sandeep Gopalan (2004), The Creation of International Commercial Law: Sovereignty Felled?, 5 *San Diego International Law Journal* 295.

[87] Renata Brazil-David (2011), Harmonization and Delocalization of International Commercial Arbitration, 28 *Journal of International Arbitration* 453.

[88] Fabio Morosini (2005), Globalization & Law: Beyond Traditional Methodology of Comparative Legal Studies and an Example from Private International Law, 13 *Cardozo Journal of International and Comparative Law* 552.

jurisdictions. That is to say and can be reflected by the above discussion regarding harmonization and diversity of arbitration laws, harmonization adds extra benefits, and does not have to be to the cost of the advantages of diversity of arbitration laws at the same time. Therefore, this book states that harmonization is a preferred approach in international commercial arbitration for essential aspects, including the enforceability of interim measures made by emergency arbitrators.

7.3 Necessity of Harmonization Regarding the Enforceability of Interim Measures Granted by an Emergency Arbitrator

Given the above discussion on the conflict between harmonization and diversity, in the context of international commercial arbitration, it is beneficial to have a harmonized regime to guarantee the effectiveness and efficiency of dispute resolution. This section analyzes the necessity of harmonization regarding the enforceability of the interim measures under the emergency arbitrator mechanism in two aspects: the advantages of the emergency arbitrator mechanism and the irreplaceability of the emergency arbitrator mechanism compared to other bodies that can issue interim measures.

7.3.1 Advantages of the Emergency Arbitrator Mechanism

7.3.1.1 Availability of Arbitral Interim Measures Before the Constitution of Arbitral Tribunals

An interim measure is an essential remedy in international commercial arbitration. Due to the period between the commencement of arbitral proceedings and the appointment of arbitrators for a tribunal, the subject-matter or crucial evidence may disappear and substantial and non-compensatory harm may also occur.[89] Moreover, the right of a party in a final award can be frustrated, and such an award may be meaningless if there are no available interim protection measures to guarantee the enforcement of the final award in the early stages of arbitration. For example, this can happen when an uncooperative party involved in a requested interim measure moves, disposes of or replaces the assets in a jurisdiction, making the enforcement of a final award "cumbersome or otherwise impossible".[90] Interim measures are

[89] Stefan Michael Kröll, Julian D. M. Lew & Loukas A. Mistelis (2003), *Comparative International Commercial Arbitration*, Kluwer Law International, p. 586.

[90] Marianne Roth (2012), Interim Measures, 2 *Journal of Dispute Resolution* 425. See also Sundaresh Menon & Elaine Chao (2006), Reforming the Model Law Provisions on Interim Measures of Protection, 2 *Asian International Arbitration Journal* 17.

likely to be even more critical in international commercial arbitration. Because of the cross-border nature, evidence or assets may be “more readily moved or concealed”.[91]

However, it takes time to appoint arbitrators for an arbitral tribunal due to “globalization, complexity, bureaucratization and institutionalization of arbitration”.[92] Institutional arbitration can be “painfully slow” in forming arbitral tribunals.[93] For instance, in the ICC Arbitration Rules 2017, any disputes should be decided by a sole arbitrator or by three arbitrators in a tribunal.[94] In the case of a sole arbitrator, if parties fail to nominate a sole arbitrator within 30 days from the date of receiving the request for arbitration by the other party, the ICC will appoint a sole arbitrator for the parties.[95] The period can be extended. In the case of three arbitrators, parties are required to nominate one arbitrator in their submissions, respectively, and the ICC shall appoint a third arbitrator as president of the tribunal.[96] Parties can choose to nominate the third arbitrator by themselves within 30 days from the confirmation of other co-arbitrators or within any other time limit agreed by the parties or fixed by the ICC. If the parties fail to nominate, the ICC will step in to appoint arbitrators for the parties.[97] It can be seen that the procedure of nominating and appointing arbitrators is time-consuming. The period can be even longer when there is a possible challenge of nominated or appointed arbitrators. If parties wait for the constitution of a tribunal to seek interim measures, it will be too late for them in urgent situations.

The emergency arbitrator mechanism acts as a gap-filler in issuing interim measures during arbitral proceedings. Once an arbitral proceeding starts, parties can apply for interim measures from an emergency arbitrator. In some institutions, for example in the ICC,[98] the HKIAC,[99] the LCIA,[100] and the SCC,[101] parties can apply for the emergency arbitrator mechanism at any time prior to the constitution of a tribunal, even without the requirement for a request for arbitration to be submitted to the institutions. The emergency arbitrator mechanism provides parties with an opportunity to seek interim measures at a very early stage of arbitration, ensuring the protection of parties’ contractual and judicial rights. Additionally, when choosing arbitration to settle a dispute, parties may not want to be forced to turn to a state

---

[91] Alan Redfern (2014), Interim Measures, in Lawrence W. Newman & Richard D. Hill, *The Leading Arbitrators’ Guide to International Arbitration*, Juris, p. 373.

[92] Ali Yesilirmak (2005), *Provisional Measures in International Commercial Arbitration*, Kluwer Law International, p. 114.

[93] Ali Yesilirmak (2005), *Provisional Measures in International Commercial Arbitration*, Kluwer Law International, p. 114.

[94] Article 12 (1), ICC Arbitration Rules 2021.

[95] Article 12 (3), ICC Arbitration Rules 2021.

[96] Article 12 (4) & 12(5), ICC Arbitration Rules 2021.

[97] Article 12 (5), ICC Arbitration Rules 2021.

[98] Article 29(1), ICC Arbitration Rules 2021.

[99] Article 23.1 & Article 1 of Schedule 4, HKIAC Arbitration Rules 2024.

[100] Article 9.4, LCIA Arbitration Rules 2020.

[101] Article 1 of Appendix II, SCC Arbitration Rules 2023.

court for interim measures due to concerns about confidentiality or inconvenience.[102] Sometimes, state courts may decline to grant interim measures either because they conclude that seeking judicial interim measures is not compatible with arbitration agreements or that it is not desirable for courts to intervene in arbitral proceedings.[103]

The essence is that the emergency arbitrator mechanism gives parties a choice and availability to apply for interim measures within the regime of international commercial arbitration, avoiding unnecessary intervention by a state court. It is noted that the jurisdiction of an emergency arbitrator is not exclusive, as it is limited by party autonomy and the concurrent jurisdiction of state courts.

7.3.1.2 Efficiency of the Emergency Arbitrator Proceedings

The emergency arbitrator proceedings are generally fast, which guarantees the efficiency of overall arbitral proceedings. The appointment of an emergency arbitrator is rapid. The appointment of an emergency arbitrator under the ICC Arbitration Rules 2021 is within two days[104]; under the ICDR Arbitration Rules 2021 it is one business day[105]; under the HKIAC Arbitration Rules 2024 it is 24 h[106]; under the LCIA Arbitration Rules 2020 it is three days[107]; under the SIAC Arbitration Rules 2016 it is one day[108]; and under the SCC Arbitration Rules 2023 it is 24 h.[109]

Additionally, the decision-making period is based on a fast-track procedure. The time limit set by institutions for an emergency arbitrator to issue a decision is 15 days under the ICC Arbitration Rules 2021,[110] 14 days under the HKIAC Arbitration Rules 2024,[111] 14 days under the LCIA Arbitration Rules 2020,[112] 14 days under the SIAC Arbitration Rules,[113] and only 5 days under the SCC Arbitration Rules 2023.[114] Generally, their timelines for issuing a decision were respected.[115]

---

[102] Michael Dunmore (2012), Interim Measures by Arbitral Tribunals: The Enforceability Conundrum, 8 *Asian International Arbitration Journal* 222.

[103] Raymond J. Werbicki (2010), Arbitral Interim Measures: Fact or Fiction?, in *American Arbitration Association Handbook on International Arbitration and ADR*, Juris Publishing, p. 90.

[104] Article 2 of Appendix V, ICC Arbitration Rules 2021.

[105] Article 7(2), ICDR Arbitration Rules 2021.

[106] Article 4 of Schedule 4, HKIAC Arbitration Rules 2024.

[107] Article 9.6, LCIA Arbitration Rules 2020.

[108] Article 3 of Schedule 1, SIAC Arbitration Rules 2016.

[109] Article 4(1) of Appendix II, SCC Arbitration Rules 2023.

[110] Article 6(4) of Appendix V, ICC Arbitration Rules 2021.

[111] Article 12 of Schedule 4, HKIAC Arbitration Rules 2024.

[112] Article 9.8, LCIA Arbitration Rules 2020.

[113] Article 8 of Schedule 1, SIAC Arbitration Rules 2016.

[114] Article 8(1) of Appendix II, SCC Arbitration Rules 2023.

[115] Raja Bose & Ian Meredith (2012), Emergency Arbitration Procedures: A Comparative Analysis, 5 *International Arbitration Law Review* 189–190; Grant Hanessian & E. Alexandra Dosman (2016), Songs of Innocence and Experience: Ten Years of Emergency Arbitration, 27 *American Review of International Arbitration* 220.

7.3.1.3 Settling Disputes Without Proceeding Further to an Arbitral Tribunal

Although it is not an original purpose of the emergency arbitrator mechanism, parties may use it to test the merits of their disputes and they may consider settling the cases afterwards. In some instances, the emergency arbitrator mechanism also unexpectedly performs "a useful, if unintended, function as a form of early ADR".[116] According to the ICC Commission Report on Emergency Arbitrator Proceedings, the settlement rate of cases that started with the emergency arbitrator mechanism was relatively high.[117] Out of the first 80 ICC emergency arbitration cases studied in this report, at least 25 of them were settled before the issuance of final awards by arbitral tribunals.[118] Among the 25 ICC emergency arbitrator cases, four reached settlements before the decisions by emergency arbitrators.

The reasons for this can be summarized after a closer examination. First, when the requested interim measures are closely related to the merits of cases, the emergency arbitrator mechanism contributes to the resolution of disputes. Second, sometimes an emergency arbitrator may express his or her own view about the merits of a dispute, although they are not legally binding, but which can contribute to the resolution of controversies. Lastly, an emergency arbitrator can help parties to obtain a consent order or award. A consent order or award refers to a type of arbitral decision upon agreed terms by parties and arbitrators.[119]

7.3.2 Irreplaceability of the Emergency Arbitrator Mechanism Compared to Other Bodies that Can Issue Interim Measures

Although there are alternatives that can render interim measures in international commercial arbitration before the constitution of an arbitral tribunal, the emergency arbitrator mechanism has unique advantages over the other various procedures.

---

[116] James Hosking, Emergency Arbitration: Innovation for Innovation's Sake?, p. 6, available at https://www.aminz.org.nz/Attachment?Action=Download&Attachment_id=835 (16 June 2020).

[117] ICC, ICC Arbitration and ADR Commission Report on Emergency Arbitrator Proceedings, 2019, p. 9, available at https://iccwbo.org/news-publications/arbitration-adr-rules-and-tools/emergency-arbitrator-proceedings-icc-arbitration-and-adr-commission-report/ (1 June 2024).

[118] ICC, ICC Arbitration and ADR Commission Report on Emergency Arbitrator Proceedings, 2019, p. 9, available at https://iccwbo.org/news-publications/arbitration-adr-rules-and-tools/emergency-arbitrator-proceedings-icc-arbitration-and-adr-commission-report/ (1 June 2024).

[119] Margaret L. Moses (2017), *The Principles and Practice of International Commercial Arbitration*, Cambridge University Press, 2017, p. 205.

7.3.2.1 Accessibility of the Emergency Arbitrator Mechanism

Compared to seeking interim measures from state courts, the application of interim measures under the emergency arbitrator proceedings is more accessible for parties in international commercial arbitration. Firstly, seeking interim measures from a state court may violate party autonomy. Parties in an arbitration agreement "may reasonably expect" that any disputes arising between them will be resolved by the agreed dispute resolution method.[120] As agreed by the parties in the first place, the emergency arbitrator mechanism respects party autonomy by responding to the request for interim measures according to the willingness of parties.

Secondly, when choosing arbitration, parties wish to have their dispute decided "in a neutral forum, rather than in the national court of one or the other".[121] To seek interim measures in a local court may cause extra expenses for hiring additional experts who are familiar with the local legal system and even in a foreign language, traveling and accommodation fees. Neutrality and impartiality can also be a problem. A party may have concerns that a local court may be protective in relation to the other party that is located in the court's jurisdiction or be concerned about any other "home court advantage".[122] With regard to the emergency arbitrator mechanism, however, neutrality and fairness can be guaranteed in the proceedings.

Thirdly, the court proceedings regarding interim measures may be lengthy. There are many explanations for this. For example, an over-burdened judiciary and the possibility to appeal. The so-called "Italian Torpedo" is one typical example of lengthy processes.[123] Instead, the emergency arbitrator mechanism is designed to be a fast-track procedure and a quick way to solve claims in urgent situations. Abuse of interim measures in state courts can be a procedural weapon.[124] The underlying principle for interim measures is that "no party right should be damaged or affected due to the duration of adjudication".[125] The emergency arbitrator mechanism ensures this principle very well.

Moreover, a possible reason for parties to choose international commercial arbitration as the dispute resolution method is that they may want to "avoid publicity which frequently accompanies proceedings in court and which could be damaging

---

[120] Michael Dunmore (2012), Interim Measures by Arbitral Tribunals: The Enforceability Conundrum, 8 *Asian International Arbitration Journal* 222; D. Alan Redfern (1995), Arbitration and the Courts: Interim Measures of Protection—Is the Tide About to Turn?, 30 *Texas International Law Journal* 72.

[121] D. Alan Redfern (1995), Arbitration and the Courts: Interim Measures of Protection—Is the Tide About to Turn?, 30 *Texas International Law Journal* 72.

[122] Marianne Roth (2012), Interim Measures, 2 *Journal of Dispute Resolution* 425.

[123] Trevor C. Hartley (2015), *International Commercial Litigation: Text, Cases and Materials on Private International Law*, Cambridge University Press, p. 281; Niek Peters (2017), *The Fundamentals of International Commercial Arbitration*, Maklu, p. 44.

[124] Ali Yesilirmak (2003), Provisional Measures in International Commercial Arbitration, *PhD thesis of the Queen Mary University of London*, p. 135.

[125] Ali Yesilirmak (2003), Provisional Measures in International Commercial Arbitration, *PhD thesis of the Queen Mary University of London*, p. 30.

to one or both of them".[126] Confidentiality is the opposite of publicity, and has been considered as an important advantage and attractiveness of international commercial arbitration.[127] Confidentiality usually refers to the obligations not to disclose information regarding an arbitral proceeding to third parties,[128] which is considered as an important element of arbitration. It "serves to centralize the parties' dispute in a single forum and to facilitate an objective, efficient and commercially-sensible resolution of the dispute, while also limiting disclosure of the parties' confidences to the press, public, competitors, and others".[129] For example, if one party is at risk of insolvency without compensation in one dispute, and meanwhile it has contracts with other trade partners, it is certainly not ideal for this party to seek interim measures in a local court, which may reveal the possibility of insolvency. On the contrary, the emergency arbitrator mechanism is more accessible. As an arbitral procedure, the emergency arbitrator mechanism can guarantee the confidentiality of disputes. Most of the institutional rules ensure that both arbitral proceedings and arbitral decisions are confidential and private.[130]

Admittedly, interim measures granted by an emergency arbitrator or a tribunal have limitations. Arbitrators lack the power to order interim measures against third parties, such as commercial banks, which are relevant when seeking to freeze financial accounts.[131] Arbitrators also have no coercive power to enforce interim measures.[132] When "highly coercive measures involving the exercise of public authority are requested",[133] a state court is a proper forum to seek interim measures. However, the emergency arbitrator mechanism provides for the concurrent jurisdiction of state courts to issue interim measures in aid of arbitration. Therefore, under the emergency arbitrator mechanism, seeking interim measures from state courts is possible, but all the other benefits of seeking interim measures from arbitrators are also available at the same time.

---

[126] D. Alan Redfern (1995), Arbitration and the Courts: Interim Measures of Protection—Is the Tide About to Turn?, 30 *Texas International Law Journal* 72.

[127] Elza Reymond-Eniaeva (2019), *Towards a Uniform Approach to Confidentiality of International Commercial Arbitration*, Springer, p. 1.

[128] Gary B. Born (2021), *International Commercial Arbitration*, Kluwer Law International, p. 3005.

[129] Gary B. Born (2021), *International Commercial Arbitration*, Kluwer Law International, p. 3005.

[130] Article 22 (3), ICC Arbitration Rule 2021; Article 40, ICDR Arbitration Rules 2021; Article 45, HKIAC Arbitration Rules 2024; Article 30, LCIA Arbitration Rules 2020; Article 39, SIAC Arbitration Rules 2016; Article 3 & Article 9 of Appendix I, SCC Arbitration Rules 2023.

[131] Walter G. Semple (1993), The UNCITRAL Model Law and Provisional Measure in International Commercial Arbitration, 6 *International Business Law* 769.

[132] Margaret L. Moses (2017), *The Principles and Practice of International Commercial Arbitration*, Cambridge University Press, 2017, p. 92.

[133] Marianne Roth (2012), Interim Measures, 2 *Journal of Dispute Resolution* 433.

7.3.2.2 Efficiency and Effectiveness of the Emergency Arbitrator Mechanism

Compared to the "standalone"[134] ICC Pre-Arbitral Referee Procedure, the emergency arbitrator mechanism is more convenient for parties. The decision made by an emergency arbitrator has a greater chance of being recognized and enforced than a decision issued by an ICC pre-arbitral referee.

Firstly, although the bases of both the emergency arbitrator mechanism and the ICC Pre-Arbitral Referee Procedure are the same, i.e., party autonomy, the emergency arbitrator mechanism is more convenient for parties due to the opt-out approach. In this case, parties do not need to agree separately on the application of the emergency arbitrator mechanism, since it is included in the institutional arbitration rules. However, in the use of the ICC Pre-Arbitral Referee Procedure, as it is a separate procedure rather than a part of the ICC arbitration rules, parties have to agree expressly upon the adoption of this procedure. A mere reference to arbitration according to the ICC arbitration rules "does not encompass the Pre-Arbitral Referee Procedure".[135] Despite its promotion by the ICC, because of such an opt-in approach, the ICC Pre-Arbitral Referee Procedure was invoked "only rarely".[136]

Secondly, the emergency arbitrator mechanism is more efficient than the ICC Pre-Arbitral Referee Procedure. Concerning the appointment of an emergency arbitrator by an arbitral institution, the period varies from 24 h to three days. For the appointment of an ICC pre-arbitral referee, parties have to agree on the nomination and appointment. Parties can choose a referee before or after an application for the ICC Pre-Arbitral Referee Procedure.[137] At the latest, the responding party must submit its opinion on the appointment of a referee within eight days after the receipt of such an application.[138] An arbitral institution makes sure that the appointment of an emergency arbitrator takes place sufficiently fast. Moreover, acting as a gatekeeper, an institution can also exclude applications that are inadmissible in order to save time for the overall arbitral proceedings.[139] Additionally, the period for an emergency arbitrator to render a decision is from 5 to 15 days depending on the rules of the different institutions. However, the limit for an ICC pre-arbitral referee is 30 days

[134] Michael Dunmore (2012), Interim Measures by Arbitral Tribunals: The Enforceability Conundrum, 8 *Asian International Arbitration Journal* 223.

[135] Michael McIlwrath & John Savage (2010), *International Arbitration and Mediation: A Practical Guide*, Kluwer Law International, p. 282.

[136] James Hosking, & Erin Valentine (2011), Pre-Arbitral Emergency Measures of Protection: New Tools for an Old Problem, *Commercial Arbitration: New Developments and Strategies for Efficient, Cost-Effective Dispute Resolution*, p. 3, available at http://www.chaffetzlindsey.com/wp-content/uploads/2011/10/000954671.PDF (1 June 2024).

[137] Article 4.1, ICC Rules for a Pre-Arbitral Referee Procedure 1990.

[138] Article 3.4, ICC Rules for a Pre-Arbitral Referee Procedure 1990.

[139] Grant Hanessian & E. Alexandra Dosman (2016), Songs of Innocence and Experience: Ten Years of Emergency Arbitration, 27 *American Review of International Arbitration* 220.

after the receipt of related files.[140] The request for interim measures in urgent situations asks for a rapid procedure, which is also the primary and initial concern in such procedures. In this scenario, the 30-day limit of the ICC Pre-Arbitral Procedure is not expedited enough to meet the needs of the parties compared to the emergency arbitrator mechanism.

Lastly, the ICC Pre-Arbitral Referee Procedure is predominantly considered contractual in nature,[141] while the emergency arbitrator mechanism is judicial in nature as well as contractual in nature. This difference in nature leads to an enforceability difference. The intent of parties to submit their claims conclusively to be settled by a natural third party entrusted with a jurisdictional nature is missing in the ICC Pre-Arbitral Referee Procedure.[142] An order made by an ICC referee is not an arbitral award but a "purely a creature of contract".[143] As discussed in *Société Nationale des Pétroles du Congo and République du Congo v. TotalFinaElf E&P Congo*, the Paris Court of Appeals concluded that a referee under the ICC arbitration was not a proper arbitrator and the referee had no intention to act in the capacity of an arbitrator.[144] The order issued by a referee had no more of a binding effect than an agreement between parties.[145] Therefore, a decision made by an ICC pre-arbitral referee cannot be recognized or enforced by state courts under the current regime of international commercial arbitration.

In contrast, as indicated in Chap. 4, an emergency arbitrator is "a full-fledged arbitrator".[146] An emergency arbitrator has the full power of a regularly-constituted tribunal to conduct proceedings and to grant interim measures that are deemed appropriate.[147] The intention of an emergency arbitrator to act as an arbitrator and to

---

140 Article 6.2, ICC Rules for a Pre-Arbitral Referee Procedure 1990.

141 Baruch Baigel (2014), The Emergency Arbitrator Procedure under the 2012 ICC Rules: A Juridical Analysis, 31 *Journal of International Arbitration* 3; Michael Dunmore (2012), Interim Measures by Arbitral Tribunals: The Enforceability Conundrum, 8 *Asian International Arbitration Journal* 225.

142 Christine Lécuyer-Thieffry (2003), First Court Ruling on the ICC Pre-Arbitral Referee Procedure, 20 *Journal of International Arbitration* 604.

143 Ian Meredith & Marcus Birch, The ICC's Pre-Arbitral Referee Procedure: How Valuable Is It?, available at https://files.klgates.com/files/publication/ab0be67f-01ef-4206-9c12-6e91f5b4837e/presentation/publicationattachment/bae41c65-1f1b-43c3-b963-7de5c496b5bc/article_meredith_icc_0108.pdf (1 June 2024).

144 Michael Dunmore (2012), Interim Measures by Arbitral Tribunals: The Enforceability Conundrum, 8 *Asian International Arbitration Journal* 226.

145 Emmanuel Gaillard (2003), First Court Decision on Pre-Arbitral Referee, 229 New York Law Journal, available at https://www.shearman.com/~/media/Files/NewsInsights/Publications/2003/06/First-Court-Decision-on-PreArbitral-Referee/Files/Download-PDF-First-Court-Decision-on-PreArbitral__/FileAttachment/IA_060503.pdf (16 June 2020).

146 Fabio G. Santacroce (2015), The emergency arbitrator: a full-fledged arbitrator rendering an enforceable decision?, 31 *Arbitration International* 283.

147 Grant Hanessian (2014), Emergency Arbitrators, in Lawrence W. Newman & Richard D. Hill, *The Leading Arbitrators' Guide to International Arbitration*, Juris, p. 349.

determine an issue is clear.[148] More and more jurisdictions have recognized the emergency arbitrator mechanism, and state courts show their willingness to enforce the interim measures granted by an emergency arbitrator. While the ICC Pre-Arbitral Referee Procedure was the forerunner of the attempts to address interim measures before the constitution of an arbitral tribunal, "it may be about to become obsolete".[149] In international commercial arbitration, parties expect to have access to interim measures efficiently and effectively. Unfortunately, compared to the emergency arbitrator mechanism, the ICC Pre-Arbitral Referee Procedure fails to satisfy the needs in both ways.

7.3.2.3 Fewer Limits of the Emergency Arbitrator Mechanism

Traditionally, arbitration is considered to be a less expensive and faster dispute resolution system than litigation in state courts. As international cases become more complicated, and international commercial arbitration becomes more popular, concerns have arisen regarding the increased time and costs of arbitration.[150] In order to provide "a streamlined arbitration with reduced scales of fees",[151] many institutions have introduced expedited arbitration. Expedited arbitration is a procedure that can simplify and accelerate the normal arbitration proceedings in cases without complicated issues.[152] The arbitrators in expedited arbitration enjoy full power including granting interim measures. However, expedited arbitration is not a perfect solution for interim measures.

Firstly, not all institutions adopt a common framework of expedited arbitration. Generally, there are two approaches in the application of expedited arbitration, i.e., automatic application and elective application.[153] The ICC adopts an automatic application of the expedited arbitration procedure. By agreeing to arbitration under the ICC Arbitration Rules 2021, it is assumed that parties agree that the expedited arbitration provisions and rules "shall take precedence over any contrary terms of the

---

[148] Michael Dunmore (2012), Interim Measures by Arbitral Tribunals: The Enforceability Conundrum, 8 *Asian International Arbitration Journal* 228.

[149] James Hosking & Erin Valentine (2011), Pre-Arbitral Emergency Measures of Protection: New Tools for an Old Problem, *Commercial Arbitration: New Developments and Strategies for Efficient, Cost-Effective Dispute Resolution*, p. 3, available at http://www.chaffetzlindsey.com/wp-content/uploads/2011/10/000954671.PDF (16 June 2020).

[150] Peter Morton (2010), Can a World Exist Where Expedited Arbitration Becomes the Default Procedure?, 26 *Arbitration International* 103.

[151] ICC, Expedited Procedure Provision, available at https://iccwbo.org/dispute-resolution/dispute-resolution-services/arbitration/rules-procedure/expedited-procedure/ (1 June 2024).

[152] Yas Banifatemi (2017), Expedited Proceedings in International Arbitration, in Laurent Lévy & Michael Polkinghorne, *Expedited Procedures in International Arbitration*, International Chamber of Commerce, p. 12.

[153] Lisa Allenden, Expedited Arbitration: Paris v. Stockholm: Full Steam Ahead, available at http://arbitrationblog.practicallaw.com/expedited-arbitration-paris-v-stockholm-full-steam-ahead/ (1 June 2024).

arbitration agreement".[154] Parties can always opt out of the expedited procedure provisions by adding the following or similar wording: "[t]he Expedited Procedure Provisions shall not apply".[155] The ICDR takes a similar approach to the ICC.[156] The HKIAC and the SIAC adopt an elective approach.[157] The expedited arbitration under the SCC asks that parties consent expressly regardless of the disputed amount or any other circumstance.[158] The SCC Rules for Expedited Arbitrations is not even a part of its regular SCC Arbitration Rules. Parties have to agree expressly on the application of the SCC expedited arbitration provisions. The LCIA only provides the possibility for an expedited formation of an arbitral tribunal in the case of exceptional urgency.[159] However, in the emergency arbitrator mechanism, a common framework is adopted by arbitral institutions.

Secondly, usually, the disputed amount in expedited arbitration cannot exceed a maximum. Every arbitral institution regulates the maximum disputed amount differently. In the ICC Arbitration Rules 2021, the disputed amount should not exceed 3,000,000 USD.[160] Under the ICDR Arbitration Rules 2021, the maximum amount is 500,000 USD.[161] If a party's claim or counterclaim does not exceed 100,000 USD, excluding interest and other arbitration costs, there will be no oral hearings, unless an appointed arbitrator for the expedited procedure determines otherwise.[162] The HKIAC does not set an exact amount in its Arbitration Rules 2024 but it refers to it on its official website.[163] Currently, the applicable monetary threshold of the HKIAC expedited arbitration has been raised from 250,000 USD to 25,000,000 HKD (over 3.2 million USD).[164] The SIAC requires that the amount in dispute cannot exceed the equivalent amount of 6,000,000 SGD (over 4.4 million USD).[165]

Thirdly, the enforceability of decisions made by a sole arbitrator in expedited arbitration may be questioned due to the number of arbitrators agreed upon initially by the parties. This dilemma is reflected in two cases with conflicting judgments. Both cases were arbitrated under the administration of the SIAC.

---

[154] Article 30(1), ICC Arbitration Rules 2021.

[155] ICC Arbitration Clauses, ICC Arbitration Rules 2021.

[156] Article 1(4), ICDR Arbitration Rules 2021.

[157] Lisa Allenden, Expedited Arbitration: Paris v. Stockholm: Full Steam Ahead, available at http://arbitrationblog.practicallaw.com/expedited-arbitration-paris-v-stockholm-full-steam-ahead/ (1 June 2024).

[158] Javier Tarjuelo (2017), Fast Track Procedures: A New Trend in Institutional Arbitration, 11 *Dispute Resolution International* 109.

[159] Article 9A, LCIA Arbitration Rules 2020.

[160] Article 1(2) of Appendix VI, ICC Arbitration Rules 2021.

[161] Article 1(4), ICDR Arbitration Rules 2021.

[162] Article 1(4), ICDR Arbitration Rules 2021.

[163] Article 42.1, HKIAC Arbitration Rules 2024.

[164] HKIAC, Expedited HKIAC Arbitration, available at https://www.hkiac.org/arbitration/process/expedited-hkiac-arbitration (1 June 2024); HKIAC, the 2024 Schedule of Fees, available at https://hkiac.org/content/2024-schedule-fees (1 June 2024).

[165] Article 5.1(a), SIAC Arbitration Rules 2016.

The first case is *AQZ v. ARA*,[166] which is the first reported judgment regarding the SIAC expedited arbitration,[167] and the other case is *Nobles Resources Pte. Ltd. v. Shanghai Good Credit International Trade Co., Ltd.*,[168] which is the first SIAC expedited arbitration award was set aside. The critical issue in both cases was whether an arbitral award can be set aside when the composition of an arbitral tribunal is not in accordance with an arbitration agreement. In these two cases, the issue regarding the composition of an arbitral tribunal referred to the appointment of a sole arbitrator in the SIAC expedited arbitrations, instead of three arbitrators in the arbitration agreements. In *AQZ v. ARA*, the Singapore High Court upheld the decision made by the sole arbitrator in the expedited procedure, stating that it would be "a commercially sensible approach" to interpret a parties' agreement with the recognition of the SIAC's discretion to appoint a sole arbitrator in expedited arbitration.[169] The judge concluded that the SIAC expedited arbitration procedure "can override parties' agreement for arbitration before three arbitrators".[170] The Singapore High Court recognized that parties implicitly consent to empower the SIAC to refer the case to a sole arbitrator in expedited arbitration by submitting a dispute to the SIAC arbitration rules, regardless of the arbitration agreement.[171]

Conversely, two years later, after the Singapore judgment, in *Nobles Resources Pte. Ltd. v. Shanghai Good Credit International Trade Co., Ltd.*, the Shanghai No. 1 Intermediate People's Court refused to enforce the award issued by a sole arbitrator in a SIAC expedited arbitration, holding that the composition of the arbitral tribunal was not in accordance with the arbitration agreement. Since both parties had agreed on a tribunal with three arbitrators, and they did not exclude such a composition in expedited arbitration, the SIAC still appointed a sole arbitrator regardless of the objections. Such arbitral proceedings violated Article V (1)(d) of the New York Convention 1958. Therefore, the Shanghai No. 1 Intermediate People's Court set the award aside.

Different from expedited arbitration, the emergency arbitrator mechanism enjoys "a common, general procedural framework"[172] in leading arbitral institutions. For the cases that can be submitted to an emergency arbitrator, there is no limit in the

---

[166] *AQZ v. ARA* [2015] SGHC 49 (High Court, Supreme Court of Singapore, 2015).

[167] Gary B. Born, & Jonathan W. Lim, AQZ v. ARA: Singapore High Court Upholds Award Made under SIAC Expedited Procedure, available at http://arbitrationblog.kluwerarbitration.com/2015/03/09/aqz-v-ara-singapore-high-court-upholds-award-made-under-siac-expedited-procedure/ (1 June 2024).

[168] *Nobles Resources Pte. Ltd. v. Shanghai Good Credit International Trade Co., Ltd.* (2016) (来宝资源国际私人有限公司与上海信泰国际贸易有限公司申请承认和执行外国仲裁裁决案，[2016]沪01协外认1号), available at http://wenshu.court.gov.cn/website/wenshu/181107ANFZ0BXSK4/index.html?docId=3977ca869daa4df39c87a7e0016e1525 (16 June 2020).

[169] *AQZ v. ARA* [2015] SGHC 49 (High Court, Supreme Court of Singapore, 2015), para. 132.

[170] *AQZ v. ARA* [2015] SGHC 49 (High Court, Supreme Court of Singapore, 2015), para. 135.

[171] Javier Tarjuelo (2017), Fast Track Procedures: A New Trend in Institutional Arbitration, 11 *Dispute Resolution International* 112.

[172] Fabio G. Santacroce (2015), The emergency arbitrator: a full-fledged arbitrator rendering an enforceable decision?, 31 *Arbitration International* 285.

maximum amount in the disputes. Moreover, jurisdictions and courts adopt a positive view of the emergency arbitrator mechanism gradually. That is to say that there are fewer limits but more certainty in the emergency arbitrator mechanism than in expedited arbitration.

7.4 Possible Proposals to Harmonize the Enforceability of the Interim Measures Granted by an Emergency Arbitrator

Despite the theoretical debate on harmonization, practical efforts have been made to harmonize international commercial arbitration generally.[173] This section examines the possibility of the harmonization of the enforceability of the emergency arbitrator mechanism together with proposals regarding different approaches, including mandatory methods and non-mandatory methods.

7.4.1 Mandatory Methods

In the last century, most trading jurisdictions have entered into international conventions to facilitate the recognition and enforcement of arbitration agreements and arbitral awards.[174] These international conventions contribute to a widely-accepted, stable and effective system for international commercial dispute resolution and ultimately help to promote international trade and business.[175] Multilateral and bilateral treaties and subsequent implementation in arbitration laws are mandatory harmonizing methods.[176] This subsection discusses the possibility and proposals for mandatory methods to harmonize the enforceability of the interim measures granted by an emergency arbitrator in international commercial arbitration.

7.4.1.1 A Protocol to the New York Convention 1958

The New York Convention 1958 is "one of the few examples where a transnational commercial law instrument… became a true success story".[177] During 60 years of

---

[173] Katherine Lynch (2003), *The Forces of Economic Globalization: Challenges to the Regime of International Commercial Arbitration*, Kluwer Law International, p. 203.

[174] Gary B. Born (2021), *International Commercial Arbitration*, Kluwer Law International, p. 98.

[175] Gary B. Born (2021), *International Commercial Arbitration*, Kluwer Law International, p. 98.

[176] Katherine Lynch (2003), *The Forces of Economic Globalization: Challenges to the Regime of International Commercial Arbitration*, Kluwer Law International, p. 204.

[177] Herbert Kronke (2010), Introduction: The New York Convention Fifty Years on: Overview and Assessment, in Herbert Kronke & Patricia Nacimiento, *Recognition and Enforcement of Foreign*

practice, it "has never ceased to fascinate the arbitration community".[178] Despite the success, there is a continuous debate on whether it is necessary to amend the Convention for improvements as time goes by.

One view is that the New York Convention 1958 should be amended. The reasoning behind this position is based on substantial criticism of the current provisions. Firstly, the ambiguity of the terms in the Convention raises difficulties in actual implementation by different jurisdictions. For example, the meaning and scope of "arbitral awards" and "public policy" are not clear. Moreover, the texts of the Convention in all the official languages of the United Nations are "equally authentic".[179] In all of the other five languages, the content of Article V (1)(e) has the same meaning, i.e., the recognition and enforcement may be refused if "the award has not yet become binding". However, in the Russian text, it states that the recognition and enforcement may be refused if "the award has not yet become final". This difference could result in confusion and even mistakes in court decisions. Secondly, the text of the Convention contains a logical loophole. Under Article V (1)(e), an arbitral award may be refused to be recognized or enforced if it "has been set aside or suspended by a competent authority of the country in which, or under the law of which, that the award was made". Consequently, a refusal of recognition and enforcement can be determined under local laws, which is not included in the narrow grounds listed in Article V.[180] Lastly, some parts of the Convention are considered to be outdated.[181] After more than 60 years, it is time to consider partial replacements, "additional reading glass, crutches to enable the treaty to last another 60 years".[182] Otherwise, the Convention may "gradually phase out" at the same time as the rise of the United Nations Convention on International Settlement Agreements Resulting from Mediation 2018[183] and the Convention on the Recognition and Enforcement of Foreign Judgments in Civil

---

Arbitral Awards: A Global Commentary on the New York Convention, Kluwer Law International, p. 1–2.

[178] Stavros Brekoulakis (2008), Enforcement of Foreign Arbitral Awards: Observations on the Efficiency of the Current System and the Gradual Development of Alternative Means of Enforcement, 19 *American Review of International Arbitration* 416.

[179] Article XVI, New York Convention 1958.

[180] Margaret L. Moses (2017), *The Principles and Practice of International Commercial Arbitration*, Cambridge University Press, 2017, p. 238.

[181] Albert van den Berg (2008), New York Convention v. Hypothetical Convention: A Closer Look at the Proposed "New York Convention", 3 *Global Arbitration Review* 14, available at https://www.arbitration-icca.org/media/1/13318252772820/new_ny_conv.pdf (1 June 2024).

[182] Marike R. P. Paulsson,, The Eve of the New York Convention's 60th Anniversary and the Birthday Party: How to Prepare with too Many Guests at the Table, available at http://arbitrationblog.kluwerarbitration.com/2018/06/21/eve-new-york-conventions-60th-anniversary-birthday-party-prepare-many-guests-table-il-ne-faut-pas-melanger-les-tables/ (1 June 2024); Marike Paulsson & Supritha Suresh (2019), The New York Convention's 60th Anniversary: A Restatement for the New York Convention?, in Katia Fach Gómez, Rodriguez Lopez & Ana Mercedes, *60 Years of the New York Convention: Key Issues and Future Challenges*, Kluwer Law International, p. 292.

[183] UNCITRAL, United Nations Convention on International Settlement Agreements Resulting from Mediation (New York, 2018) (the "Singapore Convention on Mediation"), available

or Commercial Matters 2019.[184] Modernization of the New York Convention 1958 is necessary to "remain relevant and suitable for the years to come",[185] since it cannot be achieved by merely interpretation and guidance.[186]

The opposite view is that the New York Convention 1958 should not be amended. The reasons are as follows. The Convention is a "constitutional" instrument by imposing "uniform international standards" while "leaving a substantial role for national law and national courts to play in the arbitral process".[187] By stipulating a minimum standard, the New York Convention 1958 allows contracting parties to adopt more liberal and higher standards in recognizing and enforcing foreign arbitral awards. In other words, the Convention "cannot freeze the development of arbitration law".[188] Although it has few provisions, it is even said, extra-judicially, that "the New York Convention is both the Best Thing since Sliced Bread and also whatever was the Best Thing before Sliced Bread replaced it as the Best Thing".[189] Additionally, with a significant number contracting parties to the Convention (161),[190] there is "no hope" they would agree to an amended version.[191]

Although amending the New York Convention 1958 may be unrealistic, an optional protocol regarding a uniform interpretation and clarification on the recognition and enforcement of interim measures is one effective option to be considered.[192] Different from an amendment directly to the New York Convention 1958, a protocol "amends, supplements or clarifies a multilateral treaty" in a less formal manner,

at https://uncitral.un.org/en/texts/mediation/conventions/international_settlement_agreements (1 June 2024).

[184] Hague Conference on Private International Law (HCCH), Convention on the Recognition and Enforcement of Foreign Judgments in Civil or Commercial Matters (concluded 2 July 2019), available at https://www.hcch.net/en/instruments/conventions/full-text/?cid=137 (1 June 2024).

[185] Paula Hodges, Alastair Henderson, Gitta Satryani, Vanessa Naish & Hannah Ambrose, 60 Years of the New York Convention: A Triumph of Trans-National Legal Co-operation, or A Product of its Time and in Need of Revision, available at https://www.herbertsmithfreehills.com/latest-thinking/60-years-of-the-new-york-convention-a-triumph-of-trans-national-legal-co-operation (1 June 2024).

[186] Albert van den Berg (2008), New York Convention v. Hypothetical Convention: A Closer Look at the Proposed "New York Convention", 3 *Global Arbitration Review* 14, available at https://www.arbitration-icca.org/media/1/13318252772820/new_ny_conv.pdf (1 June 2024).

[187] Gary B. Born (2021), *International Commercial Arbitration*, Kluwer Law International, p.118; *Yugraneft Corporation v. Rexx Management Corporation*, [2010] 1 R.C.S. 649, 661 (Supreme Court of Canada, 2010).

[188] Emmanuel Gaillard (2009), The Urgency of Not Revising the New York Convention, 50 Years of the New York Convention, 14 *ICCA Congress Series* 692.

[189] V. V. Veeder (2010), Is there a Need to Revise the New York Convention?, 1 *Journal of International Dispute Settlement* 500.

[190] UNCITRAL, Status: Convention on the Recognition and Enforcement of Foreign Arbitral Awards (New York, 1958)(the "New York Convention"), available at https://uncitral.un.org/en/texts/arbitration/conventions/foreign_arbitral_awards/status2 (1 June 2024).

[191] Gaillard, Emmanuel, The Urgency of Not Revising the New York Convention, 50 Years of the New York Convention, 14 ICCA Congress Series 2009, Kluwer Law International, 2009, p. 692.

[192] Ali Yesilirmak (2005), *Provisional Measures in International Commercial Arbitration*, Kluwer Law International, p. 266.

focusing a specific aspect "in greater detail".[193] The advantage is that a protocol does not bind all contracting parties, but it is open to the parties who are willing to accept changes. Such a protocol can reflect current international practice and bring more consistency.

Despite two core objectives of the Convention, i.e., ensuring that arbitration agreements are respected and that guaranteeing arbitral awards are recognized and enforced, there is "a broader goal of encouraging international commerce by means of an efficient and neutral process of dispute resolution".[194] As an inevitable aspect of international commercial arbitration, the practical importance of arbitral interim measures is well understood.[195] Without an international legal regime to enforce arbitral interim measures, parties' legal rights can be jeopardized, which could affect the status of arbitration as a preferred dispute resolution method in international commerce.

The proposed protocol should contain regulations regarding the recognition and enforcement of interim measures, not only issued by an arbitral tribunal but also by an emergency arbitrator. It can be achieved with two different approaches. One approach is that the protocol includes interim measures in the interpretation of "arbitral awards". The other approach is to distinguish interim measures from arbitral awards and to ensure the enforceability of interim measures made by arbitrators, including emergency arbitrators. Even if interim measures cannot be recognized as awards under the New York Convention 1958, they "can be at least as, or even more important than, an award".[196] Furthermore, the protocol needs to limit the scope of applicable interim measures. In the case of purely procedural interim measures, they should be excluded from the protocol.

7.4.1.2 Mutual Recognition and Enforcement

As an option in a subsidiary manner, harmonization can be achieved at regional levels. There are several international treaties in almost all regions of the world. Every region has its own objectives and goals to achieve. Hence regions can adopt different levels of harmonizing regarding arbitration, including the emergency arbitrator mechanism. For example, in the European Union (EU), the foundation for legal harmonization is

---

[193] Treaty Section of the Office of Legal Affairs of the UN (2012), *Treaty Handbook*, p. 49, available at https://treaties.un.org/doc/source/publications/THB/English.pdf (1 June 2024).

[194] Marike R. P. Paulsson (2016), *The 1958 New York Convention in Action*, Kluwer Law International, p. 1.

[195] Raymond J. Werbicki (2010), Arbitral Interim Measures: Fact or Fiction?, in *American Arbitration Association Handbook on International Arbitration and ADR*, Juris Publishing, p. 89.

[196] V. V. Veeder (1999), *Provisional and Conservatory Measures, in Enforcing Arbitration Awards under the New York Convention: Experience and Prospects*, United Nations Publication, p. 21, available at https://www.newyorkconvention.org/media/uploads/pdf/9/5/95_colloquia-1999-enforcingarbawardsunderthenyc.pdf (1 June 2024).

based on "a sufficient common core or a sufficient set of shared values",[197] despite the existing diversity in legal and cultural traditions in the Member States.

As an important forum to solve commercial disputes, arbitration may be one of the best ways to "initiate a bottom-up influence on the harmonisation of procedural rules".[198] The differences in the EU Member States' arbitration laws could be an obstacle to the "sound operation of the internal market",[199] and may create unpredictability in parallel dispute resolution proceedings and conflicting results.[200]

The European Commission, in its 2009 Green Paper on the review of the Brussels I Regulation No 44/2001, emphasized that addressing certain aspects is not meant to regulate arbitration, but "in the first place to ensure the smooth circulation of judgments in Europe and prevent parallel proceedings".[201] Article 81 of the Treaty on the Functioning of the European Union (TFEU) refers to the principle of mutual recognition to develop judicial cooperation to adopt measures for the internal market. Such a principle does not only apply to judgments but also to "decisions in extrajudicial cases"[202] which "can well be construed as referring also to arbitral awards."[203] Arbitration should be seen as a necessary part of civil and commercial judicial cooperation in the EU Member States and should also be subject to EU law.

7.4.2 *Non-mandatory Methods*

Many modern laws, rules, regulations, and usages in international commerce have been harmonized through intergovernmental institutions.[204] Due to the limitation of attempting harmonization by mandatory and binding international conventions, another less ambitious approach in international commercial arbitration can achieve

---

[197] Thomas Pfeiffer (2014), The Contribution of Arbitration to the Harmonization of Procedural Laws in Europe, 19 *Uniform Law Review* 206.

[198] Thomas Pfeiffer (2014), The Contribution of Arbitration to the Harmonization of Procedural Laws in Europe, 19 *Uniform Law Review* 206.

[199] Recital (2), Council Regulation (EC) No 44/2001 of 22 December 2000 on Jurisdiction and the recognition and enforcement of judgments in civil and commercial matters (Brussels I), available at https://eur-lex.europa.eu/legal-content/EN/TXT/PDF/?uri=CELEX:32001R0044&from=EN (1 June 2024).

[200] Massimo V. Benedettelli (2011), 'Communitarization' of International Arbitration: A New Spectre Haunting Europe? 27 *Arbitration International* 599.

[201] Commission of the European Communities (2009), Green Paper on the Review of Council Regulation (EC) No 44/2001 on Jurisdiction and the Recognition and Enforcement of Judgments in Civil and Commercial Matters, p. 8, available at https://eur-lex.europa.eu/legal-content/EN/TXT/PDF/?uri=CELEX:52009DC0175&from=EN (1 June 2024); John Gaffney (2017), Should the European Union Regulate Commercial Arbitration?, 33 *Arbitration International* 92.

[202] Article 81(2)(b), Treaty on the Functioning of the European Union, available at https://eur-lex.europa.eu/legal-content/EN/TXT/?uri=celex%3A12012E%2FTXT (1 June 2024).

[203] Massimo V. Benedettelli (2011), 'Communitarization' of International Arbitration: A New Spectre Haunting Europe? 27 *Arbitration International* 599.

[204] Jarrod Wiener (1999), *Globalization and the Harmonization of Law*, Pinter, p. 151.

a similar result.[205] Much harmonization is "exogenous" to the legal system.[206] Non-mandatory methods play an essential role in "providing tested procedural solutions and predictability in international arbitrations".[207] They not only provide necessary guidelines for practitioners but they also help parties to tailor arbitration to their individual needs. The following part gives the possibility and proposals of non-mandatory methods to harmonize the enforceability of the interim measures granted by an emergency arbitrator in international commercial arbitration.

7.4.2.1 An Amendment to the UNCITRAL Model Law 2006

As arbitrators lack coercive power and public authority, court intervention is ultimately needed if interim measures made by an emergency arbitrator are not implemented voluntarily by parties. The question of whether interim measures rendered by arbitrators qualify for recognition and enforcement under the New York Convention 1958 "was left entirely open by the 1985 version of the Model Law".[208] This issue was addressed during the drafting history of the UNCITRAL Model Law 2006.

Initially, the UNCITRAL considered that, with steps "leading to the establishment of uniform standards of arbitral procedure", a model law "would be the most appropriate way to achieve the desired uniformity", taking into account "the specific features of international commercial arbitration and modern arbitration practice".[209] After the adoption of the UNCITRAL Model Law 1985, in 1999, the UNCITRAL published a note, expressly meant to address the enforceability of interim measures in its future work.[210] Recognizing that the number of interim measures was increasing and the effectiveness of arbitration depended on the enforceability of interim measures, the UNCITRAL obtained general support to prepare "a legislative regime governing the enforcement of interim measures of protection" by arbitrators.[211]

The UNCITRAL Model Law 2006 allows the recognition and enforcement of interim measures, aiming at harmonizing various arbitration laws by "providing a

---

[205] Katherine Lynch (2003), *The Forces of Economic Globalization: Challenges to the Regime of International Commercial Arbitration*, Kluwer Law International, p. 204.

[206] Katherine Lynch (2003), *The Forces of Economic Globalization: Challenges to the Regime of International Commercial Arbitration*, Kluwer Law International, p. 203.

[207] Gary B. Born (2021), *International Commercial Arbitration*, Kluwer Law International, p.224.

[208] Renaud Sorieul (2008), The Influence of the New York Convention on the UNCITRAL Model Law on International Commercial Arbitration, 2 *Dispute Resolution International* 31.

[209] UNCITRAL (1979), Note by the Secretariat: Further Work in Respect of International Commercial Arbitration (A/CN.9/169), p. 109, available at https://documents.un.org/doc/undoc/gen/nl7/902/28/pdf/nl790228.pdf?token=obDMRqqN2A2Yc8McLL&fe=true (1 June 2024).

[210] UNCITRAL (1999), International Commercial Arbitration, Possible Future Work in the Area of International Commercial Arbitration, Note by the Secretariat (A/CN.9/460), p. 1, available at https://undocs.org/en/A/CN.9/460 (1 June 2024).

[211] UNCITRAL (2000), Report of Working Group on Arbitration on the work of its thirty-second session (A/CN.9/468), p. 14, available at https://undocs.org/en/A/CN.9/468 (1 June 2024).

common regime for recognition and enforcement of interim measures".[212] Article 17 H states that "[a]n interim measure issued by an arbitral tribunal shall be recognized as binding and, unless otherwise provided by the arbitral tribunal, enforced upon application to the competent court, irrespective of the country in which it was issued",[213] subject to the grounds for the refusal of recognition and enforcement in Article 17 I.[214] These two articles are "the most significant of the amendments".[215] As a result, the jurisdictions that have incorporated the UNCITRAL Model Law 2006 "tend to favour the enforceability" of the interim measures issued by emergency arbitrators.[216] For the jurisdictions where the UNCITRAL Model Law 2006 "has only inspired the local arbitration law",[217] or does not affect the arbitration law, the enforceability of interim measures is uncertain.

One of the major criticisms of the current UNCITRAL Model Law 2006 provisions regarding interim measures is "the difficulty of acquiring interim measures before the tribunal's formation".[218] In order to maintain consistency in the implementation and practice of the UNCITRAL Model Law, to make the UNCITRAL Model Law provisions more comprehensive and to "establish a reliable and efficient system of interim relief",[219] some future steps need to be considered. The first step is to include an emergency arbitrator into the definition of an arbitral tribunal in Article 2(b) of the UNCITRAL Model Law 2006. As reflected in Chap. 4 concerning the issuance of interim measures pending the constitution of an arbitral tribunal, an emergency arbitrator acts as a proper arbitrator, and the interim measures granted must be seen as an arbitrator's decision. Secondly, despite the widespread support for the UNCITRAL Model Law 2006, the majority of jurisdictions have not incorporated it into their own arbitration laws. From the total of 125 jurisdictions that have adopted the UNCITRAL Model Law, only 48 have adopted the 2006 amendments.[220] However, even without adopting the UNCITRAL Model Law, many jurisdictions modernized their arbitration laws taking the relevant provisions of the

212 Marianne Roth (2012), Interim Measures, 2 *Journal of Dispute Resolution* 434.

213 Article 17 H, UNCITRAL Model Law 2006.

214 Article 17 I, UNCITRAL Model Law 2006.

215 Michael Dunmore (2012), Interim Measures by Arbitral Tribunals: The Enforceability Conundrum, 8 *Asian International Arbitration Journal* 229.

216 ICC, ICC Arbitration and ADR Commission Report on Emergency Arbitrator Proceedings, 2019, p. 30, available at https://iccwbo.org/news-publications/arbitration-adr-rules-and-tools/emergency-arbitrator-proceedings-icc-arbitration-and-adr-commission-report/ (1 June 2024).

217 ICC, ICC Arbitration and ADR Commission Report on Emergency Arbitrator Proceedings, 2019, p. 30, available at https://iccwbo.org/news-publications/arbitration-adr-rules-and-tools/emergency-arbitrator-proceedings-icc-arbitration-and-adr-commission-report/ (1 June 2024).

218 Dana Bucy (2010), How to Best Protect Party Rights: The Future of Interim Relief in International Commercial Arbitration under the Amended UNCITRAL Mode Law, 25 *American University International Law Review* 606.

219 Marianne Roth (2012), Interim Measures, 2 *Journal of Dispute Resolution* 435.

220 UNCITRAL, Status: UNCITRAL Model Law on International Commercial Arbitration (1985), with amendments as adopted in 2006, available at https://uncitral.un.org/en/texts/arbitration/modellaw/commercial_arbitration/status (1 June 2024).

UNCITRAL Model Law into account.[221] Therefore, updating the provisions of the UNCITRAL Model Law 2006 with new developments, including the emergency arbitrator mechanism, promotes the modernization of global arbitration laws.

7.4.2.2 A Uniform Interpretation of International Conventions

As an alternative to adding protocols to international conventions, a flexible approach is to adopt a uniform interpretation of the practice of current international conventions, especially for the New York Convention 1958. It can be said that international conventions effectively derive their authority from the manner in which state courts interpret and apply those conventions.[222] Moreover, too much uncertainty has been raised regarding the current provisions of international conventions with new mechanisms, new technologies, and the changing environment of international arbitration. Therefore, "over the past decade the cracks are showing and it is time to ensure predictability" for the coming years.[223]

The predictability concern can be addressed by "a growing consensus around adopting international norms to resolve the merits of applications and best practice".[224] When it comes to the enforceability of the interim measures granted by an emergency arbitrator, a uniform interpretation of the practice from the New York Convention 1958 can be a solution. The relevant critical issues in the emergency arbitrator mechanism are the interpretation of "arbitral awards" and the finality test under the New York Convention 1958. Such a uniform interpretation may be led by the UNCITRAL, as was the case before in the UNCITRAL Secretariat Guide on the Convention on the Recognition and Enforcement of Foreign Arbitral Awards 2006.[225] In cooperation with law firms and law schools, the UNCITRAL also assisted in building a database to provide information on the implementation of the New York Convention 1958 to promote a uniform and effective interpretation and application throughout the world.[226]

---

[221] Pieter Sanders (1999), *Quo Vadis Arbitration? Sixty Years of Arbitration Practice: A Comparative Study*, Kluwer Law International, p. 84.

[222] Albert van den Berg (1981), *The New York Arbitration Convention of 1958: Towards a Uniform Judicial Interpretation*, Kluwer Law and Taxation Publishers, p. 5.

[223] Marike Paulsson & Supritha Suresh (2019), The New York Convention's 60th Anniversary: A Restatement for the New York Convention?, in Katia Fach Gómez, Rodriguez Lopez & Ana Mercedes, *60 Years of the New York Convention: Key Issues and Future Challenges*, Kluwer Law International, p. 269.

[224] James Hosking, Emergency Arbitration: Innovation for Innovation's Sake?, p. 7, available at https://www.aminz.org.nz/Attachment?Action=Download&Attachment_id=835 (16 June 2020).

[225] UNCITRAL, UNCITRAL Secretariat Guide on the Convention on the Recognition and https://uncitral.un.org/sites/uncitral.un.org/files/media-documents/uncitral/en/2016_guide_on_the_convention.pdf (1 June 2020).

[226] See the Introduction of the website, available at http://newyorkconvention1958.org/ (1 June 2020).

Additionally, the International Council for Commercial Arbitration (ICCA) also provides relevant court decisions in its Yearbook Commercial Arbitration with editors' commentaries.[227] The included court decisions not only concern the New York Convention 1958 but also other regional conventions. When different interpretations of international conventions are published and commented upon, this "may ultimately lead to some harmonisation".[228] In this way, judges, arbitrators, lawyers, institutions, and other practitioners in arbitration can seek guidance from previous court decisions in various jurisdictions and academic commentaries concerning the current interpretation and practice of the emergency arbitrator mechanism.

7.4.2.3 Harmonization by Arbitral Institutions to Promote the Emergency Arbitrator Mechanism

A good degree of harmonization in arbitration is achieved in practice within arbitral institutions.[229] To adapt to the changing needs of international commercial arbitration, arbitral institutions can take action in various ways. The following are two examples. The ICC provides "the perfect illustration of the influence of non-state actors on the evolution of arbitration law".[230] It can be said that the ICC initiated the drafting process of the New York Convention 1958. It also contributes to the development of the arbitration culture with the ICC's national committees,[231] and it helps to establish "a truly multicultural arbitration community able to meet the needs of a global economy".[232] Not only the ICC, but the LCIA also acts as "a platform to realise and take into account regional diversities", but also to harmonize various arbitral practices in different regions.[233] Arbitral institutions can push legislators to

[227] ICCA, ICCA Yearbook Commercial Arbitration, available at https://www.arbitration-icca.org/icca-yearbook-commercial-arbitration (1 June 2024).

[228] Pieter Sanders (1999), *Quo Vadis Arbitration? Sixty Years of Arbitration Practice: A Comparative Study*, Kluwer Law International, p. 70.

[229] Pierre Lalive (1995), The Internationalisation of International Arbitration: Some Observations, in Martin Hunter, Arthur Marriott & V. V. Veeder, *The Internationalisation of International Arbitration: The LCIA Centenary Conference*, Graham & Trotman/ Martinus Nijhoff, p. 50; S. C. Nirwani (1983), Contributions Which Conventions, Treaties, and Agreements among Institutions Can Make to the Development of Arbitration (Scope of Commercial Arbitration, Suggestions for Improvement in the System and the Need for Voluntary Initiative by Arbitral Institutions), in Pieter Sanders, New Trends in the Development of International Commercial Arbitration and the Role of Arbitral and Other Institutions, 1 *ICCA Congress Series* 98.

[230] Gabrielle Kaufmann-Kohler (2010), Soft Law in International Arbitration: Codification and Normativity, 1 *Journal of International Dispute Settlement* 294.

[231] ICC, National Committees, available https://iccwbo.org/national-committees/ (1 June 2024).

[232] Fabien Gélinas (2000), Arbitration and the Challenge of Globalization, 17 *Journal of International Arbitration* 118.

[233] Karl-Heinz Böckstiegel (1995), The Internationalisation of International Arbitration: Looking Ahead to the Next Ten Years, in Martin Hunter, Arthur Marriott & V. V. Veeder, *The Internationalisation of International Arbitration: The LCIA Centenary Conference*, Graham & Trotman/ Martinus Nijhoff, p. 73.

adapt legal frameworks to the demands of the international arbitration community for efficient dispute resolution mechanisms,[234] for example, the emergency arbitrator mechanism.

Within the leading arbitral institutions, there has been an increasing tendency for the "expansion and universalization of institutional arbitration rules to attract the parties from any jurisdiction, representing any legal tradition".[235] The globalization of arbitral institutions also leads to "increased unification of the practices of most prominent arbitral institutions".[236] It is also true in the provisions of the emergency arbitrator mechanism. According to the comparison of the arbitration rules, the ICC, the ICDR, the HKIAC, the LCIA, the SIAC, and the SCC all share "a common, general procedural framework"[237] despite various unique characteristics depending on each arbitral institution.

Harmonization of the emergency arbitrator mechanism led by arbitral institutions can be achieved in the following ways. Firstly, arbitral institutions can publish guidelines or handbooks for clarification and interpretation of the emergency arbitrator provisions. For example, the ICC provides practice notes, forms and checklists as guidance for the conduct of the ICC administrated arbitration, as well as the Secretariat's Guide to ICC Arbitration.[238] In this way, arbitral institutions can guide parties and arbitrators on how to operate under the emergency arbitrator mechanism and how to harmonize the practice in principle during the proceedings with first-hand information.

Secondly, arbitral institutions may provide case decisions delivered by emergency arbitrators, anonymously if necessary. Due to the confidentiality requirements in arbitration, it is difficult to access previous decisions by arbitrators. Some arbitral institutions have already done so, which provides valuable information as a reference. For example, the ICC publishes an ICC Dispute Bulletin, including extracts from awards granted by arbitrators, comments from experts, reference documents, and other informative resources from the institution.[239] The SCC makes its emergency arbitration cases available online. The SCC Practice Note includes the emergency arbitrator decisions issued from 2010 to 2022.[240]

---

[234] Karl-Heinz Böckstiegel (2014), Perspectives on Future Developments in International Arbitration, in Lawrence W. Newman & Richard D. Hill, *The Leading Arbitrators' Guide to International Arbitration*, Juris, p. 329.

[235] Barbara Alicja Warwas (2017), *The Liability of Arbitral Institutions: Legitimacy Challenges and Functional Responses*, T.M.C. Asser Press, p. 43.

[236] Barbara Alicja Warwas (2017), *The Liability of Arbitral Institutions: Legitimacy Challenges and Functional Responses*, T.M.C. Asser Press, p. 43.

[237] Fabio G. Santacroce (2015), The emergency arbitrator: a full-fledged arbitrator rendering an enforceable decision?, 31 *Arbitration International* 285.

[238] ICC, The Secretariat's Guide to ICC Arbitration, available at https://jusmundi.com/en/document/publication/en-foreword-2 (1 June 2024).

[239] ICC, ICC Dispute Resolution Bulletin, available at https://jusmundi.com/en/icc-dispute-resolution-library/bulletins (1 June 2024).

[240] SCC, Practice Note Emergency Arbitrator Decisions, available at https://sccarbitrationinstitute.se/en/news-events/news/new-scc-practice-note-emergency-arbitrator-decisions (1 June 2024).

Lastly, arbitral institutions can initiate research and draft reports. They can amend their arbitration rules in accordance with the current needs of the parties and suggest the removal of practical difficulties concerning local arbitration laws and procedures in line with their experience.[241] For instance, in April 2019, the ICC launched the Report of the ICC Commission on Arbitration and ADR Task Force on Emergency Arbitrator Proceedings.[242] It provides a comprehensive introduction to the emergency arbitrator mechanism administered by the ICC so far. Although the content does not endorse or impose any obligations on how arbitrators conduct the emergency arbitrator proceedings, it nevertheless provides essential guidance and inside information on the emergency arbitrator mechanism.

7.5 Concluding Remarks

Different domestic laws are perceived as "an obstacle to international trade".[243] Harmonization in international commercial arbitration does not have to eliminate the advantages of diversity according to the discussion. Therefore, in this regard, the advantages outweigh the disadvantages of harmonization in international commercial arbitration. Harmonization is probably the best solution to the enforceability problem related to interim measures granted by an emergency arbitrator. In the area of international commercial arbitration, a minimum harmonization of laws is ideal and beneficial for the development of international dispute resolution and international commerce.

[241] Vinod Kalra (1983), New Trends in the Development of International Commercial Arbitration and the Role of Arbitral and Other Institutions, in Pieter Sanders, New Trends in the Development of International Commercial Arbitration and the Role of Arbitral and Other Institutions, 1 *ICCA Congress Series* 83.

[242] ICC, ICC Arbitration and ADR Commission Report on Emergency Arbitrator Proceedings, 2019, available at https://iccwbo.org/news-publications/arbitration-adr-rules-and-tools/emergency-arbitrator-proceedings-icc-arbitration-and-adr-commission-report/ (1 June 2024).

[243] Ingeborg Schwenzer (2013), Who Needs a Uniform Contract Law, and Why, 58 *Villanova Law Review* 723.

Chapter 8
Conclusion

International commercial arbitration has continued to be a preferred method of resolving cross-border disputes in international commerce. The guaranteed enforceability of arbitral awards is considered the "most valuable characteristic".[1] With the growing complexity of international commerce, parties expect not only a final resolution of disputes, but they also expect that their rights can be protected pending final arbitral awards. Before the introduction of the emergency arbitrator mechanism, parties faced difficulties in seeking interim measures in urgent situations before the constitution of an arbitral tribunal. The emergency arbitrator mechanism fills this gap effectively. The emergency arbitrator mechanism addresses "a longstanding weakness of international arbitration" by providing an immediate, efficient procedure for applications for interim measures prior to the constitution of arbitral tribunals.[2] The experience to date regarding the emergency arbitrator mechanism has demonstrated that it is effective in solving the related claims, even in the most complex situations.

With the development of the emergency arbitrator mechanism, the enforceability of interim measures made by an emergency arbitrator is questioned. This uncertainty leads to the hesitation of legal practitioners to apply the emergency arbitrator mechanism in practice.[3] Interim measures are used to protect parties' rights pending a final arbitral award and guarantee the final decision. If the enforceability of interim measures made by an emergency arbitrator cannot be ensured, it may also lead to a meaningless final award. The recognition and enforcement of foreign arbitral decisions are essential to the prosperity of modern international commercial arbitration. International commercial arbitration has contributed to the long-term development

[1] Queen Mary University of London and White & Case LLP, 2018 International Arbitration Survey: The Evolution of International Arbitration, p. 7, available at http://www.arbitration.qmul.ac.uk/media/arbitration/docs/2018-International-Arbitration-Survey---The-Evolution-of-International-Arbitration-(2).PDF (16 June 2020).

[2] Hanessian, Grant, Emergency Arbitrators, in Newman, Lawrence W. & Hill, Richard D., The Leading Arbitrators' Guide to International Arbitration, Juris, 2014, p. 366; see also Chapter 7.4.

[3] See Chapter 1.1.3.

J. Zhang, *The Enforceability of the Interim Measures Granted by an Emergency Arbitrator in International Commercial Arbitration*,
https://doi.org/10.1007/978-981-97-6536-2_8

of cross-border transactions and trade. To some extent, the enforceability of interim measures made by an emergency arbitrator will inevitably affect international trade.

From the comparison between different arbitral institutions, it can be seen that the emergency arbitration procedures all share "a common, general procedural framework",[4] despite having various unique characteristics depending on each arbitral institution. However, under the current legal framework, there is no international convention regulating the enforceability of interim measures made by arbitrators despite different approaches taken by jurisdictions. Considering the different views of the jurisdictions, the tendency is that more and more jurisdictions allow for the power of arbitrators to issue interim measures and support the enforceability of interim measures granted by arbitrators including emergency arbitrators. For example, China's Ministry of Justice has published a Draft Revision to the Arbitration Law for public consultation, in which includes an emergency arbitrator's authority to grant interim measures. However, the conflicts between different jurisdictions regarding the enforceability of interim measures granted by an emergency arbitrator still exist. When multiple legal systems are involved in a dispute, potential legal risks and conflicts are highly possible. Parties will have to face unpredictable results when seeking enforcement of interim measures in different jurisdictions.

Harmonization is always an on-going controversial topic in legal research. In the scenario of international commercial arbitration, harmonization is beneficial, because it can provide a neutral interface for dispute resolution, a predictable legal system, and modernization and a reform of arbitration laws in different jurisdictions. Harmonization does not have to compromise the benefits of legal diversity. With a minimum harmonization of the emergency arbitrator mechanism, regulatory competition and innovation can be retained within the legal systems in various jurisdictions. The mandatory and non-mandatory methods of harmonization proposed by the book took the interests of parties and various jurisdictions into account, filling the gap caused by different regulations regarding the enforceability of interim measures at the international level, and avoiding potential legal conflicts that may cause extra expenses.

Some proposals seem too ambitious at first sight. However, "[c]hanges and improvements can only be effected by people".[5] Daring "[t]o dream the impossible dream"[6] is a strong motivation for future improvements and innovation. An arbitral award in international commercial arbitration is enforceable by a state court under international conventions or by reference to its arbitration law. "Such awards

---

[4] See Chapter 2.8.

[5] Karl-Heinz Böckstiegel (1995), The Internationalisation of International Arbitration: Looking Ahead to the Next Ten Years, in Martin Hunter, Arthur Marriott & V. V. Veeder, *The Internationalisation of International Arbitration: The LCIA Centenary Conference*, Graham & Trotman/ Martinus Nijhoff, p. 83.

[6] The Lyrics are from The Impossible Dream written by Joe Darion, in the 1965 Broadway musical Man of La Mancha. See also Howard M. Holtzmann (1995), A Task for the 21st Century: Creating a New International Court for Resolving Disputes on the Enforceability of Arbitral Awards, in Martin Hunter, Arthur Marriott & V. V. Veeder, *The Internationalisation of International Arbitration: The LCIA Centenary Conference*, Graham & Trotman/ Martinus Nijhoff, p. 109.

are blessed; but for too long, there have been difficulties enforcing an arbitrator's order for interim measures, both abroad and domestically".[7] Now is the proper time to make some changes.

[7] V. V. Veeder (1999), P*rovisional and Conservatory Measures, in Enforcing Arbitration Awards under the New York Convention: Experience and Prospects*, United Nations Publication, p. 21, available at https://www.newyorkconvention.org/media/uploads/pdf/9/5/95_colloquia-1999-enforcingarbawardsunderthenyc.pdf (1 June 2024).

Bibliography

International Conventions and Instruments

Arab Convention on Commercial Arbitration (Amman Convention) 1987, available at http://www.arbitrations.ru/userfiles/file/Law/Treaty/Arab%20convention%20on%20commercial%20arbitration%20eng_rus.pdf (1 June 2024).

Convention on the Execution of Foreign Arbitral Awards 1927 (the Geneva Convention of 1927), available at https://treaties.un.org/Pages/LONViewDetails.aspx?src=LON&id=549&chapter=30&clang=_en (1 June 2024).

Convention on the Recognition and Enforcement of Foreign Arbitral Awards, New York (the New York Convention), 10 June 1958, United Nations Treaty Series, vol. 330, p. 3, available at https://treaties.un.org/Pages/ViewDetails.aspx?src=TREATY&mtdsg_no=XXII-1&chapter=22&clang=_en (1 June 2024).

Convention on the Settlement by Arbitration of Civil Law Disputes Arising out of Economic, Scientific and Technical Co-operation Relationships1972, available at https://treaties.un.org/Pages/showDetails.aspx?objid=080000028011 0b20&clang=_en (1 June 2024).

Convention on the Settlement of Investment Disputes between States and Nationals of Other States (the ICSID Convention) 1965, available at https://icsid.worldbank.org/en/Documents/icsiddocs/ICSID%20Convention%20English.pdf (1 June 2024).

Council Regulation (EC) No 44/2001 of 22 December 2000 on Jurisdiction and the recognition and enforcement of judgments in civil and commercial matters (Brussels I), available at https://eur-lex.europa.eu/legal-content/EN/TXT/PDF/?uri=CELEX:32001R0044&from=EN (1 June 2024).

European Convention on International Commercial Arbitration, Geneva, 21 April 1961, United Nations Treaty Series, vol. 484, p. 349, available at https://treaties.un.org/Pages/ViewDetails.aspx?src=TREATY&mtdsg_no=XXII-2&chapter=22&clang=_en (1 June 2024).

European Convention Providing a Uniform Law on Arbitration 1966, available at https://rm.coe.int/CoERMPublicCommonSearchServices/DisplayDCTMContent?documentId=090000168006ff61 (1 June 2024).

Inter-American Convention on International Commercial Arbitration 1975, available at https://treaties.un.org/doc/Publication/UNTS/Volume%201438/volume-1438-I-24384-English.pdf (1 June 2024).

Protocol on Arbitration Clauses 1923 (the Geneva Protocol of 1923), available at https://treaties.un.org/Pages/LONViewDetails.aspx?src=LON&id=548&chapter=30&clang=_en (1 June 2024).

Treaty on the Functioning of the European Union, available at https://eur-lex.europa.eu/legal-content/EN/TXT/?uri=celex%3A12012E%2FTXT (1 June 2024).

J. Zhang, *The Enforceability of the Interim Measures Granted by an Emergency Arbitrator in International Commercial Arbitration*,
https://doi.org/10.1007/978-981-97-6536-2

UNCITRAL Model Law on International Commercial Arbitration (1985), with amendments as adopted in 2006, available at https://uncitral.un.org/sites/uncitral.un.org/files/media-documents/uncitral/en/07-86998_ebook.pdf (1 June 2024).

Institutional Rules

ACICA Arbitration Rules 2021, available at https://acica.org.au/wp-content/uploads/2022/11/ACICA_Rules_2021-WFF7.pdf (1 June 2024).
BAC Arbitration Rules 2015, available at https://www.bjac.org.cn/english/page/data_dl/zcgz_en.pdf (1 June 2024).
BAC Arbitration Rules 2022, available at https://www.bjac.org.cn/page/data_dl/zcgz_en_2022.pdf (1 June 2024).
CIETAC Arbitration Rules 2015, available at http://www.cietac.org/index.php?m=Page&a=index&id=106&l=en (16 June 2020).
CIETAC Arbitration Rules 2024, available at http://cn.cietac.org/index.php?m=Page&a=index&id=531&l=en (1 June 2024).
CMAC Arbitration Rules 2018, available at http://www.cmac.org.cn/wp-content/uploads/2018/09/2018%E4%BB%B2%E8%A3%81%E8%A7%84%E5%88%99%E8%8B%B1%E6%96%87.pdf (16 June 2020).
CMAC Arbitration Rules 2021, available at https://www.cmac.org.cn/data/upload/image/20231221/1703127891516407.pdf (1 June 2024).
HKIAC Arbitration Rules 2013.
HKIAC Arbitration Rules 2018, available at https://www.hkiac.org/arbitration/rules-practice-notes/hkiac-administered-2018 (1 June 2024).
HKIAC Arbitration Rules 2024, available at https://www.hkiac.org/arbitration/rules-practice-notes/hkiac-administered-2024 (1 June 2024)
ICC Arbitration Rules 1975.
ICC Arbitration Rules 2012.
ICC Arbitration Rules 2017, available at https://iccwbo.org/dispute-resolution-services/arbitration/rules-of-arbitration/ (1 June 2024).
ICC Arbitration Rules 2021, available at https://iccwbo.org/dispute-resolution/dispute-resolution-services/arbitration/rules-procedure/2021-arbitration-rules/ (1 June 2024).
ICC Rules for a Pre-Arbitral Referee Procedure 1990, available at https://iccwbo.org/dispute-resolution-services/pre-arbitral-referee/rules/ (1 June 2024).
ICDR Arbitration Rules 2006.
ICDR Arbitration Rules 2009.
ICDR Arbitration Rules 2014, available at https://www.icdr.org/sites/default/files/document_repository/ICDR_Rules.pdf (1 June 2024).
ICDR Arbitration Rules 2021, available at https://www.icdr.org/sites/default/files/document_repository/ICDR_Rules_1.pdf?utm_source=icdr-website&utm_medium=rules-page&utm_campaign=rules-intl-update-1mar (1 June 2024)
LCIA Arbitration Rules 2014, available at https://www.lcia.org/Dispute_Resolution_Services/lcia-arbitration-rules-2014.aspx (1 June 2024).
LCIA Arbitration Rules 2020, available at https://www.lcia.org/Dispute_Resolution_Services/lcia-arbitration-rules-2020.aspx#Article%209B (1 June 2024).
SCC Arbitration Rules 2010.
SCC Arbitration Rules 2017, available at https://sccinstitute.com/our-services/rules/ (16 June 2020).
SCC Arbitration Rules 2023, available at https://sccarbitrationinstitute.se/en/resource-library/rules-and-policies/scc-rules (1 June 2024).
SIAC Arbitration Rules 2010.
SIAC Arbitration Rules 2013.

SIAC Arbitration Rules 2016, available at https://www.siac.org.sg/our-rules/rules/siac-rules-2016 (16 June 2020).
Swiss Arbitration Rules 2012, available at https://www.swissarbitration.org/Arbitration/Arbitration-Rules-and-Laws (16 June 2020).
The China (Shanghai) Pilot Free Trade Zone Arbitration Rules 2015, available at http://www.shiac.org/Trade/arbitrate_rules_detail_E.aspx?id=14 (16 June 2020).
UNCITRAL Arbitration Rules 2010, available at https://www.uncitral.org/pdf/english/texts/arbitration/arb-rules-revised/arb-rules-revised-2010-e.pdf (16 June 2020).

Legislations

Belgium

Belgian Judicial Code 1985, available at https://www.ejustice.just.fgov.be/cgi_loi/arch_a.pl (16 June 2020).
Belgian Judicial Code 1998, available at https://www.ejustice.just.fgov.be/cgi_loi/arch_a.pl?=&sql=(text+contains+(%27%27))&language=fr&rech=1&tri=dd+AS+RANK&numero=1&table_name=loi&F=&cn=1967101006&caller=archive&fromtab=loi&la=F&ver_arch=003 (16 June 2020).

Czech Republic

Act of the Czech Republic No. 216/1994 Sb. on arbitration proceedings and on enforcement of arbitration awards, available at https://is.muni.cz/el/1422/jaro2008/SOC026/um/216-1994_EN.pdf (16 June 2020).

Finland

Finland Arbitration Act 754/2015, available at https://www.finlex.fi/fi/laki/kaannokset/1992/en19920967.pdf (16 June 2020).

Netherlands

The Dutch Arbitration Act, Dutch Code of Civil Procedure 2015, available at http://www.dutchcivillaw.com/legislation/civilprocedure044.htm (1 June 2024).

New Zealand

Arbitration Amendment Act 2016, available at http://www.legislation.govt.nz/act/public/2016/0053/latest/DLM6943708.html (16 June 2020).
New Zealand Arbitration Act 1996, available at http://www.legislation.govt.nz/act/public/1996/0099/latest/whole.html#DLM403282 (16 June 2020).
Versions and amendments, New Zealand Arbitration Act 1996, available at http://www.legislation.govt.nz/act/public/1996/0099/latest/versions.aspx (16 June 2020).

People's Republic of China

Hong Kong SAR

Arbitration Ordinance (Cap. 609) 2015, available at https://www.elegislation.gov.hk/hk/cap609 (16 June 2020).

Mainland China

Arbitration Law of the People's Republic of China (中华人民共和国仲裁法) 2017, translation available at http://en.pkulaw.cn/display.aspx?cgid=83c8fbd6da8a6eb8bdfb&lib=law (16 June 2020).

Arrangement between the Mainland and the Macau Special Administrative Region on Reciprocal Recognition and Enforcement of Arbitration Awards 2007 (最高人民法院关于内地与澳门特别行政区相互认可和执行仲裁裁决的安排), translation available at is https://pkulaw.com/en_law/48ef3f989a7b54d0bdfb.html (16 June 2020).

Arrangement Concerning Mutual Enforcement of Arbitral Awards between the Mainland and the Hong Kong Special Administrative Region 2000 (最高人民法院关于内地与香港特别行政区相互执行仲裁裁决的安排), the English version is available at https://www.doj.gov.hk/eng/topical/pdf/mainlandmutual2e.pdf (16 June 2020).

Arrangement Concerning Mutual Assistance in Court-ordered Interim Measures in Aid of Arbitral Proceedings by the Courts of the Mainland and of the Hong Kong Special Administrative Region 2019 (最高人民法院、香港特别行政区政府关于内地与香港特别行政区法院就仲裁程序相互协助保全的安排), the English version is available at https://www.doj.gov.hk/pdf/2019/arbitration_interim_e.pdf (16 June 2020).

Civil Procedure Law of the People's Republic of China (中华人民共和国民事诉讼法) 2023, translation available at http://en.pkulaw.cn/display.aspx?id=e55237a87e2e1d04bdfb&lib=law (1 June 2024).

Interpretation of the Supreme People's Court on the Application of the Civil Procedure Law of the People's Republic of China 2022 (最高人民法院关于适用《中华人民共和国民事诉讼法》的解释, 法释[2022]11号)

Notice of the Supreme People's Court on Implementing the Convention on the Recognition and Enforcement of Foreign Arbitral Awards Acceded to by China 1987 (最高人民法院关于执行我国加入的《承认及执行外国仲裁裁决公约》的通知), translation is available at http://en.pkulaw.cn/display.aspx?cgid=b96476088a462bafbdfb&lib=law (16 June 2020).

Provisions of the Supreme People's Court on Recognition and Enforcement of the Arbitral Awards of the Taiwan Region 2015 (最高人民法院关于认可和执行台湾地区仲裁裁决的规定), translation is available at http://en.pkulaw.cn/display.aspx?cgid=4fb6671c00b52a90bdfb&lib=law (16 June 2020).

Relevant Provisions of the Supreme People's Court on Issues concerning Applications for Verification of Arbitration Cases under Judicial Review 2017 (最高人民法院关于仲裁司法审查案件报核问题的有关规定), translation is available at http://en.pkulaw.cn/display.aspx?cgid=41864b6840cb509abdfb&lib=law (16 June 2020).

Singapore

Arbitration Act of the Statutes of the Republic of Singapore (Cap. 10) 2016, available at https://sso.agc.gov.sg/Act/AA2001?ValidDate=20160801&ProvIds=legis#legis (16 June 2020).

International Arbitration Act of the Statutes of the Republic of Singapore (Cap. 143A) 2012, available at https://sso.agc.gov.sg/Act/IAA1994 (16 June 2020).

Thailand

Thailand Arbitration Act B.E. 2545/2002, available at https://arbitrationlaw.com/sites/default/files/free_pdfs/Thailand%20Arbitration%20Act.pdf (16 June 2020).

United Kingdom

English Arbitration Act 1996, available at http://www.legislation.gov.uk/ukpga/1996/23/contents (16 June 2020).

United States of America

Federal

Federal Arbitration Act, United States Code Annotated 2002.
Federal Rules of Civil Procedure for the United States District Courts, United States Code Annotated 1991.
Restatement of the U.S Law of International Commercial and Investor-State Arbitration 2019, available at https://www.ali.org/projects/show/international-commercial-arbitration/ (16 June 2020).
Uniform Arbitration Act 2000, available at https://www.uniformlaws.org/viewdocument/final-act-2?CommunityKey=a0ad71d6-085f-4648-857a-e9e893ae2736&tab=librarydocuments (1 June 2024).

States

Alaska Statutes Annotated 2004.
Arizona Revised Statutes Annotated 2011.
Arkansas Code Annotated 2011.
Annotated California Codes 1988.
Colorado Revised Statutes Annotated 2004.
Connecticut General Statutes Annotated 1989.
Delaware Code Annotated 2015.
District of Columbia Code Annotated 2008.
Florida Statutes Annotated 2010.
Florida Statutes Annotated 2013.
Code of Georgia Annotated 2012.
Hawaii Revised Statutes Annotated 2001.
Illinois Complied Statutes Annotated 1998.
Kansas Statutes Annotated 2018.
Louisiana Statutes Annotated 2006.
Michigan Compiled Laws Annotated 2013.
Minnesota Statutes Annotated 2011.
Nevada Revised Statutes Annotated 2001.

New Jersey Statutes Annotated 1987.
New Jersey Statutes Annotated 2003.
New Mexico Statutes Annotated 2001.
Civil Practice Law and Rules, Consolidated Laws of New York, available at https://www.nysenate.gov/legislation/laws/CVP (16 May 2020).
North Carolina General Statues Annotated 2017.
North Dakota Century Code Annotated 2003.
Ohio Revised Code Annotated 1991.
Oklahoma Statutes Annotated 2006.
Oregon Revised Statutes Annotated 1991.
Oregon Revised Statutes Annotated 1993.
Pennsylvania Statutes and Consolidated Statutes 2019.
Texas Statutes and Codes Annotated 1997.
Utah Code Annotated 2008.
Revised Code of Washington Annotated 2015.
Annotated Code of West Virginia 2015.

Cases

Arbitral Decisions

A v. Z, Order, 2 April 2002, 21 ASA Bulletin 2003.
Burlington Resources Inc. and others v. Republic of Ecuador and Empresa Estatal Petróleos del Ecuador (PetroEcuador) (ICSID Case No. ARB/08/5, Procedural Order No. 1 on Burlington Oriente's Request for Provisional Measures, 2009, available at https://www.italaw.com/sites/default/files/case-documents/ita0104.pdf (16 June 2020).
Chevron Corporation and Texaco Petroleum Company v. The Republic of Ecuador (Fourth Interim Award on Interim Measures, 2013, available at https://www.italaw.com/sites/default/files/case-documents/italaw1274.pdf (16 June 2020).
ICC Case 12361, Interim Award, 22 ICC International Court of Arbitration Bulletin (Special Supplement) 2011.
Interim Award ICC Case No. 7929, XXV Yearbook Commercial Arbitration 2000.
Interim Award in Case 7544, Extracts from ICC Awards Referring to Interim and Conservatory Measures, 11 ICC International Court of Arbitration Bulletin (Issue 1) 2000.
Interim Award in Case 8786, Extracts from ICC Awards Referring to Interim and Conservatory Measures, 11 ICC International Court of Arbitration Bulletin (Issue 1) 2000.
Interim Award in Case 8879, Extracts from ICC Awards Referring to Interim and Conservatory Measures, 11 ICC International Court of Arbitration Bulletin (Issue 1) 2000.
Ipp, Anja Havedal, SCC Practice Note Emergency Arbitrator Decisions Rendered 2015–2016, available at https://sccarbitrationinstitute.se/sites/default/files/2022-11/ea-practice-note-emergency-arbitrator-decisions-rendered-2015-2016.pdf (1 June 2024).
Knapp, Lotta, SCC Practice Emergency Arbitrator Decisions Rendered 2014, available at https://sccarbitrationinstitute.se/sites/default/files/2022-11/scc-practice-emergency-arbitrators-2014_final.pdf (1June 2024).
Lundstedt, Johan, SCC Practice: Emergency Arbitrator Decisions, 1 January 2010 -31 December 2013, available at https://sccarbitrationinstitute.se/sites/default/files/2022-11/scc-practice-2010-2013-emergency-arbitrator_final.pdf (1 June 2024).
Partial Award in Case 8113, Extracts from ICC Awards Referring to Interim and Conservatory Measures, 11 ICC International Court of Arbitration Bulletin (Issue 1) 2000.

Partial Award in Case 12040, in Yesilirmak, Ali, Interim and Conservatory Measures in ICC Arbitral Practice, 1999–2008, 22 ICC International Court of Arbitration Bulletin (Special Supplement) 2011.
Sergei Paushok, CJSC Golden East Company and CJSC Vostokneftegaz Company v. The Government of Mongolia (Order on Interim measures, 2008, available at http://opil.ouplaw.com.ezproxy.ub.unimaas.nl/abstract/10.1093/law:iic/351-2008.case.1/law-iic-351-2008-IIC351(2008)D.pdf (16 June 2020).
Texaco Overseas Petroleum Company, California Asiatic Oil Company v. The Government of the Libyan Arab Republic, IV Yearbook Commercial Arbitration 1979 (Award by Dupuy, René-Jean, 1977).
Texaco Overseas Petroleum Company, California Asiatic Oil Company v. The Government of the Libyan Arab Republic, Lauterpacht, E., 53 International Law Reports 1979.
Wahlström, Evelina T., SCC Practice Note, Emergency Arbitrator Decisions 2017–2018, available at https://sccarbitrationinstitute.se/sites/default/files/2022-11/scc_practise_note_dec2020.pdf (1 June 2024).
Wahlström, Evelina T., SCC Practice Note, Emergency Arbitrator Decisions 2019–2022, available at https://sccarbitrationinstitute.se/sites/default/files/2023-10/scc_practice-note_emergency-arbitrator-decisions-2019-2022.pdf (1 June 2024).

Court Judgments

Australia

Australia No. 11, Resort Condominiums International Inc. v. Ray Bolwell and Resort Condominiums, Pty. Ltd., Supreme Court of Queensland, 389, 29 October 1993, in Van den Berg, Albert Jan, 20 Yearbook Commercial Arbitration 1995, p. 628.
Australia No. 42, Giedo van der Garde BV et al. v. Sauber Motorsport AG, Supreme Court of Victoria, Commercial Court, 11 March 2015, Supreme Court of Victoria, Court of Appeal, 12 March 2015 and Supreme Court of Victoria, Commercial Court, Arbitration List, 27 March 2015, in Van den Berg, Albert Jan, 40 Yearbook Commercial Arbitration 2015, p. 372–376.
American Diagnostica v. Gradipore, 44 N.S.W.L.R. 312, 328 (Supreme Court of New South Wales, 1998).
Cargill International SA v. Peabody Australia Mining Ltd, [2010] NSWSC 887 (New South Wales Supreme Court, 210), para. 84.
Kaspersky Lab UK Ltd v. Hemisphere Technologies Pty Ltd, No. 2016/257298, [2016] NSWSC 1476 (Supreme Court New South Wales, 2016).
Resort Condominiums International Inc. v. Ray Bolwell and Resort Condominiums (Australasia) Pty. Ltd., MOT. No. 389 of 1993 (The Supreme Court of Queensland, 1993), available at https://www.queenslandjudgments.com.au/caselaw/qsc/1993/351 (1 June 2024).
Sauber Motorsport AG v. Giedo van der Garde BV and Giedo Gijsbertus Gerrit van der Garde, [2015] VSCA 37(The Supreme Court of Victoria, 2015), available at http://www8.austlii.edu.au/cgi-bin/viewdoc/au/cases/vic/VSCA/2015/37.html (1 June 2024).

Canada

Yugraneft Corporation v. Rexx Management Corporation, [2010] 1 R.C.S. 649, 661 (Supreme Court of Canada, 2010).

France

Braspetro Oil Services Company-Brasoil v. The Management and Implementation Authority of the Great Man-Made River Project, Cour d' Appel [Court of Appeal], 1 July 1999, in Van den Berg, Albert Jan, 24 Yearbook Commercial Arbitration 1999, p. 297.
General National Maritime Transport Company v. Société Gotaverken Arendal A.B, 20 I.L.M. 884 (Paris Court of Appeal, 1980), available at http://newyorkconvention1958.org/index.php?lvl=notice_display&id=111 (1 June 2024).
Marquis de Santa Cristina et al. v. Princesse del Drago et al., 29 Journal du Droit International Privé et de la Jurisprudence Comparée 1902, p. 314 (Court of Appeal Paris, 1901).
Roses v. Moller et Cie, I Dalloz 25 (1938) (Cour de cassation, 1937), available in French at https://gallica.bnf.fr/ark:/12148/bpt6k5810054r/f34.image (1 June 2024).
Société Almira Films v. Pierrel ès qual, Revue de l'Arbitrage, 1989 (Court of Appeal Paris, 1989).
Société Nationale des Pétroles du Congo et République du Congo v. Total Fina Elf E&P Congo (Court of Appeal Paris, 2003), Revue de l'Arbitrage, 2003, pp. 1296–1299.

New Zealand

Pathak v. Tourism Transport Ltd [2002] 3 NZLR 681 (Auckland High Court, 2002).
Sensation Yachts Ltd v. Darby Maritime Ltd, No. CIV 2005–404–1908 (Auckland High Court, 2005).

People's Republic of China

Hong Kong SAR

GD v. HY, [2021] HKCFI 3900 (High Court of the Hong Kong Special Administrative Region, Court of First Instance, 2021).
The "Lady Muriel" v. Transorient Shipping Ltd. [1995] HKCA 615 (Hong Kong Court of Appeal, 1995).

Mainland China

Hemofarm DD, MAG International Trade Holding DD & Suramu Media Ltd. v. Jinan Yongning Pharmaceutical Co., Ltd., Letter of Reply of the Supreme People's Court to a Request for Instructions on the Non-Recognition and Non-Enforcement of an Arbitration Award of the ICC International Court of Arbitration, 2008 (最高人民法院关于不予承认和执行国际商会仲裁院仲裁裁决的请示的复函，[2008]民四他字第11号), translation is available at http://en.pkulaw.cn/display.aspx?cgid=445d02b47bfe3f3ebdfb&lib=law (1 June 2024).
Letter of Reply of the Supreme People's Court on Request for Instructions on Application of ED & F (Hong Kong) Co. Ltd. for Recognition and Enforcement of the Arbitral Award of London Sugar Association 2003 (最高人民法院关于ED & F曼氏(香港)有限公司申请承认和执行伦敦糖业协会仲裁裁决案的复函,[2003]民四他字第3号), original text is available at http://www.pkulaw.cn/fulltext_form.aspx?Db=chl&Gid=9b28920402971a45bdfb&keyword=%e5%85%ac%e5%85%b1%e6%94%bf%e7%ad%96&EncodingName=&Search_Mode=accurate&Search_IsTitle=1 (1 June 2024).
Letter of Reply of the Supreme People's Court to a Request for Instructions on the Recognition and Enforcement of a Foreign Arbitration Award applied by Castel Electronics Pty Ltd., 2013

(最高人民法院关于申请人Castel Electronics Pty Ltd.申请承认和执行外国仲裁裁决一案请示的复函,[2013]民四他字第46号), original text is available at http://www.pkulaw.cn/fultext_form.aspx?Db=chl&Gid=63a8559603999347bdfb&keyword=%e5%85%ac%e5%85%b1%e6%94%bf%e7%ad%96&EncodingName=&Search_Mode=accurate&Search_IsTitle=0 (1 June 2024).

Nobles Resources Pte. Ltd. v. Shanghai Good Credit International Trade Co., Ltd., 2016 (来宝资源国际私人有限公司与上海信泰国际贸易有限公司申请承认和执行外国仲裁裁决案,[2016]沪01协外认1号), available at http://wenshu.court.gov.cn/website/wenshu/181107ANFZ0BXSK4/index.html?docId=3977ca869daa4df39c87a7e0016e1525 (1 June 2024).

Ocean Eleven Shipping Corporation v. Lao Kaiyuan Mining Sole Co. Ltd. (海洋十一航运公司与老开元矿业有限公司仲裁程序案件、申请保全案件民事诉讼保全裁定书案 [鄂72 财保427号],武汉海事法院), available at http://www.pkulaw.cn/case/pfnl_1970324876955896.html?keywords=%E6%B5%B7%E6%B4%8B%E5%8D%81%E4%B8%80%E8%88%AA%E8%BF%90%E5%85%AC%E5%8F%B8%E4%B8%8E%E8%80%81%E6%8C%9D%E5%BC%80%E5%85%83%E7%9F%BF%E4%B8%9A%E6%9C%89%E9%99%90%E5%85%AC%E5%8F%B8%E4%BB%B2%E8%A3%81%E7%A8%8B%E5%BA%8F%E6%A1%88%E4%BB%B6&match=Exact (1 June 2024).

Reply of the Supreme People's Court on Request for Instructions Re Application of Zhoushan Zhonghai Cereals & Oils Industry Co., Ltd. for Non-Enforcement of Arbitration Award of Hong Kong International Arbitration Centre, 2009 (最高人民法院关于舟山中海粮油工业有限公司申请不予执行香港国际仲裁中心仲裁裁决一案的请示报告的复函,[2009]民四他字第2号).

Reply of the Supreme People's Court to the Request for Instructions on Non-Recognition of No. 07–11 (Tokyo) Arbitral Award of the Japan Commercial Arbitration Association, 2010 (最高人民法院关于不予承认日本商事仲裁协会东京07–11号仲裁裁决一案的请示的复函,[2010]民四他字第32号), translation is available at http://en.pkulaw.cn/display.aspx?cgid=9c1fb82b51eb96a4bdfb&lib=law (1 June 2024).

Singapore

AQZ v. ARA [2015] SGHC 49 (High Court, Supreme Court of Singapore, 2015).

CVG v. CVH [2022] SGHC 249 (High Court, Supreme Court of Singapore, 2022), available at https://www.singaporelawwatch.sg/Portals/0/Docs/Judgments/2022/2022%20SGHC%20249.pdf (1 June 2024).

Front Carriers Ltd v. Atl. & Orient Shipping Corp. [2006] SGHC 127 (High Court of Singapore, 2006).

Maldives Airports Co Ltd and another v. GMR Malé International Airport Pte Ltd [2013] SGCA 16 (Court of Appeal of Singapore, 2013), available at https://www.uncitral.org/docs/clout/SGP/SGP_130213_FT.pdf (1 June 2024).

NCC Int'l AB v. Alliance Concrete Singapore Pte Ltd [2008] SGCA 5 (Singapore Court of Appeal, 2008).

Star Engineering Pte Ltd v. Pollisum Engineering Pte Ltd and Great Eastern General Insurance Ltd [2024] SGHC 137 (High Court, Supreme Court of Singapore, 2024), available at https://www.singaporelawwatch.sg/Portals/0/Docs/Judgments/2024/[2024]%20SGHC%20137.pdf (1 June 2024).

The Bank of East Asia Ltd v. Quah Su-Ling [2014] SGHC 52 (High Court, Supreme Court of Singapore, 2014), available at https://www.singaporelawwatch.sg/Portals/0/Docs/Judgments/[2014]%20SGHC%2052.pdf (1 June 2024).

Ukraine

Ukraine No. 7, JKX Oil & Gas PLC et al. v. State of Ukraine, represented by the Ministry of Justice of Ukraine, Pechersk District Court, Kyiv City, Case No. 757/5777/15-ц, 8 June 2015, in Van den Berg, Albert Jan, 40 Yearbook Commercial Arbitration 2015, para. 33 in Excerpt.
Ukraine No. 8, The Ministry of Justice of Ukraine v. JKX Oil Plc et al., Court of Appeals of the City of Kiev, Case No. 22-ц/796/9284/2015, 17 September 2015, in Van den Berg, Albert Jan, 41 Yearbook Commercial Arbitration 2016, Kluwer Law International, p. 580.
Ukraine No. 9, Ministry of Justice of Ukraine v. JKX Oil Plc et al., Supreme Court, 24 February 2016 and Court of Appeal, Kyiv, 17 May 2016, in Van den Berg, Albert Jan, 41 Yearbook Commercial Arbitration 2016, Kluwer Law International, p. 583.

United Kingdom

Channel Tunnel Group Ltd. and Another v. Balfour Beatty Construction Ltd. and Others, [1993] A.C. 334 (House of Lords, 1993).
Gerald Metals S.A. v. Timis & Ors, No: HC-2016–002321, [2016]EWHC 2327 (CH) (High Court of Justice Chancery Division Commercial Court, 2016).
Richardson v. Mellish, (1824) 2 Bingham 229 (Court of Common Pleas, 1824).
Star Shipping AG v. China National Foreign Trade Transportation Corp (The Star Texas), 2 Lloyd's Rep. 445 (Court of Appeal, Civil Division, 1993).
Vita Food Products Inc. Unus Shipping Company. Limited, [1939] UKPC 7 (Judicial Committee of the Privy Council, 1939).

United States of America

A & C Discount Pharmacy, L.L.C. d/b/a Medcore Pharmacy v. Caremark, L.L.C., et al., Civil Action No. 3:16-CV-0264-D, 2016 WL 3476970 (United States District Court, N.D. Texas, Dallas Division, 2016).
Al Raha Group for Technical Services v. PKL Services, Inc., Civil Action. No. 1:18-cv-04194-AT, 2019 WL 4267765 (United States District Court, N.D. Georgia, 2019).
Allied-Bruce Terminix Companies, Inc. v. Dobson, 513 U.S. 265 (Supreme Court of the United States, 1995).
Baker Marine (Nig.) Ltd v. Chevron (Nig.) Ltd and Chevron Corp., Inc., 191 F.3d 194 (United States Court of Appeals, Second Circuit, 1999).
Blue Cross Blue Shield of Michigan v. Medimpact Healthcare Systems, Inc., 2010 WL 2595340 (United States District Court, E.D. Michigan, Southern Division, 2010).
Chinmax Medical Systems Inc., v. Alere San Diego, Inc., No. 10cv2467 WQH (NLS), 2011 WL 2135350 (United States District Court, S.D. California, 2011).
Corporación Mexicana de Mantenimiento Integral, S. de R.L. de C.V. v. Pemex Exploración y Producción, 832 F. 3d 92 (United States Court of Appeals, Second Circuit, 2016).
Corporacion Mexicana de Mantenimiento Integral, S. de R.L. de C.V. v. Pemex-Exploracion y Produccion, 962 F. Supp. 2d 642 (United States District Court, S.D. New York, 2013).
Chromalloy Aeroservices v. The Arab Republic Egypt, 939 F. Supp. 907 (United State District Court, District of Columbia, 1996).
Davis v. Prudential Securities, Inc., 59 F. 3d 1186 (United States Court of Appeals, Eleventh Circuit, 1995).
DRC, INC. v. Republic of Honduras, 774 F. Supp. 2d 66 (Unites States District Court, District of Columbia 2011).

Energy Transport, Ltd. and PT Cabot Indonesia v. M.V. San Sebastian, her freights etc. in rem, Oilmar Co. Ltd., 348 F. Supp. 2d 186 (United States District Court, S.D. New York 2004).
Gulf Petri Trading Co., Inc. v. Nigerian Nat'l Petroleum Corp., 512 F. 3d 742 (United States Courts of Appeals, Fifth Circuit, 2008).
Island Creek Coal Sales Company. v. City of Gainesville, Florida, 729 F. 2d 1046 (United States Court of Appeals, Sixth Circuit, 1984).
James Gold, et al. v. Michael Maurer, 251 F. Supp. 3d 127 (United States District Court, District of Columbia, 2017).
Karaha Bodas Co. L.L.C. v. Perusahaan Pertambangan Minyak Dan Gas Bumi Negara, 364 F. 3d 274 (United States Court of Appeals, Fifth Circuit, 2004).
M/S Bremen v. Zapata Off-Shore Co., 407 U.S.1 (Supreme Court of the United States, 1972).
Martin I. Spier v. Calzaturificio Tecnica S.p.A., 71 F. Supp. 2d 279 (United States District Court, S.D. New York, 1999).
Metallgesellschaft A.G. v. M/V Capitan Constante, 790 F. 2d 280 (United States Court of Appeals, Second Circuit, 1986).
Ministry of Def. & Support for the Armed Forces of the Islamic Republic of Iran v. Cubic Def. System, Inc., 665 F. 3d 1091 (United States Court of Appeals, Ninth Circuit, 2011).
Mitsubishi Motors Corp. v. Soler Chrysler-Plymouth, Inc., 473 U.S. 614 (Supreme Court of the United States, 1985).
Moses H. Cone Memorial Hosp v. Mercury Construction Corp., 460 U.S. 1 (Supreme Court of the United States, 1983).
Pacific Reinsurance Management Corp. v. Ohio Reinsurance Corp., 935 F. 2d 1019 (United States Court of Appeals, Ninth Circuit, 1991).
Parsons & Whittemore Overseas Co., Inc., v. Société Générale de l' Industrie du Papier (RAKTA), 508 F. 2d 969 (United Startes Court of Appeals, Second Circuit, 1974).
Publicis Communication and Publicis S.A. v. True North Communications Inc., 206 F. 3d 725 (United States Court of Appeals, Seventh Circuit, 2000).
ReliaStar Life Insurance Company of New York v. EMC National Life Company, 564 F. 3d 81 (United States Court of Appeals, Second Circuit, 2009).
Rocky Mountain Biologicals, Inc., and Skyway Purified Solutions, Inc. v. Microbix Biosystems, Inc., and Irvine Scientific Sales Company, Inc., 986 F. Supp. 2d. 1187 (United States District Court, D. Montana, Missoula Division, 2013).
Scherk v. Alberto-Culver Co., 417 U.S. 506 (Supreme Court of the United States, 1974).
Sharp Corporation and Sharp Electronics Corporation v. Hisense USA Corporation and Hisense International (Hong Kong) America Investment Co. Ltd., Civil Action No. 17–1648 (JEB), 2017WL5449805 (United States District Court, District of Columbia, 2017).
Smart Technologies ULC v. Rapt Touch Ireland Ltd, et al., 197 F. Supp. 3d 1204 (United States District Court, N.D. California, 2016).
Southern Seas Navigation Limited of Monrovia v. Petroleos Mexicanos of Mexico City, 606 F. Supp. 692 (United States District Court, S.D. New York, 1985).
T-Mobile USA Inc. v. Verity Wireless Inc., No. 2:21-cv-00733-RAJ-BAT, 2021 WL 4295845 (United States District Court, W.D. Washington, 2021).
TermoRio S.A.E.S.P. v. Electranta S.P., 487 F. 3d 928 (United States Court of Appeals, District of Columbia Circuit, 2007).
Thrivest Specialty Funding, LLC v. William E. White, 2019 WL 6124955 (United States District Court, E.D. Pennsylvania).
United Paperworkers International Union, AFL-CIO, et al., v. Misco, Inc., 484 U.S. 29 (Supreme Court of the United States, 1987).
Vimar Seguros y Reaseguros, S.A. v. M/V Sky Reefer, 515 U.S. 528 (Supreme Court of the United States, 1995).
Yahoo! Inc. v. Microsoft Corporation, 983 F. Supp. 2d 310 (United States District Court, S.D. New York, 2013).

Books

Baker, Stewart Abercrombie & Davis, Mark David, The UNCITRAL Arbitration Rules in Practice: the experience of the Iran-United States Claims Tribunal, Kluwer Law and Taxation Publishers, 1992.

Berger, Klaus Peter, International Economic Arbitration, Kluwer Law and Taxation Publishers, 1993.

Bockstiegel, Karl-Heinz, The Role of Party Autonomy in International Commercial Arbitration, American Arbitration Association Handbook on International Arbitration and ADR, Juris, 2010.

Born, Gary B., International Commercial Arbitration: Commentary and Materials, Kluwer Law International, 2001.

Born, Gary B., International Commercial Arbitration, Kluwer Law International, 2014.

Born, Gary B., International Arbitration: Law and Practice, Kluwer Law International, 2015.

Born, Gary B., International Arbitration: Cases and Materials, Kluwer Law International, 2015.

Born, Gary B., International Arbitration and Forum Selection Agreements: Drafting and Enforcing, Kluwer Law International, 2016.

Born, Gary B., International Commercial Arbitration, Kluwer Law International, 2021.

Brunet, Edward & Speidel, Richard E. & Sternlight, Jean R. & Ware, Stephen J., Arbitration Law in America: A Critical Assessment, Cambridge University Press, 2006.

Buckland, W. W. & McNair, A. D., Roman Law and Common Law: A Comparison in Outline, Cambridge University Press.

Carbonneau, Thomas E., Cases and Materials on the Law and Practice of Arbitration, Juris Publishing, 2003.

Carbonneau, Thomas E., Carbonneau on International Arbitration: Collected Essays, Juris Publishing, 2011.

Carbonneau, Thomas E., The Law and Practice of Arbitration, Juris Publishing, Inc., 2014.

Caron, David D., & Caplan, Lee, The UNCITRAL Arbitration Rules: A Commentary, Oxford University Press, 2013.

Collins, Lawrence, et al., Dicey, Morris and Collins on the Conflict of Laws, Sweet & Maxwell, 2012.

Derains, Yves & Schwartz, Eric A., A Guide to ICC Rules of Arbitration, Kluwer Law International, 2005.

David, René, Chapter 5 The International Unification of Private Law, Volume II The Legal Systems of the World: Their Comparison and Unification, International Encyclopedia of Comparative Law, J.C.B. Mohr & Mouton & Oceana Publications Inc., 1971.

Dean, Lewis, The Interpretation and Uniformity of the UNCITRAL Model Law on International Commercial Arbitration: Australia, Hong Kong and Singapore, Kluwer Law International, 2016.

Elkind, Jerome B., Interim Protection: A Functional Analysis, Martinus Nijhoff Publishers bv, 1981.

Fan, Kun, Arbitration in China: A Legal and Cultural Analysis, Hart Publishing, 2013.

Friedman, Lawrence M., The Legal System: A Social Science Perspective, Russell Sage Foundation, 1975.

Gaillard, Emmanuel & Savage, John, Fouchard Gaillard Goldman on International Commercial Arbitration, Kluwer Law International, 1999.

Gisberger Daniel & Voser, Nathalie, International Arbitration: Comparative and Swiss Perspectives, Kluwer Law International, 2016.

Hale, Thomas, Between Interests and Law: The Politics of Transnational Commercial Disputes, Cambridge University Press, 2015.

Hanessian, Grant, Emergency Arbitrator, in Newman, Lawrence W. & Hill, Richard D., The Leading Arbitrators' Guide to International Arbitration, Juris Publishing, 2014.

Harris, Philip & Moran, Robert, Managing Culture Differences, Gulf, 1991.

Hartley, Trevor C., International Commercial Litigation: Text, Cases and Materials on Private International Law, Cambridge University Press, 2015.

Jarrosson, Charles, La notion d'arbitrage, Libr. générale de droit et de jurisprudence 1987.

Jones, Geoffrey, The Evolution of International Business: An Introduction, Routledge, 1996.
Kröll, Stefan Michael & Lew, Julian D.M. & Mistelis, Loukas A., Comparative International Commercial Arbitration, Kluwer Law International, 2003.
Karrer, Pierre A. & Straub, Peter A., Practitioner's Handbook on International Commercial Arbitration, 2009.
Kurkela, Matti & Turunen, Santtu, Due Process in International Commercial Arbitration, Oxford University Press, 2010.
Lew, Julian D. M., Applicable Law in International Commercial Arbitration, Oceana Publications, 1978.
Lew, Julian D.M., Contemporary Problems in International Arbitration, Springer, 1987.
Lynch, Katherine, The Forces of Economic Globalization: Challenges to the Regime of International Commercial Arbitration, Kluwer Law International, 2003.
Mcllwrath, Michael & Savage, John, International Arbitration and Mediation: A Practical Guide, Kluwer Law International, 2010.
Menon, Sundaresh, Arbitration in Singapore: A Practical Guide, Sweet & Maxwell, 2014.
Merkin, Robert & Hjalmarsson, Johanna, Singapore Arbitration Legislation: annotated, Informa Law from Routledge, 2016.
Mohmeded, Shadat, A Critical Analysis of Arbitral Provisional Measures in England and Wales, PhD thesis of Brunel University, 2014.
Moses, Margaret L., The Principles and Practice of International Commercial Arbitration, Cambridge University Press, 2017.
Moser, Michael & Bao, Chiann, A Guide to the HKIAC Arbitration Rules, Oxford University Press, 2017.
Murphy, D., The Structure of Regulatory Competition: Corporations and Public Policies in A Global Economy, Oxford University Press, 2004.
Nairn, Karyl & Heneghan, Patrick, Arbitration World: Jurisdictional and Institutional Comparisons, Sweet & Maxwell, 2015.
Nieuwveld, Lisa Bench & Sahani, Victoria Shannon, Third-Party Funding in International Arbitration, Kluwer Law International, 2016.
Odoe, Levi Onyeisi Wilson, Party Autonomy and Enforceability of Arbitration Agreement and Awards as the Basis of Arbitration, PhD thesis of University of Leicester, 2014.
Örücü, Esin, The Enigma of Comparative Law: Variations on a Theme for the Twenty-First Century, Springer Science+Business Media, 2004.
Paulsson, Marike R. P., The 1958 New York Convention in Action, Kluwer Law International 2016.
Peters, Niek, The Fundamentals of International Commercial Arbitration, Maklu, 2017.
Petrochilos, Georgios, Procedural Law in International Arbitration, Oxford University Press on Demand, 2004.
Pillet, Antoine, Traité pratique de droit international privé, Imprimerie J. Allier, 1924.
Randel, Don Michael, The New Harvard Dictionary of Music, The Belknap Press of Harvard University Press, 2003.
Redfern, Alan & Hunter, Martin & Blackaby, Nigel & Partasides, Constantine, Law and Practice of International Commercial Arbitration, Sweet & Maxwell, 2004.
Redfern, Alan, & Hunter, J. Martin, et al., Redfern and Hunter on International Arbitration, Oxford University Press, 2015.
Reymond-Eniaeva, Elza, Towards a Uniform Approach to Confidentiality of International Commercial Arbitration, Springer, 2019.
Rubellin-Devichi, J. & Vincent, Jean, L'arbitrage: Nature juridique; Droit interne et droit international privé. Librairie générale de droit et de jurisprudence, 1965.
Rubino-Sammartano, Mauro, International Arbitration: Law and Practice, Juris, 2014.
Salama, Nadia Ramzy, Nature, Extent, and Role of Parties' Autonomy in the Making of International Commercial Arbitration Agreements, PhD thesis of The University of Manchester, 2015.
Sanders, Pieter, Quo Vadis Arbitration? Sixty Years of Arbitration Practice: A Comparative Study, Kluwer Law International, 1999.

Samuel, Adam, Jurisdictional Problems in International Commercial Arbitration: A Study of Belgian, Dutch, English, French, Swedish, Swiss, US, and West German Law, Schulthess Polygraphischer Verlag, 1989.
Schlosser, Peter, Das Recht der internationalen privaten Schiedsgerichtsbarkeit, Mohr Siebeck, 1989.
Scherer, Maxi & Richman, Lisa et al., Arbitration under the 2014 LCIA Rules: A User's Guide, Kluwer Law International, 2015.
Schreuer, Christoph H. & Malintoppi, Loretta & Reinich, August & Sinclair, Anthony, The ICSID Convention: a Commentary, Cambridge University Press, 2009.
Schwartz, Eric A., The Practices and Experience of the ICC Court, in Conservatory and Provisional Measures in International Arbitration, International Chamber of Commerce, 1993.
Steingruber, Andrea Marco, Notion, Nature and Extent of Consent in International Arbitration, PhD thesis of the Queen Mary University of London, 2009.
Tao, Jingzhou, Arbitration Law and Practice in China, Kluwer Law International, 2008.
Yang, Fan, Foreign-related Arbitration in China: Commentary and Cases, Cambridge University Press, 2016.
Van den Berg, Albert, The New York Arbitration Convention of 1958: Towards a Uniform Judicial Interpretation, Kluwer Law and Taxation Publishers, 1981.
Verbist, Herman & Schfer, Erik, et al., ICC Arbitration in Practice, Kluwer Law International, 2015.
Von Wunschheim, Clarisse, Enforcement of Commercial Arbitral Awards in China, Sweet & Maxwell, 2014.
Waincymer, Jeffrey, Procedure and Evidence in International Arbitration, Kluwer Law International, 2012.
Warwas, Barbara Alicja, The Liability of Arbitral Institutions: Legitimacy Challenges and Functional Responses, T.M.C. Asser Press, 2017.
Webster, Thomas H. & Bühler, Michael, Handbook of ICC Arbitration: Commentary, Precedents, Materials, Sweet & Maxwell, 2014.
Werbicki, Raymond J., Arbitral Interim Measures: Fact or Fiction?, in American Arbitration Association Handbook on International Arbitration and ADR, Juris Publishing, 2010.
Wiener, Jarrod, Globalization and the Harmonization of Law, Pinter, 1999.
Yesilirmak, Ali, Provisional Measures in International Commercial Arbitration, PhD thesis of the Queen Mary University of London, 2003.
Yesilirmak, Ali, Provisional Measures in International Commercial Arbitration, Kluwer Law International, 2005.
Zeller, Bruno, CISG and the Unification of International Trade Law, Routledge-Cavendish, 2007.

Book Chapters

Andersen, Camilla Baasch, Uniformity and Harmonization by Case Law: The CISG and the Global Jurisconsultorium, in Fogt, Morten M., Unification and Harmonization of International Commercial Law: Interaction or Deharmonization?, Kluwer Law International, 2012, pp. 175–189.
Andreadakis, Stelios, Regulatory Competition or Harmonisation: the Dilemma, the Alternatives and the Prospect of Reflexive Harmonisation, in Andenas, Mads & Andersen, Camila Baasch, Theory and Practice of Harmonisation, Edward Elgar, 2011, pp. 52–64.
Banifatemi, Yas, Expedited Proceedings in International Arbitration, in Lévy, Laurent & Polkinghorne, Michael, Expedited Procedures in International Arbitration, International Chamber of Commerce, 2017, pp. 9–33.
Beechey, John & Kenny, Gareth, How to Control the Impact of Time Running between the Occurrence of the Damage and its Full Compensation: Complementary and Alternative Remedies in

Interim Relief Proceedings, in de Ly, F.J.M. & Lévy, Laurent, Interest, Auxiliary and Alternative Remedies in International Arbitration, International Chamber of Commerce (ICC), 2008, pp. 91–130.

Berger, K., Pre-Arbitral Referees: Arbitrators, Quasi-Arbitrators, Hybrids, or Creature of Contract Law?, in Aksen, G. (eds), Global Reflections on International Law, Commerce and Dispute Resolution: Liber Amicorum in Honor of Robert Briner, International Chamber of Commerce, 2005, pp. 73–87.

Bian, Cheng & Li, Yuwen, Elements of Public Policy in the Making of the China-EU Comprehensive Agreement on Investment, in Li, Yuwen & Qi, Tong & Bian, Cheng (eds), China, the EU and International Investment Law: Reforming Investor-state Dispute Settlement, Routledge, 2019, Chapter 4.

Böckstiegel, Karl-Heinz, Public Policy and Arbitrability, in Sanders, Pieter, Comparative Arbitration Practice and Public Policy in Arbitration, 3 ICCA Congress Series 1987, Kluwer Law International, 1987, pp. 177–204.

Böckstiegel, Karl-Heinz, The Internationalisation of International Arbitration: Looking Ahead to the Next Ten Years, in Hunter, Martin & Marriott, Arthur & Veeder, V. V., The Internationalisation of International Arbitration: The LCIA Centenary Conference, Graham & Trotman/ Martinus Nijhoff, 1995, pp. 71–84.

Boog, Christopher, The Laws Governing Interim Measures in International Arbitration, in Ferrari, Franco & Kröll, Conflict of Laws in International Arbitration, Sellier, 2011, pp. 409–457.

Boog, Christopher, Chapter 4, Part II: Commentary on the ICC Rules, Article 29 [Emergency arbitrator], in Arroyo, Manuel, Arbitration in Switzerland: The Practitioner's Guide, Kluwer Law International, 2013, pp. 814–825.

Boog, Christopher, Chapter 13, Part III: Interim Measures in International Arbitration, in Arroyo, Manuel, Arbitration in Switzerland: The Practitioner's Guide, Kluwer Law International, 2013, pp. 1355–1369.

Boog, Christopher, Chapter 17, Part II: Commentary on the ICC Rules, Article 29 [Emergency Arbitrator], in Arroyo, Manuel, Arbitration in Switzerland: The Practitioner's Guide, Kluwer Law International, 2018, pp. 2380–2398.

Braghetta, Adriana, The Framework of the International Arbitration System: the Challenge Derived from the Improper Conduct of Judicial Courts', in Van den Berg, Albert, International Arbitration: The Coming of a New Age?, 17 ICCA Congress Series 2013, Kluwer Law International, 2013, pp. 431–455.

Bull, Cavinder, Commencing Arbitration, in Van den Berg, Albert, International Arbitration: The Coming of a New Age?, 17 ICCA Congress Series 2013, Kluwer Law International, 2013, pp. 135–173.

Carlevaris, Andrea, Chapter 20: The Geography of International Arbitration – Places of Arbitration: the Old Ones and the New Ones, in Brekoulakis, Stavros & Lew, Julian David Mathew, et al., The Evolution and Future of International Arbitration, Kluwer Law International, 2016, pp. 331–340.

Chan, Leng Sun, Making Arbitration Work in Singapore, in Reyes, Anselmo & Gu, Weixia, The Developing World of Arbitration: A Comparable Study of Arbitration Reform in the Asia Pacific, Hart Publishing, 2018, pp. 143–162.

De Cossío, Francisco González, Interim Measures in Arbitration: Towards a Better Injury Standard, in Van den Berg, Legitimacy: Myths, Realities, Challenges, 18 ICCA Congress Series 2015, Kluwer Law International, 2015, pp. 260-277.

Duca, Louis Del & Welsh, Nancy A., Interpretation and Application of the New York Convention in the United States, in Bermann, George A., Recognition and Enforcement of Foreign Arbitral Awards: The Interpretation and Application of the New York Convention by National Courts, Springer International Publishing AG, 2017, pp. 995–1052.

Faure, Michael G., How Law and Economics May Contribute to the Harmonisation of Tort Law in Europe, in Zimmerman, R., Grundstrukturen des Europäischen Deliktsrechts, Nomos Verlagsgesellschaft, 2003, pp. 31–82.

Feinerman, James V., The History and Development of China's Dispute Resolution System, in (Hunter, Chris), Dispute Resolution in China—A Practical Guide to Litigation & Arbitration in China, Asia Law & Practice, 1995, pp. 5–21.

Gaillard, Emmanuel, The Urgency of Not Revising the New York Convention, 50 Years of the New York Convention, 14 ICCA Congress Series 2009, Kluwer Law International, 2009, pp. 689–696.

Garimella, Sai Ramani & Sooksripaisarnkit, Poomintr, Chapter 5: Emergency Arbitrator Awards: Addressing Enforceability Concerns Through National Law and the New York Convention, in Gomez, Katia Fach & Lopez-Rodriguez, Ana M., 60 Years of the New York Convention: Key Issues and Future Challenges, Kluwer Law International, 2019, pp. 67–84.

Hanessian, Grant, Emergency Arbitrators, in Newman, Lawrence W. & Hill, Richard D., The Leading Arbitrators' Guide to International Arbitration, Juris, 2014, pp. 343–366.

Henderson, Alastair & Mahendra, Vikas, Interlocutory Applications (Interim Measures), in Menon, Sundaresh, Arbitration in Singapore: A Practical Guide, Sweet & Maxwell, 2014, pp. 300–313.

Hobér, Kaj, Interim Measures by Arbitrators, in Van den Berg, Albert, International Arbitration 2006: Back to Basics?, 13 ICCA Congress Series 2007, Kluwer Law International, 2007, pp. 721–750.

Holtzmann , Howard M., A Task for the 21st Century: Creating a New International Court for Resolving Disputes on the Enforceability of Arbitral Awards, in Hunter, Martin & Marriott, Arthur & Veeder, V. V., The Internationalisation of International Arbitration: The LCIA Centenary Conference, Graham & Trotman/ Martinus Nijhoff, 1995, pp. 109–114.

Jeyaretnam, Philip & Teh, Lawrence, Domestic and International Arbitration Framework in Singapore, in Menon, Sundaresh, Arbitration in Singapore: A Practical Guide, Sweet & Maxwell, 2014, pp. 95–104.

Kalra, Vinod, New Trends in the Development of International Commercial Arbitration and the Role of Arbitral and Other Institutions, in Sanders, Pieter, New Trends in the Development of International Commercial Arbitration and the Role of Arbitral and Other Institutions, 1 ICCA Congress Series 1983, Kluwer Law International 1983, pp. 82–85.

Kim, Kap-You (Kevin) & Satish, Bhushan, Legal Criteria for Granting Relief in Emergency Arbitrator Proceedings: Where Are We Now and Where Do We Go from Here? in Kaplan, Neil & Moser, Michael J., Jurisdiction, Admissibility and Choice of Law in International Arbitration: Liber Amicorum Michael Pryles, Kluwer Law International, 2018, pp. 175–192.

Kronke, Herbert, Introduction: The New York Convention Fifty Years on: Overview and Assessment, in Kronke. Herbert & Nacimiento, Patricia, Recognition and Enforcement of Foreign Arbitral Awards: A Global Commentary on the New York Convention, Kluwer Law International, 2010, pp. 1–18.

Lalive, Pierre, The Internationalisation of International Arbitration: Some Observations, in Hunter, Martin & Marriott, Arthur & Veeder, V. V., The Internationalisation of International Arbitration: The LCIA Centenary Conference, Graham & Trotman/ Martinus Nijhoff, 1995, pp. 49–58.

Lalive, Pierre, Transnational (or Truly International) Public Policy and International Arbitration, in Sanders, Pieter, Comparative Arbitration Practice and Public Policy in Arbitration, 3 ICCA Congress Series 1987, Kluwer Law International, 1987, pp. 257–320. .

Leathley, Christian & Villaggi, Florencia, Chapter 25: The Panama Convention in the United States: Chapter 3 of the FAA, in Shore, Laurence & Cheng, Tai-Heng & Chiusa, Jenelle E. & Schaner, Lawrence & Senn, Mara V. J., International Arbitration in the United States, Kluwer Law International, 2017, pp. 599–615.

Lew, Julian D.M., The Case for the Publication of Arbitration Awards, in Schultsz, Jan C. & Van den Berg, Albert Jan, The Art of Arbitration: Essays on International Arbitration, Kluwer Law and Taxation Publishers, 1982, pp. 223–232.

Lew, Julina, The Law Applicable to the Form and Substance of the Arbitration Clause, in Van den Berg, Albert, Improving the Efficiency of Arbitration Agreements and Awards: 40 Years of Application of the New York Convention, 9 ICCA Congress Series 1999, Kluwer Law International, 1999, pp. 114–145.

Lo, Amy, International Arbitration in Hong Kong, in Balthasar, Stephan, International Commercial Arbitration: International Conventions, Country Reports and Comparative Analysis, C. H. BECK·Hart·Nomos, 2016, pp. 407–446.

Lohse, Eva J., The Meaning of Harmonisation in the Context of European Union Law—a process in need of definition, in Andenas, Mads & Andersen, Camilla Baasch, Theory and Practice of Harmonisation, Edward Elgar, 2011, pp. 282–313.

Łopatka, Adam, Cultural Diversity and Cultural Human Rights, in Doeker-Mach, Guenther & Ziegert, Klaus A., Law and Legal Culture in Comparative Perspective, Franz Steiner Verlag Stuttgart, 2004, pp. 216-221.

Mistelis, Loukas, Is Harmonisation a Necessary Evil? The Future of Harmonisation and New Sources of International Trade Law, in Ian Fletcher, Lukas Mistelis & Marise Cremona (eds), Foundations and Perspectives of International Trade Law, Sweet & Maxwell, 2001, pp. 3–27.

Niedermaier, Tilman, International Arbitration in the U.S., in Balthasar, Stephan, International Commercial Arbitration: International Conventions, Country Reports and Comparative Analysis, C. H. BECK·Hart·Nomos, 2016, pp. 660–692.

Nirwani, S. C., Contributions Which Conventions, Treaties, and Agreements among Institutions Can Make to the Development of Arbitration (Scope of Commercial Arbitration, Suggestions for Improvement in the System and the Need for Voluntary Initiative by Arbitral Institutions), in Sanders, Pieter, New Trends in the Development of International Commercial Arbitration and the Role of Arbitral and Other Institutions, 1 ICCA Congress Series 1983, Kluwer Law International 1983, pp. 95–99.

Norberg, Charles Robert, General Introduction to Inter-American Commercial Arbitration, in Sanders, Pieter, 3 Yearbook Commercial Arbitration 1978, Kluwer Law International, 1978, pp. 1–14.

Otto, Dirk & Elwan, Omaia, Article V (2), in Kronke, Herbert & Nacimiento, Patricia et al., Recognition and Enforcement of Foreign Arbitral Awards: A Global Commentary on the New York Convention, Kluwer Law International, 2010, pp. 345–414.

Paulsson, Marike & Suresh, Supritha, The New York Convention's 60th Anniversary: A Restatement for the New York Convention?, in Gómez, Katia Fach & Lopez Rodriguez, Ana Mercedes, 60 Years of the New York Convention: Key Issues and Future Challenges, Kluwer Law International, 2019, pp. 269–293.

Peters, Philipp & Koller, Christian, [Chapter III: The Award and the Courts—]The Notion of Arbitral Award: An Attempt to Overcome a Babylonian Confusion, in Zeiler, Gerold & Welser, Irene, et al., Austrian Yearbook on International Arbitration 2010, pp. 137–169.

Procaccia, Uriel, The Case Against Lex Mercatoria, in Ziegel, Jacob S., New Developments in International Commercial and Consumer Law: Proceedings of the 8th Biennial Conference of the International Academy of Commercial and Consumer Law, pp. 87–95.

Redfern, Alan, Interim Measures, in Newman, Lawrence W. & Hill, Richard D., The Leading Arbitrators' Guide to International Arbitration, Juris, 2014, pp. 367–404.

Reisman, W Michael, Law International Public Policy (So-called) and Arbitral Choice in International Commercial Arbitration, in Van den Berg, Albert, Jan, International Arbitration 2006: Back to Basics?, 13 ICCA Congress Series 2007, Kluwer Law International, 2007, pp. 849–856.

Sanders, Pieter, The History of the New York Convention, in Van den Berg, Albert, Improving the Efficiency of Arbitration Agreements and Awards: 40 Years of Application of the New York Convention, 9 ICCA Congress Series 1999, Kluwer Law International, 1999, pp. 11–14.

Selvaraj, Ramesh & Liang, Tan Kai, International Arbitration in Singapore, in Balthasar, Stephan, International Commercial Arbitration: International Conventions, Country Reports and Comparative Analysis, C. H. Beck·Hart·Nomos, 2016, pp. 540–567.

Schwartz, Eric A., The Practices and Experience of the ICC Court, in Conservatory and Provisional Measures in International Arbitration, International Chamber of Commerce, 1993, pp. 45–69.

Schwarz, Franz, Limits of Party Autonomy in International Commercial Arbitration, in Knahr, Christina & Koller, Christian & Rechberger, Walter & Reinisch, August (eds), Investment and

Commercial Arbitration—Similarities and Divergences, Eleven International Publishing, 2010, pp. 73–95.

Shaughnessy, Patricia, The Emergency Arbitrator, in Shaughnessy, Patricia & Tung Sherlin, The Powers and Duties of an Arbitrator: Liber Amicorum Pierre A. Karrer, Kluwer Law International, 2017, pp. 339–348.

Sills, Robert, The Continuing Role of the Courts in the Era of the Emergency Arbitrator, in Van den Berg, Albert, Legitimacy: Myths, Realities, Challenges, 18 ICCA Congress Series 2015, Kluwer Law International, 2015, pp. 278–298.

Van den Berg, Albert, The New York Convention of 1958: An Overview, in Gaillard, Emmanuel & Di Pietro, Domenico, Enforcement of Arbitration Agreements and International Awards: The New York Convention in Practice, Cameron May, 2008, pp. 39–68.

Von Segesser, Georg & Boog, Christopher, Chapter 6: Interim Measures, in Geisinger, Elliott & Voser, Nathalie, International Arbitration in Switzerland: A Handbook for Practitioners, Kluwer Law International, 2013, pp. 107–130.

Werbicki, Raymond J., Arbitral Interim Measures: Fact or Fiction?, in American Arbitration Association Handbook on International Arbitration and ADR, Juris Publishing, 2010, pp. 89–103.

Wittich, Stephan, The Limits of Party Autonomy in Investment Arbitration, in Knahr, Christina & Koller, Christian & Rechberger, Walter & Reinisch, August (eds), Investment and Commercial Arbitration—Similarities and Divergences, Eleven International Publishing, 2010, pp. 47–71.

Xavier, Francis & Rong, Tng Sheng, Role of the Court, in Menon, Sundaresh, Arbitration in Singapore: A Practical Guide, Sweet & Maxwell, 2014, pp. 34–69.

Xiong, Qi & Shang Yong, International Arbitration in China (People's Republic), in Balthasar, Stephan, International Commercial Arbitration: International Conventions, Country Reports and Comparative Analysis, C. H. BECK·Hart·Nomos, 2016, pp. 266–299.

Zamora, José María Abascal, The Art of Interim Measures, in Van den Berg, Albert, International Arbitration 2006: Back to Basics?, 13 ICCA Congress Series 2007, Kluwer Law International, 2007, pp. 751–767.

Ziegel, Jacob, Harmonization of Private Laws in Federal Systems of Government: Canada, the USA, and Australia, in Cranston, Ross, Making Commercial Law: Essays in Honour of Roy Goode, Clarendon Press Oxford, 1997, pp. 131–166.

Journal Articles

Abedian, Hossein, Judicial Review of Arbitral Awards in International Arbitration: A Case of an Efficient System of Judicial Review, 28 Journal of International Arbitration 2011, pp. 553–590.

Aden, Menno, Wrong Answers to Wrong Questions? A New Approach to Judicial Review of International Arbitral Awards, 12 Revista Brasileira de Arbitragem 2015, pp. 55–69.

Andersen, Camilla Baasch, Defining Uniformity in Law, 12 Uniform Law Review 2007, pp. 5–54.

Baigel, Baruch, The Emergency Arbitrator Procedure under the 2012 ICC Rules: A Juridical Analysis, 31 Journal of International Arbitration 2014, pp. 1–18.

Bassler, William G., The Enforceability of Emergency Awards in the United States: or when interim means final, 32 Arbitration International 2016, pp. 559–574.

Bates, Bethany M., Reconciliation after Winter: The Standard for Preliminary Injunctions in Federal Courts, 111 Columbia Law Review 2011, pp. 1522–1556.

Belohlavek, Alexander J., Importance of the Seat of Arbitration in International Arbitration: Delocalization and Denationalization of Arbitration as an Outdated Myth, 31 ASA Bulletin 2013, pp. 262–292.

Benedettelli, Massimo V., 'Communitarization' of International Arbitration: A New Spectre Haunting Europe?, 27 Arbitration International 2011, pp. 583–622.

Beraudo, J.P., Recognition and Enforcement of Interim Measures of Protection Ordered by Arbitral Tribunals, 22 Journal of International Arbitration 2005, pp. 245–254.

Blessing, Marc, Globalization (and Harmonization?) of Arbitration, 9 Journal of International Law 1992, pp. 79–90.

Boodman, Martin, The Myth of Harmonization of Laws, 39 American Journal of Comparative Law 1991, pp. 699–724.

Boo, Lawrence & Lim, Charles, Overview of the International Arbitration Act and Subsidiary Legislation in Singapore, 12 Journal of International Arbitration 1995, pp. 75–89.

Bond, Stephen, How to draft an arbitration clause (revisited), 1 ICC International Court of Arbitration Bulletin 1990, pp. 14–21.

Born, Gary B., Arbitrability and Public Policy, 5 World Arbitration and Mediation Review 2011, pp. 293–300.

Bose, Raja & Meredith, Ian, Emergency Arbitration Procedures: A Comparative Analysis, 5 International Arbitration Law Review 2012, pp. 186–194.

Brazil-David, Renata, Harmonization and Delocalization of International Commercial Arbitration, 28 Journal of International Arbitration 2011, pp. 445–466.

Brekoulakis, Stavros, Enforcement of Foreign Arbitral Awards: Observations on the Efficiency of the Current System and the Gradual Development of Alternative Means of Enforcement, 19 American Review of International Arbitration 2008, pp. 415–446.

Bucy, Dana, How to Best Protect Party Rights: The Future of Interim Relief in International Commercial Arbitration under the Amended UNCITRAL Model Law, 25 American University International Law Review 2010, pp. 579–609.

Bühler, Michael & Heitzmann, Pierre, The 2017 ICC Expedited Rules: From Softball to Hardball?, 34 Journal of International Arbitration 2017, pp. 121–148.

Calliess, Gralf-Peter & Buchmann, Insa, Global Commercial Law between Unity, Pluralism, and Competition: the case of the CISG, 21 Uniform Law Review 2016, pp. 1–22.

Carbonneau, Thomas E. & Janson, Francois, Cartesian Logic and Frontier Politics: French and American Concepts of Arbitrability, 2 Tulane Journal of International and Comparative Law1994, pp. 193–222.

Carlevaris, Andrea & Feris, José Ricardo, Running in the ICC Emergency Arbitrator Rules: The First Ten Cases, 25 ICC International Court of Arbitration Bulletin (Issue 1) 2014, pp. 25–38.

Cavalieros, Philippe & Kim, Janet, Emergency Arbitrators Versus the Courts: From Concurrent Jurisdiction to Practical Considerations, 35 Journal of International Arbitration 2018, pp. 275–306.

Carlston, Kenneth S, Theory of the Arbitration Process, 17 Law and Contemporary Problems 1952, pp. 631–651.

Cary, William L., Federalism and Corporate Law: Reflections Upon Delaware, 83 Yale Law Journal 1974, pp. 663–705.

Chan, Leng Sun, Developments in Arbitration Laws, 14 Singapore Academy of Law Journal 2002, pp. 49–68.

Chan, Ray Y., The Enforceability of Annulled Foreign Arbitral Awards in the United States: A Critique of Chromalloy, 17 Boston University International Law Journal 1999, pp. 141–214.

Choi, Dongdoo, Joinder in International Commercial Arbitration, 35 Arbitration International 2019, pp. 29–55.

Collins, Erin, Pre-Tribunal Emergency Relief in International Commercial Arbitration, 10 Loyola University Chicago International Law Review 2012, pp. 105–124.

Cremades, Bernardo M., Overcoming the Clash of Legal Cultures: The Role of Interactive Arbitration, 14 Arbitration International 1998, pp. 157–172.

Dolinger, Jacob, World Public Policy: Real International Public Policy in the Conflict of Law, 17 Texas International Law Journal 1982, pp. 167–194.

Drahozal, Christopher R., New York Convention and the American Federal System, The Symposium, Journal of Dispute Resolution 2012, pp. 101–118.

Dunmore, Michael, Interim Measures by Arbitral Tribunals: The Enforceability Conundrum, 8 Asian International Arbitration Journal 2012, pp. 222–231.

Engle, Rachel, Party Autonomy in International Arbitration: Where Uniformity Gives Way to Predictability, 15 The Transnational Lawyer 2002, pp. 323–356.

Fassberg, Celia Wasserstein, Lex Mercatoria – Hoist with Its Own Petard?, 5 Chicago Journal of International Law 2004, pp. 67–82.

Feigerlová, Monika, Emergency Measures of Protection in International Arbitration, 18 International and Comparative Law Review 2018, pp. 155–177.

Fitzmaurice, Gerald, The Law and Procedure of the International Court of Justice, 1951–4: Questions of Jurisdiction, Competence and Procedure, 34 British Year Book of International Law 1958, pp. 1–161.

Fry, Jason, The Emergency Arbitrator—Flawed Fashion or Sensible Solution?, 7 Dispute Resolution International 2013, pp. 179–198.

Gaffney, John, Should the European Union Regulate Commercial Arbitration?, 33 Arbitration International 2017, pp. 81–98.

Gaillard, Emmanuel & Pinsolle, Philippe, The ICC Pre-Arbitral Referee: First Practical Experience, 20 Arbitration International 2004, pp. 13–38.

Garnett, Richard, International Arbitration Law: Progress towards Harmonisation, 3 Melbourne Journal of International Law 2002, pp. 400–414.

Gélinas, Fabien, Arbitration and the Challenge of Globalization, 17 Journal of International Arbitration 2000, pp. 117–122.

Genschel, Philipp & Plumper, Thomas, Regulatory Competition and International Cooperation, 4 Journal of European Public Policy 1997, pp. 626–642.

Goldstein, Marc J, Annulled Awards in the US Courts: How Primary Is" Primary Jurisdiction"?, 25 American Review of International Arbitration 2014, pp. 19–45.

Gopalan, Sandeep, The Creation of International Commercial Law: Sovereignty Felled?, 5 San Diego International Law Journal 2004, pp. 267–322.

Hanessian, Grant & Dosman, E. Alexandra, Songs of Innocence and Experience: Ten Years of Emergency Arbitration, 27 American Review of International Arbitration 2016, pp. 215–237.

Hamama, Olga & Sendetska, Olga, Interim Meaures in Support of Arbitration in Ukraine: lessons from JKX Oil & Gas et al v. Ukraine and the Recent Reform of Ukrainian Legislation, 34 Arbitration International 2018, pp. 307–315.

Hanotiau, Bernard & Caprasse, Olivier, Arbitrability, Due Process, and Public Policy Under Article V of the New York Convention, 25 Journal of International Arbitration 2008, pp. 721–741.

Hanotiau, Bernard & Block, Guy, The Law of 19 May 1988 amending Belgian Arbitration Legislation, 15 Arbitration International 1999, pp. 97–100.

Helmer, Elena V., International Commercial Arbitration: Americanized, "Civilized," or Harmonized?, 19 Ohio State Journal on Dispute Resolution 2003, pp. 35–68.

Heiskanen, Veijo, Jurisdiction v. Competence: Revisiting a Frequently Neglected Distinction, 5 Finnish Yearbook of International Law 1994, pp. 1–33.

Hill, Jonathan, Is an Interim Measure of Protection Ordered by an Arbitral Tribunal an Arbitral Award?, 9 Journal of International Dispute Settlement 2018, pp. 590–608.

Howell, David & Duthie, Leigh & Lim, Mark, International Arbitration in Singapore – Opting out of the UNCITRAL Model Law, 19 Journal of International Arbitration 2002, pp. 39–50.

Husserl, Gerhart, Public Policy and Ordre Public, 25 Virginia Law Review 1938–1939, pp. 37–67.

Jalili, Mahir, Amman Arab Convention on Commercial Arbitration, 7 Journal of International Arbitration 1990, pp.139–152.

Jarvin, Sigvard, The Sources and Limits of the Arbitrator's Powers, 2 Arbitration International 1986, pp. 140–163.

Juenger, Friedrich K., Conflict of Laws, Comparative Law and Civil Law: The Lex Mercatoria and Private International Law, 60 Louisiana Law Review 2000, pp. 1133–1150.

Kah Cheong & Yeo, Chuan Tat & Miller, William, Legal Status of the Emergency Arbitrator under the SIAC 2010 Rules, 23 Singapore Academy of Law Journal 2011, pp. 93–124.

Kaufmann-Kohler, Gabrielle, Soft Law in International Arbitration: Codification and Normativity, 1 Journal of International Dispute Settlement 2010, pp. 283–299.
Kim, Joongi, International Arbitration in East Asia: From Emulation to Innovation, 4 Arbitration Brief 2014, pp. 1–30.
Köll, Stephan, The Non-Enforceability of Decisions Rendered in Summary Arbitral Proceedings Pursuant to the NAI Rules under the New York Convention, 23 American Review of International Arbitration 2012, pp. 75–102.
Lago, Carlos de Los Santos & Bonnin, Victor, Emergency Proceedings under the New ICC Rules, 13 Spain Arbitration Review 2012, pp. 5–19.
Lainé, Armand. De l'Execution en France des Sentences Arbitrales Entrangeres, 26 Journal du Droit International Privé et de la Jurisprudence Comparée 1899, pp. 641–654.
Lécuyer-Thieffry, Christine, First Court Ruling on the ICC Pre-Arbitral Referee Procedure, 20 Journal of International Arbitration 2003, pp. 599–607.
Leebron, David W., Claims for Harmonization: A Theoretical Framework, 27 Canadian Business Law Journal 1996, pp. 63–107.
Lemenez, Guillaume & Quigley, Paul, The ICDR's Emergency Arbitrator Procedure in Action: Part I: A Look at the Empirical Data, 63 Dispute Resolution Journal 2008, pp. 66–71.
Lew, Julian D.M., Commentary on Interim and Conservatory Measures in ICC Arbitration Cases, 11 ICC International Court of Arbitration Bulletin (Issue 1) 2000, pp. 23–30.
Lim, Charles, The Development Life Cycle of International Arbitration Legislation – Singapore IAA Case Study, 7 Asian International Arbitration Journal 2011, pp. 1–28.
Locknie, Hsu, The Adoption of the UNCITRAL Model Law on International Commercial Arbitration in Singapore, 2 Singapore Journal of Legal Studies 1994, pp. 387–416.
Lorenzen, Ernest G., Commercial Arbitration—Enforcement of Foreign Awards, 45 Yale Law Journal 1935, pp. 39–68.
Lye, Kah Cheong & Yeo, Chuan Tat & Miller, William, Legal Status of the Emergency Arbitrator under the SIAC 2010 Rules, 23 Singapore Academy of Law Journal 2011, pp. 93–124.
Livingstone, Mia Louise, Party Autonomy in International Commercial Arbitration: Popular Fallacy or Proven Fact? 25 Journal of International Arbitration 2008, pp. 529–535.
Mann, Frederick A, Lex Facit Arbitrum, 2 Arbitration International 1986, pp. 241–261.
Mantilla-Serrano, Fernando & Adam, John, UNCITRAL Model Law: Missed Opportunities for Enhanced Uniformity, 31 University of New South Wales Law Journal 2008, pp. 307.
Mason, Paul Eric, The Arbitrator as Mediator, and Mediator as Arbitrator, 28 Journal of International Arbitration 2011, pp. 541–551.
Menon, Sundaresh & Chao, Elaine, Reforming the Model Law Provisions on Interim Measures of Protection, 2 Asian International Arbitration Journal 2006, pp. 1–31.
Mirabito, A. Jason, The United Nations Convention on the Recognition and Enforcement of Foreign Arbitral Awards: The First Four Years, 5 Georgia Journal of International and Comparative Law 1975, pp. 471–504.
Mistelism, Loukas, Regulatory Aspects: Globalization, Harmonization, Legal Transplants, and Law Reform—Some Fundamental Observations, 34 International Lawyer 2000, pp. 1055–1069.
Mohan, Mahdev, The New International Arbitration (Amendment) Bill: A Broader Framework for Interim Relief or Just a Tune-Up, 22 Singapore Academy of Law Journal 2010, pp. 299–332.
Morosini, Fabio, Globalization & Law: Beyond Traditional Methodology of Comparative Legal Studies and an Example from Private International Law, 13 Cardozo Journal of International and Comparative Law 2005, pp. 541–561.
Morton, Peter, Can a World Exist Where Expedited Arbitration Becomes the Default Procedure?, 26 Arbitration International 2010, pp. 103–114.
Muller, Christoph & Pearson, Sabrina, Waving the Green Flag to Emergency Arbitration under the Swiss Rules: the Sauber Saga, 33 ASA Bulletin 2015, pp. 808–824.
Muñoz, Edgardo, How Urgent Shall an Emergency Be?—The Standards Required to Grant Urgent Relief by Emergency Arbitrators, 4 Yearbook on International Arbitration 2015, pp. 43–68.

Murphy, Kent, The Traditional View of Public Policy and *Ordre Public* in Private International Law, 11 Georgia Journal of International and Comparative Law 1981, pp. 591–616.

Mustill, Michael, Arbitration: History and Background, 6 Journal of International Arbitration 1989, pp. 43–56.

Ostrowski, Stephen T. & Shany Yuval, Chromalloy: United States Law and International Arbitration at the Crossroads, 73 New York University Law Review 1998, pp. 1650–1693.

Pair, Lara M., Cross-Cultural Arbitration: Do the Differences between Cultures Still Influence International Commercial Arbitration Despite Harmonization?, 9 ILSA Journal of International and Comparative Law 2002, pp. 57–74.

Pallieri, Giorgio Balladore, L'arbitrage privé dans les rapports internationaux, 51 Recueil des Cours 1935, pp. 287–404.

Paraguacuto-Maheo, Diana & Christine Lecuyer-Thieffry, Emergency Arbitrator: A New Player In The Field-The French Perspective, 40 Fordham International Law Journal 2016, pp. 749–778.

Paulsson, Jan, Delocalization of International Commercial Arbitration: When and Why It Matters, 32 The International and Comparative Law Quarterly 1983, pp. 53–61.

Paulsson, Jan, Arbitration Unbound: Award Detached From the Law of Its Country of Origin, 30 International and Comparative Law Quarterly 1981, pp. 358–387.

Pertegás, Marta & Marshall, Brooke Adele, Party Autonomy and Its Limits: Convergence through the New Hague Principles on Choice of Law in International Commercial Contracts, 39 Brooklyn Journal of International Law 2014, p. 975–1003.

Pfeiffer, Thomas, The Contribution of Arbitration to the Harmonization of Procedural Laws in Europe, 19 Uniform Law Review 2014, pp. 199–217.

Pisar, Samuel, The United Nations Convention on Foreign Arbitral Awards, 33 Southern California Law Review 1959, pp. 14–30.

Poznanzki, Bernard G., The Nature and Extent of an Arbitrator's Power in International Commercial Arbitration, 4 Journal of International Arbitration 1987, pp. 71–108.

Pryles, Michael, Reflections on Transnational Public Policy, 24 Journal of International Arbitration 2007, pp. 1–8.

Quigley, Leonard V., Accession by the United States to the United Nations Convention on the Recognition and Enforcement of Foreign Arbitral Awards, 70 Yale Law Journal 1961, pp. 1049–1082.

Rau, Alan Scott, The Culture of American Arbitration and the Lessons of ADR, 40 Texas International Law Journal 2005, pp. 449–536.

Read, Pippa, Delocalization of International Commercial Arbitration: Its Relevance in the New Millennium, 10 American Review of International Arbitration 1999, pp. 177–201.

Redfern, D. Alan, Arbitration and the Courts: Interim Measures of Protection—Is the Tide About to Turn?, 30 Texas International Law Journal 1995, pp. 71–88.

Reymond, Claude, Where Is an Arbitral Award Made?, 108 Law Quarterly Review 1992, pp. 1–6.

Roth, Marianne, Interim Measures, 2 Journal of Dispute Resolution 2012, pp. 425–435.

Rubins, N., The Arbitral Seat is No Fiction: A Brief Reply to Tatsuya Nakamura's Commentary, 16 Mealey's International Arbitration Report 2001, pp. 23–28.

Sabater, Aníbal, When Arbitration Begins Without a Seat, 27 Journal of International Arbitration 2010, pp. 443–472.

Santacroce, Fabio G., The emergency arbitrator: a full-fledged arbitrator rendering an enforceable decision?, 31 Arbitration International 2015, pp. 283–312.

Santerns, Ank A. & Kudrna, Jaroslav, The State of Play of Enforcement of Emergency Arbitrator Decisions, 34 Journal of International Arbitration 2017, pp. 1–15.

Sauser-Hall, George, L'arbitrage en droit international privé, 44-I Annuaire de l'Institut de droit international, 1952, pp. 469–613.

Schäfer, Jan K., Borrowing and Cross-Fertilising Arbitration Laws – A Comparative Overview of the Development of Hong Kong and Singapore Legislation for International Commercial Arbitration, 16 Journal of International Arbitration 1999, pp. 41–99.

Schellaars, Rogier & Lentsch, Martje Verhoeven-de Vries, Arbitral Emergency Proceedings—à la Hollandaise: Twenty Years of Practice, Tijdschrift voor Arbitrage 2020, pp. 15–18.

Schütze, Rolf A., The Precedential Effect of Arbitration Decisions, 11 Journal of International Arbitration 1994, pp. 69–75.

Schwebel, Stephen M., A Celebration of the United Nations New York Convention on the Recognition and Enforcement of Foreign Arbitral Awards, 12 Arbitration International 1996, pp. 83–88.

Schwenzer, Ingeborg, Who Needs a Uniform Contract Law, and Why, 58 Villanova Law Review 2013, pp. 723–732.

Semple, Walter G., The UNCITRAL Model Law and Provisional Measure in International Commercial Arbitration, 6 International Business Law 1993, pp. 765–781.

Sever, Jay R., Comment, The Relaxation of Inarbitrability and Public Policy Checks on U.S. and Foreign Arbitration: Arbitration Out of Control?, 65 Tulane Law Review 1991, pp. 1661–1697.

Shaughnessy, Patricia, Pre-arbitral Urgent Relief: The New SCC Emergency Arbitrator Rules, 27 Journal of International Arbitration 2010, pp. 337–360.

Shihata, Ibrahim F.I. & Parra, Antonio R., The Experience of the International Centre for Settlement of Investment Disputes, 14 ICSID Review—Foreign Investment Law Journal 1999, pp. 299–361.

Smit, Hans, A-national Arbitration, 63 Tulane Law Review 1989, pp. 629–646.

Sorieul, Renaud, The Influence of the New York Convention on the UNCITRAL Model Law on International Commercial Arbitration, 2 Dispute Resolution International 2008, pp. 27–42.

Stephan, Paul B., The Futility of Unification and Harmonization in International Commercial Law, 39 Virginia Journal of International Law 1999, pp. 743–798.

Sun, Chan Leng & Tan, Weiyi, Making Arbitration Effective: Expedited Procedures, Emergency Arbitrators and Interim Relief, 6 Contemporary Asia Arbitration Journal 2013, pp. 349–371.

Tarjuelo, Javier, Fast Track Procedures: A New Trend in Institutional Arbitration, 11 Dispute Resolution International 2017, pp. 105–116.

Trappe, Johannes, The Arbitration Proceedings: Fundamental Principles and Rights of the Parties, 15 Journal of International Arbitration 1998, pp. 93–102.

Van den Berg, Albert, The New York Convention 1958 and Panama Convention 1975: Redundancy or Compatibility?, 5 Arbitration International 1989, pp. 214–229.

Van Haersolte-Van Hof, J, Revision of the Dutch Arbitration Act: Making the Netherlands an Even Better Place for Arbitration, 31 Journal of International Arbitration 2014, pp. 425–437.

Veeder, V. V., Is there a Need to Revise the New York Convention?, 1 Journal of International Dispute Settlement 2010, pp. 499–506.

Voser, Nathalie, Interim Relief in International Arbitration: The Tendency towards a More Business-Oriented Approach, 1 Dispute Resolution International 2007, pp. 171–185.

Wahl, Philipp, Enforcement of Foreign Arbitral Awards Set Aside in their Country of Origin: The Chromalloy Case Revisited, 16 Journal of International Arbitration 1999, pp. 131–140.

Wong, Ronald, Interim Relief in Aid of International Commercial Arbitration – A Critique on the International Arbitration Act, 24 Singapore Academy of Law Journal 2012, pp. 499–532.

Xiao, Yongping & Huo, Zhengxin, Ordre Public in China's Private International Law, 53 American Journal of Comparative Law 2005, pp. 653–677.

Yesilirmak, Ali, Interim and Conservatory Measures in ICC Arbitral Practice, 11 ICC International Court of Arbitration Bulletin 2000, pp. 31–36.

Yesilirmak, Ali, Interim and Conservatory Measures in ICC Arbitral Practice, 1999–2008, 22 ICC International Court of Arbitration Bulletin (Special Supplement) 2011, pp. 5–11.

Yimer, Gebreyesus Abegaz, Standards for Provisional and Protective Measures in Civil Litigation: What Ethiopian Courts May Learn from US Courts, 24 African Journal of International and Comparative Law 2016, pp. 329–345.

Zhao, Xiuwen, Refusing Recognition and Enforcement of Foreign Arbitral Awards on the Ground of Public Policy from the Case of Yongning Corporation (从永宁公司案看公共政策作为我国法院拒绝执行外国仲裁裁决的理由), 4 The Jurist (法学家) 2009, pp. 98–105.

Other Online Sources

ACICA, Introduction, available at https://acica.org.au/ (1 June 2024).

Allenden, Lisa, Expedited Arbitration: Paris v. Stockholm: Full Steam Ahead, available at http://arbitrationblog.practicallaw.com/expedited-arbitration-paris-v-stockholm-full-steam-ahead/ (1 June 2024).

American Law Institute, Frequently Asked Questions, available at https://www.ali.org/publications/frequently-asked-questions/ (16 June 2020).

BAC, Beijing Arbitration Commission, available at http://www.bjac.org.cn/english/page/gybh/introduce_index.html (1 June 2024).

Born, Gary B. & Lim, Jonathan W., AQZ v. ARA: Singapore High Court Upholds Award Made under SIAC Expedited Procedure, available at http://arbitrationblog.kluwerarbitration.com/2015/03/09/aqz-v-ara-singapore-high-court-upholds-award-made-under-siac-expedited-procedure/ (1 June 2024).

Cheng, Tai-Heng & Peck, Julia, Arbitration Procedures and Practice in the United States: Overview, available at https://uk.practicallaw.thomsonreuters.com/0-502-1714?transitionType=Default&contextData=(sc.Default)&firstPage=true&bhcp=1 (1 June 2024).

CIETAC, Introduction, available at http://cn.cietac.org/index.php?m=Page&a=index&id=34&l=en (1 June 2024).

Civil Law (Third-Party Funding) Regulations 2017, available at https://sso.agc.gov.sg/SL-Supp/S68-2017/Published/20170224?DocDate=20170224 (1 June 2024).

CMAC, Introduction, available at http://www.cmac.org.cn/?page_id=283&lang=en (1 June 2024).

Commission of the European Communities, Green Paper on the Review of Council Regulation (EC) No 44/2001 on Jurisdiction and the Recognition and Enforcement of Judgments in Civil and Commercial Matters, 2009, available at https://eur-lex.europa.eu/legal-content/EN/TXT/PDF/?uri=CELEX:52009DC0175&from=EN (1 June 2024).

Committee on Arbitration of the Association of the Bar of the City of New York, The Inter-American Convention on International Commercial Arbitration, 9 University of Miami Inter-American Law Review 1977, available at https://repository.law.miami.edu/cgi/viewcontent.cgi?referer=https://www.google.com.hk/&httpsredir=1&article=2022&context=umialr (1 June 2024).

ECOSOC, Report of the Committee on the Enforcement of International Arbitral Awards, 1955, available at http://newyorkconvention1958.org/index.php?lvl=notice_display&id=3423&opac_view=6 (1 June 2024).

Freimane, Natalja, Arbitrability: Problematic Issues of the Legal Term, Master Thesis of Riga Graduate School of Law, 2012, available at https://sccarbitrationinstitute.se/sites/default/files/2022-11/arbitrability-problematic-issues.pdf (1 June 2024).

Gaillard, Emmanuel, First Court Decision on Pre-Arbitral Referee, 229 New York Law Journal 2003, available at https://www.shearman.com/~/media/Files/NewsInsights/Publications/2003/06/First-Court-Decision-on-PreArbitral-Referee/Files/Download-PDF-First-Court-Decision-on-PreArbitral__/FileAttachment/IA_060503.pdf (16 June 2020).

Hague Conference on Private International Law (HCCH), Convention on the Recognition and Enforcement of Foreign Judgments in Civil or Commercial Matters (concluded 2 July 2019), available at https://www.hcch.net/en/instruments/conventions/full-text/?cid=137 (1 June 2024).

HKIAC, 2023 Statistics, available at https://www.hkiac.org/about-us/statistics (1 June 2024).

HKIAC, About HKIAC, available at http://www.hkiac.org/about-us (1 June 2024).

HKIAC, At A Glance, available at https://www.hkiac.org/about-us (1 June 2024).

HKIAC, Expedited HKIAC Arbitration, available at https://www.hkiac.org/arbitration/process/expedited-hkiac-arbitration (1 June 2024).

HKIAC, HKIAC Average Costs and Duration, available at http://www.hkiac.org/content/costs-duration (1 June 2024).

HKIAC, the 2024 Schedule of Fees, available at https://hkiac.org/content/2024-schedule-fees (1 June 2024).

Ho, Peng Kee, International Arbitration Bill, 63 Official Report – Parliamentary Debates (Hansard) 1994, available at https://sprs.parl.gov.sg/search/topic?reportid=027_19941031_S0004_T0010 (16 June 2020).

Hodges, Paula & Henderson, Alastair & Satryani, Gitta & Naish, Vanessa & Ambrose, Hannah, 60 Years of the New York Convention: A Triumph of Trans-National Legal Co-operation, or A Product of its Time and in Need of Revision, available at https://www.herbertsmithfreehills.com/latest-thinking/60-years-of-the-new-york-convention-a-triumph-of-trans-national-legal-co-operation (1 June 2024).

Hosking, James & Valentine, Erin, Pre-Arbitral Emergency Measures of Protection: New Tools for an Old Problem, Commercial Arbitration 2011: New Developments and Strategies for Efficient, Cost-Effective Dispute Resolution, available at http://www.chaffetzlindsey.com/wp-content/uploads/2011/10/000954671.PDF (1 June 2024).

Hosking, James, Emergency Arbitration: Innovation for Innovation's Sake?, available at https://www.aminz.org.nz/Attachment?Action=Download&Attachment_id=835 (16 June 2020).

HSBC, Margin Trading Facilities, available at https://www.hsbcprivatebank.com/en/bank/margin-trading-facilities (1 June 2024).

Judiciary of the Hong Kong Special Administrative Region of the People's Republic of China, available at https://legalref.judiciary.hk (1 June 2024).

IBA Guidelines on Conflicts of Interest in International Arbitration 2024, available at https://www.ibanet.org/resources#Practice%20Rules%20and%20Guidelines (1 June 2024).

IBA Rules on the Taking of Evidence in International Arbitration 2020, available at https://www.ibanet.org/resources#Practice%20Rules%20and%20Guidelines (1 June 2024).

ICCA, ICCA Yearbook Commercial Arbitration, available at https://www.arbitration-icca.org/icca-yearbook-commercial-arbitration (1 June 2024).

ICC, ICC Arbitration and ADR Commission Report on Emergency Arbitrator Proceedings, 2019, p. 9, available at https://iccwbo.org/news-publications/arbitration-adr-rules-and-tools/emergency-arbitrator-proceedings-icc-arbitration-and-adr-commission-report/ (1 June 2024).

ICC, Expedited Procedure Provision, available at https://iccwbo.org/dispute-resolution/dispute-resolution-services/arbitration/rules-procedure/expedited-procedure/ (1 June 2024).

ICC, ICC Dispute Resolution 2020 Statistics, available at https://jusmundi.com/en/document/publication/en-2020-icc-dispute-resolution-statistics (1 June 2024).

ICC, ICC Dispute Resolution Bulletin, available at https://jusmundi.com/en/icc-dispute-resolution-library/bulletins (1 June 2024).

ICC, ICC International Court of Arbitration, available at https://iccwbo.org/dispute-resolution-services/arbitration/icc-international-court-arbitration/ (16 June 2020).

ICC, National Committees, available https://iccwbo.org/national-committees/ (1 June 2024).

ICC, Pre-Arbitral Referee, available at https://iccwbo.org/news-publications/arbitration-adr-rules-and-tools/rules-pre-arbitral-referee-procedure/ (1 June 2024).

ICC, Report and Preliminary Draft Convention adopted by the Committee on International Commercial Arbitration at its meeting of 13 March 1953, 9 ICC International Court of Arbitration Bulletin 1998, available at http://library.iccwbo.org/content/dr/COMMISSION_REPORTS/CR_0011.htm?l1=Bulletins&l2=ICC+International+Court+of+Arbitration+Bulletin+Vol.+9%2FNo.1+-+Eng (16 June 2020).

ICC, The Secretariat's Guide to ICC Arbitration, available at https://jusmundi.com/en/document/publication/en-foreword-2 (1 June 2024).

ICDR, 2022 ICDR Case Data Infographic, https://www.adr.org/sites/default/files/document_repository/AAA430_ICDR_Case_Data_2022.pdf (1 June 2024).

Introduction of the website, available at http://newyorkconvention1958.org/ (1 June 2024).

Jie, Xu, Emergency Arbitrator Proceedings and the GKML Case, 2018, available at http://www.bjac.org.cn/news/view?id=3330 (1 June 2024).

Jiménez de Aréchaga, Separate Opinion of President Jiménez de Aréchaga, 1976, available at https://www.icj-cij.org/files/case-related/62/062-19760911-ORD-01-01-EN.pdf (1 June 2024).

Jkx Oil & Gas PLC, Poltava Gas B.V. and Poltava Petroleum Company JV v. The State of Ukraine, in Kravchenko, Oksana & Petrov, Yaroslave & Tkachova, Anna, JKX Oil & Gas PLC, Poltava Gas B.V. and Poltava Petroleum Company JV v. The State of Ukraine seeking to grant permission for enforcement of a foreign arbitral award dated 14 January 2015, issued by the Emergency Arbitrator Rudolf Dolzer under the Arbitration Rules of the Stockholm Chamber of Commerce, Supreme Specialized Court of Ukraine for Civil and Criminal Cases, No. 757/5777/15-ц, 17 May 2016; A contribution by the ITA Board of Reporters, available at http://www.kluwerarbitration.com.ezproxy.ub.unimaas.nl/document/kli-ka-16-25-005?q=%22Jkx%20oil%22 (16 June 2020).

Kalderimis, Daniel, New Zealand, The Asia-Pacific Arbitration Review 2016, available at https://www.chapmantripp.com/Publication%20PDFs/The%20Asia-Pacific%20Arbitration%20Review%202016.pdf (16 June 2020).

Kalderimis, Daniel & Yesberg, Kate, Recent Amendments to New Zealand's Arbitrating Act, available at http://arbitrationblog.kluwerarbitration.com/2016/11/28/recent-amendments-to-new-zealands-arbitration-act/#_ftn1 (1 June 2024).

Legislative History, Arbitration Act of the Statutes of the Republic of Singapore (Cap. 10) 2016, available at https://sso.agc.gov.sg/Act/AA2001?ValidDate=20160801&ProvIds=xv-#xv- (1 June 2024).

Legislative History, International Arbitration Act of the Statutes of the Republic of Singapore (Cap. 143A) 2016, available at https://sso.agc.gov.sg/Act/IAA1994#xv- (1 June 2024).

LCIA, History, available at http://www.lcia.org/LCIA/history.aspx (1 June 2024).

LCIA, Introduction, available at http://www.lcia.org/LCIA/introduction.aspx (1 June 2024).

LCIA, Reports, available at https://www.lcia.org/LCIA/reports.aspx (1 June 2024).

LCIA, Schedule of LCIA Arbitration Cost (2014), available at http://www.lcia.org/Dispute_Resolution_Services/schedule-of-costs-lcia-arbitration.aspx (1 June 2024).

LCIA, Schedule of LCIA Arbitration Cost (2023), available at https://www.lcia.org/Dispute_Resolution_Services/schedule-of-arbitration-costs-2023.aspx (1 June 2024).

Li, Haifeng, First Emergency Arbitrator Proceedings in China and Enforcement in Hong Kong, 2018, available at https://globalarbitrationnews.com/first-emergency-arbitrator-proceedings-in-china-and-enforcement-in-hong-kong/ (1 June 2024).

Lim, Steven, Interim Relief in International Arbitration, available at http://www.siac.org.sg/2013-09-18-01-57-20/2013-09-22-00-27-02/articles/444-interim-relief-in-international-arbitration (16 June 2020).

Meredith, Ian & Birch, Marcus, The ICC's Pre-Arbitral Referee Procedure: How Valuable Is It?, available at https://files.klgates.com/files/publication/ab0be67f-01ef-4206-9c12-6e91f5b4837e/presentation/publicationattachment/bae41c65-1f1b-43c3-b963-7de5c496b5bc/article_meredith_icc_0108.pdf (1 June 2024).

Michaelson, Peter L., Emergency Arbitration: Fast, Effective and Economical, available at https://ccarbitrators.org/wp-content/uploads/PLMichaelson-Emerg-Arb(ABA-JustResolutions-03-2016)(final-complete).pdf (16 June 2020).

Moses, Margaret, Public Policy: National, International and Transnational, available at http://arbitrationblog.kluwerarbitration.com/2018/11/12/public-policy-national-international-and-transnational/ (1 June 2024).

Morrison & Foerster LLP, Singapore Considers Amendments to Its International Arbitration Act, available at https://www.lexology.com/library/detail.aspx?g=2f8a6fb4-76b7-46ba-8258-91931f4a8156 (1 June 2024).

Newyorkconvention1958, available at http://newyorkconvention1958.org/ (1 June 2024).

Park, William W., Arbitral Jurisdiction in the United States: Who Decides What?, 11 International Arbitration Law Review 2008, available at http://williamwpark.com/documents/Arbitral%20Jurisdiction%20%20IALR.pdf (1 June 2024).

Paulsson, Marike R. P., The Eve of the New York Convention's 60th Anniversary and the Birthday Party: How to Prepare with too Many Guests at the Table, available at http://arbitrationblog.kluwerarbitration.com/2018/06/21/eve-new-york-conventions-60th-anniversary-birthday-party-prepare-many-guests-table-il-ne-faut-pas-melanger-les-tables/ (1 June 2024).

Preamble, International Arbitration Act of the Statutes of the Republic of Singapore (Cap. 143A) 2016, available at https://sso.agc.gov.sg/Act/IAA1994 (1 June 2024).

Queen Mary University of London and White & Case LLP, 2010 International Arbitration Survey: Choices in International Arbitration, available at http://www.arbitration.qmul.ac.uk/media/arbitration/docs/2010_InternationalArbitrationSurveyReport.pdf (1 June 2024).

Queen Mary University of London and White & Case LLP, 2015 International Arbitration Survey: Improvements and Innovations in International Arbitration, available at http://www.arbitration.qmul.ac.uk/media/arbitration/docs/2015_International_Arbitration_Survey.pdf (1 June 2024).

Queen Mary University of London and White & Case LLP, 2018 International Arbitration Survey: The Evolution of International Arbitration, available at http://www.arbitration.qmul.ac.uk/media/arbitration/docs/2018-International-Arbitration-Survey---The-Evolution-of-International-Arbitration-(2).PDF (1 June 2024).

Queen Mary University of London and White & Case LLP, 2021 International Arbitration Survey: Adapting Arbitration to a Changing World, available at https://arbitration.qmul.ac.uk/research/2021-international-arbitration-survey/ (1 June 2024).

Samuel, Adam, Separability of Arbitration Clauses-Some Awkward Questions about the Law on Contracts, Conflict of Laws and the Administration of Justice, available at http://www.adamsamuel.com/separabi.pdf (16 June 2020).

Savola, Mika, Interim Measures and Emergency Arbitrator Proceedings, Presentation at the 23rd Croatian Arbitration Days: Access to Arbitral Justice, 2015, available at https://arbitration.fi/wp-content/uploads/sites/22/2016/04/23-cad-savola-interim-measures-and-emergency-arbitrator-proceedings.pdf (16 June 2020).

SCC, About the SCC, available at http://www.sccinstitute.com/about-the-scc/ (16 June 2020).

SCC, Statistics 2022, Emergency Arbitrator Proceedings 2022, available at https://sccarbitrationinstitute.se/en/about-scc/scc-statistics (1 June 2024).

SCC, Statistics 2021, Emergency Arbitrator Proceedings 2021, available at https://sccarbitrationinstitute.se/sites/default/files/2023-02/scc-statistics-2021.pdf (1 June 2024).

SCC, SCC Statistics 2010–2023, available at https://sccarbitrationinstitute.se/en/about-scc/scc-statistics-0 (1 June 2024).

Shanmugam, K, International Arbitration (Amendment) Bill, 86 Official Report – Parliamentary Debates (Hansard) 2009, Column: 1627, available at https://sprs.parl.gov.sg/search/topic?reportid=020_20091019_S0004_T0002 (16 June 2020).

Shanmugam, K, International Arbitration (Amendment) Bill, 89 Official Report – Parliamentary Debates (Hansard) 2009, available at https://sprs.parl.gov.sg/search/topic?reportid=024_20120409_S0003_T0004 (16 June 2020).

SHIAC, FTZ Court of Arbitration, available at https://www.shiac.org/pc/Trade?moduleCode=introduction (1 June 2024).

Shore, Laurence, Defining "Arbitrability": The United States vs. the rest of the world, New York Law Journal, 2009, available at https://indiacorplaw.in/wp-content/uploads/2016/08/shore-definingarbitrability.pdf (1 June 2024).

SIAC, SIAC Annual Report 2023, available at https://siac.org.sg/wp-content/uploads/2024/04/SIAC_AR2023.pdf (1 June 2024).

SIAC, The Emergency Arbitrator and Expedited Procedure in SIAC: A New Direction for Arbitration in Asia, available at http://www.siac.org.sg/2013-09-18-01-57-20/2013-09-22-00-27-02/articles/420-the-emergency-arbitrator-and-expedited-procedure-in-siac-a-new-direction-for-arbitration-in-asia (16 June 2020).

Smith, G., The Emergence of Emergency Arbitrations, Dec. Arbitrator & Mediator Journal 2015, available at http://www.gordonsmithlegal.com.au/resources/Emergency%20Arbitrations%20(12082016).pdf (1 June 2024).

Siusel, Ihor & Omelyannovich, Olesya, Ukraine: Enforceability of Emergency Arbitral Awards (JKX Oil & Gas PLC v. Ukraine), 2019, available at https://globalarbitrationnews.com/ukraine-enforceability-of-emergency-arbitral-awards-jkx-oil-gas-plc-v-ukraine/ (1 June 2024).

Sun Wei, First Emergency Arbitrator Proceeding in Mainland China: Reflections on How to Conduct an EA Proceeding from Procedural and Substantive Perspectives, 2018, available at http://arbitrationblog.kluwerarbitration.com/2018/09/01/first-ea-proceeding-mainland-china-reflections-conduct-ea-proceeding-procedural-substantive-perspectives/ (1 June 2024).

Tat, Lim, Arbitration Procedures and Practice in Singapore: overview, 2017, available at https://uk.practicallaw.thomsonreuters.com/3-381-2028?transitionType=Default&contextData=(sc.Default)&firstPage=true&bhcp=1#co_anchor_a382816 (16 June 2020).

The American Law Institute, Restatement of The U.S. Law of International Commercial and Investor-State Arbitration Is Approved, available at https://www.ali.org/news/articles/restatement-us-law-international-commercial-and-investorstate-arbitration-approved/(16 June 2020).

The Supreme People's Court of the People's Republic of China, Guiding Cases, available at http://www.court.gov.cn/fabu-gengduo-77.html (16 June 2020).

The ICC, History, available at https://iccwbo.org/about-icc-2/our-mission-history-and-values/ (1 June 2024).

Treaty Section of the Office of Legal Affairs of the UN, Treaty Handbook, 2012, available at https://treaties.un.org/doc/source/publications/THB/English.pdf (1 June 2024).

UNCITRAL, International Commercial Arbitration, Possible Future Work in the Area of International Commercial Arbitration, Note by the Secretariat (A/CN.9/460), 1999, available at https://undocs.org/en/A/CN.9/460 (1 June 2024).

UNCITRAL, Note by the Secretariat: Further Work in Respect of International Commercial Arbitration (A/CN.9/169), 1979, available at https://documents.un.org/doc/undoc/gen/nl7/902/28/pdf/nl790228.pdf?token=obDMRqqN2A2Yc8McLL&fe=true (1 June 2024).

UNCITRAL, Reports of the United Nations Commission on International Trade Law on the work of its resumed fortieth and its forty-first session, 2009, A/RES/63/120, available at https://documents.un.org/doc/undoc/gen/n08/477/99/pdf/n0847799.pdf?token=5bv7z0RYg7NEOoNnC6&fe=true (1 June 2024).

UNCITRAL, Report of Working Group on Arbitration on the work of its thirty-second session (A/CN.9/468), 2000, available at https://undocs.org/en/A/CN.9/468 (1 June 2024).

UNCITRAL, Status: Convention on the Recognition and Enforcement of Foreign Arbitral Awards (New York, 1958)(the "New York Convention"), available at https://treaties.un.org/Pages/ViewDetails.aspx?src=TREATY&mtdsg_no=XXII-1&chapter=22&clang=_en (1 June 2024).

UNCITRAL, Status: UNCITRAL Model Law on International Commercial Arbitration (1985), with amendments as adopted in 2006, available at https://uncitral.un.org/en/texts/arbitration/modellaw/commercial_arbitration/status (1 June 2024).

UNCITRAL, UNCITRAL Arbitration Rules, https://uncitral.un.org/en/texts/arbitration/contractualtexts/arbitration (1 June 2024).

UNCITRAL, UNCITRAL Secretariat Guide on the Convention on the Recognition and Enforcement of Foreign Arbitral Awards, 2006, available at https://uncitral.un.org/sites/uncitral.un.org/files/media-documents/uncitral/en/2016_guide_on_the_convention.pdf (1 June 2024).

UNCITRAL, United Nations Convention on International Settlement Agreements Resulting from Mediation (New York, 2018) (the "Singapore Convention on Mediation"), available at https://uncitral.un.org/en/texts/mediation/conventions/international_settlement_agreements (1 June 2024).

Uniform Law Commission, Overview, available at https://www.uniformlaws.org/aboutulc/overview (1 June 2024).

Van den Berg, Albert, New York Convention v. Hypothetical Convention: A Closer Look at the Proposed "New York Convention", 3 Global Arbitration Review 2008, available at https://www.arbitration-icca.org/media/1/13318252772820/new_ny_conv.pdf (1 June 2024).

Van den Berg, Albert, Introductory Note, Convention on the Recognition and Enforcement of Foreign Arbitral Awards, available at http://legal.un.org/avl/ha/crefaa/crefaa.html (1 June 2024).

Van Zelst, Bas, The End of Justice(s): Perspectives and Thoughts on Automation in Dispute Resolution, Inaugural Lecture at Maastricht University, 2018, available at https://pdfs.semanticscholar.org/a321/e1245440c3786790303aa0e21e6740ddc930.pdf (1 June 2024).

Vasani, Sarah Zagata, The Emergency Arbitrator: Doubling as an Effective Option for Urgent Relief and an Early Settlement Tool, available at https://www.lexology.com/library/detail.aspx?g=e786221a-8823-4f25-8307-d28df1078fdc (1 June 2024).

Veeder, V. V., Provisional and Conservatory Measures, in Enforcing Arbitration Awards under the New York Convention: Experience and Prospects, United Nations Publication, 1999, available at https://www.newyorkconvention.org/media/uploads/pdf/9/5/95_colloquia-1999-enforcingarbawardsunderthenyc.pdf (1 June 2024)

Vivekananda, N., The SIAC Emergency Arbitrator Experience, available at http://siac.org.sg/2013-09-18-01-57-20/2013-09-22-00-27-02/articles/338-the-siac-emergency-arbitrator-experience (16 June 2020).

World Economic Forum, The Global Competitiveness Report 2019, available at http://www3.weforum.org/docs/WEF_TheGlobalCompetitivenessReport2019.pdf (1 June 2024).

Working Group II (Arbitration and Conciliation) of United Nations Commission on International Trade Law, Settlement of commercial disputes: Revision of the UNCITRAL Arbitration Rules: Note by the Secretariat, A/CN.9/WG/II/WP.154/Add.1, 2009, available at https://documents.un.org/doc/undoc/ltd/v09/855/86/pdf/v0985586.pdf?token=TBS2qyWnzP0IytNcNP&fe=true (1 June 2024).

Yuen, Peter & Shi, Helen H. & McDonald, Damien & Boltenko, Olga & Townsend, Matthew, Hong Kong and Mainland China Agree upon Bilateral Arrangement Regarding Interim Measures for Arbitration, 2019, available at http://arbitrationblog.kluwerarbitration.com/2019/04/02/hong-kong-and-mainland-china-agree-upon-bilateral-arrangement-regarding-interim-measures-for-arbitration/ (1 June 2024)

The manufacturer's authorised representative in the EU is Springer
Nature Customer Service Centre GmbH, Europaplatz 3, 69115 Heidelberg,
Germany. If you have any concerns regarding our products, please
contact ProductSafety@springernature.com

Printed and bound by CPI Group (UK) Ltd, Croydon, CR0 4YY
01/10/2026
02225963-0003